THE RUSSIAN REVOLUTION, 1905–1921

SERIES ADVISORS
Geoff Eley, University of Michigan
Lyndal Roper, University of Oxford

Mark D. Steinberg, a professor of history at the University of Illinois in Urbana-Champaign, is the author of many books and articles, including *The Fall of the Romanovs: Political Dreams and Personal Struggles in a Time of Revolution* (1995), *Voices of Revolution, 1917* (2001), *Proletarian Imagination: Self, Modernity, and the Sacred in Russia, 1910–1925* (2002), *Petersburg Fin-de-Siècle* (2011), and recent editions of the late Nicholas Riasanovsky's *A History of Russia*. His research and teaching interests include histories of cities, working-class culture, emotions, violence, revolutions, and utopia.

The Russian Revolution, 1905–1921

MARK D. STEINBERG

OXFORD
UNIVERSITY PRESS

OXFORD
UNIVERSITY PRESS

Great Clarendon Street, Oxford, OX2 6DP,
United Kingdom

Oxford University Press is a department of the University of Oxford.
It furthers the University's objective of excellence in research, scholarship,
and education by publishing worldwide. Oxford is a registered trade mark of
Oxford University Press in the UK and in certain other countries

First Edition published in 2017

Impression: 1

Published in the United States of America by Oxford University Press
198 Madison Avenue, New York, NY 10016, United States of America

British Library Cataloguing in Publication Data
Data available

Library of Congress Control Number: 2016941738

ISBN 978-0-19-922762-4 (hbk.)
     978-0-19-922763-1 (pbk.)

Printed in Great Britain by
Clays Ltd, St Ives plc

ACKNOWLEDGMENTS

Like the revolution itself, the history of this book has deep roots. It began with an intriguing invitation from Christopher Wheeler, an editor at Oxford University Press, to submit a proposal for a new series of books that sought authors with "something fresh to say" about major events and topics in history and who would communicate to both students and lay readers the excitement of our changing understandings of the past. I was honored and stimulated by the invitation to write such a book on the Russian Revolution and am grateful to him for asking me.

All scholarship, of course, stands on the shoulders of work that has gone before (even if we often kick at those past authors' heads a bit). This is doubly true of books on topics like the Russian Revolution, which must consider the work of dozens of accomplished historians. I have tried to say something different and fresh, to bring a distinctive "attitude" to the project (as Wheeler asked for in his first announcement), while trying to avoid the convention of demonstrating originality by dissing my elders and colleagues. I could not have written the book without the huge body of existing research and interpretation, from whom I have borrowed and reworked a great deal. In this sense, the notes and the bibliography can be seen as a type of acknowledgment of people to whom I am indebted and grateful.

More immediately, I have been reminded again of the generosity of scholars in taking time from their own full lives of research, writing, teaching, and other work to read and critique the work of others (we do so much for so little pay). This book is many times better and more interesting thanks to their criticisms, suggestions, and encouragement. These critical readers include historians and literary scholars, graduate students, and independent authors. Some critiqued early drafts of chapters at workshops, especially the Russian Studies Circle (Kruzhok) at the University of Illinois and the biannual Midwest Russian History Workshop. More recently, a number of individuals were kind enough to agree to read the whole manuscript or parts of chapters. Diane Koenker, Boris Kolonitsky, Roshanna Sylvester, and (Steve Smith as anonymous reader for Oxford University Press) offered wise and essential critical readings of the entire manuscript. Heather Coleman, Barbara Engel, Gregory Freidin, Nina Gourianova, Adeeb Khalid, Harriet Murav, and Christine Worobec read chapters where they have particular expertise. I am very grateful to them all. That I did not always take their good advice should underscore the fact that, while I have been inspired by so many scholars, I am alone responsible for whatever you might not like or agree with in this book.

I also want to thank my graduate research assistants—Andy Bruno, Maria Cristina Galmarini, Stephen Jug, and Jesse Murray—who helped enormously with the time-consuming and challenging task of reading through endless microfilm copies of Russian newspapers. The talented librarians at the University of Illinois and the Slavic Reference Service, especially Christopher Condill and Joseph Lenkart, solved many research problems, large and small, with skill and generosity with their time. I am also grateful to the staff at the Russian National Library in St Petersburg, especially Alexander Sapozhnikov, Alexander Kashtaner, and their colleagues in the newspaper division, where I have spent a great deal of time over the years.

At Oxford University Press, Christopher Wheeler, Matthew Cotton, Robert Faber, and Cathryn Steele have been a pleasure to work with— I thank them all for their intelligence, encouragement, and patience. I am also very grateful for the fine editing, proofreading, indexing, and production work by Jane Robson, Linda Miller, R. A. Marriott, and Manikandan Chandrasekaran.

Finally, this book is dedicated to the memory of Jane Taylor Hedges (1951–2015), an extraordinary scholarly editor and my beloved partner in life for more than thirty-five years until cancer overcame her strength and vitality, which still sustains me. She and I discussed every idea in this book and she is deeply part of it. And I thank our fabulous son Sasha (also a sharp critic of ideas), and my friends, who have all kept me looking and living forward.

CONTENTS

LIST OF ILLUSTRATIONS

LIST OF ILLUSTRATIONS

INTRODUCTION
EXPERIENCING THE RUSSIAN REVOLUTION

> Reading books on the history of the revolution is more pleasant than experiencing the revolution.
>
> (Nikolai Berdyaev, "Thoughts on the Russian Revolution," 1923)

> History: that vile scholar's lie among whose printed lines not a drop of spilled blood can be found, where nothing remains of the passion, the pain, the fear, and the violence of men.
>
> (Victor Serge, *Conquered City*, 1932)

This pair of comments about the Russian revolution and history by two writers who personally experienced those events—a conservative religious philosopher and a left-wing activist—suggest something of what this book tries to do: tell the story of the Russian revolution as *experience*, as people thinking and feeling about history as it unfolded in their own lives and as they took part in making history. The story of the Russian revolution has been told and interpreted in as many ways as there are of telling and interpreting history itself. Traditional approaches focus on causes: why, for example, did the tsarist autocracy collapse in February 1917 and then the liberal government that replaced it fall to the Bolsheviks after only months in power? The usual answers emphasize the role of institutions, leaders, and ideologies, and the unfolding story itself as a causative structure: events shaped the events that followed.

"Revisionist" social history, now itself a tradition, encourages us to look to societal structures and groups for explanations. In interpreting the Russian revolution, this has meant recognizing the "deepening social polarization between the top and bottom of Russian society" as the main cause and driver of events.[1] As social history evolved into a new cultural history, historians have looked more to the complex and elusive world of mentalities and attitudes beneath the surfaces of events, structures, and ideologies: toward "discourse"—words, images, symbols, rituals, and myths—as not only revealing attitudes but shaping how people are able to understand their world and act in it.[2]

"Experience" intersects with all of these traditions and innovations as we ask what the past meant to people then, as lived history. The definition of experience is much debated. The historian Martin Jay has offered one of the better definitions: it is our inward dialogue with our external world, the self's encounter with existence outside the self, especially the "encounter with otherness," which can change us in unpredictable ways.[3] Older definitions tended to define experience as mature and developed knowledge of the world (the opposite of "innocence"),[4] or as a more authentic knowledge than that imposed or indoctrinated by authority, such as that of ideology or religion. Recent definitions have been more skeptical, warning against the temptation to enshrine experience as a raw, genuine, unmediated truth about reality. As the historian Joan Scott famously argued, experience is "always already an interpretation."[5] Past experience is doubly difficult to interpret, of course, for our access is limited and shaped by the evidence left to us. Our knowledge and interpretations of the past are unavoidably shaped by the past's own knowledge and interpretations of itself. Historians may wish to reach the utopian ground of genuine experience in past lives, but we know (or should know) that we will never arrive. The journey can be full of discovery, but it has no final end in "the truth."

In this journey, "the archive" (all the evidence of the past) is where the historian seeks answers to old questions and reasons to ask new ones. Every student is taught that "primary sources" (documents created during the time under study) are better than secondary sources as more direct reflections of the past itself. Of course, there is as much desire as science in this. We want something approaching a face-to-face encounter with the living past (many historians literally dream of it) and find that primary documents offer as much of this experience as possible, especially when we are attentive and open in reading texts and knowledgeable about historical contexts. But most historians understand that all we have to work with are traces and interpretations. We try not to be seduced by the appearance of immediacy and guilelessness in the voices in documents. We try to be wary of the influence of interpreting contemporaries who created the evidence and to be aware of the social, cultural, and political pressures that shaped what they thought and what they said, and what they did not or could not say. We try to hear what is absent or silent. We try to keep in mind that the meanings authors intended at the time may not be transparent to us now. At the same time, we tend to be suspicious of the claim, more common in literary studies, that texts are so laden with intentions, deceptions, repressions, and silences that only the most skeptical and critical interpretive work can suggest what might be hidden there. Most historians (at least this is my preference) approach the evidence of experience with a mixture of receptiveness and critical suspicion, immersing ourselves in evidence generated from people's lives and listening to their voices while asking hard questions about the interpreting already being done there.[6]

Newspapers are a frequent source in this book. The great essayist Walter Benjamin, while working in the 1930s on a new type of history of modernity, tried to explain his approach with the comment that "to seize the essence of history, it suffices to compare Herodotus and the morning newspaper."[7] The comparison was informed by the two German words for "experience," *Erfahrung* and *Erlebnis*. *Erfahrung* is experience that is coherent and continuous, the result of a process of ordering facts—the "journey" (*Fahrt*) that is the etymological heart of the word. *Erlebnis* is experience that is more immediate and particular, closer to everyday "life" (*Leben*), hence often translated as "lived experience."[8] On the surface, *Erfahrung*-experience is the terrain of the professional historian who tells a narratively well-integrated, expertly constructed, and directional story of the historical process, while *Erlebnis*-experience is that of the newspaper journalist telling history's story at its most fresh, unprocessed, and unorganized. For the historian of experience, the newspaper would seem to give us the past's own present, lived historical experience before it was rewritten to fit a story of "History."

I admit to the seductiveness of this ideal. I have long been drawn to newspapers as sources, and this book reflects this. But I try not to be naive, for newspaper writers certainly were not. Journalists knew that the stories they reported were filtered by incomplete evidence, unreliable or false witnesses, and their own choices and purposes. They had stories to tell and motives in telling them, ranging from selling papers to advancing a political cause—and Russian journalists had the added pressure of government censorship. To be sure, some writers insisted that the newspaper was nothing more than a "mirror" held up to life "as it is."[9] But most of them understood that the newspaper was much more than a mirror, just as most historians today recognize that history is much more than a simple factual story of "how it really was" (the definition of the historical method made famous by Leopold von Ranke in the nineteenth century). Russian journalists, even those working for the mass-circulation newspapers whose readers were assumed to want to be entertained by the most sensational stories, also believed themselves to be serious commentators about their times, even moral witnesses to the age—making objectivity less important than commentary and judgment. The point and the challenge for journalists, as for historians, is bringing together the daily news and the long narration, historical experience as the immediate present of the past and the sense of living in the meaningful flow of time linking past, present, and future. This is especially necessary when the goal, as it is for this book, is to discover how people in the past—and not only classes and categories of people, much less "the people" as an imagined national whole, but specific individuals in specific times and places—tried to understand, interpret, and shape their own history.

Large questions weave through the many stories and voices in this book:

- The human person (the self, the individual, *lichnost'* in Russian) as the acting subject of history but also as a value people fought to promote and defend.
- Inequality, especially when connected to social, economic, gender, and ethnic differences.

- Power and resistance, including as expressed and experienced through violence.
- History as an experience of time, especially the feeling in the past that they were living in "historical" times.
- And, perhaps most important because we are talking about a revolution, how people understood, lived, and practiced "freedom"—possibly as an answer to all these questions.

The structure of this book is shaped by these questions. Part I, "Documents and Stories," considers some exemplary and evocative primary texts, allowing the sources themselves to stand out front, ahead of the usual way of telling history.[10] I chose these documents less because they are "typical" (an elusive goal) than because they are *telling*: because they speak to us of how people tried to make sense of their experience of revolution, both intellectually and emotionally. I focus on a single dramatic moment in this history: the "springtime of freedom" in 1917. And I focus on one protean and elusive question: the meaning of "freedom." It is this first chapter's conceit (in the literary sense of an extended metaphor governing a text) that I imagine we can walk the streets of the revolution and ask people what they thought and felt about their experience of revolution and freedom.

Part II, "Histories," is a chronological narrative of the entire period, but with a twist. All the usual events are here, from "Bloody Sunday" in 1905 to the final shots of the civil war in 1921. And so are familiar questions of interpretation. Was Russia on a path to avoid another revolution thanks to the reforms of 1905–6? What were the effects of World War I on the fate of the autocracy? Why did the democratic Provisional Government that replaced the autocracy after February 1917 lose support so quickly? How did the Bolsheviks come to power and stay there against all odds? These events, trends, and explanations, however, are viewed through the doubled perspective of the professional historian looking backward and the contemporary journalist reporting and interpreting history as it happened. The historian's narrative viewpoint is that of retrospective and cohesive narration, based on available evidence and current scholarly interpretation: what professional historians now generally agree happened, what mattered, and why. The journalist's narrative viewpoint is rather different, at least at first glance: they were "historians of the present tense," as it has been famously said, who "record and interpret history at the moment of its making."[11]

Both narrative points of view, however, are still only stories about stories. It is our human nature to tell stories and want to hear them, and history stories are among the most important to us. Because the past, like the present, tends toward disorder and incoherence, we want to make it into "history" by putting its fractured pieces in some meaningful order, overlooking the many gaps in what we know or understand, highlighting connections and patterns, especially how events were connected causatively to the past and would shape what was to come (the definition of history as change over time), and, through all of this, focusing on what we judge to be true and important according to whatever criteria we favor. Journalists then and historians now faced many of the same challenges: the testimony of witnesses is often untrustworthy; evidence is incomplete; understanding is influenced by their own experiences and values and those of their sources; and, not least, they both must select out of the commotion of the everyday what they believe most matters.

Part III, "Places and People," turns to particular social spaces and individual perspectives across the entire period. The first place (Chapter 5) is that of the city and especially "the street" as both location and symbol. In almost every revolution, the street is the epicenter of public action and political meaning: a tangible social and political space for doing things and a symbol of "the crowd" and all that is out of control. The Russian street was a place of peril and pleasure, of crime and violence, but also of wandering and discovery and more illicit pleasures. The street was also the space of history, a place to challenge order and demonstrate belief in a different reality. Not least, the street was the heart of democracy: the place where people, especially "*the* democracy," as Russians called the rising class of the non-privileged, demanded recognition and inclusion, where they experienced and made history.

Chapter 6 turns to the countryside, so important in a country where most people remained peasants or had only recently left their villages. But rather than assume, as we usually do in writing history, that the evidence of *men's* experiences and actions (most of the available evidence, to be sure) can stand for the history of both men and women, I look for the perspective of village women in the revolution, and ask how women's experiences, especially of difference and inequality, might unsettle our assumptions, remind us of the diversity of "peasant" experiences and attitudes, and make us look at the history of peasant revolution differently.

Chapter 7 looks to the spaces of empire. In Russia, national and ethnic difference could be enjoyed, celebrated, and accommodated, or experienced as a threat and problem to solve. It was a story of inequality, exclusion, prejudice, and violence, but also of negotiation, opportunity, and invention. In light of the huge variety of imperial experiences in the revolution, rather than offer an overview from the heights or select the history of a few groups as "typical," I look at three individuals as they encountered and engaged with difference and participated in the unmaking of empire in Russia: the Central Asian Muslim activist Mahmud Khoja Behbudi, the Ukrainian writer and political leader Volodymyr Vynnychenko, and the enigmatic Jewish author Isaac Babel.

The final chapter looks at another trio of rebels: the radical feminist Alexandra Kollontai, the professional revolutionary Lev Trotsky, and the "futurist" poet Vladimir Mayakovsky. All three devoted their lives to revolution and worked actively to build the new society of their dreams, especially after the Bolsheviks, their party, came to power. I call them "utopians" against their own insistence to the contrary, for I am using the term not in the usual dismissive way (their way) to speak of impossible dreams of perfection built out of nothing but imagination, fantasy, and desire. I am thinking, rather, of a definition of utopia as a critical negation of that which merely *is* in the name of what *should be*, as a radical challenge to conventional assumptions about what is possible and impossible in the present, as a vision of time and history as containing the possibility of an explosive "leap" (in the famous Marxist phrase) "from the kingdom of necessity to the kingdom of freedom." To be sure, their utopian impulses would collide with the stubborn realities of the present and the heavy weight of necessity. But I prefer to conclude this book—for this speaks more strongly of the history of the revolution as it was then experienced—with their early boldness of hope than their later tragedies of disappointment.

Chronology is itself interpretation. Books on the Russian revolution have defined its timespan as February through October 1917 (from the demonstrations and mutinies that toppled the tsar to the uprising that brought the Bolsheviks to power), as 1917–18 (until the civil war), as 1917–21 (including the civil war), as 1917–29 (until the Stalinist "Great Turn"), as 1917–38 (through the end of the "Great Terror"), as 1914–21 (from war through war, as it were), as 1891–1924 (from the first "revolutionary crisis" to Lenin's death), and other variations.[12] In making these choices, each author is also making an argument about history and revolution and Russia's experience of both. My book treats the years from 1905 to 1921 as an era of linked crises, upheavals, radical change, and possibility. My question, of course, is what this all meant to people at the time, how *they* saw the connections and ruptures.

The words used by contemporaries to speak of their experiences suggest something of the range of possible answers. Many people would have agreed with the anonymous woman who stopped a writer on the street in 1918 and declared, "Everyone is saying that Russia has perished, that it's been going downhill for thirteen years!"[13] Others looked back at 1905 as a "dress rehearsal" (Lenin's famous phrase) and opening battle, and at the years in between as a time to prepare and organize. And a great many people described something much less definite: a sense that they were living across these years in "times of trouble," "catastrophe," "uncertainty," "confusion," "instability," "indeterminacy," and "groundlessness," but also times of "heroism," "hope," "light," "salvation," and "resurrection." This was not a stable set of interpretations even for individuals: one judgment or mood could shift to another. No single interpretation or emotion explained enough. Nor should it be enough for us now looking back.

Notes

1. Ronald Grigor Suny, "Revision and Retreat in the Historiography of 1917: Social History and its Critics," *Russian Review,* 53/2 (April 1994): 167.
2. See Ronald Grigor Suny, "Toward a Social History of the October Revolution," *American Historical Review,* 88/1 (February 1983): 31–52; Suny, "Revision and Retreat"; Steve Smith, "Writing the History of the Russian

Revolution After the Fall of Communism," *Europe-Asia Studies,* 46/4 (1994): 563–78; Edward Acton, "The Revolution and its Historians," in Edward Acton, Vladimir Cherniaev, and William Rosenberg (eds), *Critical Companion to the Russian Revolution* (Bloomington, IN, 1997), 3–17; Mark D. Steinberg, *Voices of Revolution, 1917* (New Haven, 2001), 1–35; Sheila Fitzpatrick, *The Russian Revolution,* 3rd edn (Oxford, 2008), 4–13; S. A. Smith, "The Historiography of the Russian Revolution 100 Years On" and Boris I. Kolonitskii, "On Studying the 1917 Revolution: Auto-biographical Confessions and Historiographical Predictions," *Kritika: Explorations in Russian and Eurasian History,* 16/4 (Fall 2015): 733–68.

3. Martin Jay, *Songs of Experience: Modern American and European Variations on a Universal Theme* (Berkeley, CA, 2005), 401–9.

4. A contrast reaching back at least to William Blake's *Songs of Innocence and Experience* (1789).

5. Joan Scott, "The Evidence of Experience," *Critical Inquiry,* 17 (Summer 1991): 797.

6. See E. H. Carr, *What is History?* (London 1961); Joyce Appleby, Lynn Hunt, and Margaret Jacob, *Telling the Truth about History* (New York, 1994); Richard Evans, *In Defense of History* (New York, 1999); Lynn Hunt and Victoria Bonnell, *Beyond the Cultural Turn* (Berkeley, CA, 1999); Charles Megill, *Historical Knowledge, Historical Error: A Contemporary Guide to Practice* (Chicago, 2007); Lynn Hunt, *Writing History in the Global Era* (New York, 2014).

7. Walter Benjamin, "Paris, Capital of the Nineteenth Century: Exposé [1939]," in Walter Benjamin, *The Arcades Project,* tr. Howard Eiland and Kevin McLaughlin (Cambridge, MA, 1999), 14.

8. See Jay, *Songs of Experience,* 11–12, 224–9, 340–1, and passim.

9. O. Gridina, "Zerkalo ne vinovato," *Gazeta-kopeika,* 31 October 1910, 3.

10. The editor at Oxford University Press who developed the plan for "Oxford Histories," Christopher Wheeler, suggested that these books open with "a key document (or possibly several)...as a sharply focused encounter with the book's subject and a way of framing the subsequent account. The aim is to arrest the attention of readers with some striking evidence from the archive, vividly establishing the importance of the topic and opening up the range of analytical opportunities—in both familiar and unexpected or unsettling ways." I am grateful to him for this idea.

11. "Lauds Journalists as True Historians," *New York Times,* 19 December 1930 (a speech by Dr John Finley, associate editor of the *New York Times*).

12. Many authors comment on their chronological definition of "the revolution." See e.g. Fitzpatrick, *The Russian Revolution,* 1–4. See the Bibliography for a selection of histories.

13. Ivan Bunin, *Cursed Days: Diary of a Revolution*, tr. and ed. Thomas Gaiton Marullo (Chicago, 1998), 27–8.

PART I

DOCUMENTS AND STORIES

CHAPTER 1
SPRINGTIME OF FREEDOM
WALKING THE PAST

Modern revolutions are bacchanalias of words. When Bessie Beatty, a reporter for *The San Francisco Bulletin*, arrived in early June 1917 in the Russian capital, Petrograd (the Germanic-sounding name of the capital, St Petersburg, had been patriotically changed at the start of the World War), she found the streets and squares near the train station filled with crowds of people talking: "students, peasants, soldiers, workmen, pouring a torrent of words into the night." When she asked what was going on—"is it another revolution?" she wondered—she was told that "nothing is happening. They are just talking, It has been like this since March . . . They talk all day and all night, all the time."[1] The editors of one of Russia's leading newspapers observed the same in early autumn, though with less wide-eyed admiration: "There is no authority, no legality, and no effective political action in Russia, but there is an abundance of political words."[2]

The revolution did indeed unleash a flood of words as people tried to make sense of these historic days. People talked about revolution on the streets and squares, in factories and villages, in soldiers' barracks, in trams and trains, and in taverns, not to mention at meetings organized by various groups. Much of this talk has been lost. But a great deal was recorded in newspapers, pamphlets, leaflets, posters, and other publications that poured from the now uncensored presses and passed hand to hand—arousing more words, including a rising mountain of resolutions, appeals, and petitions approved at meetings. Words had become the defining attribute of civic life and the main way to practice politics—indeed, many complained, often a substitute for real action. Political theorists have argued that a lively "public sphere"—a social space of collective association and the free exchange of opinion concerning matters of civic concern—is essential for the development of a "civil society," which is the essential foundation for a democratic society. Russia, after the fall of the monarchy, had become a republic of words. Among these words, "freedom" was preeminent, not least because of its power to capture and express, as both idea and as emotion, the meaning of these sudden and dramatic events. Maria Pokrovskaya, perhaps Russia's most prominent liberal feminist in those years, put it simply and typically, "Russia has suddenly turned a new page in her history and inscribed on it: Freedom!"[3]

What remains of this flood of words forms the historian's archive, which I approach in this chapter by reversing the usual way historians write with documents. Usually, we build carefully constructed narratives and arguments out of a large body of evidence, revealing our primary sources in purposeful fragments—in quotes and notes—as proof and illustration. In this chapter, the documents themselves lead, as they do in other "Oxford Histories." This approach is not necessarily more "true" than when a historian's interpretation shapes the telling. As I noted in the Introduction, most historians are painfully aware that the archive of primary sources is already interpreted: shaped, for example, by conventions of writing for newspapers or in resolutions, by considerations of audience, by political values and purposes, and, not least, by what they thought was important. Historians mediate the archive further by making choices. Given the approach I described in the Introduction, it will not be a surprise when I reveal my hand: I have selected documents for this chapter, out of many thousands I read, not because they are typical (an illusory ideal, in any case) but because they are *telling*: these documents speak to us of how people tried to make sense of their experiences, intellectually and emotionally.

In choosing documents to illuminate the history of the revolution, I might have focused on a single voice—perhaps a history-maker like Lenin, or a more modest individual, an industrial worker, for example, who helped make history at the ground level—across all of the major events of this era, including Bloody Sunday in 1905; the October

Manifesto and new Fundamental Laws establishing a semi-constitutional monarchy in 1905 and 1906; the outbreak of what would become a devastating war in the summer of 1914; the demonstrations, strikes, and mutinies in February 1917 that toppled the tsar's government; the formation of a Provisional Government of elite liberals alongside the Soviet of Workers' and Soldiers' Deputies led by socialists; the overthrow of the Provisional Government, in the name of the Soviet, by the Bolshevik wing of the Russian Social Democratic Workers' Party; the new devastations of a civil war.

Instead, this chapter looks at multiple perspectives on a critical moment in time—and one that is more an aftermath than an event: the "springtime of freedom" of 1917. I want to imagine that we can walk through the streets during these first months of revolution: go to the demonstrations and meetings, listen to speeches, talk with people in public or where they work, and read everything at hand. Above all, I want to imagine we can ask people what they meant by that great, inclusive, and yet vague idea that everyone insisted defined the revolution: "freedom." We can do this aided by what has been left behind of that flood of words—including the reporting of Russian journalists who actually were walking the streets, listening and recording, trying to capture what revolution and freedom meant, while also making their case for what it should mean.

Springtime has long been a metaphor associated with political struggles for freedom, since at least Europe's 1848 "springtime of the peoples" and forward to recent revolutionary upheavals such as the "Arab spring." The political power of the metaphor draws on the physical experience of nature—increasing light and warmth, thaw and rebirth. In Christian cultures, it draws on associations with Easter, the sacred time of resurrection and salvation. The first named political "spring" in Russia was in 1904, though this referred to liberalizing reforms from above rather than revolution from below. In the last decades of the old regime, Russian artists and writers—most famously, Igor Stravinsky in his 1913 ballet *Rite of Spring* (*Vesna sviashchennaia*, literally *Sacred Spring*)—repeatedly used the theme of spring to explore the metaphoric end of darkness and cold, dramatic awakening, and the promise of a new and happier life.

15

When the autocracy abruptly collapsed at the beginning of March 1917, "freedom" was proclaimed the watchword of the revolution and associated with a flood of meanings already at hand from a long history of Russian political opposition: ending coercion, liberating the individual to realize his (sometimes her) full human capacities, creating a vital public sphere for political and civic participation. Freedom was often attached to emotions: pleasure and happiness, or at least the expectation of these, and a sense of living in a time of miracle, of experiencing the improbable arrival of salvation amidst exceptional disaster, loss, and ruin. This was complicated, as will be seen, by a tension deep in the meanings of "freedom" that was literally part of the language: the difference in Russian between *volia* and *svoboda*, though the distinctions are not as sharp in life as dictionaries have it. In English, we often distinguish these terms as "liberty" and "freedom." Authoritative Russian dictionaries explain, also too simply, that *volia* is the freedom of the individual, of the spirit, and especially of the will (the word *volia* also means "the will"), and *svoboda* is freedom connected to social relationships, groups, and laws that both emancipate and protect. In other words, *volia*-freedom is defined as the lack of restrictions, associated in Russian culture and history with the open spaces of steppe, rebels, and bandits: *volia* is freedom at its most free, though not always kind or gentle. *Svoboda*-freedom, in this explanation, becomes the pursuit of desires, needs, and interests in concert with the freedom of others. In nineteenth-century Russia, this notion of *svoboda*-freedom was associated with the history of European political struggles, especially the opening figure in the famous trinity of "liberté, égalité, fraternité," usually rendered in Russian as *svoboda, ravenstvo, i bratstvo*.[4] For the lower classes, *svoboda* was a less familiar term than *volia*, though it became increasingly popular in 1917—perhaps precisely because it was less familiar or clear, so it had an openness that well suited new experiences, ideas, and desires.

The peculiarities of Russian meanings should not be overstated. Russians were part of ongoing European and global debates about the meanings of freedom and liberty. Even on the streets and in popular newspapers during 1917, one can hear, for example, the universal tension between what has been called "negative" liberty and "positive" freedom: between freedom as liberation from constraints and freedom as emancipating justice, between freedom as allowing individuals the pursuit of happiness and freedom as guaranteeing the conditions for happiness, between inner freedom and freedom fully realized in political and social life.[5] We can also hear in the daily life of the revolution echoes of a definition of freedom as unlikely miracle, undoing the realities of a harsh everyday material life, oppressive social and political structures, and even the limitations on human possibility. Later in the twentieth century, Hannah Arendt would define freedom in this way as a radical "new beginning," an "improbable miracle," an "infinite improbability" that is nonetheless inevitable, for such is the nature of human existence, the very creation of which was infinitely improbable. Therefore, she argued, it is completely natural and realistic for humans to "look for the unforeseeable and unpredictable, to be prepared for and to expect 'miracles' in the political realm," even though the scales of reality "are weighted in favor of disaster."[6] Years earlier, in the midst of a second world war, Walter Benjamin, a friend of Arendt, agreed that human history is inclined toward "catastrophe," but insisted that it contains in its nature the possibility, however elusive and rare, of deliverance, redemption, and salvation—of miraculous new beginnings, of "spring-time."[7] Revolutions have been one of human history's strongest expressions of this desire, vision, and possibility. As Benjamin put it, revolutions "blast open the continuum of history"—the steady march of time where the present so shapes the emerging future that change can be only incremental and based on what *is* rather than what might be— and allow humanity to "leap in the open air of history" (*Sprung unter dem freien Himmel der Geschichte*), literally in the "free air": history as radical possibility.[8] Or as Karl Marx and Friedrich Engels famously used this same metaphor, revolution is "humanity's leap from the kingdom of necessity to the kingdom of freedom."[9]

But enough heady theory: it is time to walk through the streets of revolution.

1

If we arrived in Russia at the turn of the new year, 1917, picking up a local newspaper to orient ourselves to the events and moods of the day, we would notice a familiar tradition: New Year reflections about the passing of the old and the coming of the new, about history in its daily march. As 1917 began, now deep into the third year of war and economic crisis, no one imagined that revolution was only weeks away. On the contrary, the main feeling was that nothing would change, at least not for the better. If we were in Petrograd reading the 1 January edition of the popular *Kopeck Gazette* (*Gazeta-kopeika*), we would have surely noted the editorial asking rhetorically why we celebrate the coming of the new year at midnight, in the deep darkness of the night. Because, the editor concluded, we are ashamed. "We are ashamed of the past, ashamed of our indifference and apathy toward life around us—and so, as a type of self-justification, we shout about a better and brighter time. But the better has gone, and we are becoming worse and worse."[10] Other editorial writers were more optimistic, or refused to give in to disillusionment, insisting that people must hope, if for no other reason than that Russians have suffered for so long. For example, if we were in Moscow, we would have noticed the following first-page essay on New Year's Day in the *Daily Kopeck Gazette* (*Ezhednevnaia gazeta-kopeika*), a similar mass-circulation newspaper, titled "In 1917," written by the regular columnist P. Borchevsky (about whom we know nothing apart from his byline). He offered this interpretation of the traditional Russian New Year's greeting, "For a new year and new happiness" (*S novym godom, s novym schast'em*).

We must believe, without any self-delusion, that we have the full right to expect happiness from the new year without uncertainty. This happiness is coming! It will be real change and a solution to problems that are now so abundant, so strained, so tightened into a painful knot.

The necessity of hope, the faith that trust in the future would finally be justified, was an argument that had become typical in New Year's editorials. But this was more plea than argument, a profession of faith grounded more in impatience with hopelessness than in certainty of coming change. Borchevsky acknowledged the doubts plaguing the public mood:

We can speak of what is happening now in Russia only with feelings of confusion.... Completely unable to imagine what is coming, we hungrily

devour every rumor and live in a world thick with guesses and hints. This tension in the political atmosphere cannot continue much longer. There has been too much in Russia in recent times, even in these last days, that one may say about what causes us to tremble with nervous anticipation of the future: "What is ahead?! How will it all end?!" It will end. It must find resolution. This will happen in 1917.

The new year will bring "decisive answers," though not necessarily good answers. But uncertainty is worse than well-defined problems. Readers of the censored press knew perfectly well the troubles that could not be stated aloud in print, especially the enormous suffering caused by war, economic crisis, and government failure. But what would be the answer?

So much that is still unsettling and troubling will be revealed and made clear. And then things will become easier. This is the happy relief—the happiness of clear danger or clear good—that awaits us in 1917.[11]

There was no obvious reason to expect this. All the more reason to hope for a miracle.

2

On 2 March 1917 (on the Julian calendar, used in Russia at the time, which was thirteen days behind the Western European Gregorian calendar), the emperor Nicholas II abdicated the Russian throne. He acted under pressure from generals and other elites when the troops he ordered to bring a stop to protests in Petrograd mutinied, transforming street disorders into political revolution. Few expected the tsar would step down, though his authority had been eroding steadily during the war. When he did, crowds poured into the streets to celebrate. Newspapers tried to capture the mood:

The dazzling sun appeared. Foul mists were dispersed. Great Russia stirred! The long-suffering people arose. The nightmare yoke fell. Freedom and happiness—forward.
   "Hurrah! Hurrah! Hurrah!"
   With thunderous roar, the thousand-voiced cry of the elated people cheer the student-orator.
   From end to end are carried excited voices.

Every face is tense, eyes shining, gestures bold and free.

People admire the red flags fluttering high above their heads, look around, gather in large crowds, share impressions of the new and the unexpected.

Many embrace, kiss, congratulate one another, and throw themselves greedily at the distributed proclamations.

They read loudly, abruptly, agitatedly.

From mouth to mouth passes the long-awaited joyous news: "Freedom! Freedom! Freedom!"

Tears glisten in the eyes of many.

Uncontainable, wild joy.[12]

In both style and substance we feel in reports like this from the streets something of the sense of a miracle, of a sudden new beginning, of the improbable birth of the new, but also the sense that this deliriously joyous new "now" might just as easily vanish. But for the moment, it seemed that "freedom" had the magical power to cut through contradictory ideas and feelings, including through uncertainty and fear. The euphoric aura of "freedom" was palpable everywhere. And everyone seemed to share the hyperbolic, emotional, and usefully vague understanding of freedom as a "Great Joy," a "sacred" time of "Resurrection," a promise of "Happiness." Capital letters and exclamation points seemed essential to make clear that these were not ordinary feelings and beliefs. In the face of the catastrophes of war and economic and political failure, everything now seemed possible and everyone to be as one. But not for long.

3

As we imagine walking, listening, reading, and inquiring about the meanings of "freedom," we would surely notice, along with vague and hyperbolic declarations about a new and happy time, the ubiquity of soldiers, often riding around in vehicles and shooting festively into the air. Consider this scene inside the capital's military garrison (Figure 1). Wanting to commemorate their role in the revolution, these soldiers posed for a photograph beside their armored vehicle. Painted or chalked on the vehicle, in large and bold letters, is the Russian word "SVOBODA!"

Figure 1. Soldiers posing by armored vehicle, 28 February 1917. Russian State Archive of Film and Photographic Documents (Rossiiskii gosudarstvennyi arkhiv kinofotodokumentov), Moscow.

(FREEDOM!). We might read this revolutionary mise-en-scène as an interpretation of the word. At the least, they seem to be insisting on their role in history. Drawn below the turret is the outline of a flag identifying their unit, the Armored Division, and a date, 28 February 1917. The 27th of February was the defining moment for the revolution in the Russian capital: the day when mostly working-class street demonstrators were joined by mutinying garrison troops (also heavily working-class), which deprived the tsarist government of power over the streets, especially the essential power of violence to silence opponents. So, the 28th is the day "freedom" began, for which soldiers could take historic credit. The posed scene also speaks of the relationship between freedom and force: not only the elimination of the state's ability to use violence to suppress disorders, but also the threat of new violence in defense of freedom and perhaps in pursuit of the positive good that freedom should bring. With their martial pose and displayed weapons, these soldiers seem determined to argue that freedom depends on who holds the power of violence. The soldier at the door, a military dagger at his waist, is pointing his pistol at the camera. The men in front are armed and ready for combat, crouched beneath the vehicle's gun muzzles. We might interpret the scene's message as also about men and masculinity. Though the revolution was launched by women who courageously took to the streets of Petrograd in late February, this image speaks of the armed courage and vigilance of men. But there are dissonant notes. While one of the men perched above "Freedom!" has his pistol in hand and a fierce look on his face, the other seems to be lounging and slightly smiling. And on the wall of the garage behind this posed scene is the command "smoking is strictly forbidden." These are chance not purposeful words in the picture, simply part of the location at a storage base for weapons. But it may not be too fanciful to see this as symbolic: a commentary on the looming persistence of authority and restrictions amidst inflammables, a suggestion of the necessity of limitations on freedom.

4

This was the "springtime of freedom," everyone was saying. Of course, the seasonal metaphor of spring contained the possibility of the return of fall and winter. The soldiers posing for the photo above seemed to say "this is why you need us and our weapons." In mid-March, an editorial, signed only "B," appeared in Moscow's *Daily Kopeck Gazette* titled "The Springtime of Russia" (*Vesna Rossii*). "The first springtime of Russia," the author wrote, favoring abrupt, declarative opening phrases to convey a mood. "The springtime of resurrection and renewal. The springtime of freedom." Such phrases were typical and familiar, including the suggestions of the sacred and a syntax that sounded more like shouts in the street or declaimed verses than prose. "B" tried to capture the feelings of freedom with other expressions typical of the moment. Metaphors were preferred, for ordinary words seemed inadequate.

The long harsh winter of arbitrary power (*proizvol*) and force has been defeated.

No longer does the vision of a new Russia, as it was still written "yesterday," appear as merely a future promise. It now appears as a real possibility, as a wide horizon.

The great Russian revolution, so quickly, so unexpectedly, like oxygen to a dying man, came to save the Russian people at the very moment when those in authority did not expect it.

All revolutions come unexpectedly. This is the real grandeur of their arrival.

They are born spontaneously (*stikhiino* [literally, like the elements]). They fly in, like a hurricane, and tear out freedom for the exhausted people.

"As it was, so it shall be."

Words, the author recognized, contained power in this liberating storm. Freedom of speech became essential to the freedom that had been wrested from the old authority. And this meant not merely the formal absence of censorship or even mere legal protections for speech and the press, but a radical change in the very spirit of public language:

The old toothless words, the worn and exhausted clichés, the age-old "Aesopian language" [a traditional Russian reference to the need, in the face of censorship and repression, to express critical arguments indirectly, through allusion and analogy]—have disappeared with the last shadows of the eternal Russian "1001 nights" [the famous Arabic tales as analogies for Russia's "Asiatic" political backwardness and tyranny].

With convulsions and death-throes, twisting and vanishing, they were dispersed with the first rays of the sun.

But the new was still fragile and weak, and freedom must be defended, especially the freedom to speak.

The "quotation marks" [around words] have been laid bare. The "spells of the dead" (*nav'i chary*) over Russian reality have disappeared. The permanent guard-post for watching over the shackled speech of the Russian press has been demolished.

They are no more. A new guard has come and replaced the bureaucratic police watch.

And this guard stands ready to defend our newly won gains.

It must stand as a trusted honor guard, having met the dawn of renewal in this first spring of a new Russia.

Though still only hints, the worry can be felt. And worry, and warnings, would increase as the months passed. But for now, the author concluded, miraculous results were assured if the newly freed people of Russia were responsible and vigilant:

A springtime of life has come.

A springtime of enormous state construction, of fundamental reforms and the growth of a young Russia.

And you, meeting the first spring in a free country, must remember that it depends entirely on you, on your own ability, reasonableness (takt), and organization, whether we will meet such a springtime every year.

So be on guard in defense of our conquered freedom and you will be rewarded with a dazzling life.[13]

5

In reading newspapers in these opening days of the revolution, we would have been sure to read *Izvestiia* (News), the paper of the Petrograd Soviet of Workers' and Soldiers' Deputies, an organization of elected representatives and socialist activists, formed at the same moment as the new Provisional Government, which tried to serve as the voice of the lower classes, of "the democracy." And we would have surely noticed the poems included in almost every issue, often submitted by workers and soldiers. Poetry had special appeal in these days of revolution, not least to working-class Russians, many of whom turned their hand to poetry to express feelings and thoughts about freedom and revolution, often sending their efforts to newspapers. In the last days of March, Stepan Stepanov, a navy seaman (*matros*—the lowest rank) in the 9th Division of the Baltic Fleet, sent this carefully handwritten poem to *Izvestiia*:

> **Dawn has broken. Arise, tribe oppressed,**
> **Arise, oh people bound in chains.**
> **Seed once sown under the brutal yoke,**
> **Has now brought forth bountiful fruit.**

Unbend your mighty shoulders,
Who would dare block your path bought with blood?
No henchmen of monarch's thrones,
Will take away your progress, your freedom flag!

Who would trespass on your temple holy,
Or dare defile that sacred site?
No one, for you are a hero, a mighty titan,
All men fall silent in your sight.

Like the armored car labeled "freedom," and appeals to be "on guard" for freedom's defense, freedom and force are tied together. And while undemocratic and oppressive power is sustained by blood and fetters, freedom is guarded by its own awe-inspiring authority. Freedom, we are told, requires temples and guns.

Seaman Stepanov followed his poem with a note to the editors apologizing for his limited education and so "lack of knowledge of the rules of versification." But he politicized this lack by blaming "the accursed despot" who had "not let me study since my childhood days," along with the poor quality of his backward and provincial school. Such marks of a history of inequality are why that the revolution needed his verses, he implied. "Now is a great and awe-inspiring (*groznoe*) time and all of us must work tirelessly, never letting up. I want very much to be useful and to help in some way the great cause, the people's cause."[14] What his words lacked in technique, he suggested, was compensated for by their honest and authentic truth; indeed, his "apology" for ignorance of the "rules" only reinforced the value of his words as truth. And true words, in the spring of 1917, were thought to have the power to set one free.

6

The second day of April 1917 was Easter Sunday in the Orthodox calendar. Greeting cards were a relatively modern innovation. These two speak of many of the ideas and feelings people had about that year. In Figure 2, a rooster, beneath the traditional Easter greeting, "Christ has Risen," is crowing the dawn, the words "Freedom of Russia" (*Svoboda Rossii*) inscribed on a large red Easter egg. In Figure 3, under

Figure 2. Postcard "Freedom of Russia," Easter 1917. Department of Prints, Russian National Library, St Petersburg. I am also grateful to Boris Kolonitsky and Ella Saginadze for help in obtaining prints and permissions for Figures 2 and 3.

Figure 3. Postcard "Long Live the Republic," Easter 1917. Department of Prints, Russian National Library, St Petersburg.

the same greeting, before a rising sun, a worker and a soldier grasp hands in solidarity across an even larger red Easter egg inscribed "Long Live the Republic!" While we might find odd this mixing of secular and sacred (and nature and Christianity) to define freedom, this merging the resurrection of Christ with the resurrection of Russia was completely characteristic of the times.

7

Women's role in the revolution surprised socialist activists, who tended to view women as politically backward, inexperienced, and timid. The Bolshevik paper *Pravda* (Truth, but also Justice), a week after the revolution, praised working women for being first to take to the streets in demonstrations on Women's Day, for encouraging men to come out on strike, and for persuading solders not to shoot at the massing crowds. But *Pravda* did not mention that Bolshevik activists had told women not to strike at that time but "to show restraint and discipline," fearing that women's actions would lack "purpose." Even now, the party viewed women's boldness as rooted in traditional female concerns and feelings: "heartache for those close to them taken away by the war alternated with distress for their hungry children." The reality of women's activism was more complex. Side by side with stories of women tearfully begging soldiers not to shoot at "your mothers and sisters," and demanding bread to feed their hungry families, were women joining in violent attacks on police, breaking into police stations to burn documents, and looting stores.[15]

And women continued to take to the streets. In our imagined wandering of the streets of Petrograd in search of meanings, we would have surely gone to the giant women's march of 19 March, organized by feminist activists to demand voting rights for women, though many of the banners carried by working-class and peasant-class women addressed social and economic issues of concern to them.

Figure 4 shows women, working-class judging by their dress, before a banner offering an explicit commentary on "freedom": "If the woman is

Figure 4. Women's march, 19 March 1917. Russian State Archive of Film and Photographic Documents, Moscow.

a Slave, there will be no Freedom. Long live the Woman with Equal Rights." Figure 5 is a photograph of soldiers' wives (*soldatki*), whose banners declare: "Increase the Pay Packets for Families of Soldiers, the Defenders of Freedom and a People's Peace" and "Feed the Children of Defenders of the Motherland."

Rights and needs were often included in definitions of freedom, especially by groups with few rights and much material need. Advocates of equal rights for women would often cite the actions of women in the February revolution as argument for transforming the role of women in society. "Weren't we women the first out on the streets to fight for freedom, together with our brothers, and, if necessary, to die for it?" the Bolshevik-feminist Alexandra Kollontai asked in *Pravda* in late March. "So why now, just when we are starting to build a new Russia, are we

Figure 5. Soldiers' wives at women's march, 19 March 1917. "The Russian Revolution—Events and Personalities: An Album of Photographs. Collected by Bessie Beatty." Unpublished. The New York Public Library, p. 42 (date incorrectly stated as 9 April 1917). Slavic and Baltic Division. The New York Public Library, Astor, Lenox and Tilden Foundations.

feeling the fear that freedom...will ignore half the population of liberated Russia?"[16] The hesitation by both the Provisional Government and the Soviet to agree to women's suffrage was the immediate spur for this criticism. But after the vote was granted, in response to this mass demonstration, women continued to demand equal political and civil rights beyond suffrage.

Were we in Moscow in early March, we might have attended a meeting hosted on 6 March by the Moscow chapter of the League for Women's Equal Rights, to which representatives of women workers and of many women's organizations were invited. There, we would have heard "freedom" defined as including equal pay for women's work; social protections for maternity and child-rearing; abolition of laws allowing regulated prostitution and of other laws applying only to women, which "degrade women's human dignity"; the appointment of women to government posts at all levels, though especially when these concerned the "interests of the female population"; and opening to women the legal profession, the factory inspectorate, and all areas of "public service." If these measures are not taken, a resolution adopted at this meeting declared with frustration and anger, "this will be an open declaration that 'free citizen' implicitly means only men."[17]

8

Notwithstanding women's activism, the record of women's voices, especially the voices of non-elite women, is surprisingly sparse. As I worked in Russian archives reading through thick folder after folder of letters, appeals, and even lengthy essays that had been sent by individuals and groups to the new Provisional Government, the Petrograd Soviet, prominent political figures, and diverse newspapers, I encountered the words of thousands of men—including huge numbers of workers, peasants, and soldiers, some barely literate, but still determined to write—but very few women, least of all working-class or peasant women. Of course, silences in the historical record are as telling as what we do hear. Historians of women have emphasized that the paucity of women's own voices in the public sphere itself speaks strongly of histories of exclusion and subordination, of the male-dominated character of public life.

As if to underscore this silence, men sometimes wrote in a woman's voice, speaking in the first person in a language gendered female (Russian indicates the speaker's gender), instructing women about the "new life" that the revolution promised them and the proper meaning of freedom. In our explorations of public life and experience in these months, we would have surely rushed to read the newspaper for women, the *Woman Worker* (*Rabotnitsa*), launched by the Bolshevik party in May. In the first issue, we would have found this poem, written by a soldier at the front named E. Andreev (the author made no attempt to hide that he was a man), ventriloquizing a woman singing of freedom to her beloved, to whom she sent news of the "new dawn":

> My head spins,
> With joyous cries, the people's cries.
> We now have liberty, we now are free,
> And women have been given rights!
>
> A mighty faith, a massive strength,
> Awakened in my young breast;
> My heart has wished so long for freedom,
> And craved a different life....
>
> My dear, my sweet, understand my joy,
> And look tenderly into my eyes,
> For stormy passions have awakened in my breast,
> And fire has ignited in my eyes.[18]

This soldier imagined the "feminine" voice as stereotypically emotional and sentimental. And the women editors of *The Woman Worker* willingly selected it for their first issue. In supporting the struggles of women, including bolder demands for political equality and rights, the editors also hewed carefully to their party's ideological insistence that the class unity of proletarian men and women, as opposed to feminist gender separatism, was the only way women could realize the "light and freedom" the revolution promised.[19]

9

A great many documents from 1917—our window into the flood of words we might encounter on the streets of the revolution—treat freedom as positive, active, and transformative. Even the popular image of liberty as broken fetters was defined in positive ways, not least as the negation of physical harm: no more would workers be punished with fist and rods, no more would the poor go hungry, no more would citizens be sent to war, no more would activists be sent to prison or Siberia for speaking out.[20] Many voices looked beyond smashed shackles in defining freedom. True freedom, most Russians seemed to assume, must be a force for change for the better. The breaking of shackles must bring the rising sun, another ubiquitous image in 1917. And this new dawn was a social one. Freedom must not only free individuals from constraints, it must also create a free society of "citizens" living in conditions of justice. Liberal political philosophers have long warned against this illiberal confusion of "liberty with her sisters, equality and fraternity." It is a dangerous mistake, the argument goes, to conflate the freedom that emancipates the individual from external interference, that allows an active life in the pursuit of happiness, with the freedom that promotes happiness directly by changing society. Worse, the argument continues, this confuses individual happiness with social happiness, confuses individual freedom with the very different goal (perhaps laudable but not belonging to the proper definition of freedom) of ensuring "recognition" of the dignity and value of individuals who have been treated as different and subordinate because of their class, gender, race, ethnicity, or religion.[21] In other words, "freedom" should not be mistaken to mean rights and justice. This conflation of liberty and her "sisters," of course, has been precisely how freedom has been understood and acted on in modern revolutions, from late eighteenth-century France to our own time. During Russia's revolutionary spring, a great many workers, peasants, and soldiers insisted—notably in letters and petitions to the Soviet in Petrograd, viewed as the people's representatives—that liberty required the active creation of social equality and fraternity. Concretely, this meant not only reining in "the bourgeoisie," who would "rather die than give us our freedom,"[22] but solving the most pressing material problems of the day: providing food, controlling prices, giving all of the land to the people who work it, expanding education.[23] Most Russian commoners would have found it hard to understand the liberal warning that "confounding liberty with her sisters" equality and fraternity was not only a definitional mistake but might undermine true freedom.[24] For what sort of freedom could there be without recognition for all, prosperity for all, power for all, happiness for all?

And yet, as so often in the revolution, no single view could represent all people, even all men of the same class. Many lower-class Russians did embrace a conception of freedom as liberty from all constraints, though in more radical than liberal terms. Toward the end of March, a self-described "insignificant worker" who signed his name as A. Zemskov wrote a long and rambling letter about "freedom" to the Minister of Justice, Alexander Kerensky, who was the only socialist in the cabinet in these early months, offering "the truth that only a working man capable of speaking the pure truth can feel."

Ever since the last Russian autocrat fell from his high throne, you have been hearing on all sides laudatory hymns to the new state order and freedom. The new order is drawn in golden colors, freedom has its praises sung to the ringing of bells—these are the sounds of the revolutionary days we have known. I who expose this noise for what it is, am an enemy of state order no matter what it is, but I would sing the praises of freedom more loudly and triumphantly than you would, you slaves of the sinful earth, if freedom were ever to appear to us from somewhere. The whole question, though, is whether it is freedom's praises you are singing. Aren't you singing the praises of new chains that are only going by the name of freedom? The facts of the political reality we know speak so clearly that there is not even any need to refer to history or the opinions of the great many bourgeois scholars who have been reckless enough to hint at a certain portion of the truth, to say without error that freedom and state order are incompatible.... That the tsar is gone the Russian worker has heard—and believes deeply and naively that the hour of his liberation has come, and the honorable Milyukov [leader of the liberal Constitutional Democratic Party] and the ignoble press declared back on 2 March that "the chains have been lifted from the people." In fact, though, we never had freedom for a single second even at the very height of the revolution.... Before the old autocratic yoke could be lifted, a horse collar was made up in rough-and-ready fashion at the Tauride Palace [seat of both the new Provisional Government and the Petrograd Soviet] and put on the people's neck to songs and hymns, while the cry went out all around the world: "Freedom!!" In actual fact, however, it's a horse collar.... That is how badly the people's vision has been spoiled: they can't tell the difference between those two things, the collar and freedom!...

At times, Zemskov could be philosophical in explaining why this new freedom was a "blatant lie."

Every state authority (even in democratic states) is founded on coercing its own subjects.... Where there is freedom there cannot be coercion, and where there is coercion, there cannot be freedom.

But mostly he defined freedom around questions of social power—and not as abstractions about who controlled the means of production (the Marxist definition of class) but as concrete forms of power over the very bodies of the poor.

The slogan of our era is "Freedom!" "Down with coercion!" Nonetheless, all the leaders of our revolutionary movement who have proclaimed these slogans are professing and energetically supporting harsh military discipline among the troops—that crudest form of coercion....They shout at the top of their lungs that "the chains have been broken and freedom has come!" But, damn it, what kind of freedom is it when millions of voiceless slaves are still being led like sheep to the cannons and machine guns and the officer is still treating the slave as if he were a mere thing, when still only crude coercion restrains the multi-million army of gray slaves?

Zemskov's class feelings were strong, so much so that he lumped together as "oppressors of the people" not only the capitalist "bourgeoisie" but also "the entire intelligentsia (especially the socialist intelligentsia)." Indeed, he felt particular contempt for socialist intellectuals who claimed that the revolution "is guided by a single goal—the desire for freedom, happiness, and every good for the people."

How stupid to believe these words. Do the people really want you to look after them, take care of them, etc.? No, the people want you to get off their backs. If you want good, happiness, and all the rest for the people, then climb down off the people's mighty back, which you have been riding on and squeezing all the juice from. Don't live by its labor, don't stuff yourselves on what belongs to others....After all, you're oppressing the people, who have long known that you're riding on their back: the noble and the merchant and the scholar and the poet and the journalist and the lawyer and the priest. You're all nothing but greedy predators making off with the products of our labor. That is what the people are suffering from and this is where the root of social evil lies. The people need only for you parasites to stop riding on their backs, and once that happens, freed from your yoke, they will govern themselves, and worrying about them will be none of your business. Though probably they will have no reason to create a state....I ask you not to not to christen me with the name of anarchist. I am no anarchist. I am a proletarian free of prejudice.[25]

10

In our walks through revolutionary Petrograd, we would surely want to visit the writer Maxim Gorky—perhaps we might rest in his apartment (he welcomed many different people) and ask his thoughts on the revolution and the meaning of freedom. One of Russia's most influential public voices, especially among literate commoners and left-leaning intellectuals, Gorky was himself a great wanderer in search of stories. By origins from the provincial lower middle class, as a young man he had worked his way across Russia, employed variously as an apprentice and errand-boy in a drafting workshop, a cook's helper on a Volga steamboat, a construction worker, a sales assistant at a public market, a newspaper reporter, and other jobs. He became interested in socialism after encountering an illegal student circle in Kazan. Above all, he was a major writer, perhaps the most popular contemporary fiction author in Russia at the time, especially for his stories and plays about restless plebeians living and wandering on the fringes of society. Politically, he was close to the Bolshevik party, which he often aided financially, and to Lenin personally, though he hesitated to formally join the party.

During the spring of 1917, he launched a newspaper in Petrograd, the *New Life* (*Novaia zhizn'*). He titled his personal editor's column "Untimely Thoughts," for he viewed himself as a voice of inconvenient truths, of conscience within the revolutionary camp. As he liked to say, with pride, he was "a heretic everywhere."[26] The first issue appeared on the international workers' holiday May Day (18 April on Russia's calendar). Gorky's first editorial focused on a favorite theme: the relationship between "revolution and culture," between political change and the intellectual and moral life of society and individuals. Freedom was at the heart of this relationship. Gorky worried about the "devastating" legacy of autocracy, bureaucracy, and violence, especially on the human "spirit." And he warned that overthrowing the monarchy, which had achieved only negative liberty, could not "spiritually cure" Russians, and might even push the disease deeper into the "organism."[27] He continued these thoughts in his second column, insisting on the enormous transformation required if the new freedom was to be true freedom.

The new structure of political life demands from us also a new structure of the soul. One cannot be reborn in two months, of course. But the sooner we attend to cleansing ourselves of the dirt and filth of the past, the stronger will be our spiritual health and the more productive will be the work of creating new forms of social existence. We live in a storm of political emotions, in the chaos of a struggle for power, a struggle that arouses dark instincts alongside good feelings. This is natural, but it cannot but threaten a certain distortion of the psyche, an unnatural one-sided development. Politics is the soil in which the nettle of poisonous enmity, evil suspicions, shameless lies, slander, morbid ambitions, and lack of respect for the person (*lichnost'*) grows rapidly and abundantly.[28]

Gorky's worries were reinforced a few days later, on 21 April, by a violent incident on Nevsky Prospect in the heart of Petrograd, in which three men were reported killed and several wounded when someone opened fire during a clash between demonstrators and soldiers. Gorky was less concerned about who was to blame for this violence than about the conditions of liberty that were threatening true freedom.

The bright wings of our young freedom are spattered with innocent blood.... It is criminal and vile to kill one another now, when we have the beautiful right to argue honestly, to disagree with one another honestly. Those who think otherwise are incapable of feeling and recognizing that that they are free people. Murder and violence are the arguments of despotism.... The great happiness of freedom must not be darkened by crimes against the person (*lichnost'*). Otherwise we will kill freedom with our own hands. We must understand, it is time to understand, that the most dreadful enemy of freedom and rights is within us: our stupidity, our cruelty, and all that chaos of dark, anarchistic feelings, which have been cultivated in our souls by the monarchy's shameless oppression, by its cynical cruelty. Are we capable of understanding this? If not, if we cannot refrain from the most flagrant use of force over man, then we have no freedom. It is simply a word that we do not have the strength to fully endow with its proper content.[29]

What was this "proper content" of "freedom?" Negation of restraints was clearly not enough. Freedom must be "fully endowed" with positive purpose, especially overcoming the moral and emotional damage caused by both the abusive past and the disrupted present. Gorky placed at the center of this vision the human person, the self, the individual in society—captured in the single Russian word, which he often used, *lichnost'*. This term had become, since the mid-nineteenth century, a keyword among Russian intellectuals for recognizing the existence and value of the inward but always social self: the essential core of every person that gives rise to the equal and natural dignity of all human beings and thus the natural equal rights of all. As such, the notion of *lichnost'* became the benchmark for measuring, and condemning, the harm caused by political and social conditions that degraded individuals, whether caused by Russia's economic and political backwardness or by the experience of rapid industrial and urban modernization.[30]

Gorky shared the widespread belief that freedom must protect and enrich *lichnost'* and that this required going beyond overcoming external constraints on the individual to establish social conditions that would enable the person to flourish individually and in society. Such freedom required transforming mind and spirit, a "cleansing" of intellectual and moral traces of the unemancipated past. In time, this vision could have brutal implications: for Gorky personally, this partly justified his support of Stalin's modernizing revolution from above and efforts to "engineer the human soul." But for now, in 1917, Gorky was attached to the nineteenth-century liberal insistence that true or "just" freedom demands "recognition" of the "freedom of the other." Hence, Gorky's disgust and anger at acts of street violence that violated the liberty and rights of others. But liberal definitions of freedom also felt too modest and restrained for revolutionaries like Gorky: freedom must do more than recognize the freedom of the other; freedom must bring positive change, a "new life" for society and the individual, a miraculous new beginning.

11

Traveling to Moscow later that spring, we might have sought out the great modernist author Andrei Bely, and found him working on his essays on the revolution, published later that year under the title *Revolution and Culture*, the same title Gorky had chosen for his first editorial in his *New Life* newspaper. The author most recently of the brilliant novel *Petersburg* (1916), Bely perceived the revolution as an elemental force of nature:

Like a quake deep in the earth, breaking everything, the revolution appears before us: it appears like a hurricane, sweeping aside forms.... The revolution recalls nature: storms, floods, waterfalls. Everything in it breaks "across boundaries"; everything in it is excessive.[31]

But this violent breaking of boundaries could also be compared to the birth of new life:

In the mechanistic view of existence, revolution is an explosion, breaking the dead form into formless chaos. But it is really otherwise: it is rather the pressing force of an emerging shoot, the tearing of the shoot through the seed's membrane, the germination of the maternal organism in the mysterious act of birth.[32]

Bely's vocabulary (including the gendered images of destruction and creation) drew on symbolist theories and mystical philosophy, but also on popular images of revolution as a springtime of rebirth, destructive storms, resurrection, and new life.

In some ways, Bely answered Gorky's concern that violent emotions and acts threatened freedom.

The act of revolution is a duality: an act of force and an act of freedom, the death of old forms and the birth of the new. These two manifest-ations are two branches from a single root.... The kick of revolution is proof that the infant is stirring in the womb. Revolutionary force is like a stream from an artisanal well: at the beginning the source spews dirt, and the sluggishness of earth flows in its streams; but the stream becomes cleansed. Revolutionary cleansing is the organization of chaos into the supple movement of newborn forms.

So the disorder and uncertainties of revolution should not be feared:

The first moment of revolution is the formation of vapor; the second is its condensation into lithe and flowing form: a cloud. A cloud in motion can be anything you like: a giant, a city, a tower. Metamorphosis reigns within it. Colors appear in it. It speaks with thunder: thunderous voices in mute and formless vapor are the miracle of life's birth in the depths of the revolution.[33]

And the new life that was being born was nothing less than "the kingdom of freedom." Bely dwelled at length on this idea, originating, of course, in the Judeo-Christian prophesy of a messianic "kingdom of God" or "kingdom of heaven." For Marx and Engels, we have seen, this idea was adapted to a definition of revolution as a "leap from the kingdom of necessity to the kingdom of freedom," a leap from existence shaped by the material limitations of nature and history to a radically new life where human action would be a matter of desire and possibility and people would be able, as never before, to "fashion their own history with full consciousness."[34] A more immediate source for Bely was Lev Tolstoy, who had insisted, in his 1894 pamphlet, *The Kingdom of God is Within You*, that this knowledge alone, not the authority of churches or states, was the way to a redeemed, just, and truly free society.[35]

Bely took this further. He applied the idea of a revolutionary leap first to the world of art, to the need to "break free from the necessity of creativity into the land of its freedom." He expanded on Tolstoy: "the kingdom of freedom is already within us! It shall be outside of us!"[36] This extended far beyond art:

The first act of creativity is the creation of a world of art. The second act: one's own self-creation in the image and likeness of the world. But the world of created forms does not allow the creator into the kingdom of freedom he has constructed. Standing at the threshold is a sentry, which is our own conservative "I".... Act three: entry into the kingdom of freedom and the new union of unconditionally free people for the creation of communities of life in the image and likeness of new names, inscribed secretly within us by spirit.[37]

As to how we enter into this "kingdom of freedom," Bely found the Marxist metaphor of the leap weak and wanting:

The revolution of the spirit is a comet flying toward us from a reality beyond boundaries. Overcoming necessity in the kingdom of freedom, envisioned as a social leap, is not at all a leap: it is a comet falling on us. But even this fall is an optical illusion, a reflection in the firmament of what is happening in our heart.[38]

Like Halley's comet, which excited a great deal of public interest (and fear) in Russia when it approached in 1910,[39] this image of the revolution as a comet can be read as an argument about a miraculous reality, an improbable but true reality beyond normal, everyday facts. But this future world of freedom, this more true but alien reality, Bely explained, is not an external force from distant space, but "our own image within us, like a star; it cannot be seen; it is given as a bundle of glints."[40] Walter Benjamin, responding to a different historical crisis and inspired by different philosophical and political ideas, would similarly describe "present time" as "shot through with splinters of messianic time" and a future time of redemption that can only be "grasped" as "an image" when it "flashes up in a moment of danger."[41] Returning to where we began this chapter, we might suggest, with the help of Bely and Benjamin, what many Russians seemed to believe and feel during this springtime of freedom: that these glints and splinters, if grasped, could "blast open the continuum of history" and allow a "leap in the open air" toward a "kingdom of freedom" beyond the boundaries of the present as they knew it.

Notes

1. Bessie Beatty, *The Red Heart of Russia* (New York, 1918), 8. Another American journalist arriving that summer, John Reed, was also struck by the torrent of public talk. See John Reed, *Ten Days that Shook the World* (New York, 1919), 14.
2. "Politika i ekonomika," *Russkie vedomosti*, 19 September (2 October) 1917, 3.
3. *Zhenskii vestnik*, 3 March 1917, 1, quoted in Rochelle Goldberg Ruthchild, *Equality and Revolution: Women's Rights in the Russian Empire, 1905–1917* (Pittsburgh, PA, 2010), 223.
4. Svetlana Boym, *Another Freedom: The Alternative History of an Idea* (Chicago, 2010), 78–9. See also the most authoritative and influential of Russian dictionaries, by Vladimir Dal' and by Dmitrii Ushakov.
5. Especially influential discussions of these distinctions and tensions are Isaiah Berlin, "Two Concepts of Liberty" (1958), in his *Four Essays on Liberty* (New York, 1990), and Hannah Arendt, "What is Freedom?" (1958) in her *Between Past and Future* (New York, 2006).
6. Arendt, "What is Freedom?," 165–9.
7. Walter Benjamin, "On the Concept of History" (1940), *Selected Writings*, ed. Howard Eiland and Michael W. Jennings, 4 vols. (Cambridge, MA, 2003), iv. 389–411; Michael Löwy, *Fire Alarm: Reading Walter Benjamin's 'On the Concept of History'* (London, 2005).

8. Benjamin, "On the Concept of History," *Selected Writings*, iv, especially 395 and 397 (Theses XIV and A). See also Löwy, *Fire Alarm*, 87–9, 99–102.

9. Friedrich Engels, *Herrn Eugen Dühring's Umwälzung der Wissenschaft* [Herr Eugen Dühring's Revolution in Science, or Anti-Duhring, 1878], sect. 3 (Socialism), ch. 2 (Theoretical), in Karl Marx and Friedrich Engels, *Werke: Herausgegeben vom Institut für Marxismus-Leninismus beim ZK der SED*, xx (Berlin, 1962), 264. A similar argument can be found in Karl Marx, *Capital: A Critique of Political Economy*, iii (Chicago, 1909), ch. 48 (pp. 952–5). See also Andrzej Walicki, *Marxism and the Leap to the Kingdom of Freedom: The Rise and Fall of the Communist Utopia* (Stanford, CA, 1995).

10. M. Gorodetskii, "Na Novyi god," *Gazeta-kopeika*, 1 January 1917, 3.

11. P. Borchevskii, "V 1917 godu," *Ezhednevnaia gazeta-kopeika*, 1 January 1917, 1.

12. "Soldaty idut...," *Ezhednevnaia gazeta-kopeika*, 6 March 1917, 3.

13. B., "Vesna Rossii," *Ezhednevnaia gazeta-kopeika*, 11 March 1917, 1.

14. "Razsvelo," by the sailor Stepan Stepanov, 28 March 1917. State Archive of the Russian Federation (GARF), f. 1244, op. 2, d. 31, ll. 43, 44ob. Manuscript.

15. Ruthchild, *Equality and Revolution*, 218–23; Choi Chatterjee, *Celebrating Women: Gender, Festival Culture, and Bolshevik Ideology* (Pittsburgh, PA, 2002), ch. 2.

16. Aleksandra Kollontai, "Rabotnitsy i uchreditel'noe sobranie," *Pravda*, 21 March 1917, 3.

17. "Liga ravnopraviia zhenshchin," *Smolenskii vestnik*, 9 March 1917, 4. I am grateful to Michael C. Hickey for a copy of this text, which he used and translated in his edited collection, *Competing Voices from the Russian Revolution: Fighting Words* (Santa Barbara, CA, 2011), 167–8.

18. Soldat E. Andreev, "My vmeste s toboiu," *Rabotnitsa*, 1–2, 10 May 1917, 6.

19. See P. F. Kudelli, "Pamiati pavshikh bortsov," *Rabotnitsa*, 10 May 1917, 2.

20. Mark Steinberg, *Voices of Revolution, 1917* (New Haven, 2001), passim.

21. Berlin, "Two Concepts of Liberty," 154–66. An older and likely influential argument is G. W. F. Hegel's concept of "recognition" (*Anerkennung*), developed in his Jena Lectures of 1805–6, published as *The Spirit of Philosophy*, as "recognition" of an individual's "personhood," "being," "will," and "existence" to be an essential human need.

22. Handwritten appeal to the Petrograd Soviet from Matvei Frolov, 25 April 1917, GARF, f. 6978, op. 1, d. 354, ll. 10b.-2.

23. e.g. resolution of the workers of the "Old Parviainen" factory, 13 April 1917, in Steinberg, *Voices of Revolution*, 95.

24. Berlin, "Two Concepts of Liberty," 154–70.
25. Handwritten letter to Minister of Justice Alexander Kerensky from A. Zemskov, 26 March 1917. State Archive of the Russian Federation (GARF), f. 6978, op. 1, d. 296, ll. 39–450b.
26. M. Gor'kii, "O polemike," *Novaia zhizn'*, 25 April (8 May) 1917, 1.
27. M. Gor'kii, "Revoliutsiia i kul'tura," *Novaia zhizn'*, 18 April (1 May) 1917, 1.
28. M. Gor'kii, "Nesvoevremennye mysli," *Novaia zhizn'*, 20 April (3 May) 1917, 5.
29. M. Gor'kii, "Ob ubiistve," *Novaia zhizn'*, 23 April (6 May) 1917, 1.
30. For more discussion, see V. V. Vinogradov, *Istoriia slov* (Moscow, 1994), 271–309; Derek Offord, "Lichnost': Notions of Individual Identity," in Catriona Kelly and David Shepherd (eds), *Constructing Russian Culture in the Age of Revolution, 1881–1940* (Oxford, 1998), 13–25; Laura Engelstein and Stephanie Sandler (eds), *Self and Story in Russian History* (Ithaca, NY, 2000); and Mark D. Steinberg, *Proletarian Imagination: Self, Modernity, and the Sacred in Russia, 1910–1925* (Ithaca, NY, 2002), 2–5, 62–101.
31. Andrei Belyi, *Revoliutsiia i kul'tura* (Moscow, 1917), 3.
32. Ibid. 12–13.
33. Ibid. 13–14.
34. Marx and Engels, *Werke,* xx. 264.
35. L. N. Tolstoi, *Tsarstvo Bozhie vnutri vas* (The Kingdom of God is Within You) (Berlin, 1894).
36. Belyi, *Revoliutsiia i kul'tura*, 17.
37. Ibid. 24.
38. Ibid. 30.
39. See e.g. *Vesna* 1910/3: 23 and 1910/11: 86 (a letter from Lev Tolstoy).
40. Belyi, *Revoliutsiia i kul'tura*, 29.
41. Benjamin, "On the Concept of History," 390–1, 397.

PART II

HISTORIES

CHAPTER 2
REVOLUTION, UNCERTAINTY, AND WAR

The 1905 Revolution

On Sunday, 9 January 1905, soldiers fired on a demonstration by thousands of workers and their families marching toward the Winter Palace in St Petersburg carrying a petition for the tsar, Nicholas II. Hundreds were wounded and at least 130 people were killed according to the official government count. "Bloody Sunday" ignited a gigantic political and social upheaval that quickly spread throughout the empire.[1] The unprecedented mass march to the tsar's palace had a bizarre origin: it was organized by an Orthodox priest, Father Georgii Gapon, who was also an agent of the political police, which had organized an government-sponsored "Assembly of Russian Factory Workers" with the aim of luring workers away from radical politics by helping them address their everyday material needs and show the concern of the government. Although Gapon worked for the police, his sympathies were complex and his relations with the government may have been partly duplicitous. Certainly, the petition carried to the Winter Palace was a contradictory mix of the traditional tones of a humble people beseeching their "tsar-father" to protect and help them and quite bold and modern demands for a constitutional and representative political system, to be established by a Constituent Assembly elected through universal, secret, and equal suffrage; state intervention to improve working and living conditions and reduce poverty; legalization of trade unions and strikes; and guaranteed "freedom and inviolability of the person, freedom of speech and press, freedom of assembly, and freedom of conscience in the practice of

religion." Socialist participants in Gapon's police-affiliated labor movement, whose motives for taking part were also complex, helped draft
these modern political demands.[2]

The petition, the march, and the revolution it ignited were shaped by
years of history: the negative experience of living under a bureaucratic
and authoritarian government, of strong limits on individual and civic
freedom, of deep inequalities of class, ethnicity, religion, and gender,
and, most recently and continuing, of a disastrous war with Japan; but
also the positive experience of educated elites (and gradually a widening
range of Russians) embracing and promoting liberal and radical arguments about natural and universal human dignity and rights and about
the necessity of a society of citizens with protected freedoms, fundamental civil rights, and participation in both local and national government.
These histories of perceived injustice and imagined alternatives were
echoed in the petition carried on Bloody Sunday: not only in the reforms
proposed, but especially in the vocabulary used, which described past
and present as "despotism," "arbitrary power," and the "lack of rights";
blamed "bureaucrats" and "capitalist-exploiters" for people's suffering; and
declared "human rights" (*chelovecheskie prava*) to be the principal goal.

In the weeks and months that followed, the government faced the
nightmare it had been trying to prevent through organizations like
Gapon's police union for workers. The number of strikes and strikers
during 1905, a movement that spread across the empire, was greater than
in all previous years combined; illegal trade unions proliferated and
were joined in October by city-wide workers' "soviets," or councils, in
which socialist intellectuals were influential; streets were filled with
demonstrations, occasionally violent; and demands grew more political
and uncompromising. In the countryside, peasants soon joined in,
though concentrating more on immediate concerns than national political arrangements: they assaulted estates, seized grain, illegally cut wood,
and generally refused to obey their landlords. A handful of mutinies
erupted in the army and especially the navy, sometimes violent (as in the
famous uprising on the Battleship *Potemkin* in the Black Sea) and always
violently suppressed. Violence was also taken up by non-elites, especially
right-wing gangs known as "black hundreds," who opposed the revolution and its values, for which they blamed and attacked students,

intellectuals, and Jews. In the non-Russian borderlands of the Russian empire, the revolution tended more quickly to turn radical and violent. In the Caucasus, the Baltic Provinces, and Poland, local activists attacked symbols of Russian rule and demanded national independence.

The climax of the revolution was the October general strike, which brought millions of people into the streets, especially workers, students, white-collar employees, and professionals. The main demands were everywhere the same: civil liberties and elections to establish a new constitutional order, which growing numbers believed must be a republic not a constitutional monarchy. Hoping to calm the country, the tsar listened to the advice of some of his officials (he would later regret this) and promised, in his October Manifesto, to establish a parliament representing "all classes," to be called the State Duma, adapting an old word for a council of advisors, which would have the power to decide on all laws and to "supervise the legality" of the actions of all government officials (though not the tsar himself) and "to grant to the population the unshakeable foundations of civil freedom, based on the principles of genuine inviolability of the person and freedom of conscience, speech, assembly, and association."[3] This was an astonishing concession. The Manifesto promised exactly what the tsar had sworn he would never do, and about which he predicted catastrophe if it ever occurred: share political power with representatives of society. Moderate liberals were satisfied that this was enough; and they reasonably feared that continued struggle might produce a social revolution that would threaten more than political structures. But many Russians wanted more; and many doubted the tsar would keep his promises, anyway.

*   *   *

This is the story historians tell—a relatively authoritative retrospective account based on available evidence and current scholarly interpretation. Another viewpoint, which will continue in dialogue with the professional historians' tale in these three narrative chapters of Part II, is the writing of history by journalists "in the present tense" at the "moment of its making," as it was once famously said.[4] One of the best known Russian newspapers at the time was the Moscow daily *Russian Word* (*Russkoe slovo*), a vaguely liberal paper that claimed to reflect the views and interests of the "man-on-the street," even "the mood of the crowd."[5]

The rebellion in the wake of Bloody Sunday was understood to be a historic turning point, even a new beginning. Reporters described these events as the "dawn of new life," with the country standing "on the eve of its liberation," on the boundary between "impenetrable darkness" and a "bright, luminous, and spacious" future, as a historic time of "renewal," "rebirth," and "renaissance."[6] The sense that history was being made was felt even more strongly after the October Manifesto: "Today begins a new life. Russian history has gone onto a new path. Throughout the centuries of Russia's servile existence we have never known a stronger, happier moment."[7] "Newness" was a refrain: Russia was entering a "new life," a time of "creation," a new "beginning," a time of becoming "new people" with a renewed spirit.[8]

"Freedom" was the leitmotif that defined the heart of the new, especially as desire and experience. Russia, a columnist declared in typical phrases, was finally joining "the common family of bold peoples advancing toward freedom and happiness."[9] The road would not be easy, another observed: this was a "fight to the death between two giants: the new life with its freedom and freshness, and the old one, decrepit and ulcerous, but still able to bite sharply in its final convulsions." The outcome was inevitable, however: "freedom of thought, speech, and the person (*lichnosti*),"[10] or in the phrase, common after the October Manifesto, that harkened back to the French Revolution and thus linked the Russian revolution to a presumed universal human struggle, Russians would win "liberty, equality, and fraternity."[11] Freedom was imagined with practical acts—electing a legislature with democratic representation, ensuring free speech and assembly, guaranteeing the rule of law—and emotional metaphors: a treasure bought with blood and tears, a star glimpsed through the narrow prison window of past oppression, a bright comet or meteor, rays of light, burning flames, fresh wine.[12]

"Citizenship" defined this new freedom. A citizen, by definition, was protected from arbitrary oppression: the free Russia that was emerging would be a society governed by "law and rights" (*zakon i prava*).[13] But citizenship was also defined as a duty: freedom depended on an active and responsible citizenry. In this light, there was much talk of the awakening of Russia's social forces, civic culture, and spiritual strength—in other words, the birth of the "good citizen."[14] "Awakening" was a ubiquitous metaphor. The "sleeping and forgotten people" were "awakening" to the "great historical meaning" of these times.[15] They awoke to discover they were no longer children but now "men" and thus "citizens in the highest sense of the word," that they had outgrown the "clothes" that the "bureaucracy" had put on them, which were now "too tight and short."[16]

"Shadows" darkened these bright visions ("Light and Shadows" (*Svet i teni*) was the title of a regular column in the *Russian Word* by the influential journalist Sergei Iablonovskii). Even aside from skepticism about the sincerity of the tsar's commitment to real change, commentators worried about how "new" and "reborn" people really could be. Writers regularly cursed the deep and lasting wound inflicted by Russia's history. The "bureaucracy"—usually a metonym for the whole political order topped by the tsar—had tried to "squeeze the vast and diverse life of the nation into the frame of its bureaucratic understanding," thus "paralyzing" civic life.[17] This history had consequences for the present and the future: because Russians had for so long been "politically enslaved and spiritually crushed,"[18] "humiliated" and "tormented" by a patriarchal system of rule,[19] stifled and infantilized by "long years of tutelage and surveillance," the "enterprising spirit, energy, and independence of the masses" had been "eroded." How could Russians now suddenly be "capable" and "ready" to build a new, free society?[20] Most writers tried to be optimistic: the newly unshackled and awakened people could change, they would be reborn. But the worries were not without cause.

Popular violence was a particularly troubling sign to most observers. On the one hand, violence was recognized as historically necessary. How else could people free themselves from an old regime gripping desperately onto power with its "old, bony fingers"?[21] How else could "chains" be broken, "prisons" destroyed, and "torture" ended? This page in Russian history, like so many before, was being written in "terrible, bloody letters," but now for a good cause, for the people not the state.[22] At the same time, violence, however explainable by a history of oppression, was also seen as a danger for freedom. Journalists worried that the pent-up passions, resentments, anger, and ignorance among the "dark" common folk would produce a bloody "time of troubles" (*smutnoe vremia*, a phrase with a deep history in Russia for describing eras of disruption and violence, which often ended in greater authoritarianism) that would bury the newborn freedom.[23]

But optimism remained the leading mood: faith in new beginnings; faith that the "darkness" represented by the "black hundreds" (violent right-wing patriotic groups) and the remnants of the "police state" were only the pitiful "death throes" of the old order;[24] faith that that a "life" so long "locked up and restrained with force," but now free to "boil and seethe," would heal the wounds of history and create new people and a new life.[25] There was even hope that the skeptics were wrong and the government would keep its word,[26] that the day after the tsar signed the October Manifesto truly was Russia's "first day of freedom."[27] Nicholas II himself viewed these troubles with a certain optimism, but not in anticipation of greater freedom for his nation: in a letter to his mother on 27 October, he welcomed the violence of the black hundreds: "In the first days after the Manifesto the subversive elements raised their heads, but a strong reaction set in and a whole mass of loyal people suddenly made their power felt....The impertinence of the Socialists and revolutionaries had angered the people once more; and, because nine-tenths of the trouble-makers are Jews, the people's anger turned against them. That's how the pogroms happened."[28]

1906–1914: Reform, Possibility, Uncertainty, Crisis

Historians have long structured interpretations of Russian history between the 1905 revolution and the outbreak of the World War in 1914 around poles of optimism and pessimism. The simplest version is presented as a stark choice: was Russia heading inescapably toward crisis and revolution, or was Russia on a path toward resolving tensions and creating a functioning civil society with a reformed political order had it not been for the unprecedented stresses of World War I? Evidence on the side of optimism (the terminology assumes, of course, that orderly progress is good and revolution bad) includes the political reforms that created the legislative State Duma and established basic civil rights, social reforms that lessened hardships and protected the less powerful, an increasingly lively public sphere filled with voluntary associations of all sorts, continued economic development and modernization, and other signs of progress and normalization—with movement toward Western capitalist democracy the assumed norm. Pessimists could point toward the many limitations on these reforms, the persistence of social discontent and conflict, and the growing appeal of parties on the political left.[29] The evidence on both sides is strong, though perhaps the question is too simple: rather than see two alternative historical outcomes, should we not focus on the sheer contradictoriness of these years, the lack of coherence and clear direction, the potential for many different outcomes?

Contradiction and indirection were certainly plentiful after 1905. The new "Fundamental Laws" passed in May 1906 established the State Duma with legislative and budgetary rights but also restricted its authority in many ways, including a lack of parliamentary control over the appointment and actions of cabinet ministers and over large parts of the budget, plus a skewed electoral system that favored social classes and groups expected to be more conservative. Trade unions and strikes were legalized but police retained extensive authority to monitor union activities and shut down unions for the least sign of political activity. Greater press freedom was guaranteed, but publications were subject to punitive fines and closure for overstepping the bounds of tolerated free speech. The contradictions deepened when the new prime minister, Pyotr Stolypin, revised the electoral law in the summer of 1907 with the hope of ensuring a more compliant legislature (the troublesome First and Second Dumas were both dissolved by the tsar before their terms ended), reducing representation by peasants, workers, and non-Russian nationalities and increasing that of the gentry (such that the vote of one landlord to the Third Duma would now count as much as the votes of 260 peasants). In the short term, Stolypin's "coup," as critics dubbed it, worked well. The Third and Fourth Dumas were more compliant, dominated by conservative and moderate political parties. Stolypin also effectively "pacified" political and social unrest, closing disagreeable publications by the hundreds and using summary courts-martial to dispatch a great many people accused of "sedition" to prison, exile, or the gallows. So many were executed that contemporaries spoke with grim wit of "Stolypin's necktie"—the hangman's noose. Following a well-trod political tradition,

Stolypin paired repression with reform, especially an agrarian reform designed to break up the traditional peasant commune and create a new class of strong, independent, peasant farmers.[30]

In an interview with a provincial newspaper in 1909, quoted in almost every history of these years, Stolypin rejected the widespread "pessimism" in society and counseled patience: "give the state twenty years of external and internal peace and you will not recognize present-day Russia."[31] Only five more years of external peace remained before the outbreak of war, though these were, as Stolypin hoped, years of relative social peace. But signs of danger were visible even before the war. These included a campaign of terrorist assassinations of tsarist officials. Stolypin himself was killed in 1911, shot at a theatre in Kiev in the presence of the tsar. The strike movement revived in 1910 and grew especially large after the massacre of over a hundred striking workers by government troops in 1912 in the Lena goldfields in Siberia. External peace was also in doubt, evident in diplomatic and military conflicts in the Balkans in 1912 and 1913, which pitted Russia and Austria against one another over influence in the region.

Oppositional groups and ideologies flourished in these conditions, ranging from moderate liberals to radical socialists: the main political parties were a largely pro-government party of moderate liberals known as Octobrists (formally called the Union of 17 October, for the manifesto of that day was enough change for them); the left-liberal Constitutional Democratic Party (known as Kadets) who judged the reforms of 1905–6 a good start; the neo-populist Socialist Revolutionary Party (the SRs), who considered both peasants and workers to be their constituency; and the two main Marxist parties, formally united as the Russian Social Democratic Workers' Party, but divided since 1903 between Lenin's radical and disciplined Bolsheviks and the more gradualist and democratic Mensheviks. Most of these oppositional groups shared the same basic ideals: the rule of law instead of the arbitrary will of tsar, bureaucrats, and police; basic civil rights (freedom of conscience, religion, speech, assembly); an elected legislature; and social reforms, including extension of public education, land reform to put more land in the hands of peasants, and protective labor laws. For socialists these were short-term goals on the road to a society that joined democracy to social equality and communitarian solidarity. Liberals viewed these as final goals. Inspiring these programmatic ideals was a core assumption shared by almost everyone in the opposition: the natural dignity and rights of the human person. Promoting this value was assumed to be the whole point of political and social change.[32]

Often in history, expectations raised and frustrated can be a more potent inspiration to revolution than deprivation and suffering, which tend to produce fatalism and passivity. This was clearly evident across Russia after 1905. Peasants welcomed "freedom" but understood it to mean control of all the land that they worked and the products they produced—an understanding unacceptable to landlords and the state. Non-Russians (notably Poles, Ukrainians, Finns, Balts, Georgians, Armenians, Jews, and Muslims) were freer to establish and expand ethnic, national, and religious organizations—libraries, charities, credit unions, national congresses, political unions and parties, and native-language publications—but were continually reminded in practice that the expansion of "freedom" and "rights" after 1905 did not bar discrimination much less grant self-determination. Workers benefitted from the legalization of strikes and trade unions, which the government hoped (and radicals like Lenin feared) would reduce the appeal of radical politics by giving workers an effective channel to redress their grievances, but this benefit was undermined by persistent surveillance and harassment of labor unions by the police (dispersing meetings, arresting leaders, and closing publications at the very hint of criticism of the government). Urban women found greater opportunities for organization and activism after 1905, especially when they focused on women's issues such as prostitution, but were denied electoral rights and equality before the law.

Historians have emphasized the growing strength and historical importance of "civil society" in Russia by the late 1800s. The revolution of 1905 and the reformed legal order that followed unleashed civic activity as never before, evident in a proliferation of non-governmental organizations promoting literacy, temperance, sport, science, charity, and other public benefits; professional organizations representing business owners, professionals, white-collar employees, and industrial workers; a vibrant and diverse periodical press; and public spaces for sociability such as theatres, music halls, entertainment parks, nightclubs, and cinemas.[33] But as the history of the labor movement in Russia suggests, the vitality of civic organization could both encourage a sense of inclusion and give force to movements for more radical change, especially among people feeling disappointed and frustrated with the persistence of so many limitations on freedom. The revival of workers' political demands after 1910 and growing interest among workers in the less compromising Bolsheviks were early warning signs of troubles to come.[34] Or so we can now see looking back.

* * *

The press viewed "these times" (a phrase often used) as historic. A journalistic tradition marked each new year with essays on the old and the new, on the passage of time and its direction. This ritual took on increasingly worried tones after 1905. The traditional New Year's wish, "For a new year and new happiness," began to feel ironic in the face of so much evidence that the progress of each new year brought no real change and that happiness eluded most people. Across classes and ideological viewpoints, people were said to feel "depressed," even "despondent," over what seemed to be the stagnation of history, the failure of time to bring change.[35] A 1908 New Year's Day editorial in a magazine associated with the Orthodox Church offered a typical view. While people had the same hopes for the new as in years past, now "time has shattered the foundations of these hopes." A "revolution" (*perevorot*) had taken place in public attitudes such that "the old has been torn down, thrown out, condemned," leaving only "indeterminacy" (*neopredelennost'*—another word often heard in those years).[36] Religious writers had an advantage over most journalists: they could embrace the public's discovery that secular progress was a myth as a healthy disillusionment that brought an awakening to higher truths. But most writers experienced this "public mood," which they often shared, as evidence that the present was a dead end with "no exit."[37] An editorial on 1 January 1910 in the newspaper *The Modern Word* (*Sovremennoe slovo*) echoed a widespread attitude in advising readers to be skeptical about hope for the new year: for "how many times has the specter of happiness deceived us?"[38]

As the year 1913 began, often viewed in retrospect as old Russia's last days before war and revolution changed everything forever,[39] the editors of a popular magazine asked writers, businessmen, and other public figures to offer their toasts for the New Year. Many declared that they personally remained hopeful, but almost everyone agreed that the public's mood was heavy and depressed. And they claimed to understand why: New Year's wishes for change and happiness were (as the well-known psychiatrist Vladimir Bekhterev put it) only "desires" (*pozhela-niia*), while "reality does not bring happiness."[40] Or as a columnist who called himself "The Wanderer" (Skitalets, the pen name of Osip Blotermants) wrote on New Year's Day 1913 in the popular tabloid *The Kopeck Gazette* (*Gazeta-kopeika*). "We find ourselves in such troubled straits now because our reality is dismal, the year's results are nil, and hope has flown away from us." We may have wished for "new happiness" last year, but we got "nothing besides a bitter aftertaste and disillusionment."[41]

Such gloomy reviews on time and hope were not limited to New Years. Throughout these years, journalists endlessly described a worsening "epidemic" of public "pessimism," "depression," and "despair."[42] One well-known specialist on popular education commented in 1912 about the many letters he received from readers of his magazine articles: with "horrifying" regularity people were telling him that their lives had lost meaning and purpose, and that they could see no path into a better future.[43] This troubled view of history—of time as meaningful development—can be seen in the frequent used of the Russian word *bezvremen'e,* usually translated as "untimeliness," but meaning a time of difficulty, trouble, failure, and sorrow.[44] In those years, *bezvremen'e* named a troubled time of contradiction and illusion, of moral and spiritual sickness, of loss and despair, of untimely decline instead of timely progress—of time itself wandering and lost without direction.[45]

The particulars were the stuff of daily news. In documenting "signs of the times," newspapers did their best to highlight positive things: advances in scientific knowledge and technical know-how; business success and opportunities for upward mobility; the vitality of cultural institutions like museums, schools, libraries, exhibitions, and theatres. Newspapers also recorded the everyday pleasures and freedoms offered by the modern city. Advertisements reminded readers that pleasure and fun awaited even those with modest incomes and limited time free from work. For those with more income, there was opera, ballet, theater, concerts, balls, private parties, restaurants, cafés, and cabarets. For those with much less, and a desire to do something more than get drunk for leisure, there were "people's theaters," summer entertainment parks (known as "pleasure gardens"), the circus, cinema, and spectator sports. The history of "Russia at play," as the historian Louise McReynolds called it, was an important part of how contemporaries narrated for themselves the history of the years between 1905 and 1914. But to understand this story, it must be viewed against its dark social background. The pursuit of "entertainment" and "merriment" had become a public mania, reporters thought,[46] because people were desperate to escape from work and poverty, from violence and crime, from politics, "from the loud cries of the 'big questions.'"[47] Revelry was a natural response to a reality that, in the words of Olga Gridina, a leading columnist for *The Kopeck Gazette,* "has far more dark than bright sides."[48]

Newspapers constantly reminded readers of this darkness. Reporting on everyday life in the most popular newspapers leaned heavily on certain subjects, partly because they were compelling stories in their own right (entertaining in a dark key), and partly because they seemed to define the history of the present. Sex has often been a topic used to judge the state of a society (and to sell papers, of course) and was an obsessive topic in the Russian press, which read the sexual state of Russian society as a sign of fundamental "deformity" and "sickness."[49] Reporters described the nation as drowning in a "filthy torrent" of public "debauchery" that spilled over from brothels to cafés and into the street, as fallen into a "sexual bacchanalia" that had deformed Russia into a "modern Sodom."[50] This bacchanalia was linked to a still larger moral illness: rising "barbarity,"[51] people becoming more and more like savages and beasts, inspired by a "brutal and morose" egoism embodied in the modern motto, "I want!"[52]

A "bacchanalia" of violence was part of this story. Political violence, such as terrorism, state executions, and pogroms, was one aspect (though direct discussion was limited by censorship), but mostly this was an "epidemic" of everyday violence: the dark "reign of the knife" (*nozhevsh-china*) that afflicted Russian cities, and was blamed variously on "bandits" after money, sexual predators, "hooligans" (said to stab for no particular reason), and individuals overcome by momentary anger.[53]

These stories were purposefully sensational and titillating, but they also served as commentaries on "these times" and the "spirit of the age": signs of a "monstrously ugly" "spirit of evil" in the air,[54] of "something fatal" in contemporary life,[55] of some deep and ubiquitous "sickness."[56] The interpreting could be even more sweeping: commentators read this evidence as defining Russia's experience of modernity as a history of "trauma," "tragedy," and "catastrophe."[57]

The "epidemic" of suicides that struck urban Russia in 1906 and lasted until the war was viewed as a particularly troubling sign of Russia's historic illness,[58] evidence that Russian society was "fractured," "chaotic," "deformed," "rudderless," "sick," and at a "dead end." Some writers blamed the "traumas" of recent events: the Russo-Japanese War, Bloody Sunday and the 1905 revolution, uprisings, terrorism, and state repression.[59] Most commentators, though, saw a deeper "sickness," which they attributed to epochal historical changes, especially urbanization and industrialization.[60] Religious writers blamed suicide on the loss of faith and certainty brought by secular modernity.[61] But secular writers said much the same. It seemed that many people could not bear the deep contradiction between raised desires and the actual conditions of "reality."[62] Some writers saw something of a protest in suicide: as bearing witness with one's own life to the harm caused to the human spirit by "life as it is."[63] Most people responded to this disenchanted reality more modestly, with passive pessimism. Some demanded boldness and faith, including revolutionaries like Vladimir Lenin who were far from thinking that history was sick or adrift. Many, we have seen, chose pleasure-seeking, which journalists tended to interpret as "feast in the time of plague," "a wild dance at the edge of the abyss."[64] In August 1914, Russia along with the rest of modern Europe leapt into that abyss.

War

The outbreak of war across Europe in August 1914 briefly quieted political and social protest, as Russians directed their thoughts and emotions against the German and Austrian enemies, and often against the many ethnic Germans living and working in Russia. But patriotic unity, though nurtured by a strong threat to the Russian "fatherland" (as propaganda regularly reiterated), did not have deep roots and so did not last long in the conditions of protracted conflict that made unprecedented and harsh demands on the population and the economy. To be sure, generals and officials continued to boast about the brave and righteous enthusiasm of the nation's fighting men and the unflagging support of society at all levels. But a growing number of people began to ask, as the devastation mounted, whether the suffering was worth the price, and in whose interest the war was being fought.

Only five months into the war, nearly 400,000 Russian men had lost their lives and nearly a million were wounded, and these staggering losses continued. The army was in retreat by the spring of 1915. Chaotic flight, plunder, and desertion were not uncommon. By the end of the first year of war, Russian casualties reached four million men captured, wounded, or dead. In 1916, the military situation improved; there were even some modest successes, though with great loss of life. But the war continued to drain the material and human strength of the country, and not only at the front. There were ominous signs by 1915, most visibly food shortages and rising prices, that the economy was breaking down under the strain of wartime demand. The army was also increasingly fragile. A prominent historian of the Russian military during World War I described a growing crisis in morale "rooted fundamentally in the feeling of utter despair that the slaughter would ever end and that anything resembling victory could be achieved."[65] Labor strikes, though illegal, increased steadily from the middle of 1915, including in the capital, Petrograd. But mostly people did what they could to survive, wondering when and how it would all end. Government officials responsible for public order worried that patience would soon run out. In October 1916, a report from the Petrograd branch of the security police (the Okhrana) warned bluntly of "the possibility in the near future of riots by the lower classes of the empire enraged by the burdens of daily existence."[66]

The war was viewed by many liberal-minded Russians as a national crisis that proved the need to include the public fully in political life. To a degree, the government welcomed the organized work of citizens supporting economic mobilization or offering relief to wounded soldiers. The government even accepted the value of national associations like the

War Industry Committee, which was led by prominent industrialists and civic leaders, and the Union of Zemstvos and the Union of Towns, representing at the national level local bodies of rural and urban self-government. But the government preferred, as a matter of political principle, to rely on its own structures to mobilize the nation. Most pointedly, Nicholas II refused to cooperate with the majority of Duma members who pleaded for more influence over whom the tsar appointed as his ministers. Liberals and many conservatives hoped to save the political order by reforming it. By contrast, the tsar was determined to keep away from power even those who favored a greater public voice in government. If anything, his appointments to high office seemed designed deliberately to offend liberal society. Especially grating was the tsar's increasing reliance on his German-born wife and their spiritual guide, Grigory Rasputin, whose combined influence grew after the tsar appointed himself commander-in-chief and departed to the front. The reality of Rasputin's influence was bad enough—it was made worse by all sorts of rumors, including about a sexual relationship between Alexandra and Rasputin. The continual firing of ministers (sometimes on the advice of Alexandra and Rasputin) and their replacement by men less and less open to any role for the public, and often less and less competent in their jobs, were among many signs that civil society and the autocratic state were at a dangerous crossroads. The assassination of Rasputin in December 1916, engineered by right-wing and monarchist elites hoping to save the dynasty and Russia from imminent catastrophe, did little to avert disaster, and may have even hardened the unwillingness of Nicholas and Alexandra to concede anything or even recognize the severity of the crisis. That an explosion was coming seemed clear to almost everyone else. In October 1916, the priest and conservative activist Ivan Vostorgov wrote the following in a letter: "We are on a downward slide. Beneath us is a yawning abyss. Disorders and disturbances are ripening in the life of the state. The revolution has prepared itself down to the smallest detail. But where is the counterrevolution? Nowhere to be seen. Our days are waning in a bloody glow."[67]

* * *

Newspapers were filled with news of the war: daily reports on developments at the front, announcements by the government, and patriotic commentary. War coverage in the prominent Moscow daily, *The Russian Word,* studied by Louise McReynolds, was characteristic of the major papers, if slightly more liberal: welcoming the war with an almost messianic belief that this was a historic fight against authoritarian militarism; enmity toward Germany (and Germans) as a barbaric military civilization that brought cruelty to the world; admiration for the gallant and heroic Russian troops; declarations of optimism; and insistence (the liberal stance) that success demanded national unity, which required that the autocratic monarchy give a larger role to public institutions and the Duma.[68] Journalists, of course, knew that they could say no more than the government would tolerate, and military censors were keeping a close eye on the press to make sure they did not overstep. But the optimism was likely authentic, and sometimes put in grand historic terms. As an editorial in one Petrograd paper put it, though written in the dark autumn of 1915, "we live now in a time of great possibilities. Under the roar of arms...Russia, like a living organism, full of life, is finding the strength to heal its inner sores."[69] Some journalists carefully expressed their anxieties about the future, at least by acknowledging that the public was worried. A review essay on wartime literature and art, for example, described the evidence of "pain" and "hopelessness," even an atmosphere of "cold and decay" that "emanates from almost everything."[70] But the most common experience of the war years, echoed in the press, was neither bold confidence nor dark despair, but uncertainty. If these were historic times, the direction and outcome seemed far from clear.

At the same time, the war left much of everyday life untouched. Familiar stories of crime, violence, murder, suicide, accidental death, hooliganism, and prostitution still filled the newspapers. Wartime conditions, especially economic hardships, surely aggravated these old "horrors of life" (*uzhasy zhizni*)—the headline chosen by one newspaper for its daily chronicle of social disorders—though military censorship likely prevented reporters from saying so. One journalist was able to report in 1916 that many of his "Social Life" columns for the magazine *Life for Everyone* (*Zhizn' dlia vsekh*), which compiled summaries of "dismal Russian life as it is reflected in the newspapers," were rejected by the censors, who considered such dark reports to be "contemporary but not timely" (*sovremennoe no ne svoevremennoe*), in other words a reality that was not politically welcome.[71] Journalists continued to pose "eternal questions" during the war, such as why do people suffer and why is there evil in the world? The bloodshed, hatred, and material suffering of the war made these abstract questions more tangible than ever. And many journalists continued to express hope, however contrary to the evidence of the present, that a "fairytale world" of "happiness" might yet be established on earth, not least because people so thirsted for this.[72] Both suffering and hope would feed the events of 1917. The war had intensified both.

Notes

1. The following account of these upheavals draws on many studies. The most detailed and reliable is Abraham Ascher, *The Revolution of 1905*, 2 vols. (Stanford, CA, 1988 and 1992).
2. "Petition of Workers and Residents of St Petersburg for Submission to Tsar Nicholas II," 9 January 1905. For the Russian text (and discussion of different drafts), see Aleksei Shilov, "K dokumental'noi istorii 'petitsii' 9 ianvaria 1905, *Krasnaia letopis': istoricheskii zhurnal*, 1925/2(13): 33–5. An English translation can be found in Ascher, *The Revolution of 1905*, i. *Russia in Disarray* (Stanford, CA, 1988), 87–9.
3. The manifesto was published in every Russian newspaper. For a scan of Russian text on the front page of *Vedomosti Spb Gradonachal'stva*, 18 October 1905, see <https://commons.wikimedia.org/wiki/File%3AOctober_Manifesto_1.jpg> [accessed 26 August 2016] An English translation can be found in George Vernadsky et al. (eds), *A Source Book for Russian History from Early Times to 1917*, 3 vols. (New Haven, 1972), iii. 705, and Ascher, *The Revolution of 1905*, i. 228–9.
4. See Introduction.
5. See Louise McReynolds, *The News under Russia's Old Regime: The Development of a Mass Circulation Press* (Princeton, 1991), 171–9.
6. "Zaria novoi zhizni," *Russkoe Slovo*, 20 February 1905, 2; G.P., "Prostye rechi," *Russkoe Slovo*, 9 March 1905, 1–2; Aleksandr Rossov, "Katastrofa," *Russkoe slovo*, 10 June 1905, 1; Vl. Umanskii, "Pered obnovleniem," *Russkoe slovo*, 20 June 1905, 3.
7. *Russkoe slovo*, 18 October 1905, 1 (editorial placed beside the October Manifesto).
8. "Obnovlenie," *Russkoe slovo*, 18 October 1905, 1; Sergei Iablonovskii, "Svet i teni: Zvon kolokolov," *Russkoe slovo*, 18 October 1905, 2; *Russkoe slovo*,

19 October 1905, 1; Sviashchennik G. Petrov, "Beseda s gr. S. Iu. Vitte," *Russkoe slovo*, 19 October 1905, 1.

9. Vas. Nemirovich-Danchenko, "Slepaia voina," *Russkoe slovo*, 12 June 1905, 1–2.

10. Aleksandr Rossov, "Provintsial'naia zhizn': Vse po-staromu," *Russkoe slovo*, 13 June 1905, 3–4.

11. "Obnovlenie," *Russkoe slovo*, 18 October 1905, 1.

12. e.g. Tan, "Svobodnaia Moskva," *Russkoe slovo*, 21 October 1905, 1.

13. Sergei Iablonovskii, "Svet i teni: Est' iurist i iurist," *Russkoe Slovo*, 12 February 1905, 3.

14. P. Boborykin, "Gde u nas liudi?," *Russkoe Slovo*, 20 February 1905, 2.

15. Orest Smirnov, "Vazhnoe postanovlenie zemstva," *Russkoe slovo*, 14 June 1905, p. 2.

16. Aleksandr Rossov, "Provintsial'naia zhizn': Vse po-staromu," *Russkoe slovo*, 13 June 1905, 3–4; "Obnovlenie," *Russkoe slovo*, 18 October 1905, 1; Sviashchennik G. Petrov, "Lichnost' i gosudarstvo," *Russkoe slovo*, 14 June 1905, 1.

17. G.P., "Prostye rechi," *Russkoe slovo,* 9 March 1905, 1–2.

18. Orest Smirnov, "O darovitykh detiakh naroda," *Russkoe slovo*, 7 June 1905, 1–2.

19. Aleksandr Rossov, "Krest'ianskie nuzhdy," *Russkoe slovo*, 27 June 1905.

20. Vl. Umanskii, "Sumeem-li?" *Russkoe slovo*, 8 June 1905, 3.

21. Vas. Nemirovich-Danchenko, "Slepaia voina," *Russkoe slovo*, 12 June 1905, 1–2.

22. Vl. Umanskii, "Pered obnovleniem," *Russkoe slovo*, 20 June 1905, 3.

23. K. Mirov, "Krest'ianskaia smuta," *Russkoe slovo*, 11 March 1905, 1; Sergei Iablonovskii, "Svet i teni: Zhupel'," *Russkoe slovo*, 11 March 1905, 3; Sviashchennik G. Petrov, "Potrebnoe mest'," *Russkoe slovo*, 21 October 1905, 1.

24. Ia. Usmovich, "D'iavol'skii zamysel," *Russkoe slovo*, 24 October 1905, 1; Aleksandr Rossov, "Staryi poriadok umiraet," *Russkoe slovo*, 24 October 1905, 1.

25. Aleksandr Rossov, "Krest'ianskie nuzhdy," *Russkoe slovo*, 27 June 1905.

26. Sergei Iablonovskii, "Vopl' Fomy," *Russkoe slovo*, 19 October 1905, 1.

27. *Russkoe slovo*, 19 October 1905, 1.

28. *The Secret Letters of the Last Tsar: Being the Confidential Correspondence between Nicholas II and his Mother, Dowager Empress Maria Fedorovna*, ed. Edward Bing (New York, 1938), 190–1.

29. Versions of this optimist–pessimist debate—a favorite of generations of American teachers of Russian history—can be found in most English-language histories of the coming of the 1917 revolution. The most influential scholarly study to challenge the Western optimistic narrative (Soviet and Marxist scholars, of course, saw revolution as inevitable, and a good thing) was Leopold Haimson, "The Problem of Social Stability in Urban Russia, 1905–1917" (part 1), *Slavic Review*, 23/4 (December 1964): 619–42, and (part 2) 24/1 (March 1965): 1–22.

30. Abraham Ascher, *P. A. Stolypin: The Search for Stability in Late Imperial Russia* (Stanford, CA, 2001); Victoria Bonnell, *Roots of Rebellion: Workers' Politics and Organizations in St Petersburg and Moscow, 1900–1914* (Berkeley, CA, 1983).

31. Ascher, *Stolypin*, 294.

32. On liberals, see especially Shmuel Galai, *The Liberation Movement in Russia, 1900–1905* (Cambridge, 1973); William Rosenberg, *Liberals in the Russian Revolution: The Constitutional Democratic Party, 1917–1921* (Princeton, 1974), part 1; Richard Pipes, *Struve*, 2 vols. (Cambridge, MA, 1970 and 1980). On socialists, see especially Leopold H. Haimson, *The Russian Marxists and the Origins of Bolshevism* (Cambridge, MA, 1955); Oliver Radkey, *The Agrarian Foes of Bolshevism* (New York, 1958); Abraham Ascher, *Pavel Axelrod and the Development of Menshevism* (Cambridge, MA, 1972); Manfred Hildermeier, *The Russian Socialist Revolutionary Party Before the First World War* (New York, 2000).

33. On civil society, see especially Edith Clowes, Samuel Kassow, and James West, eds., *Between Tsar and People: Educated Society and the Quest for Public Identity in Late Imperial Russia* (Princeton, 1991); and Joseph Bradley, *Voluntary Associations in Tsarist Russia: Science, Patriotism, and Civil Society* (Cambridge, MA, 2009). On the press, see McReynolds, *The News under Russia's Old Regime*.

34. Haimson, "Problem of Social Stability"; Bonnell, *Roots of Rebellion*.

35. e.g. N.V. "Itogi minuvshago goda," *Vesna*, 1908/1 (6 January): 1; "Novogodnye mysli," *Tserkovnyi vestnik*, 1908/2 (10 January): 43; R. Blank, "1909-yi god," *Zaprosy zhizni* 1909/11 (29 December): 1.

36. "S novym godom," *Tserkovnyi vestnik*, 1908/1 (3 January): 1.

37. Notably, Mikh. Al. Engel'gardt, "Bez vykhoda," *Svobodnye mysli*, 35 (7 January 1908): 1.

38. "1910 god," *Sovremennoe slovo*, 1 January 1910, 5.

39. See e.g. Wayne Dowler, *Russia in 1913* (DeKalb, IL, 2010).

40. *Ogonek,* 1913/1 (6 January), n.p.

41. Skitalets, "Molchanie," *Gazeta-kopeika,* 1 January 1913, 3–4.

42. For many examples, see my *Petersburg Fin de Siècle* (New Haven, 2011), ch. 7.

43. N. Rubakin, "Dlia chego ia zhivu na svete," *Novyi zhurnal dlia vsekh,* 1912/6 (June): 67.

44. Vladimir Dal', *Tolkovyi slovar' zhivago velikorusskago iazyka,* 2nd edn (St Petersburg, 1880); D. N. Ushakov (ed.), *Tolkovyi slovar' russkogo iazyka* (Moscow, 1935).

45. e.g. V. Lavretskii, "Tragediia sovremennoi molodezhi," *Rech',* 30 September 1910, 2; I. Brusilovskii, "Smysl' zhizni," *Sovremennoe slovo,* 13 March 1910, 1; Mikhail Kovalevskii, "Zatish'e," *Zaprosy zhizni,* 1911/12 (23 December): 705; M. Slobozhanin, "Iz sovremennykh perezhivanii," part 4: "'Ia' i okruzhaiiushchaia sreda," *Zhizn' dlia vsekh,* 1913/7: 1019–21, and part 3: "Ob estetikh noveishei formatsii i estetizme voobshche," *Zhizn' dlia vsekh,* 1913/3–4 (March–April): 461.

46. Rabotnichek, "Bezumnaia zhizn'," *Peterburgskii listok,* 23 February 1914, 3.

47. Vas. Reginin, "K chitateliam," *Argus,* 2 (February 1913): 3 (a list of problems that reading this new magazine would help readers escape).

48. Ol'ga Gridina, "Odna zhenshchina," *Gazeta-kopeika,* 6 June 1910, 5.

49. For an important account and analysis, see Laura Engelstein, *Keys to Happiness; Sex and the Search for Modernity in Fin-de-Siècle Russia* (Ithaca, NY, 1992).

50. D., "Polovaia vakkhanaliia," *Gazeta-kopeika,* 27 July 1909, 3; O. Gridina, "Griaznyi potok," *Gazeta-kopeika,* 27 February 1910, 3; S. Liubosh, "Griznaia volna," *Sovremennoe slovo,* 1910/811 (7 April): 1; O. Gridina, "Kamni," *Gazeta-kopeika,* 18 May 1911, 3; Vadim, "Svet vo t'me," *Gazeta-kopeika,* 3 March 1913, 5–6.

51. V. Trofimov, "'Zhestoki u nas nravy'…," *Gazeta-kopeika,* 4 April 1909, 3.

52. O. Gridina, "Griaznyi potok," *Gazeta-kopeika,* 27 February 1910, 3.

53. e.g. "Nozhevshchina," *Gazeta-kopeika,* 6 April 1910, 7; Skitalets, "Plokhoi matematik," *Gazeta-kopeika,* 17 October 1909, 3; Skitalets, "Chelovek umer," *Gazeta-kopeika,* 8 February 1913, 3. On hooliganism, see Joan Neuberger, *Hooliganism: Crime, Culture, and Power in St Petersburg, 1900–1914* (Berkeley, CA, 1993). On murder, see Louise McReynolds, *Murder Most Russian: True Crime and Punishment in Late Imperial Russia* (Ithaca, NY, 2013). See also Chapter 5 in this volume.

54. Vadim, "Dukh zla (po povodu ankety o samoubiistvakh)," *Gazeta-kopeika,* 16 February 1913, 3.

55. Podpischik zhurnala "Zhizn' dlia vsekh," "Golos iz nedr neveshestva," *Zhizn' dlia vsekh*, 1913/9 (September): 1289–90.

56. Az., "Deti-nozhevshchiki," *Gazeta-kopeika*, 9 December 1908, 4.

57. Steinberg, *Petersburg Fin de Siècle*, 254–61.

58. See also Susan Morrissey, *Suicide and the Body Politic in Imperial Russia* (Cambridge, 2006), chs. 10–11.

59. Zhbankov, "Sovremennye samoubiistva," *Sovremennyi mir*, 1910/3 (March): 27, 29, 40, 53.

60. Rozenbakh, "Prichiny sovremennyi nervoznosti i samoubiistv," *Peterburgskaia gazeta*, 26 April 1909, 3.

61. "K samoubiistvam molodezhi," *Tserkovnyi vestnik*, 1910/12 (25 March): 362; "Sovremennost' i dumy," *Tserkovnyi vestnik*, 1913/31 (1 August): 948; "Tragediia sovremennoi kul'tury," *Tserkovnyi vestnik*, 1914/27 (3 July): 811.

62. Ol'ga Gridina, "Smert' otvetila!" *Gazeta-kopeika*, 5 March 1910, 3.

63. N. Ia. Abramovich, "Samoubiistvo," in *Samoubiistvo: sbornik obshchestvennykh, filosofskikh i kriticheskikh statei* (Moscow, 1911), 113.

64. Leonid Galich, "Mysli: Nauchnyi optimizm i meshchane," *Rech'*, 11 July 1907, 2. See also Skitalets, "Vavilon na chas," *Gazeta-kopeika*, 2 January 1911, 4–5; Stepan Felenkin, "Nasha molodezh'," *Gazeta-kopeika*, 8 February 1910, 3.

65. Allan Wildman, *The End of the Russian Imperial Army*, i. *The Old Army and the Soldiers' Revolt (March-April 1917)* (Princeton, 1980), 106.

66. "Doklad petrogradskogo okhrannogo otdeleniia osobomu otdelu departamenta politsii," October 1916, *Krasnyi arkhiv*, 17 (1926): 4–35 (quotation on p. 4).

67. I. I. Vostorgov to N. Ch. Zaionchkovsky, 4 October 1916, GARF, f. 102, op. 265, d. 1056, l. 692, quoted in Mikhail Lukianov, "Pervaia mirovaia voina i differentsiatsiia rossiiskoi pravoi, iul' 1914 – fevral' 1917 g.," forthcoming in translation as "The First World War and the Polarization of the Russian Right, July 1914–February 1917," *Slavic Review* (Winter 2016).

68. McReynolds, *The News*, 259–68, analyzing *Russkoe slovo* from July 1916 to January 1917.

69. *Gorodskoe delo*, 1915/15–16 (1–15 August): 799.

70. M. Nevedomskii, "Chto stalos' s nashei literaturoi," *Sovremennik*, 1915/5 (May): 254.

71. V. Posse, "Obshchestvennaia zhizn'" *Zhizn' dlia vsekh*, 1915/8–9 (August–September), 1317 (on his purposes); 1916/6 (June), 752 (on the censor).

72. E. N. Liubin, "Vechnyi vopros," *Zhizn' dlia vsekh*, 1915/7 (July), 979–82.

CHAPTER 3
1917

Historians have told the story of 1917 in many ways. Not least, the evolution of history as a discipline has changed how we understand, interpret, and narrate 1917—though this "scientific" reason has been inseparably entwined with political and ideological inclinations (what a historian thinks of revolutions, socialism, liberalism, the state, and popular action—not to mention the Soviet Union itself) and even ethical values (what they think, for example, about such still difficult issues as inequality, social justice, and violence). Historians, like the people we study, differ over what counts as belonging in the narrative we call "history." Not long ago, the main innovation was to decenter the focus away from political leaders, state institutions, geographic centers, men, and Russians, in order to pay more attention to the roles of commoners (especially soldiers, workers, and peasants), women, nationalities, provinces, and the margins of empire. More recent scholarly attention to subjectivities—not only people's stated ideas and demands but the much hazier terrain of values and emotions—has added another enriching and complicating dimension to this narrative. But scholars have also recently reemphasized the importance of big structures in shaping history: economic modernization, capitalism, law, the global movement of ideologies and ideas, international relations, war. None of these different approaches, of course, is mutually exclusive. They have been combined in different ways—as I try to do in this book.

The big crisis events of 1917, especially as they unfolded in the capital, Petrograd, structure the standard narrative of the revolution: the February revolution that toppled the tsar, the April Crisis over war aims, the near-insurrection of the July Days, the failed Kornilov Mutiny in August, and the October revolution that brought the Bolsheviks to power. Behind these events stands the story of causation: the context of war, economic breakdown, social polarization, and failure of governance. This is the style of history telling with which we are most familiar: important and connected events with explainable causes and significant outcomes. The familiarity of this approach, even what is left out, does not argue against its necessity. Other chapters will return to 1917 from other perspectives. But these events and contexts are the essential structure and foundation. And, unusually, most historians agree about what happened, why, and what changed.[1]

The first crisis began on 23 February (8 March), when thousands of women textile workers in Petrograd walked out of their factories to protest shortages of bread and food, and in commemoration of International Women's Day, adding to the large numbers of men and women already on strike in the capital and other cities. This crisis, an upheaval that quickly spread across the city and the country and brought down the government in a matter of days, should not have been a surprise to those in power. Reports from secret police agents living and working undercover in the capital city described by January 1917 a rising "wave of animosity against those in authority in wide circles of the population."[2] Simmering public anger was fueled by the suffering caused by the war, increasingly desperate economic conditions, especially food shortages and rising prices, and state policies that seemed either unconcerned or inept. Among ruling elites who were attentive to the public mood, a mirror image of popular unease arose: fear that the war effort, and their own political and social survival, might be threatened by an upheaval among the lower classes. As working women and men took to the streets of the capital in increasing numbers, chants, banners, and speeches demanded bread but also an end to the war and the end to autocracy. Students, teachers, and white-collar workers joined the crowds. Scattered violence broke out, especially smashing store windows. Some demonstrators carried sticks, pieces of metal, rocks, and pistols. Although socialist activists encouraged the movement, it lacked real leadership or direction. It was an expression of discontent more than deliberate action to resolve it. As such, many socialists considered these actions to be "disorders" not "revolution."[3] Or, in the more contemptuous view of the empress Alexandra, writing to Nicholas II at the front, these demonstrations were just a "hooligan movement" making raucous trouble for its own sake.[4]

The tsar, ill-informed and unable to understand what was unfolding, responded with a fatal mixture of overconfidence and impatience, helping to turn disorders into revolution. On 25 February, he dispatched a telegram to the chief of the Petrograd military district with these fatal words: "I command you tomorrow to stop the disorders in the capital, which are unacceptable in the difficult time of war with Germany and Austria."[5] Police and local garrison soldiers followed orders and fired into the crowds, wounding and killing many. Government officials, and many socialist leaders, believed that this settled matters. But the next day, soldiers came out on the streets on the side of the demonstrators. This collapse of effective military authority in the capital created panic in the halls of power, especially as the upheaval spread to cities across the country, with locally garrisoned soldiers often joining demonstrators on the streets. On 27 February, the cabinet of ministers prorogued the State Duma, blaming its leaders (who continued to insist that only a reform of government could bring calm to Russia and allow the war to continue) for contributing to the upheavals, and then itself resigned. Perhaps most decisively, top military leaders tried to persuade Nicholas II that only a new government controlled by the Duma could "calm minds" and stop "anarchy spreading to the whole country," which would lead to the disintegration of the army, the collapse of the war effort, and the "seizure of power by extreme left elements."[6] Facing what amounted to a revolt of his generals, Nicholas felt betrayed, but understood he had no choice. Hoping to rescue the war effort and save the monarchy, he abdicated on 2 March and named his brother Mikhail, who was thought to be more inclined to compromise, to succeed him on the throne. Mikhail refused the crown, a quiet gesture that dramatically ended the 300-year old Romanov dynasty and made the Russian empire a de facto republic. But the revolution was only beginning.

The rest of 1917 was a series of crises shaped by the struggle over who would take hold of this power and be able to keep it. In large part, this struggle was embodied in the peculiar institution of "dual power": the tense political relationship between the Soviet (Council) of Workers' and Soldiers' Deputies in Petrograd (created through elections at workplaces and garrisons, and led by socialists, which soon become a national Soviet of Workers', Soldiers', and Peasants' Deputies, with representatives sent to the capital by local soviets all over the country) and the new Provisional Government (established by members of the State Duma in an agreement with the Petrograd Soviet). But this was only the most prominent aspect of "dual power," which was truly an empire-wide phenomenon, embodied in almost every power relationship in the country: in the army between the officer corps and soldiers' committees, in factories between management and workers' committees, in villages between the traditional commune and peasant committees, in schools between school administrations and student councils (soviets). Generation, as much of social position, was part of this story: the committee and soviet "class," as some called them, tended to be young men, often soldiers returned from the front. Dual power looks simpler than it was: not only was the degree of cooperation and conflict between sides varied and changeable across the country and over time, but in many parts of the empire bodies representing local nationalities or other groups complicated these relationships still further.

In general, especially in the early months of 1917, power was a problem to figure out as much as a struggle for ascendancy over others. The Provisional Government and the Soviet both felt uncertain about the legitimacy and scope of their authority. The liberal leaders of the new government, who believed strongly in legality, were painfully aware that they were essentially a self-appointed committee of members of the closed State Duma, which itself had been elected on a restricted and biased franchise. The "provisional" name they chose for the new government made it quite clear that they accepted state power only as a temporary move until proper democratic elections were held, which required elections for a Constituent Assembly that would establish the foundation for a legitimate constitutional order. In its turn, although the Soviet would regularly challenge government policies and actions on behalf of the social groups they represented, and their power to bring workers and soldiers into the streets made them a real political force, the socialist leaders of the Soviet insisted that their role was to advocate for particular classes not represent the whole nation. Talk of "Soviet power" was unacceptable to them, even insane. Their political reluctance was shaped by ideological beliefs, ideas about history, and views of reality. They believed that the immediate task of the revolution was to establish democracy and civil rights, tasks traditionally associated (especially in the Marxist view of history) with the historical role of the liberal bourgeoisie. The idea of overthrowing this class and building socialism seemed premature at best, even suicidal, given the ongoing war but also because Russia was far too underdeveloped socially and culturally for such a radical experiment. The Soviet leaders made it clear that they wanted to influence the government not to control it: to push the hesitant but properly empowered "bourgeoisie" to establish a republic, guarantee civil rights, and prepare elections for a future Constituent Assembly.

The Provisional Government launched a bold program of civic and political reform: they freed thousands of political prisoners and exiles; proclaimed freedom of speech, press, assembly, and association; endorsed the right of workers to go on strike; abolished flogging, exile to Siberia, and the death penalty; removed legal restrictions based on nationality or religion; restored a constitution to Finland, promised independence to Poland, and generally favored greater authority for institutions of local government across Russia and the empire; granted women the right to vote and run for office (after some initial hesitation, which quickly yielded to protests by women, including street demonstrations by women workers); and began preparing for elections to a Constituent Assembly on the basis of universal, secret, direct, and equal suffrage. This was surely the most liberal government in the world at that time, and in actions not only words. But the government also found it difficult, for both ideological and practical reasons, to solve three critical problems. First, they could not immediately satisfy the demand of peasants for more land. To be sure, they started work on land reform. But they also insisted that final decisions about redistributing property had to wait for a government with true democratic authority. Second, they could not end economic shortages and disruptions. At the least, this would have required a degree of government control of social and economic life that as liberals they could not accept. Third, they could not end the war. Nor were they willing to withdraw Russia unilaterally from a fight they viewed as the struggle of democratic nations against German militarism and authoritarianism.

St Petersburg was not Russia, Nicholas II liked to say: the loyal population of peasants and townspeople in the interior were not like troublesome capital-city residents. Yet the revolution in February resonated immediately and strongly throughout Russia and the empire. In provincial towns, enthusiastic demonstrators filled the streets (initially dispersed by local police and Cossacks), singing revolutionary songs, carrying banners supporting the new order, and attending endless protest meetings. Parties and soviets were established. New local authorities arrested and disarmed the military and police defenders of the old regime, and replaced local bureaucrats with administrators favoring the new government. In the non-Russian areas of the empire, the same story unfolded with the important addition of demands for ethnic and national autonomy. Indeed, perhaps the most immediate effect of the revolution outside the capital was a strong localism, not least because the government in Petrograd lacked the means to exercise local power. In villages, where most of the population lived, peasants responded to news of the revolution with their own version of support and enthusiasm: seizing (and sometimes beating up) old-regime officials and police, organizing village committees, and, above all, telling anyone who would listen that the main goal of the revolution ought to be transferring all land into the hands of those who actually worked it.[7]

Each crisis event of 1917 had an immediate and concrete cause: a leaked diplomatic note, a street demonstration by radicals, an attempted military coup, a Bolshevik insurrection. But the deeper cause of every crisis, in the view of many contemporaries and most later historians, was the "impassable abyss" dividing educated elites from the common people. As one liberal army officer explained to his family in mid-March, based on his experiences among rank-and-file soldiers, the common people believe that "what has taken place was not a political but a social revolution, in which, according to them, we are the losers and they the winners. . . . Previously we ruled, now they themselves want to rule. Within them speak the unavenged insults of centuries past. A common language between us cannot be found."[8] This class abyss would increasingly threaten the "dual power" arrangement, which itself embodied these divisions, and would shape the process and outcome of 1917.

The war was the subject of the first crisis for the new revolutionary state. Pressured by the Petrograd Soviet to renounce the annexationist war aims of the tsarist government, the Provisional Government issued a declaration in late March insisting that "the goal of free Russia is not mastery over other people, nor to take away their national property, nor to forcibly seize foreign territories—but to support a stable peace on the basis of national self-determination."[9] At the same time, the foreign minister, Paul Miliukov, sent a diplomatic note to the Allies assuring them of Russia's determination to fight to victory and readiness to impose on the defeated powers the usual sorts of "guarantees and sanctions," which most people assumed included Russian control of the Dardanelle straits and Constantinople, as agreed upon with the Allies in 1915. When this note was leaked to the press and published on 20 April, the consequences were explosive, for this seemed directly to contradict the foreign policy line of the Petrograd Soviet and the government's own declaration, which now looked like a hypocritical sop to the Soviet. Huge crowds of enraged protesters, including armed soldiers, took to the streets of Petrograd and Moscow denouncing "Miliukov-Dardanelskii," the "capitalist ministers," and the "imperialist war." Miliukov was forced to resign and the cabinet had to be reorganized to include socialists, which helped restore popular confidence in the government but also made the parties that led the Soviet implicitly responsible for future government failures. The only major socialist party that refused to allow its members to join the "bourgeois" coalition government was Lenin's still relatively marginal Bolsheviks.

To help strengthen support for their position, the Soviet leadership organized a "unity" demonstration in Petrograd for Sunday 18 June. Slogans proposed included "Unity of Revolutionary Forces," "Down with Civil War," "Support the Soviet and the Provisional Government." What occurred instead, in the recollection of a Soviet leader, was "a stinging flick of the whip in the face of the Soviet majority and the bourgeoisie."[10] Amidst a scattering of Soviet-endorsed slogans, most of the banners that marchers carried bore Bolshevik slogans, such as "Down with the Ten Capitalist Ministers," "They've Deceived us with Promises,

Prepare to Fight," "Peace to the Hovels, War against the Palaces," and
the increasingly popular "All Power to the Soviets."

This was, indeed, only a "flick of the whip" compared to the "July
Days" two weeks later. On 3 July, tens of thousands of soldiers, sailors,
and workers, a great many of them armed, took to the streets of the
capital. They occupied the city center, seized automobiles, fought with
police and Cossacks, and emphasized their insurrectionary mood by
frequently firing their guns into the air. By 2:00 a.m., 60,000–70,000
men, women, and children were in the streets, mostly near the Soviet
headquarters in the Tauride Palace, and the crowds were continuing to
grow in size and belligerence. Resolutions passed at mass meetings
demanded an immediate end to the war, no more "compromises" with
"the bourgeoisie," and "all power to the Soviets." Few demonstrators
seemed clear as to how to achieve these goals, especially as the Soviet
leadership rejected the very idea that they should hold "all power." In the
most famous scene of the July Days, the Soviet leaders sent the Socialist
Revolutionary Victor Chernov into the streets to calm the crowd. His
appeals were answered by an angry demonstrator who shook his fist and
shouted at Chernov, "Take power, you son of a bitch, when it is handed
to you." The moderate leaders of the Soviet blamed the Bolsheviks for all
this. And the Bolsheviks themselves surely encouraged the movement.
But they were not ready or not willing to lead it to power. Without
leadership, the uprising disintegrated. Heavy rain on the evening of
4 July chased the last of the crowds off the streets.[11]

Historians still debate whether the July Days were a carefully orchestrated, but failed, attempt by the Bolshevik party to seize power. Or part
of a Bolshevik strategy for testing the waters for a later coup. Or an effort
by rank-and-file Bolshevik radicals to force a reluctant leadership to act.
Or even an uncoordinated action by radicalized soldiers and workers,
which the party at first agreed to support, and briefly considered using to
take power, before backing away as it became clear that success was
impossible. Most historians agree that rank-and-file Bolshevik activists
played a huge role in these events and that a great many workers and
soldiers looked to the party for leadership. And there is little doubt that
overthrowing the Provisional Government was on the Bolshevik agenda.
The question was: when?

Contrary to stereotypes of provincial backwardness, the disintegration of support for the Provisional Government and for unity across classes occurred even more rapidly in the provinces than in Petrograd or Moscow. In Saratov, for example, as Donald Raleigh has documented, a local liberal newspaper reported in June that "power not only in the city but throughout the province has actually passed to the [local] soviet of workers' and soldiers' deputies." The rupture between moderate and radical socialists also moved more quickly than in the center: the Bolsheviks quit the Saratov soviet in May to protest cooperation with the liberal bourgeoisie. Likewise, local workers, soldiers, and peasants more quickly lost patience with compromise and favored immediate and direct solutions to their problems, which meant turning to the Bolsheviks.[12] In other provincial towns, such as Kazan and Nizhny-Novgorod, and in the surrounding countryside, as Sarah Badcock has shown, the essence of local "politics" for most people was not party affiliation, or participation in elections, but the direct fight for economic and social needs. The distrust of all elites was perhaps even more intense among provincial commoners than in the capital cities.[13] Even many Cossacks of the Don region, widely viewed as the fiercest supporters of a strong disciplinary state, favored local over central power.[14] Such localism and fragmentation of power defined the revolution as much if not more than political decisions and struggles for state power in Petrograd. The authority of the government eroded rapidly, undermined by the growing power of local soviets, committees, unions, and other institutions.

Social authority across Russia fragmented even more precipitously, stimulated by the worsening economic crisis, which made direct action seem the only possible solution, but also by intense distrust of "the bourgeoisie" and the political elites associated with them. Soldiers disregarded officers and would listen only to elected soldiers' committees. Peasants stopped waiting for land reform when there was little to stop them from taking land and expelling landlords. Workers took direct action to control workplace conditions: in many factories "workers' control"—an idea born and evolving in practice rather than being a theory to apply—deepened as factory committees began not only overseeing decisions by management but making important managerial decisions themselves. When employers or managers threatened lay-offs due to fuel shortages, for example, factory committees might seek new fuel supplies and arrange for delivery and payment, arrange for more economical use of available fuel, demand control over company expenditures, authorize everyone's hours to be cut equally, or insist on the workers' collective right to decide who should be laid off. In a small number of cases, usually when employers intended to close a factory, workers' committees decided to run the factories themselves.[15] To many observers this was "anarchy" and "chaos." To many others it was "democracy" from the bottom up.

The central government, restructured after the July crisis with a socialist majority and led by the socialist lawyer Alexander Kerensky, could not accept this fragmentation of power and weakening of the state. They declared a war against "anarchy."[16] But the government's "statism," as it has been called, may have only aggravated the situation, stimulating the next political crisis and thus further weakening state authority. The July Days may have made the wrong danger clear, producing the wrong solutions: the easily identifiable threat of Bolshevik sedition overshadowed the greater and more difficult threat of social, national, and regional polarization and fragmentation. In July, responding to the threat it understood, the government arrested hundreds of Bolshevik leaders (though Lenin was among many who eluded arrest and went into hiding). Civil liberties were restricted in the interests of public order. The death penalty was restored for soldiers at the front judged by field courts to be guilty of treason, desertion, flight from battle, refusal to fight, incitement to surrender, mutiny, or even disobeying orders. Street marches in Petrograd were banned until further notice. And General Lavr Kornilov, a tough-minded Cossack admired in conservative circles for his advocacy of military and civic discipline, was appointed as the new commander in chief. Prime Minister Kerensky wanted to be seen as a strong political executive who could overcome disorder. As he declared in a speech at the funeral of Cossacks killed fighting insurgents during the July Days, "all attempts to foment anarchy and disorder, regardless of where they come from, will be dealt with mercilessly, in the name of the blood of these innocent victims."[17] Perhaps as a symbolic gesture, but also for security reasons, Kerensky moved the offices of the Provisional Government into the Winter Palace.

The "Kornilov Affair," a strange mixture of conspiracy and confusion, was fueled by the rising torrent of talk about the dangers of disorder and the need for discipline and a strong state. The new commander in chief saw himself as the man to save Russia, a self-regard encouraged by the conservative press, right-wing politicians, and organizations of military officers, businessmen, and landowners. Kornilov appears to have believed, not without reason, that Kerensky also wished to muzzle the Soviet and its supporters, perhaps through a temporary military dictatorship. The historical record of what actually happened is full of contradictory evidence and claims. What we know is that on 26 August Kerensky learned that Kornilov had demanded the resignation of the entire government, the proclamation of martial law in the capital, the transfer of all civil and military authority into his own hands, and was moving troops to the capital to back up his demands. Kornilov's defenders would later insist that Kerensky himself had ordered this centralization of power and the movement of troops was only to protect Kerensky and the government from a rumored Bolshevik coup. Kerensky appealed to the nation to help "save" Russia and the revolution from a military coup. The Soviet leadership responded by mobilizing local soviets, trade unions, factory committees, and left-wing parties, including the Bolsheviks (the Soviet even helped arrange for Bolshevik leaders to be freed from prison). Kornilov's advancing troops were easily persuaded to stop their advance, especially when told that Kerensky did not support their actions. So the "mutiny" ended within days. But the crisis was only starting. The right blamed Kerensky for having deceived and betrayed Kornilov. The left suspected that Kerensky had plotted with the commander in chief and then turned against him. As a result, another governing coalition fell apart, torn by deepening distrust between liberals and socialists. Only in late September could a new coalition Provisional Government be formed—the third and final cabinet—headed by Kerensky, with ten socialist ministers (mostly members of the Menshevik and Socialist Revolutionary parties, though officially acting as individuals) and six liberal ministers (mostly from the Constitutional Democratic Party, the Kadets).

The Bolsheviks, as the only major left-wing party not participating in the government, became a lightning rod for people's frustration. And their unambiguously class-based platform well suited the increasingly polarized social mood. They proclaimed their goals to be redistribution of the tax burden to the rich to benefit the poor; support for the struggles of peasants against landowners, workers against employers, and soldiers against officers; and undoing "counterrevolutionary" measures such as the death penalty.[18] Especially compelling, though, were their repeated slogans: "Bread, Peace, Land" and "All Power to the Soviets"—incantations that captured every discontent and offered one simple solution. Growing Bolshevik popularity was visible already before the Kornilov Affair: in balloting for factory committees and trade unions, in new and recall elections of deputies to district and city soviets, in receptivity within the soviets to Bolshevik speakers and resolutions, and even in elections to city councils.[19] After Kornilov, which intensified fear of counter-revolution and frustration with the compromises of the moderate socialists, Bolshevik influence grew more rapidly, though paralleled by the growth among the Socialist Revolutionaries of the similarly less conciliatory "Left SRs." On 31 August, a majority of deputies in the Petrograd Soviet voted in support of a Bolshevik resolution to establish a socialist government without propertied elements.[20] By late September, the Bolsheviks had a sufficiently reliable majority in both the Petrograd and Moscow Soviets to elect a new leadership with a Bolshevik majority. In Petrograd, Lev Trotsky, who had recently joined the Bolshevik party, was elected chairman. The same was happening throughout the country. Most important, the Bolsheviks were now ready to make use of their growing popularity for a daring political gamble—an insurrection to seize state power.

The Second All-Russian Congress of Soviets of Workers' and Soldiers' Deputies opened in Petrograd on 25 October with representatives from hundreds of Soviets across the empire. The Bolsheviks were the largest single group among the deputies, and held an effective majority with the support of the Left SRs. A new presidium was elected with fourteen Bolsheviks and seven Left SRs. Mensheviks were allocated four seats but, in a move some later considered political suicide, they refused to accept their seats as a gesture of protest against the Bolshevik insurrection underway in the streets. The congress endorsed the Bolshevik slogan "All Power to the Soviets," though most deputies understood Soviet power to mean a united democratic socialist government not one-party Bolshevik rule. When the Menshevik leader Yuly Martov warned that the Bolshevik attempt to settle the question of state power by means of a "conspiracy" on the eve of the Soviet congress made "civil war" and counter-revolution more likely and proposed that negotiations begin immediately among "all socialist parties and organizations" to form a "united democratic government," this was unanimously approved. Even the Bolsheviks declared that they "were most interested in having all political factions express their point of view on the unfolding events."[21] But the plan for a multi-party socialist government, for a "revolutionary democratic authority," was overtaken by events and by a deeply ingrained Bolshevik skepticism about working with other "factions."

On the night of 24–5 October, worker "Red Guards" and radical soldiers in Petrograd seized major streets and bridges, government buildings, railway stations, post and telegraph offices, the telephone exchange, the electric power station, the state bank, and police stations, and arrested the ministers of the Provisional Government. This insurrection followed a detailed plan worked out in secret meetings of the Soviet's Military Revolutionary Committee, which Bolsheviks controlled and Trotsky chaired, though timing was a matter of intense debate within the party—for timing had potent political implications. Trotsky was insistent that the uprising wear the legitimizing mantle of a Soviet action for "Soviet power" and in "defense" of the revolution against government repression. But Lenin had worried, quite reasonably, that the Soviet congress might tie the Bolsheviks' hands by insisting on a government including all socialist parties or an even broader "democratic government" that excluded only the propertied elements, so he insisted on the necessity of presenting the congress with the overthrow of the Provisional Government as fait accompli which would be pointless to debate. When the congress opened on the 25th, the attack on the Winter Palace was underway. Menshevik and SR speakers were furious and denounced the Bolshevik action as a "criminal political adventure," an opportunistic grab for power by a single party behind the backs of the Soviet in whose name it duplicitously claimed to act. They predicted that Bolshevik actions would plunge Russia into civil war and destroy the revolution. Not wanting to "bear the responsibility" for these actions, most Mensheviks and Right SRs walked out of the congress—accompanied by Trotsky's famous taunt that they were "bankrupts" destined only for "the trash heap of history." In the predawn hours of 26 October, the congress approved Lenin's declaration that all state authority was in Soviet hands and all local power transferred to local soviets of workers', soldiers', and peasants' deputies. The congress also pledged to immediately propose peace to all nations, transfer all land to peasants' committees, defend soldiers' rights and power, establish "workers' control" in industry, and ensure the convocation of a Constituent Assembly.

* * *

Journalists understood that they were experiencing history, that 1917 was among those exceptional times when the normally steady pace of historical evolution erupts into a drama of sudden change, turning points, and fateful choices. As we saw in Chapter 1, journalists described the early weeks of revolution, in an often feverish tone, as a miraculous springtime of freedom, resurrection, and rebirth, as the long-awaited end of darkness, slavery, and suffering. We should not oversimplify this romantic embrace of revolution. Already in the spring, "wild joy" was mixed with anxiety about the fragility of this new freedom. Freedom itself was understood and used in different ways. And inclusive dreams of universal brotherhood were mixed with fierce hatred for freedom's "enemies." As utopian euphoria met the harsh realities of history as daily life, not least the severe economic problems and the continuing war, interpretations and moods become even more contradictory and torn. It would not take long, as the historian Boris Kolonitsky has written of the rapidly changing mood in 1917, for the "quasi-religious" elation of the February days "to give way to political dejection and disillusionment."[22] Worse, it seemed to a great many journalists that the revolution was falling uncontrollably into an abyss of growing anarchy, class enmity, and civil war. The sense of crisis we find in much of the non-party journalism of 1917 was more complex and fraught than the traditional historian's narrative about a series of namable political crises, and struggles for power by organized groups, leading to the Bolsheviks coming to power. These journalists perceived these crises less as a historical march of events than as an experience of deepening disorder, distrust, anger, and anxiety. More than historians usually allow, with our attention to causes and outcomes, journalists who wrote down history as it was unfolding, especially writers working independently of the main party publications, saw the centrality of disarray and uncertainty in history and the historical experience.

"Anarchy, anarchy!" was the continual cry of the mainstream press by late spring, Maxim Gorky noted with derision in his regular column in his newspaper *The New Life* (*Novaia zhizn'*).[23] The liberal papers, he complained, were especially inclined to "howl and gnash their teeth" about the coming "ruin of Russia," blaming the Russian people in tones of "inky wrath and cowardly malice." And there was harm in these words, Gorky warned: the daily dose of newspaper panic-mongering and blame nurtured in "the souls of their readers" dark and "shameful" emotions: malice, contempt, cynicism, hypocrisy, and fear.[24] Mass-circulation "boulevard papers," such as Moscow's *Daily Kopeck Gazette* (*Ezhednevnaia gazeta-kopeika*) and its successor *News for Everyone* (*Gazeta dlia vsekh*), writing for a readership mainly of urban commoners, were also preoccupied with growing anarchy and looming catastrophe. Already in the first days after the monarchy was brought down, essayists began to warn that the country's "resurrection" to a "new life" of freedom was threatened by the "discord" (*raznoglasie*) of different interests and viewpoints.[25] On 10 March, the *Daily Kopeck Gazette*'s regular columnist P. Borchevsky (we encountered in Chapter 1 his worried optimism in January 1917) appealed to readers to recognize the necessity and virtue of patience and self-control, even concerning the understandable desire for the war to be over: "Citizens. Let's wait. Let's take ourselves in hand.... Let's not sow anarchy now after doing something so great.... Let's restrain our heart-felt impulses and not allow anarchy and disintegration."[26] After the first big political crisis in April, which brought large crowds to the streets, such warnings became more frequent and urgent, with many journalists describing the revolution and Russia as threatened by disorder (especially the sense of *shameful* disorder expressed by the Russian word *bezobrazie*), chaos, anarchy, ruin, and catastrophe, producing a time of troubles (*smuta*), uncertainty, and crisis. This vocabulary had become ubiquitous by late spring. "Anarchy" was a leitmotif in essays warning of the dangers of indiscipline, irresponsibility, mutual enmity, and even too much "talk," and appealing for national unity, maturity, self-discipline, and "sober" work for the common cause.[27] And this was before the July Days, which are usually seen by historians to have been the turning point in producing fear of disorder.

Talk of "anarchy" led to talk of "who is to blame?"—one of the famous "eternal Russian questions," along with "what is to be done?" And blame easily evolved into talk of "enemies" and what to do about them. Even in blame we hear discord. Many journalists blamed the radical left, especially the Bolsheviks for their stubborn opposition to government and their allegedly demagogic and irresponsible enthusiasm for leading people into the streets. An editorial by Petrograd's *Kopeck Gazette* was typical in its blistering attack on Lenin after his return to Russia from many years of exile in Western Europe (after serving his three-year sentence in Siberia for revolutionary activities, Lenin resettled in the West, moving to neutral Switzerland during the war). The *Kopeck Gazette* was less troubled by Lenin's willingness to travel through Germany, a train journey that preoccupied a great many critics, who accused Lenin of making a deal with the enemy, than by the deeply "counter-revolutionary" danger his party represented. The Bolsheviks, this editorial insisted, were "enemies of the Russian people, preaching discord rather than unity, murder and hatred rather than brotherly love, anarchy rather than organization, and instead of the red flag of Freedom—the black flag of death and destruction."[28] Linking Bolshevism and anarchism (whose symbol was the black flag) was increasingly common. Of course, the newspapers also reported on the activities of actual anarchists, whose numbers and influence were never large, but their antics and arrests made good news copy. But Bolshevik "anarchism" was the greater concern. As a *Kopeck Gazette* reporter wrote in early June: "For two months already, Bolsheviks and anarchists have been conducting the most fierce agitation, preaching the most extreme principles." These ideas might be intended to produce "heaven on earth," this journalist sneered, but society and government "cannot be built on theories." Any attempt to implement "the Bolshevik program," in the current conditions of actual Russian life, "will bring only upheaval and destruction" (*potresenie i gibel'*).[29]

Many journalists also blamed the rising tide of anarchy on "the people." Educated Russian "society" had long worried about the perceived political and cultural backwardness of the common people. After the February revolution, many liberals and socialists translated this into open disappointment in the common people for not being "mature" and "responsible" "citizens." Even the socialist minister of justice, Alexander Kerensky, expressed in late April his bitter loss of confidence in the liberated Russian people: "I no longer have my former certainty that before us are not mutinous slaves but conscious citizens"—phrases that would be echoed widely in the following months.[30] By early summer, a reporter noted, the disdainful words "mutinous slaves" were heard at "every step—sitting in a restaurant, in the theater, on the train to the dacha, in front, behind, at your side." The class locations named here were obvious. While this journalist refuted the charge as unfair, arguing that the common people had "emerged from slavery and clearly understand freedom,"[31] other critics accepted the truth of the charge, but blamed history for the problem. Yes, the "psychology of the crowd," evident in recent cases of mob violence, can be savage, filled with "blind rage." But this was the "inescapable consequence of our long years of servile debasement, of our cultural backwardness," which would be overcome with time and effort.[32]

Gorky argued much the same in his newspaper columns. As a socialist "from the people," standing at some distance from organized parties and factions, he did not hesitate to warn that "the most dreadful enemy of freedom and rights" was the "chaos of dark anarchistic feelings" in people's "souls."[33] Like other socialists, though, he diagnosed these dark feelings as an "infection" from the past. "When I reproach our people for their tendency to anarchism, for their dislike of work, for their savagery and ignorance, I keep in mind: they cannot be different. The conditions in which they have lived could not nurture in them respect for the person, or consciousness of the rights of the citizen, or feelings of justice; for these were conditions of utter lack of legality and rights, the oppression of man, shameless lies, and bestial cruelty."[34] In condemning the "insane" and "disgusting" scenes of street violence during the July Days, Gorky insisted that the "incitement" was not the Bolsheviks, or counter-revolutionaries, or foreigners—claims by the government and much of the liberal and conservative press—but "a more vicious and stronger enemy: oppressive Russian stupidity."[35] The dark weight of history on the present also defined the most important historic task for the revolution: overcome this legacy so that people can be truly free to "create new forms of life,"[36] "temper and cleanse [the people] of the slavery in which they were raised," which can only be done with the "slow fires" of "culture." If the revolution fails in this historic challenge, Gorky bitterly warned in July, "then the revolution has been in vain, it has no meaning, and we are a people incapable of living."[37]

Class feeling fueled these worries and fears, influencing not only talk among elites about the people's backwardness but a plebian distrust of elites that helped shape behaviors that elites rejected as immature, irresponsible, and anarchic. The "wrath and malice" that Gorky blamed the liberal press for directing against the common people was heard even more loudly from below. For many workers and peasants, one word was often enough to capture a wide field of social mistrust, resentment, and anger: "bourgeois" (imported into Russian as *burzhui*). The term was conveniently imprecise in actual use: a bourgeois might be an industrialist or capitalist (the proper Marxist usage), an aristocrat, a rich peasant (kulak), a white-collar worker, a member of the intelligentsia (hence, terms like "bourgeois-socialist" intellectual), a government official, a military officer, an ideological opponent of the revolution, a supporter of the war, even a journalist working for a non-socialist paper (known on the left as "the bourgeois press"). As Kolonitsky has shown, the term was an expression of moral judgment more than social analysis: it was a way to speak of people whose actions in this historic time were judged selfish, egoistic, and greedy, caring little for the common good or the common people.[38] So, for example, when the *Daily Kopeck Gazette* warned that the "greedy appetites of the bourgeoisie" threatened the revolution,[39] the warning was also a definition of "bourgeois" as people acting from selfish greed. Or, when a provincial journalist defended the Provisional Government against accusations of being a "bourgeois government," his argument rested not on the social composition of the cabinet (most of the ministers were, in fact, industrialists or professionals) but on their moral qualities: "its members are honest, intelligent citizens who fervently love their country."[40] The popular language of class was imbued with a moral vocabulary. Class struggle, even for many working-class Marxists who had learned a social and economic understanding of class, was typically framed as a fight between right and wrong, justice and injustice, good and evil.

Even the word "democracy" acquired class meanings during 1917. On the political left, it became common to use the word less to describe a political ideal or system than to describe the political expression of class interests and values. "The democracy"—as it is often translated, for in Russian there are no articles, so the added "the" indicates that the reference is to a group of people rather than an idea or system—meant social groups who were not privileged, did not exploit others, and did not conspire against the revolution. The democracy was the common people and those who sided with them as a matter of principle and belief, especially the socialists active in the soviets. Even when democracy was used in the older sense to describe a political ideal or a system of political relationships, the meaning was less about equal rights and representation for all than political power that would act in the interests of the poor. Typical were phrases like the following in letters sent to the Soviet newspaper *Izvestiia* during the fall of 1917: "The democracy is sacrificing everything in the name of saving the country and the revolution.... But a tiny class has gripped its tentacles around these efforts."[41] "We demand that all of the democracy and the government struggle energetically to bring about a speedy conclusion to the war."[42] Liberal elites insisted that "democracy" should unite all citizens under a democratic government. But they recognized, to their great disappointment, that many commoners used the word to exclude the "bourgeoisie," including, sometimes, socialist intellectuals.[43]

By the fall, the emotional and moralistic language of class had reached fever pitch. Typical was a resolution from a soldiers' committee sent to the Soviet newspaper *Izvestiia* on 1 September: "It is time to shake off the spell of the bourgeoisie; it is time to discard it like an oozing scab, so that it doesn't do any more damage to the revolution.... [The bourgeoisie] commits the country to devastation by our bitterest enemies, it squanders our life like some trifle, and it produces disaster wherever it turns.... It is waging a deathly battle with the revolution at every step, taking cover behind fine words."[44] The Soviet newspaper was inundated with such appeals, often warning that a time of fateful action was coming. As one soldier put it a poem sent to the paper: "Who will we say is now guilty / When the settling of scores has begun? / The damnable bourgeois, those scoundrels, / To the gallows we'll send one and all."[45]

Questions about the proper role of government were a natural corollary to arguments about order versus anarchy, the common good versus class egoism, conscious citizens versus mutinous slaves, and other arguments tying the fate of the revolution and even freedom itself to social and political maturity, responsibility, discipline, and unity. By midsummer, liberal and conservative forces were looking with an increasing sense of urgency to the strong hand of the state but also to the need to inculcate a "statist" consciousness in the population. Kopeck newspapers—whose editors and lead writers leaned toward Kerensky as the embodiment of robust democratic authority—repeatedly counterpoised a "strong, authoritative government" to "continued anarchy."[46] When Kerensky became the head of the government after the July Days, an editorial in the *Kopeck Gazette* declared: "Let the new government know that the country, craving firm authority, supports them, and that if the government shows the full strength and firmness of its authority Russia will be saved."[47]

The phrase "firm authority" (*tverdaia vlast'*) was heard constantly by summertime, though there was no single vision of who should hold such power and how they should use it. Indeed, there was less and less agreement, even in the popular press, about the nature of the crisis or the solution. On the non-Bolshevik left and center, many saw Kerensky as the personification of their desire for strong authority to defend the revolution and its goals. In the *Kopeck Gazette,* for example, Kerensky progressed rapidly from "the best representative of the Russian democracy"[48] to the "favorite" of the revolution, "our leader and our conscience," the bright "son of liberated Russia," even a virtual savior, whose "faith in freedom" will enable him to "carry his cross to the end."[49] A political "cult" emerged around Kerensky—with echoes of the traditional ideal of the tsar-father and foreshadowing the cult of Lenin. Sympathetic journalists, echoing and encouraging the talk of the streets, exalted Kerensky as the "hero," "knight," "genius," "glory," and "sun" of the revolution and of "Russian freedom."[50]

Talk of heroes and saviors led, especially as the revolution seemed more vulnerable, to talk of "enemies." This, too, was a flexible term.

"Enemy" could be a social label used to define and reproach all who were rich and powerful, a political label branding those who opposed the interests of the common people, and a moral label chastising elites for self-interested egoism or commoners for irresponsibility and indiscipline. In wartime, of course, it carried associations with the external German enemy and thus implications of treason. While many conservatives viewed the chief "internal enemies" to be radical socialists and Jews, most ordinary Russians judged the rich and privileged to be the main "enemies of the people."[51] The soldiers who wrote to *Izvestiia* on 1 September (I earlier quoted their condemnations of the bourgeoisie) echoed what almost everyone was saying by that fall: "The homeland and the revolution are in danger! Like a thundering tocsin this rings out across the land."[52] The question by then was no longer whether the revolution and Russia were in danger, but only who was to blame and what was to be done.

Notes

1. My account draws on the large scholarly literature on 1917, illustrated with archival sources, memoirs, and reports in the newspaper of the Petrograd Soviet. Many of these works are cited in the notes. Others are cited in the Bibliography. Particularly influential general histories of the revolution in English include works by Orlando Figes, Sheila Fitzpatrick, Bruce Lincoln, Richard Pipes, Alexander Rabinowitch, Christopher Read, S. A. Smith, and Rex Wade.
2. Major General Globachev (head of the Petrograd Okhrana), "Dopolnenie k doneseniiu (sovershenno-sekretno)," 26 January 1917, Gosudarstvennyi arkhiv Rossiiskoi Federatsii (State Archive of the Russian Federation), henceforth GARF, fond 111, opis' 1, delo 669, listy 112–113.
3. N. N. Sukhanov, *The Russian Revolution, 1917: A Personal Memoir* (Princeton, 1984), 5.
4. Letter from Alexandra to Nicholas II, 25 February 1917, GARF, f. 601, op. 1, d. 1151, l. 490–4930b. See Mark D. Steinberg and Vladimir M. Khrustalev, *The Fall of the Romanovs* (New Haven, 1995), 73–6.
5. Quoted by Khabalov in his testimony of 22 March 1917, in *Padenie tsarskogo rezhima: stenograficheskie otchety doprosov i pokazanii, dannykh v 1917 g. v Chrezvychainoi Sledstvennoi Komissii Vremennogo Pravitel'stva*, ed. P. E. Shchegolev, 7 vols. (Moscow and Leningrad, 1924–7), i. 190–1.

6. Telegram from General Alekseev to Nicholas II, 1 March 1917, *Krasnyi arkhiv,* 21 (1927): 53–4.

7. Ronald Grigor Suny, *The Baku Commune, 1917–1918: Class and Nationality in the Russian Revolution* (Princeton, 1972), ch. 3; Donald Raleigh, *Revolution on the Volga: 1917 in Saratov* (Ithaca, NY, 1986), ch. 2; Sarah Badcock, *Politics and the People in Revolutionary Russia: A Provincial History* (Cambridge, 2007), ch. 2; Aaron B. Retish, *Russia's Peasants in Revolution and Civil War: Citizenship, Identity, and the Creation of the Soviet State, 1914–1922* (Cambridge, 2008).

8. "Iz ofitserskikh pisem s fronta v 1917 g.," *Krasnyi arkhiv,* 50–1 (1932): 200.

9. G. E. L'vov, "Zaiavlenie Vremennogo Pravitel'stva o voine" (27 March 1917), *Izvestiia Petrogradskogo Soveta rabochikh i soldatskikh deputatov* [*The News of the Petrograd Soviet of Workers' and Soldiers' Deputies,* henceforth simply *Izvestiia,* though the wording following this initial title word would change as the Petrograd Soviet evolved into a national body], 29 March 1917, 1.

10. Sukhanov, *The Russian Revolution,* 418.

11. Pavel Miliukov, *Istoriia vtoroi russkoi revoliutsii,* i (Sofia, 1921), 243–4; Alexander Rabinowitch, *Prelude to Revolution: The Petrograd Bolsheviks and the July 1917 Uprising* (Bloomington, IN, 1978), 188; Richard Pipes, *The Russian Revolution* (New York, 1990), 428–9.

12. Donald Raleigh, *Experiencing Russia's Civil War: Politics, Society, and Revolutionary Culture in Saratov, 1917–1922* (Princeton, 2002), 28–34.

13. Badcock, *Politics and the People.*

14. Peter Holquist, *Making War, Forging Revolution: Russia's Continuum of Crisis, 1914–1921* (Cambridge, MA, 2002), chs. 2–3.

15. Smith, *Red Petrograd,* chs. 6–7; David Mandel, *The Petrograd Workers and the Soviet Seizure of Power* (London, 1984), ch. 3.

16. This theme is highlighted by Peter Holquist in his *Making War, Forging Revolution,* esp. ch. 3.

17. *Izvestiia,* 119 (16 July 1917): 5. See also Rabinowitch, *The Bolsheviks Come to Power,* 39–42.

18. *Proletarii,* 6 (19 August 1917): 1.

19. Rabinowitch, *The Bolsheviks Come to Power,* 90; Orlando Figes, *A People's Tragedy: The Russian Revolution, 1891–1924* (Harmondsworth, 1996), 458–9.

20. Rabinowitch, *The Bolsheviks Come to Power,* 162.

21. *Izvestiia,* 208 (27 October 1917): 4. (The Bolshevik spokesman was Anatoly Lunacharsky.)

22. B. I. Kolonitskii, "Antiburzhuaznaia propaganda i 'antiburzhuaznoe' sozna-nie'" (a translation appeared in *Russian Review* in April 1994), in V. Iu. Cherniaev et al. (eds), *Anatomiia Revoliutsii* (St Petersburg, 1994), 199–201.

23. Maksim Gor'kii, "Nesvoevremmenye mysli," *Novaia zhizn'*, 18 (31) May 1917, 1.

24. *Novaia zhizn'*, 18 May 1917, 1; 9 June 1917, 1.

25. *Ezhednevnaia gazeta-kopeika*, 6 March 1917, 1.

26. P. Borchevskii, "Nado-li voevat'?" *Ezhednevnaia gazeta-kopeika*, 10 March 1917, 1.

27. *Gazeta dlia vsekh*, 26 May 1917, 1; 16 May 1917, 4; 27 May 1917, 2; 30 May 1917, 2; 1 June 1917, 1–2; 2 June 1917, 2.

28. *Gazeta-Kopeika*, 14 April 1917, 1. See also articles about Lenin on 6, 17, and 20 April.

29. Osip Iakovlev, "Bulat ili karton," *Gazeta-kopeika*, 18 June 1917, 6.

30. "S"ezd delegatov s fronta," *Delo naroda*, 30 April 1917, 3. See the discussion by Boris Kolonitsky in his essay " 'Vzbuntovavshiesia raby' i 'velikii grazh-danin': Rech' A. F. Kerenskogo 29 April 1917 i ee politicheskoe znachenie," *Journal of Modern Russian History and Historiography*, 7 (2014): 1–51.

31. Emigrant, "Raby-li," *Gazeta-kopeika*, 27 June 1917, 3.

32. I. Ivanov, "Pechal'no," *Gazeta dlia vsekh*, 3 June 1917, 3.

33. *Novaia zhizn'*, 23 April 1917, 1.

34. *Novaia zhizn'*, 18 May 1917, 1. See also Gorky's columns on 2 and 12 May 1917.

35. *Novaia zhizn'*, 14 July 1917, 1.

36. *Novaia zhizn'*, 18 May 1917, 1.

37. *Novaia zhizn'*, 14 July 1917, 1.

38. See Kolonitskii, "Antiburzhuaznaia propaganda," 196–7.

39. Aiaks, "K torgovym sluzhashchim!" *Ezhednevnaia gazeta-kopeika*, 7 March 1917, 4.

40. *Revel'skoe slovo*, 21 April 1917, quoted in Kolonitskii, "Antiburzhaznaia propaganda," 197.

41. Resolution sent to *Izvestiia* from the soldiers' committee of the 92nd Trans-port Battalion, 1 September 1917. GARF, f. 1244, op. 2, d. 10, ll. 55–7.

42. Appeals to the country and to soldiers from the Soviet of Soldiers' Deputies of the 12th Army, printed 7 October 1917. *Izvestiia*, 191 (7 October 1917): 3.

43. Boris Kolonitskii, " 'Democracy' in the Political Consciousness of the February Revolution," *Slavic Review*, 57/1 (Spring 1998): 95–106.

44. Resolution of the soldiers' committee of the 92nd Transport Battalion, 1 September 1917. GARF, f. 1244, op. 2, d. 10, ll. 55–7. The complete text is translated in Mark Steinberg, *Voices of Revolution* (New Haven, 2001): 220–5.

45. P. Anoshkin, in the army at the front, received 16 August 1917. GARF, f. 1244, op. 2, d. 31, ll. 3–30b. Translated in Steinberg, *Voices of Revolution*, 219.

46. Emigrant, "Na ulitsakh Petrograda," *Gazeta-Kopeika*, 5 July 1917, 2.

47. Editorial, *Gazeta-Kopeika*, 25 July 1917, 1.

48. Editorial, *Gazeta-Kopeika*, 5 July 1917, 1.

49. "Obozhanie bez palki (O Kerenskom)," *Gazeta-Kopeika*, 6 July 1917, 3; editorial, *Gazeta-Kopeika*, 15 September 1917, 3.

50. B. I. Kolonitskii, "Kul't A. F. Kerenskogo: obrazy revoliutsionnoi vlasti," *Soviet and Post-Soviet Review*, 24/1–2 (1997): 43–65; Orlando Figes and Boris Kolonitskii, *Interpreting the Russian Revolution: The Language and Symbols of 1917* (New Haven and London, 1999), 76–89.

51. For an example of this phrase in popular use, see the letter to the Petrograd Soviet from peasants in Viatka province on 26 April 1917 in Steinberg, *Voices of Revolution*, 131.

52. Resolution of the soldiers' committee of the 92nd Transport Battalion, 1 September 1917. GARF, f. 1244, op. 2, d. 10, ll. 55–7.

CHAPTER 4
CIVIL WAR

The Bolsheviks came to power holding contradictory ideas about the revolutionary socialist state. On the one hand, they embraced an emancipatory and democratic vision of mass participation grounded in unleashing ordinary people's desires and energies. As Lenin argued after his return to Petrograd in the spring of 1917, the only way to save Russia "from collapse and ruin" is to "imbue the oppressed and the working people with confidence in their own strength," to release the "energy, initiative, and decisiveness" of the people, who in this mobilized condition can perform "miracles."[1] This was the ideal of a new type of state, a "commune state" (referring to the Paris Commune of 1871) of mass participatory power, a "state apparatus of one million people" who would serve not for "fat sums" but "for the sake of high ideals."[2] The commune state ideal was reflected in the change of the official name of the party in 1918 from the "Russian Social Democratic Workers' Party (Bolshevik)" to the "Russian Communist Party (Bolshevik)." In the first months after coming to power, Lenin regularly appealed to "working people," as the "makers of history," to "remember that you yourselves are now administering the state," and so to "take matters into your own hands from below, waiting for no one."[3] Some historians have interpreted this talk as utilitarian at best and deceitful at worst—as no more than a means, in the opinion of Orlando Figes, "to destroy the old political system and thus clear the way for the establishment of his own party's dictatorship."[4] We should be cautious, however, not to let the way things turned out blind us to the extent to which many Bolsheviks believed in this emancipatory and participatory vision of revolutionary power.

But this was only one side of the Bolshevik ideology of state power. Lenin was right to insist that Bolsheviks were "not anarchists." They believed in the necessity of strong leadership, discipline, coercion, and force. "Dictatorship," understood and legitimated as the "dictatorship of the proletariat," was an essential part of Bolshevik ideas about how to make a revolution and build a socialist society. To hold onto state power and to destroy their enemies, the Bolsheviks were ready, and said so explicitly, to use the most "draconian measures" (Lenin's words), including mass arrests, summary executions, and terror. And not only against "rich exploiters," Lenin warned, but against "crooks, idlers, and hooligans," and those who spread "disintegration" in society. It was now the Bolsheviks' turn to decry "anarchy" as threatening the revolution.[5] Dictatorship was more than a matter of necessity, however. It was also a virtue: proletarian class war, as a war aiming to overcome the divisions of class that produced violence and war, was the only war in history, as Lenin put it in December 1917, "that is legitimate, just, and sacred."[6] Still, this was to be war.

In the first months, the new Soviet government acted to empower common people and establish a more egalitarian society: giving soviets local administrative power; endorsing the peasant revolution by trans- ferring all agricultural land to the peasants;[7] supporting the movement among workers to participate in decisions governing everyday factory life with laws requiring "workers' control";[8] supporting the movement among rank-and-file soldiers by giving "full power within any military unit" to soldiers' committees and soviets, with all officers democratically elected;[9] supporting struggles against Russian imperial domination by abolishing privileges and restrictions based on nationality or religion and insisting on the "equality and sovereignty" of all the empire's peoples, including the right to self-determination even "to the point of separation and the establishment of an independent state";[10] abolishing legal des- ignations of civic inequality, such as estates, titles, and ranks, in favor of the single designation of all people as "citizens";[11] and replacing existing legal institutions with "courts established on the basis of democratic elections."[12]

Most of these acts of radical democratization would be undone during the emergency conditions of the civil war, abandoned as untimely hindrances to effective mobilization and discipline. But Bolshevik state-building, from the first, already expressed the authoritarian face of Bolshevik ideology. One early sign was the willingness to establish a single-party Soviet government in the face of the widespread popular assumption that "all power to the Soviets" meant power to the unified representatives of "the democracy." One-party rule was not an immediate or absolute principle, however. There were practical reasons for the new Soviet government to include non-Bolsheviks, especially the shortage of qualified individuals for the many government offices that had to be staffed. And there were political reasons, especially pressure from workers' and soldiers' committees, from the national railroad workers' union (which threatened a national strike over the issue), from independent left-wing socialists, and from dissenting Bolsheviks. Among the latter, the most prominent were the Central Committee members Grigory Zinoviev and Lev Kamenev, who publicly criticized one-party government as contrary to the will of the majority of workers and soldiers, defensible only by "political terror," and likely to result "in the destruction of the revolution and the country."[13] In December 1917, Lenin agreed to include in the cabinet (the Council of People's Commissars, or Sovnarkom) a limited number Left Socialist Revolutionaries (a breakaway faction from the main SR party). But this did not last long. After a few months, the Left SRs, who joined the government hoping to influence Bolshevik policies, quit in frustration, sparked by the peace treaty with Germany which they opposed. In the months that followed, continual Left SR criticism of Bolshevik authoritarianism—one frustrated Left SR leader condemned Lenin in May 1918 as a "berserk dictator"—and Bolshevik frustration with constant interference by Left SR activists, led to a decisive break. After a Left SR party member assassinated the German ambassador, an act viewed as part of an "uprising" against Soviet power, the Bolsheviks purged Left SRs from the government at every level and cracked down severely on the party and its members. One-party rule was now complete and destined to last.[14]

The decision to close the long-awaited and long-idealized Constituent Assembly was viewed by many as a particularly troubling sign of Bolshevik authoritarianism. The results of these elections, held in November, were revolutionary—a vast majority of Russians, in open and democratic voting, chose a socialist path into the future: the Socialist Revolutionary Party won 38 percent of the total vote (46 percent when we include the separate Ukrainian SRs), Bolsheviks 24 percent, Mensheviks 3 percent, and other socialist parties another 3 percent, giving socialists a resounding (if divided) three-quarters of the total vote. Non-Russian nationalist parties, some inclined toward socialism, took approximately 8 percent of the total votes. The liberal Kadet (Constitutional Democratic) party polled less than 5 percent. Other non-socialists (including rightists and conservatives) won only an additional 3 percent. The Bolsheviks won a respectable quarter of the entire national vote, polling especially well in cities, the army, and in the northern industrial region—it is fair to say that they proved that they truly were the party of the working class.[15]

At the same time, the elections did not justify the Bolsheviks' dominant control of government, though they could hardly be expected to step down. Even when Lenin confirmed, on the first day of Soviet power, that the elections would be held as previously scheduled on 12 November,[16] attentive readers of Lenin's writings would have noticed early warnings about "constitutional illusions" and insistence that the "course and outcome of the class struggle" was more important than the Constituent Assembly.[17] These arguments were developed after the elections into a full-blown public case against making a "fetish" of the Assembly: the electoral lists were out of date (especially due to the formation of the Left SR party after the lists were drawn up); the "will of the people" had shifted further to the left since the elections; soviets are a "higher form of democracy" and so any government the Constituent Assembly might establish would be a step backward; the likelihood of civil war required emergency measures. Ideologically, the most important case against the Assembly was the historical argument about class struggle: the legitimacy of a parliament should be measured not by electoral formalities but by its position in this historic struggle, which depends on the extent to which it will "carry out the will of the working people, serve their interests, and defend their conquests." Concluding that it would surely fail this historic test, even though the Assembly was overwhelmingly socialist, the Bolsheviks claimed they had no choice: the logic of history and the class struggle "forced" them to disband the counter-revolutionary Constituent Assembly, which they did at its first meeting in January.[18] It is worth remembering, though, that some prominent moderate Bolsheviks opposed this move and most Left SRs approved of shutting the Assembly.

The Bolsheviks began suppressing opposition voices even before this dramatic move against the democratic body that most Russian socialists and liberals had long viewed as the holy grail of democratic revolution. The Decree on the Press, in late October, closed many newspapers, including liberal and socialist ones, that might incite "resistance or disobedience," "sow sedition by a clearly slanderous perversion of the facts," or simply "poison the minds and sow confusion in the minds of the masses."[19] In late November, the main non-socialist party, the Constitutional Democratic Party (Kadets), formally known as the Party of the People's Freedom, was outlawed as a "party of enemies of the people," its leaders arrested and all of its members put under surveillance.[20] When the few non-Bolsheviks still active in the Soviet leadership—especially Left SRs, notably Isaac Steinberg—criticized this decree, Lev Trotsky reportedly warned that this was only "mild terror" compared to what would very soon be necessary as the class war grew more fierce: "not prison but the guillotine will be ready for our enemies."[21] In December, the government established the "All-Russian Extraordinary Commission for the Struggle Against Counterrevolution and Sabotage," known as the Vecheka or simply Cheka (from its initials), a security police charged with discovering and suppressing opposition to the revolution.[22] One of the motives for establishing the Cheka, the historian Alexander Rabinowitch has shown, was to create an agency that would free the Bolsheviks from interference by the Left SRs at the very moment they were being welcomed into the government as coalition partners: as one of the Cheka leaders explained in an internal report, the Left SRs "greatly impeded the struggle against counter-revolution by pressing their 'universal' morality, humanism, and resistance to placing limitations on the right of counter-revolutionaries to enjoy free speech and freedom of the press."[23]

Civil war, as a nationwide military conflict between "Red" and "White" armies, began in earnest in the summer of 1918. In many respects, especially as experienced, the civil war was the continuation of a history of state violence begun in 1914. The Soviet state had just managed to extricate itself from the war with Germany by accepting in

March "the most onerous and humiliating peace treaty" (by the party's own judgment), though a minority of party leaders insisted that the principles of international class struggle demanded they reject the terms and fight on against imperialism and capitalism, if only in a guerilla war since the army had collapsed and troops at the front were completely "demoralized."[24] The "breathing spell" that the peace was supposed to bring lasted barely a few months before sustained warfare broke out between the White armies (a confederation of anti-Bolshevik forces, led by former tsarist officers, that began to take shape at the start of 1918) and the Red Army (the military force built in the middle of 1918 under Trotsky's leadership as War Commissar).

But the civil war was a more complex and varied experience than this simple binary of Red versus White suggests.[25] The history of the civil war included terrorism and armed struggle by Socialist Revolutionaries, anarchists, and socialists opposed to both Bolshevik "dictatorship" and the return of right-wing dictatorship that the Whites seemed to represent; "Green" armies of peasants who fought against both Reds and Whites, mainly depending on who presented the greater immediate threat to their autonomy; national independence movements across the empire; armed intervention by troops from Britain, France, the United States, and other Allied powers; and a war with Poland. By the end of 1920, out of this great diversity and through a great deal of bloodshed, the Red Army and the Soviet state prevailed: the White armies were defeated, other movements opposed to Bolshevik power were crushed (for the moment), and Soviet governments were established and defended in Georgia, Armenia, Azerbaijan, and eastern Ukraine.

How the Red Army and Soviet power prevailed has been much debated by historians. Most agree that the Communist side benefitted from military, strategic, and political advantages. Militarily, the Red Army was a surprisingly effective force given its origins in the scrappy volunteer Red Guards, especially when compared to the White Army leadership's origins in the tsarist military. It helped that, while nurturing new "Red" commanders from the ranks, the government compelled "military specialists" to serve in the Red Army, and, to bolster their authority, the army restored the traditional hierarchical structures of command. Strategically, the Red Army benefitted from working outward from a valuable geographic center: the Soviet government occupied the Russian heartland, which meant controlling most of the population, industry, and war stocks, while the Whites worked from the peripheries with only limited coordination between different armies. This was especially important as Russia's main railroads radiated outward from Moscow (effectively the new capital after March 1918, when the government fled Petrograd, expecting it would soon fall to the Germans), giving the Red Army more coherent lines of transportation and communication. On the other hand, the White armies controlled more agricultural lands and so their troops were better fed.

Above all, though, the Whites suffered from political disadvantages. White leaders understood that they could not restore the old order. But they found it difficult, given their backgrounds and ideologies, to endorse the desires of the majority of the population. Committed to the imperial ideal of "Russia one and indivisible," they rejected even the tactical temptation to offer concessions to non-Russian nationalities (who might have been a key source of support on the peripheries) and suppressed non-Russian nationalism in lands under their control. Peasants were not enthusiastic about either side in the civil war. Both Red and White armies took their grain and horses, conscripted peasants into their ranks, and used terror against suspected opponents, sometimes burning down whole villages. But what mattered most to peasants was land and the Bolsheviks had endorsed—wisely, cleverly, or hypocritically, depending on one's judgment of their motives—peasant seizures of estate lands, while White leaders worked to undo the rural revolution in the name of law and the principle of private property, not to mention in support of the landowners who were one of their base constituencies.

The civil war was a vicious affair. Both sides practiced mass incarceration, summary executions, hostage taking, and other forms of "mass terror" against suspected enemies. There were "excesses," as in every war, tolerated by authorities on both sides. On balance, Red and White violence was comparable and reciprocal. But the Bolsheviks, especially through the Cheka, made a distinctive contribution to this blood-stained history: not merely a pragmatic willingness to do whatever necessary to survive (making "extraordinary" measures normal), but a willing embrace of violence and coercion as means to remake the world and advance history. The violence of the "proletariat" (which is mostly to say those who fought the class war *in the name* of the working class) was justified as not only historically necessary, but moral and good: this was a class war to end class war, and thus to end all violence, redeem the whole of suffering humanity, and create a new world and new people.[26] Bolsheviks approached violence and coercion as part of a great and inevitable historical process, the "leap into the kingdom of freedom," that could not be won without a fight against those with a stake in the old kingdom of inequality and oppression. Bolsheviks were not afraid, as Lenin put it, of "Jacobin" methods (evoking the radicals of the French revolution and their guillotine) when used in the "interests of the nation's majority" and to "break the resistance of the capitalists."[27]

This was a matter not only of suppressing enemies. During the civil war the government and the party relied increasingly on centralized, top-down, and often coercive methods of rule in every area of life, especially the economy and society. Scholars continue to debate how much circumstance and necessity as opposed to ideological inclination shaped this authoritarian turn—particularly the economic policies that Lenin latter dubbed "war communism." Truly, it is almost impossible to disentangle these. Complicating matters further, but also suggesting deep interconnections reaching well beyond Russia and Bolshevism, many of these authoritarian policies echoed and developed practices used by governments across Europe to mobilize their economies and societies during the World War—not least, the influential though politically conservative example of German "war socialism" (*Kriegssozialismus*).[28] The "kingdom of necessity" had become exceedingly strong and harsh. A report on the condition of the economy in the spring of 1918 described "a state of collapse" due to "disorganization," "crisis," "decline," "instability," and "paralysis" in every sector.[29] Restoring the shattered economy and harnessing it to fight and to build became the greatest need. But how this was done was shaped by more than circumstance—hence the paradoxical notion of "war communism," of realizing the emancipated future under conditions of desperate necessity.

The problem of food, especially supplies to workers and soldiers, was of utmost urgency. In May 1918, the government proclaimed a "food dictatorship," which included a state monopoly on the entire grain trade, stringent price controls, suppression of private "bagmen" accused of speculating on shortages, and deploying armed detachments to requisition grain and other food products from peasants. The food dictatorship had a "revolutionary" side, when framed as class war against the rural "bourgeoisie," who were alleged to be hoarding massive "surpluses," and as a first step toward socialized agriculture. But necessity was the main driver. The peasant revolution had resulted in the increased dominance of traditional small-scale subsistence farming, rather than larger farms producing marketable produce. In any case, peasants had little economic motivation to market grain, since there was little to buy and money was increasingly worthless; so they hoarded. Yet the food dictatorship was largely a failure: not only did peasants often violently resist requisitioning and protest low prices but the state was not strong enough to substitute itself for private actors in the economy.[30]

In industry, the Bolsheviks were committed to the historic goal of abolishing market relationships and private property. But the collapse of production demanded action now. A Supreme Council of the National Economy was formed in December 1917 to develop a long-term plan for the transition to socialism. Some scattered nationalizations occurred before the civil war, but these were mostly the work of local soviets and factory committees rather than the central state. The economic crisis and the coming of civil war encouraged a more decisive turn away from the private economy. In June 1918, the government nationalized all large-scale industry (small factories were nationalized in 1920). Retail trade was largely prohibited by the end of 1918, in order to rein in the "anarchy of the market." This struggle for the economy was not limited to suppressing the bourgeoisie. The government introduced compulsory labor for all adult males, established strict workplace discipline, replaced "workers' control" with one-person management (and raised the salaries and authority of managerial and technical "specialists"), harnessed trade unions to industrial mobilization, and suppressed strikes. Local activists and institutions, inspired by ideological fervor, played a large part in moves to suppress capitalism, and these could have considerable popular appeal, especially actions such as forced contributions from local "bourgeois" and requisitioning of homes and apartments to become communal dwellings for workers.

At the same time, workers' discontent was growing. Economic suffering and resentment at increased workplace discipline encouraged a renewed interest in the arguments of Mensheviks, SRs, and even anarchists, who called for the restoration of multi-party democracy based on strong local bodies of popular power. Workers were also responding to a less formal sense that the Communist authorities had lost or betrayed the spirit of the October revolution. In Petrograd in early 1918, the main socialist opposition parties helped establish a type of counter-soviet called the Extraordinary Assembly of Factory Delegates. They argued that economic problems were due to the failure of unions, factory committees, and local soviets to function as democratic worker-run bodies rather than as bureaucratic arms of the Bolshevik state. By contrast, Bolshevik leaders argued that, since the state was a workers' state, workers owned the means of production, and therefore they could not be exploited. When the government increased the bread ration for factory workers in late May, the Assembly of Delegates encouraged workers to strike and accused the state and party of trying to "bribe" workers and to divide them from "other strata of the people," arguing that only the "restoration of people's power" would solve the problem of hunger. In response, the government suppressed the strikes and arrested the movement's leaders.[31]

Political relations were shaped by the same mixture of wartime crisis and ideological preference. The governing style of the party was marked more and more by centralization and hierarchy, rule by command and decree, suppression and punishment of dissent, and the expanding use of surveillance to monitor society. This was partly a legacy of the older Bolshevik vanguard model for how to organize a socialist revolution. But this was different, as many Bolsheviks would complain, not least because it was applied to constructing not overturning a political and social system. Local soviets and committees, the signature face of the revolution from below, were reined in. The power of factory committees and unions were marginalized in favor of one-person management and strict workplace discipline. Reductions in workplace autonomy were further reduced in 1920 by policies to "militarize the economy," which included "labor conscription" that made workers subject to military discipline and harsh punishment for infractions. Absenteeism, low productivity, "pilfering" of goods, and other acts of indiscipline were branded as "criminal" acts, "desertion," and "treason," especially in key industries like transport and munitions. Arrests, speedy trials, exile to labor camps, and some executions became normal, with the Cheka playing an increasingly pervasive role. These efforts had the desired effect: in 1920, at least according to official statistics, productivity increased.[32] On the other hand, in this new militarized political environment, the robust localism and direct democracy of 1917, once praised and endorsed, was now treated as dangerous fragmentation and anarchy.

Still, many communists believed that they were fighting to create a new society, a new culture, and new people—to leap from the kingdom of necessity to the kingdom of freedom. The civil war years were the "heroic period of the Russian revolution," in the words of an early Soviet historian of "war communism."[33] Violence could seem like a virtuous struggle against the foundations of violence. The collapse of the economy could look like the end of capitalism. This was a time of experimentation, much of it endorsed by the ruling party and state, to transform social and cultural life on every "front." One battleground was the family, sexuality, and gender relations. A special branch of the party, the Women's Section (Zhenotdel, founded 1919), worked to nurture the "new woman," freed of the unequal burdens of family life through collective kitchens and collective day care but also free, bold, and active in personality. A youth wing of the party, the Komsomol (founded 1918), worked to inspire a new collectivist spirit among young people. Communes were organized across the country, especially student and worker "house communes" in cities and a few experimental agricultural communes. Even the terrible problem of child homelessness was seen by idealists as an opportunity to raise children in a new way, free of the backward-looking attitudes and values of most parents. Seeking to transform workers' cultural life, a "proletarian culture" movement emerged at the end of 1917, with much of the initiative coming from working-class writers, poets, artists, and activists, and often nurturing a radical new "proletarian literature" inclined toward utopian visions of "crucified" humanity "resurrected" (favorite metaphors) to a shining new world, a paradise of happiness and freedom. Artists, architects, and writers—many now working with support from state institutions, especially the

Commissariat of Enlightenment—were imagining this new world and even drawing up impossible architectural plans.[34] Nothing seemed unimaginable during this historic time when the most brutal violence and the most radical visions were part of the same journey "through torment and sorrow, in unceasing struggle for liberation from all chains, toward a pyramid of light, perfection, and happiness," to borrow words describing a proposed public sculpture park in 1918.[35]

Most historians view the coercive and violent culture of the civil war as having a decisive impact on the evolution of Bolshevism, as a "formative experience" that, as Robert Tucker argued in his influential study of the origins of Stalinism, "militarized the revolutionary political culture of the Bolshevik movement," leaving a heritage of "martial zeal, revolutionary voluntarism and *élan,* readiness to resort to coercion, rule by administrative fiat, centralized administration, [and] summary justice," converting the Bolshevik ethos of "ruthlessness, authoritarianism, and 'class hatred'... into cruelty, fanaticism, and absolute intolerance of those who thought differently," and hardening the conviction that "the state was the modality through which socialism would be built."[36] The Bolsheviks were certainly not passive in this experience. As Sheila Fitzpatrick famously argued, the civil war "gave the new regime a baptism by fire," but this "was the kind of baptism the Bolsheviks had risked, and may even have sought."[37]

The end of the civil war left the Soviet economy and society in an even more catastrophic condition. Historians debate whether this was due more to the long years of war and social upheaval—a continuum of catastrophe with deep roots[38]—or to the particular effects of Soviet policies. But all agree on the cataclysmic results: a ruined economy, urban depopulation, a massive refugee crisis, peasant rebellion, strikes, and open dissidence among even communists. By 1921, industrial output had fallen to 20 percent of the prewar level. Workers, who were supposed to be the foundation of Soviet rule as a "dictatorship of the proletariat," fled the ruined and hungry cities or became soldiers or administrators, such that the size of the working class shrank to less than half of its prewar scale. This "declassing" of the proletariat, as Marxists called it, was a worrisome and paradoxical effect of the revolution: as the working-class Bolshevik and "Workers' Opposition" leader Alexander

Shliapnikov famously taunted Lenin at the 1922 party congress, "Allow me to congratulate you on becoming the vanguard of a non-existent class."[39] Peasants dramatically cut back on the land they cultivated, producing little more than what they needed for their own use. But even their own subsistence was threatened when drought brought many regions to the verge of starvation, which would arrive on a mass scale in 1921–2. On top of this was rampant illness and disease ("one of the most cataclysmic public health crises in modern history," in the words of a historian[40]); homelessness, including millions of children;[41] violent urban crime; rural banditry; massive drunkenness; and every imaginable form of dissipated and abusive behavior by demoralized people trying to survive. Lenin was not exaggerating when he told the tenth Communist party congress in March 1921 that Russia emerged from seven years of war like a "man beaten to within an inch of his life."[42] Or as some historians have argued, Russia ended the civil war in a condition of "trauma."[43]

Popular rebellion added to the sense of a damaged and traumatized revolution. After peasants no longer feared a White victory, the Bolsheviks ceased to be the lesser evil. Peasants ambushed grain requisitioning teams and attacked representatives of state authority. In western Siberia, the middle Volga, Tambov province, and Ukraine, massive uprisings broke out in late 1920. The main demands were everywhere the same: end the forced requisitioning of grain, restore free trade, and give peasants complete control of the land they worked and the products they produced. This libertarian vision was what peasants thought they had achieved in the revolution, mostly by their own hands. Some peasant groups demanded reconvening the Constituent Assembly. Unrest among urban workers was less widespread, but more unsettling politically. In early 1921, scattered protest meetings, demonstrations, and occasional strikes broke out. Workers' demands mainly concerned matters of physical survival, especially food and clothing. But economic frustration, as in the past, brought out political discontent. Workers demanded the restoration of civil rights and the end of coercive management in factories; some called for a Constituent Assembly. In March, sailors at the Kronstadt naval base, located on an island close to Petrograd, mutinied. Kronstadt sailors, who had famously supported the Bolsheviks during the July Days—Trotsky praised them at the time as "the pride and glory of the Russian revolution"—and during the October seizure of power, now demanded ending one-party rule, restoring freedom of speech and press, summoning a Constituent Assembly, transferring all power to freely elected soviets, and ending not only grain requisitioning but state control of the economy. "Down with the Commissarocracy" became a popular slogan among both sailors and workers.

Complicating this crisis was dissent among communists who felt that core principles of the revolution had been sacrificed in the struggle to survive. Dissident party factions had arisen before. In 1918, "Left Communists" opposed the Brest-Litovsk treaty as a betrayal of world revolution and criticized the introduction of strict labor discipline into industry as a violation of workers' control. In 1919, a "Military Opposition" challenged Trotsky's plan that the new Red Army employ traditional discipline and use former tsarist officers. Once the civil war was over, however, internal criticism of party policy became more open and vehement, though no more successful. "Democratic Centralists" challenged the growing authoritarian centralization and bureaucratization of the party and demanded freer discussion of issues and elections of local party officials. The "Workers' Opposition" opposed traditional discipline in industry, the use of "bourgeois specialists" in management, and the subordination of trade unions to the state.[44]

The spring of 1921 was a turning point. Dissent was silenced and crushed. The tenth party congress in March banned factions within the party, so that criticism among Communists could not coalesce around any organized force. But the suppression of opposition within the party was mild compared to the violence used to crush peasant insurrections, workers' strikes, and the Kronstadt mutiny. Lenin, Trotsky, and other Communist leaders justified these actions, perhaps even to themselves, because they were sure they were on the right side of history. At the same time, it seemed that compromise was also necessary—in the face of so much discontent but also given the "delay" of the worldwide socialist revolution, which was expected to provide the sort of internationalist support that economically underdeveloped Russia needed to solve its economic problems and progress rapidly toward socialism. In 1921, the brutality and heroism of "war communism" was abandoned in favor of a conciliatory and sober "New Economic Policy," or NEP. Much did not change. The Communist party's control of the state remained intact (reinforced with a formal ban on other political parties) and discipline within the party was reinforced (including the ban on factions). In the economy, the state retained full control of the "commanding heights": banking, large and medium industry, transportation, foreign trade, and wholesale commerce. But small-scale private enterprise and retail trade were again allowed, though regulated. And in place of the despised requisitioning of grain and produce, the government established a fixed "tax in kind," replaced later by a cash tax. NEP was a "retreat" on the road to socialism, Lenin admitted, which the more radically inclined found intolerable. But many Bolsheviks, perhaps Lenin included, began to think of NEP as a new path to socialism, suitable to a backward peasant country. During the 1920s, a debate raged in the party between advocates of a slow transformation that would raise the cultural and economic level of the population and help the population understand the benefits of socialist cooperation, and advocates of a more militant forced march into socialism, even a revival of the heroic radicalism of war communism. The debate was settled only by Stalin's "Great Turn" at the end of the 1920s, a "revolution from above" that tried to cut through complexity and compromise and leap into a new economy, society, and culture.

*　*　*

Many journalists felt that "civil war" began the day the Soviets took power.[45] Some embraced the fight: the government newspaper *Izvestiia* and the Bolshevik party newspaper *Pravda* declared that this was the start of the final battle against the bourgeoisie and other "enemies of the people," including "traitors" among socialists who refused to support the people's cause. Liberals and moderate socialists, before they were silenced, declared this battle to be pointless and barbaric fratricide that would lead not to a new life but only to more torment, sorrow, and disaster. Resolutions and letters from soldiers printed in *Izvestiia* in the first weeks of Soviet power reflected the viewpoint of the new government. The October revolution, these chosen texts insisted, had set in motion an unprecedented but long dreamed-of time: the "death throes of capital," whose "mighty chain," "which shackled laboring Russia for centuries," has now been broken, making way for a new life with "no more slaves or masters," and without oppression or violence. This was the "long-awaited Great hour . . . for the realization of the Great slogan of Liberty, Equality, and Fraternity," a time when "our long-suffering Russian Land" had become "at long last free Russia." And anyone who "stands in the way," or "betrays the cause of the people's revolution" (such as socialists who "disgraced" themselves by walking out of the Soviet congress), will be "swept aside."[46]

Liberals and moderate socialists viewed this moment very differently. The most influential liberal newspaper, *Speech* (*Rech'*), on the first day of Soviet power, condemned the Bolshevik revolution as a "coup d'etat" and defined it less as a significant turning point in history than as one more "trial" in Russia's ongoing suffering and destruction, "a new stage on its path of thorns" (a common metaphor for suffering that alluded to Christ on the path to Calvary).[47] The popular left-liberal newspaper the *Contemporary Word* (*Sovremennoe slovo*), also on 26 October, declared that "this revolution is not a step toward the kingdom of freedom and socialism but a leap into the abyss, immense and dark." Non-Bolshevik socialists said much the same. The *People's Word* (*Narodnoe slovo*), a populist newspaper, predicted only "new torments and trials" along Russia's continuing "path of thorns."[48] Likewise, on this last day before the Soviet newspaper *Izvestiia* came under Bolshevik control, the editors declared that "this is not a transfer of power to the Soviets, but the seizure of power by one party, the Bolsheviks," and predicted that the attempt to rule Russia alone, without the support of other parties, would lead only to "the bloodshed of civil war: blood and pogroms."[49]

News for Everyone (*Gazeta dlia vsekh*) was an independent left-of-center newspaper published in Moscow for "ordinary city dwellers" (*obyvateli*), a successor to the *Daily Kopeck Gazette* (*Ezhednevnaia gazeta-kopeika*). After October, the editors continued to claim that they spoke to and for the interests of the urban commoner, especially against the rich and powerful. The Soviet government tolerated the paper until June 1918, when it was shut down, as many papers were, for "spreading false rumors" along with other charges.[50] The editors shared the widespread conviction that only a socialist government representing the entire left would save Russia from catastrophe and so were immediately suspicious of the new Bolshevik government. They worried aloud that Bolshevik rule was leading Russia not forward into a new and positive historical stage but downward into more chaos, violence, and barbarism. The street battles that broke out in Moscow and other cities immediately after the declaration of Soviet power led the paper's columnists to decry the Bolshevik revolution as "fratricidal conflict" and "vandalization,"[51] and to blame the Bolsheviks for provoking the common people with "deceitful" and "empty" promises and unleashing bloody and brutal "passions."[52]

In the months following, the columnists of *News for Everyone* voiced deepening dismay about what the revolution had brought: empty promises, brutality, violence, disorder, hunger, death, and "civil war." P. Borchevsky, whom we have heard before as a lead columnist for both the *Daily Kopeck Gazette* and *News for Everyone* (his essays usually held pride of place as the left column on the front page), greeted the New Year of 1918 with doubts that it would bring the desired "new happiness." He offered his own brief history of the revolution. "The old year, 1917, was a year of catastrophes and disappointments." To be sure, the "heavy weight of gloomy reaction" had initially given way to "the bright joy of the first days of freedom." But then came months of political conflict, violence, tension, and, not least, "speeches, speeches, and more speeches." Then came the October overturn. In part, this was a good thing, for it put "talentless rulers in prison." But then

the most terrible begins. Blood pours in streams. Moscow burns and trembles under shelling. From this ocean of blood emerges a new government. With guns and bayonets in its hands.... But no peace, no bread, no freedom, no money, no work.... Only shame and fratricidal conflict. This is where we find ourselves now. No end in sight. And rumors are growing and spreading about new shame, new battles, and new misery. No end to misfortune in sight. Looking ahead: slavery, hunger, blood, despair. How can we speak of any "new happiness" here?[53]

Two days later, Borchevsky took an even more historical view of the present and the future, emphasizing the futility of ideological visions of change: "You can have all the beliefs and views you like, but then there is real life—unvarnished, cruel, and cunning. This life will break theories, fracture parties, and confound every hypothesis and conjecture."[54] In early March, another front-page columnist, Isaiah Gromov, offered his reading of the first full year of revolution: "your heart clenches and you want to weep and curse" over the many "great, joyous, and terrible" things that have unfolded in these twelve months. But the most terrible thing was that the revolution was beginning "to choke on the people's blood," to perish in the "fratricidal whirlwind" of "mutual destruction."[55] "Civil war" was a constant theme in *News for Everyone*, and typically judged in moral terms as "shameful" and "sinful" "fratricide," and as part of the catastrophic experience of disruption after October: the thick atmosphere of instability and uncertainty, egoism and selfishness, and the falling value of human life.[56]

These columnists did not hesitate to blame the Bolsheviks for all this, branding their policies and actions as "shameful,"[57] and disparaging the new leaders in the harshest terms. Borchevsky, during the elections to the Constituent Assembly, accused the Bolsheviks of having "decided to lay their hairy bestial hand on that which the whole of exhausted Russia puts its dreams, where every Russian suffering for the fate of their homeland sees salvation."[58] But *News for Everyone* writers also saw dangers that were outside the control of the government or the result of government policies, especially the looming threat of hunger, which would threaten everything of value: "with hunger we lose our reason, conscience, and discipline," which might lead to a new and more terrible revolution, "the revolution of the belly," which is stronger "than any political theory" or "all the revolution's decrees."[59]

These independent left-wing journalists, among the last with access to print, echoed what they believed many Russians were feeling in the wake of October: that "the Russian land is perishing."[60] The public mood was dark, these journalists found, marked by anxiety, confusion, exhaustion, fear, powerlessness, passivity, and a deep "longing" for a "peaceful life."[61] In February 1918, the columnist Gromov tried to describe the state of mind of the ordinary Russian (the *obyvatel'*) after a year of revolution:

So much has happened and every day brings such stunning events that one's head becomes like mush and one's spirit fills with despair and emptiness....Nerves are pulled tight. Thoughts coil into a tangle. No beginning, no end, no exit, no solution...Everyone wants to simply shout: "Can't you finally just leave us alone. I don't want a thing—not peace, not war, not joy, not despair, not your damned politics!! Give me enough to eat and I will think nothing, know nothing, and fear nothing!"[62]

Maxim Gorky's independent socialist paper, *New Life,* was more sympathetic to the revolution. But he too recognized the catastrophic experience of these days: "Yes, we live up to our necks in blood and filth," he wrote at the end of December 1917, "Thick clouds of repulsive vulgarity surround us and are blinding many. Yes, at times it seems that this vulgarity will poison and stifle all the beautiful dreams to which we have given birth in our labor and torment." But he rejected the gloomy and pessimistic mood that so many others could not escape. His optimism depended on faith—on a loosely Marxist belief that historical progress is driven by contradiction itself:

In these days of revolt, blood, and enmity, terrible for many, one must not forget that on this path of great torments and unbearable trials we are heading toward the rebirth of man, we are undertaking the earthly cause of emancipating life from the heavy, rusted chains of the past....We must believe that these frenzied days smeared with filth and blood are the great days of the birth of a new Russia....In these days of monstrous contradiction a new Russia is being born.[63]

The full weight of these "days of revolt, blood, and enmity" would be felt many times over when the "civil war" everyone was talking about became a real war. Although independent press voices had been silenced, we can get some sense of how this history was described at the moment of its making through two contrary newspaper voices from the fall of 1919: the *Poor* (*Bednota*), published by the Central Committee of the Communist Party for peasants and soldiers and the pro-White newspaper *Priazovsky Region* (*Priazovskii krai*), published in Rostov-on-the-Don, the administrative capital of a region in the south then fully controlled by White forces.

The year 1919 was an uncertain time, the outcome of the conflict still far from clear, yet both newspapers were strikingly upbeat about the weakness of their enemies, the righteousness of their cause, and their own successes and popular support. Articles in the *Poor,*[64] presented often as local reports from villages and towns in areas controlled by the

Soviet government and the Red Army, emphasized all that was being done to improve people's lives and how happy everyone was about these efforts: building schools, organizing "cultural-enlightenment" work such as reading rooms, fighting alcoholism, supporting poor peasants against rich exploiters, fighting speculators who took advantage of the poor, and aiding the families of Red Army soldiers. Peasants, young people, and townspeople were enthusiastic supporters of this "great revolution," which the "bourgeoisie" and the White armies were fighting to undo. In one typical village, for example, "an enlightenment circle has existed already for a year" with great support: "young people, even in the summer when there is so much work, do not forget about their circle: they stage contemporary plays and the room is always full."[65] The paper reported the same positive spirit during celebrations of the second anniversary of the October revolution, said to be marked throughout the Soviet lands by great joy, festivity, and unanimity: "Almost the entire population, including children, were present at the mass meeting. Tea and snacks were organized for the school-aged children, consisting of bread, an egg, and two pieces of sugar. The meaning of the holiday was explained to the children. . . . After tea there was a show, after which a Red Army choir performed a number of songs."[66] History and the people were clearly on the side of Soviet power and the Bolsheviks. And everyone was confident and happy. It is unlikely that these writers were blind to the suffering and uncertainties all around them. And it is too simple to reduce their rosy account only to the effect of censorship. The language of reporting might be seen as itself a type of performance (a "speech act" in the later lexicon of linguistics) meant not merely to reflect reality but to constitute and change it.

Reporting from the White-controlled region around the Don river and the Azov sea, an area with strong Cossack traditions, the *Priazovsky Region* newspaper also described a local population fully in support of the struggle against the Bolshevik regime, certain that this was a historic fight for the people's happiness, and confident of victory. These arguments were especially pronounced in essays celebrating a new local holiday, "The Day of the Warrior" (*Den' voina*). Citizens of all classes, readers were told, were inspired by feelings of "patriotism" and "civic conscience" and the "sacred cause of liberating the country from bandit domination" (a common term at the time for Bolshevik rule).[67] Even the local "working masses" had "sobered up from the intoxication of Bolshevism," recognizing "the unrealizable illusions of the proletarian dictatorship for which the proletariat itself has had to pay in oceans of blood." Workers were now ready to "set aside all 'class interests'" in order to rebuild their "destroyed country," and understood now that to do so was their "sacred duty." Past "dreams of a 'Leninist kingdom' had dissipated like night shadows before the coming light of day."[68]

Where Bolsheviks viewed the Communist party as the historic force for advancing the cause of class struggle and socialist transformation, the journalists of the *Priazovsky Region* embraced the military as the historic force for national salvation: "In all the difficult times of European history, during all eras of revolution and terrorism, only the military elements have been able to save the honor, dignity, and well-being of the nation."[69] The White emphasis on the historic nature of their struggle against Communism was as strong a theme as the Communist insistence on the world-historical significance of the proletarian revolution. As one journalist typically put it, this was a "titanic" battle of "bright light against the most absolute darkness, of honesty and truth against villainy and dishonor, of true freedom for all against the most terrible enslavement, such as did not exist even in the darkest times of the medieval inquisition." The White forces were "saviors." The Reds were "robbers and bandits, adventurists and cheats, the savage mob, and bands of crooks, who take advantage of the huge and age-old ignorance of the people for their dark, selfish ends."[70]

Examples were given to demonstrate these truths. Reporters described, for example, life in the Ukrainian capital of Kiev after Communists had been expelled by White forces: shuttered theaters immediately reopened, independent newspapers reappeared, civic and political work resumed, including "all parties from Mensheviks and Right SRs to monarchists," consumer prices dropped, educated people were no longer afraid to dress well, the "desperation" previously seen in people's eyes was replaced by "inspiration and hope" along with "gratitude" to the White army for their freedom, and all classes felt a new sense of unity, including workers and Ukrainian nationalists.[71]

Both sides defined the civil war in moral terms as a fight of light against darkness, good against evil, and freedom against slavery, on a global historic stage—a representation also visible in the often similar poster iconography produced by the two sides.[72] For Communists and their supporters, this was part of an international class struggle against inequality, exploitation, and oppression, inspired by universal values of liberty, equality, and fraternity. In publications supporting Bolshevik power, writers proclaimed the revolution a struggle for sacred "truth," especially for *pravda,* the moral truth of earthly justice, righteousness, honesty, love, and goodness. In the words of a worker-poet writing in the newspaper the *Workers' Life* (*Rabochaia zhizn'*) in 1920, the people have inscribed on their red banners "with rays of light" "the "inextinguishable word Love."[73] Such quasi-religious hyperbole among writers enthusiastic about the revolution was commonplace during the civil war. In "proletarian" periodicals in 1920, for example, the revolution was described as building a new church on the ruins of the old, "a Temple of Sacred Truth, Love, and Equality," a "Workers' Kingdom" of "Truth, Righteousness, and Love" (*istina, pravda, liubov'*), a "new world" of "Equality, Liberty, Fraternity, and Beauty," which would be "clean and beautiful," "holy and pure."[74]

Anti-communist journalists were no less convinced of the global historical significance of their struggle and the universal truth of their values. An essay in the *Priazovsky Region* in September 1919, for example, by an author calling himself "Schiller from Taganrog" (a town in the region), argued that the civil war was truly a global historic struggle: "the struggle against Bolshevism is a cause not only for Russia, where this social scourge found itself a cozy cradle, but for the whole of the civilized world, where the mutinous rabble are threatening ever newer disruptions." As such, "the rebirth of a free Russia as a fully-fledged member of the European family of peoples" is a goal fully in accord with the "direction of history's movement."[75] The only difference in the arguments of Communist writers was the emphasis on class struggle as the historical engine driving world progress and freedom.

Notes

1. Lenin, "Frightening the People with Bourgeois Terrors," *Pravda*, 48 (4 May 1917): 1; "Inevitable Catastrophe and Extravagant Promises," *Pravda*, 59 (17 May 1917): 1; "Can the Bolsheviks Retain State Power," written late September 1917 and published in the magazine Prosveshchenie [*Enlightenment*] 14 October 1917. Lenin's works are available in English translation at <https://www.marxists.org/archive/lenin/works> [accessed 30 July 2016] and in Russian at <http://publ.lib.ru/ARCHIVES/L/LENIN_Vladimir_Il'ich/_Lenin_V.I._PSS5_.html>. [accessed 26 August 2016]. Translations in this chapter are my own. Titles of articles are given in English.

2. From Lenin's pamphlet *The State and Revolution*, written during his post-July exile in Finland in 1917.

3. "To the Population," 5 November 1917, *Pravda*, 4 (evening edn) (6 November 1917); "How to Organize Competition" (24–7 December 1917, though unpublished at the time); and "The Immediate Tasks of Soviet Power" (printed in *Pravda*, 83 (28 April 1918)), all in V. I. Lenin, *Izbrannye proizvedeniia v chetyrekh tomakh [Selected Works in Four Volumes]* (Moscow, 1988), iii. 24, 48, 165.

4. Orlando Figes, *A People's Tragedy: The Russian Revolution, 1891–1924* (Harmondsworth, 1996), 503. This is also the argument of Richard Pipes in his *The Russian Revolution* (New York, 1990).

5. See especially his essays "How to Organize Competition" (24–7 December 1917) and "The Immediate Tasks of Soviet Power" (April 1918), in Lenin, *Izbrannye proizvedeniia*, iii. 48–55, 162–92.

6. See James Ryan, *Lenin's Terror: The Ideological Origins of Early Soviet State Terror* (London, 2012), 86–8, 97–8 (quotations 86, 98).

7. See James Bunyan and H. H. Fisher (eds), *The Bolshevik Revolution, 1917–1918: Documents and Materials* (Stanford, CA, 1961; 1st edn 1934), 124–32.

8. "Draft Decree on Workers' Control," 26–7 October 1917, in Lenin, *Izbrannye proizvedeniia*, iii. 15–16; "Decree on Workers' Control," 14 November 1917, in *Izvestiia*, 227 (16 November 1917): 6. See discussions in S. A. Smith, *Red Petrograd: Revolution in the Factories, 1917–1918* (Cambridge, 1983), 209–16, and David Mandel, *The Petrograd Workers and the Soviet Seizure of Power* (London, 1984), 364–78.

9. "Decree on the Elective Principle and on the Organization of Authority in the Army," *Izvestiia*, 254 (17 December 1917): 5.

10. "Declaration of the Rights of the Peoples of Russia," 2 November 1917, *Izvestiia*, 215 (3 November 1917): 4.

11. "On the Abolition of Estates and Civil Ranks," 10 November 1917, *Izvestiia*, 223 (12 November 1917): 6.

12. Sovnarkom decree on legal reform, 24 November 1917, in Bunyan and Fisher, *Bolshevik Revolution*, 291–2.

13. *Novaia zhizn'*, 166 (29 October 1917): 1; 167 (30 October 1917): 2; Mandel, *Petrograd Workers*, 323–42; Figes, *A People's Tragedy*, 496; *Izvestiia*, 217 (5 November 1917): 4.

14. Alexander Rabinowitch, *The Bolsheviks in Power: The First Year of Soviet Rule in Petrograd* (Bloomington, IN, 2007), 260–309 (quotation about Lenin, p. 271).

15. Oliver H. Radkey, *Russia Goes to the Polls: The Election to the All-Russian Constituent Assembly, 1917*, rev. edn (Ithaca, NY, 1989); Bunyan and Fisher, *Bolshevik Revolution*, 347–8; *Novaia zhizn'*, 182 (16 November 1917): 4. See also Pipes, *Russian Revolution*, 541–3.

16. "Resolution on the Constituent Assembly," 27 October 1917, *Izvestiia*, 209 (28 October 1917): 2.

17. Lenin, "On Constitutional Illusions" (26 July 1917), printed first in *Rabochii i soldat*, 11 (4 August 1917) and 12 (5 August 1917), in V. I. Lenin, *Sochineniia* (Moscow, 1955), xxv. 174–87. See also Robert Service, *Lenin: A Political Life*, ii (Bloomington, IN, 1991), 227–8.

18. "Theses on the Constituent Assembly," *Pravda*, 213 (13 December 1917): 3; *Izvestiia*, 242 (2 December 1917): 1; *Pravda*, 207 (6 December 1917): 2; Bunyan and Fisher, *Bolshevik Revolution*, 361–2; *Izvestiia*, 244 (6 December 1917): 6.

19. Decree on the Press, *Izvestiia*, 209 (28 October 1917): 2.

20. *Izvestiia*, 239 (29 November 1917): 1.

21. *Delo naroda*, 223 (3 December 1917): 4; Bunyan and Fisher, *Bolshevik Revolution*, 361–2; *Novaia zhizn'*, 192 (3 December 1917): 2.

22. Bunyan and Fisher, *Bolshevik Revolution*, 297–8; *Pravda*, 290 (18 December 1927): 2.

23. From a 1922 report by Martin Latsis, quoted in Rabinowitch, *The Bolsheviks in Power*, 83.

24. From the minutes of the seventh Bolshevik party congress, 8 March 1918, in Bunyan and Fisher, *Bolshevik Revolution*, 527–9.

25. Among many historians who make this point, see e.g. Rex Wade, *The Bolshevik Revolution and the Russian Civil War* (Westport, CT, 2001), ch. 4; Boris Kolonitskii, "Krasnye protiv krasnykh: K 90-letiiu okonchaniia Grazhdanskoi voiny v Rossii," *Niva*, 2010/11, at <http://magazines.russ.ru/neva/2010/11/ko4.html> [accessed 30 July 2016].

26. Donald Raleigh, *Revolution on the Volga: 1917 in Saratov* (Ithaca, NY, 1986); Peter Holquist, *Making War, Forging Revolution: Russia's Continuum of Crisis, 1914–1921* (Cambridge, MA, 2002). See also Vladimir Buldakov, *Krasnaia smuta: Priroda i posledstviia revoliutsionnogo nasiliia* (Moscow, 2010).

27. See Lenin, "Can Jacobinism Frighten the Working Class?" in *Pravda*, 7 July (24 June) 1917; "Counter-Revolution Takes the Offensive: Jacobins without the People," *Pravda*, 10 June (28 May) 1917; Service, *Lenin*, ii. 226–7; Ryan, *Lenin's Terror*, 35, 66, 80.

28. Holquist, *Making War, Forging Revolution;* David Hoffman, *Cultivating the Masses: Modern State Practices and Soviet Socialism, 1914–1939* (Ithaca, NY, 2011).

29. Prof. V. I. Grinevetskii, *Poslevoennye perspektivy russkoi promyshlennosti* (Kazan, 1919), 64. See also Bunyan and Fisher, *Bolshevik Revolution*, 621.

30. Lars Lih, *Bread and Authority in Russia, 1914–1921* (Berkeley, CA, 1990); Silvana Malle, *The Economic Organization of War Communism, 1918–1921* (Cambridge, 1985); Mary McAuley, *Bread and Justice: State and Society in Petrograd* (Oxford, 1991); Julie Hessler, *A Social History of Soviet Trade: Trade Policy, Retail Practices, and Consumption, 1917–1953* (Princeton, 2004), ch. 1.

31. On the labor movement after October, see William G. Rosenberg, "Russian Labor and Bolshevik Power after October," *Slavic Review*, 44/2 (Summer 1985): 213–56; Vladimir M. Brovkin, *Behind the Front Lines of the Civil War: Political Parties and Social Movements in Russia, 1918–1922* (Princeton, 1994); Jonathan Aves, *Workers Against Lenin: Labour Protest and the Bolshevik Dictatorship* (London, 1996); and other works cited in Chapter 5 of this volume.

32. On economic militarization, see especially Aves, *Workers against Lenin* and Lewis Siegelbaum, *Soviet State and Society between Revolutions, 1918–1929* (Cambridge, 1992), 34–8.

33. L. Kritsman, *Geroicheskii period velikoi russkoi revoliutsii (opyt analiza t.n. "Voennogo Kommunizma")*, 2nd edn (Moscow and Leningrad, 1926; 1st edn 1924).

34. William G. Rosenberg (ed.), *Bolshevik Visions: First Phase of the Cultural Revolution in Russia*, 2nd edn (Ann Arbor, 1990); Richard Stites, *Revolutionary Dreams: Utopian Vision and Revolutionary Life in the Russian Revolution* (Oxford, 1989); Lynn Mally, *Culture of the Future: The Proletkult Movement in Russia* (Berkeley, CA, 1990); Mark Steinberg, *Proletarian Imagination: Self, Modernity, and the Sacred in Russia, 1910–1925* (Ithaca, NY, 2002).

35. Ivan Shadr's proposal for a "Monument to the World's Suffering," in the cultural journal of the Moscow Soviet, *Tvorchestvo*, 5 (September 1918): 21.
36. Robert C. Tucker, "Stalinism as Revolution from Above," in Tucker (ed.), *Stalinism: Essays in Historical Interpretation* (New York, 1977), 91–2; Sheila Fitzpatrick, "The Civil War as a Formative Experience," in Abbott Gleason, Peter Kenez, and Richard Stites (eds), *Bolshevik Culture: Experiment and Order in the Russian Revolution*(Bloomington, IN, 1985), 57–76; Fitzpatrick, "The Legacy of the Civil War," in Diane P. Koenker, William G. Rosenberg, and Ronald Grigor Suny (eds), *Party, State, and Society in the Russian Civil War: Explorations in Social History* (Bloomington, IN, 1989), 385–97; Raleigh, *Experiencing Russia's Civil War*, ii. 108–9; Holquist, *Making War, Forging Revolution*; 204; Smith, *Russian Revolution*, 98.
37. Sheila Fitzpatrick, *The Russian Revolution*, 3rd edn (Oxford, 2008), 72.
38. I am echoing Peter Holquist's notion of a "continuum of crisis" in his *Making War, Forging Revolution*.
39. Quoted by almost every historian of this period (though sometimes misdated to 1921), the comment appeared in the minutes of the Eleventh Congress of the Russian Communist Party, March–April 1922. See *11-s"ezd RKP(b): Mart-Aprel' 1922, Stenograficheskii otchet* (Moscow, 1961), 103–4.
40. Raleigh, *Experiencing Russia's Civil War*, 198.
41. See Alan Ball, *And Now My Soul Is Hardened: Abandoned Children in Soviet Russia, 1918–1930* (Berkeley, CA, 1994).
42. Lenin, "Report on the Substitution of a Tax in Kind for the Surplus Grain Appropriation System," 15 March 1921. *Polnoe sobranie sochinenii*, 5th edn (Moscow, 1966–75), xliii. 68.
43. e.g. Raleigh, *Experiencing Russia's Civil War*, 207. See also Igor' Narskii, *Zhizn' v katastrofe: Budni naseleniia v 1917–1922 gg.* (Moscow, 2001).
44. The classic study is Robert V. Daniels, *The Conscience of the Revolution: Communist Opposition in Soviet Russia* (New York, 1960).
45. e.g. D. Oshanin, "Kto prav?" *Gazeta dlia vsekh*, 8 November 1917, 1.
46. Soldiers' resolutions printed in *Izvestiia*, 2 November 1917, 6–7; 21 November 1917, 8; 30 November 1917, 7. See also Steinberg, *Voices of Revolution*, 284–8.
47. *Rech'*, 252 (26 October 1917): 1. The paper was closed the following day.
48. Summary and quotations from various newspapers in "Obzor pechati," *Novaia zhizn'*, 164 (27 October 1917): 1.
49. *Izvestiia*, 207 (26 October 1917): 1.
50. "Revoliutsionnyi sud," *Gazeta dlia vsekh*, 13 June 1918, 2.

51. *Gazeta dlia vsekh*, 8 November 1917, 1–3, and many similar articles that followed.

52. "Bred sumashchedshikh" and "Dusha vopiet k nebu," *Gazeta dlia vsekh*, 10 November 1917, 1–3; Nabliudatel', "Tretii obman," *Gazeta dlia vsekh*, 12 November 1917, 3.

53. P. Borchevskii, "S novym . . . ," *Gazeta dlia vsekh*, 11 January 1917, 1.

54. P. Borchevskii, "Krov' pugaet," *Gazeta dlia vsekh*, 13 January 1918, 1.

55. Isaiia Gromov, "Budem zhdat'," *Gazeta dlia vsekh*, 1 March 1918, 1.

56. *Gazeta dlia vsekh*, 21 November 1917, 2; 1 December 1917, 3; 13 December 1917, 2; 13 January 1918, 4; 30 January 1918, 1; 1 February 1918, 3; 27 February 1918, 3.

57. *Gazeta dlia vsekh*, 26 November 1917, 1; 28 November 1918, 3; 13 December 1917, 1; 11 January 1918, 1; 16 January 1918, 3.

58. P. Borchevskii, "Net nadezhdy," *Gazeta dlia vsekh*, 25 November 1917, 1.

59. P. Borchevskii, "Revoliutsiia briukha," *Gazeta dlia vsekh*, 20 January 1918, 1. See also I. Pavlov, "V lapakh goloda," *Gazeta dlia vsekh*, 25 January 1918, 3.

60. *Gazeta dlia vsekh*, 18 November 1917, 3; 19 November 1917, 3; 24 November 1917, 3.

61. *Gazeta dlia vsekh*, 17 November 1917, 1; 7 December 1917, 1; 9 January 1918, 3; 12 January 1918, 3; 25 January 1918, 3; 30 January 1918, 1, 3.

62. Isaiia Gromov, "Ostav'te nas v pokoe," *Gazeta dlia vsekh*, 8 February 1918, 1.

63. Maxim Gorky, editorials in *Novaia zhizn'*, 24 December 1917, 1 and 31 December 1917, 1.

64. Based on reading *Bednota* from September through November 1919.

65. *Bednota,* 11 September 1919, 2.

66. *Bednota,* 27 November 1919, 2.

67. "Den' voina," *Priazovskii krai*, 14 September 1919, 2.

68. "Rabochii vopros," *Priazovskii krai*, 4 September 1919, 1.

69. Loengrin, "15 Sentiabria," *Priazovskii krai*, 14 September 1919, 2.

70. Shiller iz Taganroga, "Arabeski: Den' voina," *Priazovskii krai*, 14 September 1919, 2.

71. Leonid Teplov, "Kievskie pis'ma," *Priazovskii krai*, 17 September 1919, 2.

72. See e.g. two famous posters: "Struggle of the Red Knight with the Dark Force" (1919) and "For the Unity of Russia" (1919), portraying a white knight killing a red dragon. The image can easily be found on the internet with a search by title.

73. S. Obradovich, "Krestnyi put'," *Rabochaia zhizn'*, 1920/1–3/65–67: 20.

74. A. Platonov, "Khristos i my," *Krasnaia derevnia*, 11 June 1920; N. Rybatskii, "Ia kak-to v khrame byl," *Revoliutsionnye vskhody*, 5–6 (November 1920): 9–10; S. Obradovich, "Vol'nyi rabochii," *Rabochaia zhizn'*, 1920/5–7: 4; I. Sadof'ev, "Sil'nee smerti," *Griadushchee*, 1921/1–3: 14; Rabochii Porokhovik, *Griadushchaia kul'tura*, 3 (January 1919): 13; Aksen-Achkasov, "Iunosham," *Griadushchee*, 1918/1 (January): 12–13. See also examples and discussion in Steinberg, *Proletarian Imagination,* ch. 7.
75. "Evropeiskie perspektivy," *Priazovskii krai*, 27 September 1919, 1.

PART III

PLACES AND PEOPLE

CHAPTER 5
POLITICS OF THE STREET

"The street" is a metaphor as much as a place: signifying opportunity and danger, order and disorder, the crowd. In revolution, the street is the epicenter of public action and meaning: a tangible social and political space for doing things and a symbolic space to think and argue about. Always contradictory, even in ordinary times, the modern street signals the city's power to offer anything and everything, from the most thrilling to the most base. That these experiences are mostly in public is essential: the street is the heart of the modern "public sphere," a historically important space, scholars have argued, where citizens, or would-be citizens in societies with limited freedom and rights, build social connections, seek their place as civic actors, and challenge assumptions about who belongs there, who controls civic life, and for what ends. As such, the street is an arena for power—for its exercise and for struggles to take and reorient it—but inseparable from the lived experience of that place.

St Petersburg's Nevsky Prospect, the most famous street in the Russian empire, was an exemplar of what streets can mean. Great crowds of people came here to work, shop, eat, meet, strive, revel, and despair. And to wander, gaze, and wonder: as the street's first literary chronicler, Nikolai Gogol, famously observed in the 1800s, "although you may have had some important and necessary thing to do here, as soon as you step into this street you really forgot all about it."[1] Bureaucrats, officers, aristocrats, merchants, ladies, clerks, workers, idlers, conmen, pickpockets, and prostitutes all crossed paths on Nevsky. Writers, from journalists to poets, were inevitably attracted to this place: for the narrative power of the everyday human spectacle, but also because they could see that such a street symbolized larger things—the nation, society, the empire, human nature, the modern city, civilization, and more.

Revolution, with its crowds of people acting out unleashed desires and ideas, magnified the street's material and symbolic importance. In 1905 and 1917, actions ranging from disciplined marches and mass meetings to disorderly looting and mob violence unfolded on streets across the empire. Labor strikes brought workers out into the open when they were supposed to be inside and under control. The street became more than ever a place for the unfamiliar and extraordinary, for breaking boundaries, for demonstrating the possibility of an altogether different everyday reality. Of course, the street was also home to most of the pathologies of urban life, from crime to prostitution, along with access to most of the city's pleasures, from theaters to taverns. In many ways, the street was the heart of a certain type of democracy: an open and disorderly space where anyone could take part in political life, demand recognition, and experience history. In the language of the Russian revolution we have seen, the street was also the heart of "the democracy": the non-privileged classes, the social base for socialist parties, the revolutionary "crowd," the people. Fittingly, we sometimes speak today of a country's popular masses as "the street," especially when they have been roused to protest. The experience of revolution is nowhere more palpable than on the street.

The Everyday Street, 1900–1914

Russia's cities, reaching back into the nineteenth century, were sites of an urban revolution that was an essential context for the political and social revolutions to come. This revolution transformed the lives of millions of migrants from the countryside and small towns who sought work and opportunity in the city. Journalists narrated this upheaval in terms familiar to literatures of urbanization: moving from provincial darkness and silence to the bright lights and noisy vitality of the metropolis; naive innocence disabused and replaced by sophisticated or cynical knowledge; but also the always ambiguous experience of pleasures mixed with suffering. Newcomers marveled at the intoxicating display of urban public life: motley crowds in motion; the rumbling speed of street cars (and the press of bodies inside); construction everywhere; glittering shop windows filled with alluring goods; the shouts of advertising; and a cornucopia of places for fun, ranging from theaters, restaurants, and nightclubs to inexpensive popular stages, music halls, summer entertainment parks, and cinemas. Journalists, wandering the streets in search of material for human interest sketches or *feuilletons*, described this in vivid detail, but they also insistently reminded readers (as if they could forget) of the ubiquity of dirt and dust, trash piled up in courtyards, broken paving and peeling paint, foul smells, and the continual "noise, groans, din, and roar" of people, transport, and machines—especially in the industrial outskirts and neighborhoods with large numbers of the poor. For some, this new urban landscape was a place for adventure and discovery. But most writers, not least because they had arguments to make, dwelled on the street as "crass," "repulsive," "obscene," "monstrous," and "corrupt."[2]

"There is no deeper abyss than the sidewalk on the streets of a big city," a columnist for a popular left-leaning newspaper, the *Little Gazette* (*Malen'kaia gazeta*), observed in 1914.[3] By then, this had become a cliché. After 1905, when censorship became less strict, newspapers filled their pages with stories of crime, sexual predation, street violence, prostitution, suicide in public places, and other "sores" of modern urban life—often under the simple headline "Our Street."[4] The influential conservative newspaper *New Times* (*Novoe vremia*) relentlessly complained about the "mores of the street" that had come to define public life, particularly after 1905 when "political breakdown" contributed to "moral breakdown."[5] The tabloid journalist Olga Gridina described the city as a land of beasts: animal-like drunks, "wild tigers" who bare their "teeth" (knives) when you refuse them money, "packs of fierce wolves" preying on women and girls.[6] For journalists, "the street" was both a physical and moral space, and always ambiguously liberating, seductive, degraded, and ruinous. The street represented one of the great free spaces in an unfree society, though too often this meant, moralizing journalists complained, "freedom" for "carousing, drunken disorder, and public debauchery," freedom to live only "for the pleasures of today."[7]

Women experienced with extra force the opportunities and perils of the urban revolution. In modernizing cities, women found new opportunities to be out on the streets, to work outside the home (though especially in domestic service and women's industries like textiles), to attend school, to enjoy new public forms of entertainment, and (for the most privileged) to participate in civic life through charities, teaching, journalism, and civic advocacy (at least around "women's issues" like prostitution or schooling for girls).[8] This widening sphere was deeply unequal, of course, with opportunity and experience varying according where a women lived, her class, her age, her level of education, her family's attitudes, and the winds of chance. For women whose survival depended on labor, the experience of modern public life was often grueling. Women laboring in small workshops, mostly as seamstresses, found terrible conditions: a woman activist organizing tailoring workers in Moscow described long hours of exhausting work, filthy workshops permeated with foul odors from the toilet, a "constant noise and buzz" that wore on the nerves, the shouts and curses of managers, and sexual harassment by both male workers and supervisors. These women complained that this was "a dog's life, no one should live like this."[9] Factory work, though regulated by the state, was not much better: as a Russian priest dramatically put it in his 1906 study of woman factory workers, "there is a Hell more terrible than Dante's ninth circle. It is female labor."[10] Domestic service was another hell: the low pay, long hours of work, lack of privacy and personal life, and intense dependency led women activists at the time to describe domestic servants as "white slaves."[11] These conditions led many working-class women to prostitution—as a way to escape poverty but also as a response to traumas of sexual abuse and rape, which were more likely where unrelated men had direct power over women.[12]

Contemporaries interpreted women's everyday experience in the modernizing city in the anxious and moralizing frame of urban peril and deceit. Although women were now free to walk unaccompanied in public, they could not avoid "humiliation at the hands of impudent street rogues."[13] Voracious male wolves, it seemed, prowled every public space of the city.[14] And women's presumed innocence, purity, and weakness made them easy victims when they strayed from the domestic sphere. Newspapers and magazines offered readers endless variations (mixing fact, sensation, melodrama, and allegory) on the theme of the "innocent" and "pure" country girl, full of hope for a new life, corrupted and destroyed by the immoral and merciless life of the big city. These stories typically began with seduction and betrayal, or women tricked into dependency and prostitution, when, desperate for work (or better work), they accepted offers of jobs in shops that turned out to be fronts for brothels. The modern street was itself a seducer: young women were corrupted, it was said, by desires for fashionable clothes, jewelry, perfume, "admirers," and pleasure. A 1906 pamphlet on Nevsky Prospect described working-class women gazing enviously in shop windows "sparkling" with goods. In time, the "marketplace of fashion and beauty" lured them "like moths to a fire." Their growing "appetites" would lead to their degradation and ruin, turning many innocent daughters of the village into "cynical daughters of the street."[15]

Women were not simple victims in these stories of the revolution that urban life wrought in people's lives, as the following suggests. Headlined "A Typical Story," this series of articles about "Liza" appeared in the popular penny tabloid the *Kopeck Gazette* in St Petersburg in 1910. When the author, Olga Gridina, first encountered her, at a friend's home where Liza worked as a maid, she was 22 years old, cheerful, and pretty. Like most female domestic servants, she had likely grown up in a village. The temptations of city life made her ambitious and dissatisfied. Seeking a change, she trusted a nicely dressed woman who seemed to be offering her a better job, but was luring young women into prostitution. Liza was deceived, but she was not entirely innocent. When she quit her work as a maid, she declared to her employers, "What am I, a slave or something? I will be my own mistress!" Soon, she was seen promenading down Nevsky Prospect wearing "gaudy silk finery and a huge fashionable round hat." Her former employers wished they had reminded her of the proper virtues of "labor, honor, and modesty." But Liza had embraced a new moral argument, grounded in the spirit of individualism and capitalism: her right to choose her own way and the values of "finery, pleasures, wealth, and a life limited by nothing." Two months later, Gridina noticed Liza walking the streets and stopped to ask her about her new life. Her manner was bold and saucy. She was proud to be a "carouser" (*guliashchaia*), a term in Russian that refers to both merry-making and prostitution. She was offended that some people considered her "trash" and would even spit at her in public. Her choice of sex work, she insisted, was not only rational but morally legitimate in the modern world. Everyone sells what they can. "You sell your essays, and I sell my body—it's mine, isn't it?" And it's better work than domestic service: "When I was a servant, I sold my hands, my eyes, my legs. 'Run, look, bring, give!' Nothing more. Servile and dirty work. But now!...I see no difference in selling my body. And the work is easier and more profitable." Several months later, the journalist again noticed Liza working Nevsky Prospect. Now her beauty was gone and some of her teeth were missing. Gridina learned that her madam beat her and clients beat her. Too late, she realized that her modern philosophy had been mistaken: "I did not understand the sort of pit I had fallen into!...I gave myself to the streets and they swallowed me." Few exits remained: "I can drink myself into unconsciousness, or get beaten senseless by some man," or end it all with poison or under the wheels of a streetcar.[16]

This urban morality tale included almost every trope found in public discussions of urbanization in Russia: hardship and opportunity for young people migrating to the expanding cities, the growing desire for individual freedom and agency, the intrusion of the capitalist marketplace into the most intimate spheres, the ubiquity of deceit and illusion, the inequalities of power and possibility, violence against women, disillusionment, and suicide. Whether or not the story was completely factual should matter no more to us than it did to the author: it was a "typical story," a reflection of well-known realities and widely shared interpretations. And Gridina was determined to make the moral of the story perfectly clear: she repeatedly used her columns to warn migrants to the city from "Russia's dark corners, where age-old silence reigns," who thought they were entering a "bright temple" and hoped to feel on the street the "pulse of the age" and a "festival of the human spirit," that all they would find was a glittering mask hiding the "harsh and bitter" truth that experience would eventually reveal.[17]

These stories were artful exaggerations to make a political point. Yes, working-class individuals and families experienced the harshest sides of city life, including overcrowded and unsanitary housing, higher rates of illness and premature death (made worse by pervasive alcoholism, especially among men), a greater likelihood of becoming victims of violence, low incomes and long hours of work, and many other physical and psychological depredations of being poor and powerless.[18] At the same time, the benefits of city life were considerable. Acquiring new work skills (and often literacy) and learning the ways of the street gave poor migrants to the city a heightened sense of self-respect and confidence. The spectacle of consumer goods could stimulate longing and hope. But self-esteem, knowledge, and desire are complex things that can also nurture envy, resentment, and anger.

Unbridled sex, in the view many journalists, exemplified the ambiguities of the new urban experience. Journalists, popular writers, and public health activists described in great detail a "bacchanalia" of public "excess," which they blamed on the growing modern spirit of license, individualism, and the pursuit of pleasure, which were intensified by the upheavals and disappointments of revolution in 1905.[19] Pedophilia was an example: such men are now unashamed, newspapers complained, to seek their prey on public streets and squares and by light of day.[20] The new visibility of homosexuality was another sign, to many contemporaries, of this modern loss of control. Many found it disturbing to see what was once closeted in private spaces now walking the city streets extravagantly advertising itself. Only ten years ago, a journalist wrote in 1908, "homosexuality hid itself away in the capital's cellars, not disturbing and debauching the street," whereas now "homosexuals have crawled out of their hideouts" and "the 'lip-smacking' of these beasts of prey, hungry for fresh meat, is heard everywhere."[21]

The "bacchanalia" of urban violence was the logical twin to these stories of unbridled excess and unashamed openness, further demonstrating the precarious experience of bodies and values in the new city. "Newspapers are printed on white paper, but, really, in our times their pages seem covered with blood," the columnist calling himself "The Wanderer" (Skitalets) observed in 1913.[22] A few years earlier, a public health physician diagnosed a "traumatic epidemic of blood and violence" raging in everyday city life.[23] In addition to revolutionary terrorism and government repression, the main symptom was everyday violence.[24] "Hooliganism" typified this and drew special attention from both press and police.[25] At their most harmless, young men dubbed "hooligans" might briefly seize control of a public sidewalk and raucously threaten and mock passersby, especially those who looked respectable. Hooligans performed their own version of sexual harassment: making open and crass sexual propositions to women on the streets, at best laughing at their refusal, though this could also be a prelude to a rape or stabbing. But "hooliganism" mostly meant street violence, usually excessive and senseless: typical, in the judgment of the press, was the hooligan who stabbed a man in the neck and chest when he refused his demand for 14 kopecks to buy vodka.[26] Worst of all were the hooligan knifers who, it was reported, skipped the preliminary demands and just attacked.[27] As Joan Neuberger argued in her important study of hooliganism in St Petersburg, these acts can be interpreted as part of a fundamentally political struggle over who had the right to the streets. But hooligan acts were often experienced and interpreted less as a threat posed to social order and civilized values than as a symptom of the moral "sickness" within public life.[28] This had a class dimension: the poverty in which working-class men grew up was said to nurture moral degeneration.[29] But hooligan amorality and violence was mostly viewed as embodying the new modern ethos where people are "valued cheaper than trash"[30] and "nothing remains 'unthinkable.'"[31]

And hooliganism was only the most spectacular example of the everyday violence of the street: muggings (usually of the poor against the poor), violent fights between friends in a bar or on the street (frequently over "trifles," the press noted, often presumed insults, ending in spilled blood and sometimes death, especially when a knife was at hand), and sexual assault (newspapers frequently reported women and girls raped, and sometimes killed, by strangers, sometimes by groups of men, usually in dark streets or squares in the poorer parts of town). It seemed to many that Russia's urban revolution had released not only enormous creative energy but also the beast in man—updating the classic saying that "man is wolf to man" (*homo homini lupus*)—to the new urban world.[32]

At least, that is how it looked to moralizing journalists and civic reformers, and probably to most victims. We can only speculate about the experiences and intentions of the perpetrators. Joan Neuberger has suggested that hooligans found "pleasure" in shocking supposedly "respectable" citizens, which made their acts a form of purposeful resistance to the disciplining power of elites over public life, and thus "a new kind of power."[33] Since we are speculating, we might go further and look for answers in histories of street violence by other alienated and powerless poor people, including colonial subjects and the subaltern poor. We might ask whether the extremes of violence, such as knifing a stranger "for 14 kopecks" or stabbings among friends over "trifles," which contemporaries found to be so "senseless," did not make a certain "sense," including as a type of unconscious politics: not as deliberate and rational acts of resistance but as expressions of feelings of rage, of emotions and bodies on edge, ready to erupt at the slightest provocation. At the heart of that tension and rage, we might suggest, were social wounds inflicted by daily experiences of difference, subordination, and exclusion. One could not change, short of revolution, the material and structural conditions that made one marginal, poor, abused, both power-less and voiceless, but one could, precisely through excess and violence, make oneself visible and noticed, if only as a "problem." True, this served no practical means or end, but it can be read as a political expression, an expression of disaffection and refusal that spoke of deep and painful experience, a way of speaking of this experience with their own bodies and those of others in ways that could not be ignored.[34]

The rise of "the crowd" has long been seen as an intrinsic aspect of the urban revolution. If "the street" exemplified the multiplicity, motleyness, and dissonance of modern urban life, the "many-faced street crowd" (*mnogolikaia ulichnaia tolpa*), in the popular Russian phrase, was its living heart. Heterogeneity was its hallmark—"the crowd" could include shopkeepers, artisans, peddlers, clergy, noble-men, soldiers, workers, artists, criminals, peasants, prostitutes, beggars, tramps, hooligans, men and women, young and old, Russians and non-Russians. The crowd was defined less by class than by sensibility. The constant cussing and swearing (*skvernoslovie*) that "hangs over the streets" of even sophisticated St Petersburg was viewed as a sign of the degrading effects of the street: people of every rank and class were said to be swearing incessantly "on the street, in streetcars, in public parks, on trains, etc.—everywhere that the crowd is."[35] The street was also the crowd's theater: the crowd, journalists complained, was always ready to gather and gaze at a man run over by a tram, a fight, a fire, a suicide.[36]

Marxist writers, who believed that the modern city was the cradle of proletarian revolution, embraced the city and the street. The suffering of the poor was rationalized as part of a historical process in which the worst aspects of modern life would dialectically produce a new and happy future. "Conscious proletarians" were expected to embrace the "noisy and harsh" realm of the new modern city as "the embryo of a new life,"[37] as "the seething center where the liberating armies gather, struggling for a new world."[38] Indeed, there was something thrilling for a young provincial or peasant who came to the city for the first time and encountered the noise of the streets and the diversity of people, the glow of lamp lights, the sounds of factory whistles, the Dionysian flux of it all. The urban revolution was "dazzling and intoxicating," as one working-class poet put it.[39] But even workers who embraced the Marxist historical vision could not fail to see the dark side: the city and the street as a "cruel abyss," a devouring "vampire," a "whirlpool" of debauchery and vulgarity, a "cursed place" marked by "force, cruelty, and blood," inhabited by the "soulless" and alien "crowd."[40] The experienced truth, as always, was "many-faced."

The Revolutionary Street, 1905

In the early months of the 1905 revolution, liberal commentators, inspired by their own desires and hopes, expressed unbounded admiration for the discipline of "the people" as public actors. Typical was a report in the *Russian Word* (*Russkoe slovo*) in June 1905 about a strike movement underway since May in the industrial city of Ivanovo-Voznesensk (a textile production center near Moscow that was often dubbed the "Russian Manchester"). These mass strikes revealed the "decent and well-mannered character" (*vospitannost'*) of "our workers," despite the harshness of their lives. Even with tens of thousands in the streets, workers acted "consciously," "rationally," "peacefully," and "properly" (*korrektno*).[41] Street life changed dramatically during 1905: strikes, demonstrations, and meetings were constant, along with torrents of talk about a coming "new freedom," equal rights, and democratic power. "Public opinion," it seemed to contemporaries, had suddenly "grown up" and was no longer "a little child that can be consoled with penny candy," but "standing to its full and awesome height, replies to this penny candy with laughter."[42] Gradually, however, this awesome and defiant rising began to terrify elites. The insurgent crowd in the streets began to be judged like the everyday crowd as "dark," "ignorant," "wild," and "bestial."[43]

Public life was marked by a new mood of self-confidence, most dramatically during the "days of freedom" following the October Manifesto, when people acted as if all authority and restrictions had vanished—which was precisely what Nicholas II feared, that concessions might be viewed as a sign of weakness and stimulate more defiance. In cities and towns across the empire, streets were occupied by demonstrators, while parks, squares, schools, universities, theaters, and other public spaces were seized for meetings, whether sanctioned by the authorities or not. The world of print became a vital public sphere in new ways, too. Existing publications ignored the censorship and new liberal and radical newspapers and magazines proliferated "like mushrooms." The rise and ubiquity of political laughter was especially striking. Dozens of satirical magazines appeared in these months, often circulating widely through street sales as well as subscription. They mocked the government and political leaders, laughed with no less moral outrage and cynical irony at the old familiar "sores" of urban public life—murder, violence, rape, suicide, and hooligan "street outrages"—and also at commercial advertisements, conversations "overheard" on the street, night life, shopping, the cinema, fashion, sex, beggars, and drunks. If satire, as an influential Russian dictionary put it, is the "ridicule of weakness and vice," politics and the street both offered plenty of raw material.[44]

Another sign of this newly defiant public mood: everyone seemed to be organizing. "Underground" political groups came out into the open. Almost every social, professional, and ethnic group established organizations to defend and advance their interests. Workers' soviets proliferated in cities across the empire and began to act with more and more local authority, notably in Siberia where soviets seized complete control of several city governments. Some people sought change through "direct action" (*iavochnyi poriadok*) and "the path of seizure" (*zakhvatnyi put'*), as when factory committees and trade unions declared eight-hour work days and new work rules as if employers did not still actually have that power; employers, who insisted they did, responded with firings, lockouts, and their own organizations. In very visible and public ways, people were exercising freedom and power "as if" reality was already as they desired it—though no constitution or law guaranteed these freedoms and the government and other authorities were prepared to use the fiercest violence to suppress "disorders," reminding the public that powerful desires are not the same as powerful facts.[45]

The street was an essential space to mark politically these days as historic, even sacred. We see this vividly during funerals for those killed during the revolution, as for Nikolai Bauman, a Bolshevik activist murdered during a demonstration on 18 October by a right-wing worker who beat him to death with a metal pipe. Tens of thousands of people, representing a wide range of political and social groups and points of view, joined the funeral procession, which wound through the streets of Moscow for eight hours. People carried red flags, wreaths to lay at Bauman's grave, and banners with inscriptions memorializing him as a symbol of the struggles for "freedom," a "democratic republic," or "socialism." Marchers sang "songs of freedom," bands played "solemn music," and good order was maintained, according to reporters. The liberal newspaper *Russian Herald* (*Russkie vedomosti*) was sure that many in the crowd were uncomfortable with Bauman's politics as a Bolshevik, but for now "it was enough that he was a fighter for freedom," for the point was not partisan politics but a united "protest against arbitrariness, violence, and oppression."[46] Here, at least briefly, was the "multi-faced" street marching together in the same direction with confidence and positive feelings. When Bauman's widow at the gravesite vowed revenge, the crowd fell to their knees and chanted "We vow! We vow!" (*klianemsia*). A witness (a socialist but not a Bolshevik) stressed the intensity and sweep of positive emotions felt by the crowd: "We did not think of Bauman in these happy hours, or we thought of him without grief—it was as if this were not a corpse but a symbol of the revolution, a sacred object."[47] The symbolism of the event, but also the fractures of the street and the violence just beneath the surface, were magnified when a waiting crowd of armed men fired on students returning from the cemetery to the university. Some students, themselves armed and ready, shot back. Cossacks, stationed nearby, joined in shooting at the students. Six were killed.[48]

Violence was intrinsic to the life of the street. The revolution of 1905 began when soldiers fired into singing crowds of working-class men and women marching to the Winter Palace. After the October Manifesto, the state again found the confidence and will to use sustained violence against people in the streets. Journalists reported Cossack soldiers in cities across the empire attacking crowds who had been "peacefully marching down the street, proclaiming their love for freedom."[49] Repressive state violence, officially termed "pacification," would increase in the months following. Anti-revolutionary violence, however, also came from below, from the street. Right-wing patriotic gangs, dubbed "black hundreds" by the press, wreaked terror in hundreds of cities across the empire during and after the "days of freedom." These groups were often well organized and armed, tolerated (even backed) by police and Cossacks, and made up of large numbers of "patriotic" laborers, workers, the unemployed, clerks, and shopkeepers. These right-wing crowds, carrying national flags, portraits of the tsar, and sometimes Orthodox Church banners, took to the streets with sticks, rocks, and guns to confront the celebrating and demonstrating workers and students, including at funerals for the fallen. They would belligerently roam the streets, push pedestrians off sidewalks, force students and people who looked educated to kneel before portraits of the tsar, and beat up anyone they judged to be subversive (as all Jews and intellectuals were presumed to be), especially if anyone fought back against them. Many people were beaten to death, stabbed, and shot. Black-hundred violence resembled hooligan street violence, especially in the arbitrariness in choosing targets that reportedly made every "respectable" person afraid to go into the streets. But hooligans, who were still on the streets, claimed to hate all politics and fought anyone in their way, including right-wing street thugs.[50]

Where Jews were a large part of a city's local population, right-wing violence reached extremes, often lasting for days with little police interference. "Pogroms" erupted almost immediately after the October Manifesto, most intensely in the southern port city of Odessa, and to a lesser extent in other towns. Right-wing marchers expressing loyalty to the tsar and their acts of violence against any "revolutionaries" they could find on the streets, quickly devolved into mass anti-Jewish violence: mobs smashing and plundering Jewish neighborhoods, homes, and businesses and beating and murdering Jewish men, women, and children—or anyone thought to be Jewish or allied with Jews. Press reports described ghastly brutalities, including mutilations and rape. By early November, thousands of Jews had been killed or maimed in pogroms.[51]

Liberal journalists blamed this "disgusting" and "shameful" black-hundred violence on the ignorance of the crowd: the "dark common people" (temnyi narod) who could not understand the real reasons for the current "time of troubles," whose "passions" were inflamed by counter-revolutionaries and by "the horrors of war, material insecurity, and lack of understanding," and so carried out acts of "bloody mob justice (samosud) against those they believe to be guilty of these troubles," notably students, "the intelligentsia in general," and Jews of all classes.[52] But liberals also blamed the state for nurturing the ignorance of the crowd, preventing common people from understanding the true sources of their unhappiness. And they blamed the state directly for encouraging, supporting, and participating in the violence, though they judged this a sign of state weakness not strength: "the dying executioner is in its final agony, but, out of habit, its senseless eyes seek new victims."[53] That the state chose to ally itself with the dark street seemed, to reasoned liberals, especially shameful and disgusting.

Street violence also arose from the left, and not only in response to anti-revolutionary violence. Soviets, student groups, trade unions, and socialist parties organized self-defense squads, collected money to buy guns, arranged target practice, and advised workers in factories to make knives out of pieces of metal. "Fighting squads" (boevye druzhiny) guarded meetings and demonstrations, but they were not only defensive. Right-wing claims that demonstrators carried guns, destroyed pictures of the tsar, damaged property, and were deliberately provocative had some merit.[54] In Moscow, roving gangs of workers damaged factories that remained open during strikes and intimidated non-striking workers. Looting and violence against police and soldiers were especially common in provincial towns where administrative authority had been largely replaced by local soviet power. The police called these workers "hooligans," the same term used by left-wing groups to brand black hundreds.[55]

The radical left brought something new and different to street violence: an idealization of armed insurrection in the streets. Partly this was a heroic answer to the violence of black hundreds, police, and Cossacks. But this was also a political tradition: socialist radicals had long assumed that a workers' revolution would involve an armed seizure of power and fighting in the streets and they viewed themselves as heirs to a long, heroic, and bloody history—especially the French revolution, the revolutions of 1848, and the Paris Commune of 1871. On 6 December 1905, the Moscow soviet, with the agreement of the local Menshevik, Socialist Revolutionary, and Bolshevik party leaders, declared a general strike to overthrow the "criminal tsarist government" and establish a democratic republic, which "alone can safeguard our freedom." They expected the general strike to become an insurrection, especially once the government used force against them, and they prepared. The idea was for much more than another political strike: this was going to be "the great Russian Revolution," speakers declared.[56] If measured by the shut-down of the city, the strike was a success. And it did, indeed, produce an insurrection. But this ended in what even many radicals recalled as "the December tragedy." Catastrophe was not unexpected: activists had worried that the government would try to "provoke the proletariat with brazen tricks so as to draw it onto the streets to be shot down." But "better to perish in a struggle than be bound hand and foot without engaging in a struggle."[57] Insurrectionists built barricades out of any-thing at hand, from barrels and crates, to cut-off telegraph poles, to overturned trams and carriages. Soldiers regularly dismantled and burned the barricades, but rebels immediately and repeatedly rebuilt them. Fighting squads attacked police and soldiers and then quickly vanished. In Moscow's industrial outskirts, the streets were entirely under the control of district soviets. Strikes and uprisings in support soon broke out in other cities.

These events created heroic legends, but the insurrection could not match the violence of the state, which ordered troops to act "ruthlessly" to "exterminate gangs of insurgents," even when this required shelling working-class neighborhoods.[58] Approximately one thousand people died in the Moscow uprising, a great many of them civilians not involved in direct fighting. This was only the beginning of the state response: mass arrests, beatings of suspects (including teenage boys and girls), execu-tions without trial, and exile to Siberia soon followed. Military "punitive expeditions" were dispatched throughout the country to arrest and punish suspected subversives but also to intimidate local populations through a public display of ruthless force. Terror is the term many historians have used to interpret this repression. And we know that, to be effective, terror must be as visible as possible. The uprising drove a wedge between liberals and the radical street, drawing on a long history of anxieties about the backwardness of the plebeian crowd and the dangers of the street. Liberals blamed socialists for deceiving the crowd with impossible promises and leading them to "the slaughterhouse."[59] But most historians have shown that the masses were not simply dupes and victims: there was a large measure of independence in the street, controlled by no one, and a deep desire to stand up and fight the world as it was, however futile that effort might be.[60]

The Revolutionary Street, 1917

When the government banned alcohol consumption at the outbreak of war in August 1914, many viewed this as a "miracle" sure to transform urban public life.[61] In fact, little changed. To be sure, taverns became tearooms and streets saw fewer drunks, but there was a great deal of illegal drinking in private, including use of poisonous surrogates. The familiar everyday pleasures of city life remained: theater, cinema, the circus, sports, entertainment parks, cafés, and nightclubs. And the familiar "horrors of life" (as newspapers liked to call them) remained: muggings, hooligan "outrages," delinquent "street children," gang fights, bar-room arguments ending in violence, prostitution, injury or death beneath the wheels of trams and automobiles, and suicide in public places.[62]

But the war was gradually felt on the streets, and with increasing force. As the economy strained, inflation and shortages of food and other products produced growing tensions. People found it difficult to buy even what they could still afford. Shops closed early or entirely for lack of bread, sugar, meat, and other essentials. Lines grew for what was available. Ordinary citizens did what they could to get by: spending hours in the streets looking for stores with food and standing in lines (working-class women in Petrograd reportedly spent about forty hours a week in food lines[63]), begging, tearing down wooden fences to keep stoves heated for warmth, and grumbling about the rich. Street crime worsened, especially by working-class children, driven to the street and thievery by "hunger and lack of supervision," as so many fathers were at the front and mothers at work and searching for food.[64]

State authorities worried about the mood on the street. In the first weeks of 1917, secret police agents assigned to live among the working-class population of the capital city reported troubling signs: strikes; factories shut down by workers because they were too hungry to work and needed to search for food; meetings around workplaces where speakers complained of high prices, food shortages, and government failures; the spread of subversive leaflets and proclamations; occasional street demonstrations; assaults on businesses, especially food stores; and scattered violence against police and Cossacks. Even the usually litany of street muggings, robberies, hooliganism, and suicides now looked to these agents like signs of new and bigger troubles—though only in the context of war and open discontent did they begin to understand that the everyday social violence by the poor was always an expression of subtly political, if undirected, frustration and anger. Police agents were particularly worried about the mood among working-class women: "these mothers, exhausted from standing endlessly at the ends of lines, and having suffered so much in watching their half-starving and sick children, are perhaps much closer to a revolution than Mssrs. Miliukov, Rodichev, and Co. [leaders of the liberal Constitutional Democratic (Kadet) Party], and, of course, they are much more dangerous."[65]

When the autocracy fell in February, the streets of Petrograd, Moscow, and, very soon, cities across the country were transformed into festivals of unity and solidarity: strangers embraced and kissed ("just like at Easter," many said), café and business owners offered demonstrators food or a place to rest, people wore red ribbons on their clothes, and streets and squares were filled with celebratory parades, prayer services of thanksgiving, and (especially in provincial towns) organized "festivals of freedom."[66] Even funerals for fallen "freedom fighters" were treated as celebratory festivities of unity rather than occasions for grief or anger.[67]

The disorder and even chaos that also reigned in the streets during these first "days of freedom" did not easily fit the romantic story of a peaceful revolution inspired by national unity across classes. Victor

Shklovsky, a writer and literary critic stationed in Petrograd as an instructor in a reserve armored car division, described the scene he witnessed on the streets in the first hours and days of revolution:

> Despite scattered gunfire, many people stood around in doorways—even women and children. They looked as if they were waiting for a wedding or a magnificent funeral.... We were all being swept along by a river and the whole of wisdom consisted in yielding to its current. We fired into the air all the time, even with the cannons.... And throughout the city rushed the muses and furies of the February Revolution—trucks and automobiles piled high and spilling over with soldiers, not knowing where they were going or where they would get gasoline, giving the impression of sounding the tocsin throughout the whole city. They rushed around, circling and buzzing like bees.... The city resounded with crashes. I don't know how many collisions I saw during those days.... Later on, the city was jammed with automobiles simply left by the wayside.... I was happy with these crowds. It was like Easter—a joyous, naïve, disorderly carnival paradise.[68]

Many observers found it difficult to embrace the disorder, especially the violence: crowds breaking into weapons factories and arsenals, wandering the streets carrying guns and draped in cartridge belts, driving about in "requisitioned" cars and trucks and shooting into the air, opening prisons and releasing criminals along with revolutionaries, and attacking police stations, sometimes setting them ablaze and beating any policeman they could lay their hands on. Crowds smashing store windows, looting, and breaking into wine storehouses (and drinking) also poorly fit the narrative of peaceful restraint and unity.[69]

That women participated in disorders especially worried political leaders inclined to see women's unruliness as evidence of dangerous backwardness rather than political boldness. Women workers who took to the streets of the capital on International Women's Day, the protest that would launch the revolution, were far from "feminine" in their conduct. From the streets outside factories they shouted and chanted for men and other women to join them, threw icy snowballs and pieces of metal at factory windows, and sometimes broke in. Women were active among crowds that stopped streetcars and demanded that everyone get off to support the protests. Women led attacks on bakeries, butchers, and food warehouses and were a visible presence in raids on prisons and police stations. And women played a key role in pleading with soldiers not to shoot at demonstrators, but were also themselves quite bellicose on the streets, even provoking police and soldiers with curses and insults.[70]

Contemporaries interpreted the disorderly street stories of the February revolution in different ways. The Petrograd Soviet denounced the excesses as "hooliganism."[71] Maxim Gorky, the independent socialist writer, condemned the violence and looting as evidence of "political ignorance" and "Asiatic savagery."[72] Nikolai Sukhanov, a Menshevik member of the Soviet leadership, in his memoir of 1917, justified all "the excesses, the man-in-the-street's stupidity, vulgarity, and cowardice, the muddles, the motor-cars, the girls" as "what the revolution could not in any circumstances avoid, without which nothing similar had ever happened anywhere."[73] Lev Trotsky, in his own account of the revolution, judged the raucous crowds of February even more heroically, as the common people "stamping its boots, clanging the butts of its rifles, rending the air with its shouts, and stepping all over the feet" of people and classes representing "the past."[74] The historians Boris Kolonitsky and Orlando Figes have described these street behaviors as part of a "symbolic revolution": workers marching into city centers from the industrial outskirts were a way for "workers to claim the streets as 'theirs,'" and acts of violence against the well-dressed expressed "self-assertion" and public power.[75] Street violence, even looting, can be read as symbolic expressions of frustration, anger, refusal, and presence, as signs of oppression avenged and hierarchies overturned, of a new public power for the poor. When crowds of workers, soldiers, and other townspeople took control of city streets for meetings and demonstrations or beat up representatives of public authority (especially police), they were literally demonstrating their own authority in the public sphere. However, as the months passed, many contemporaries came to view the disorderly street quite differently: as a sign of the persistent backwardness, moral decadence, and savage brutality of the crowd.

"Street disorders" (*ulichnye bezobraziia*), "chaos," and "anarchy" became increasingly dominant themes in public discourse during 1917. Political leaders, journalists, and even most socialist activists, warned incessantly that the undisciplined and irrational street was deforming and threatening true "freedom." What they called chaos could range from relatively trivial, but telling, public acts like cab drivers driving in any direction they pleased to unsanctioned demonstrations and strikes.[76] Of particular concern was the spread of violent crime. The numbers of thefts, robberies, and murders in the capital (and the trend was probably similar in other cities) skyrocketed in 1917, with the rates increasing as the year went on—along with rates of drunkenness and prostitution.[77] By midsummer, it seemed that "blood is flowing like water." This was an old story, of course, as was the judgment that this proved how much "human life has been devalued." But old stories took on new meaning in 1917, when "freedom" was supposed to bring a new and redeemed spirit to public life.[78] Also, the forms of everyday violence had advanced in at least one important respect in 1917: shootings replaced knifings.

The revolution was itself largely to blame for the new epidemics of crime, disorder, and violence, not least thanks to the mass release of prisoners, mostly convicted criminals, the collapse of police and judicial authority, and the crowd's seizure of many thousands of guns, which often found their way into the hands of both criminals and a nervous population. The economic crisis was also surely a stimulus—to crime and violence and to the atmosphere of uncertainty, fear, and frustration, including at government authorities that seemed to have no idea of what to do or effective power to do it.[79] By late spring, and especially by early fall, normally sanguine commentators were warning of a catastrophe, of the "grim specter of hunger,"[80] of Russia "dying." Depending on class, gender, and inclination, people experienced and interpreted these conditions in different ways. Some organized or appealed to the "vital forces of the country" (a term defined according to perspective and inclination) to act. Some demanded patience and "responsible" self-discipline. Some tried to save themselves and their family by any means, from crime to flight from the city. Most just tried to get by. A few dreamed of, and prepared, a new revolution.

The psychology of the street concerned everyone. As in years past, city newspapers worried aloud about the roughness, ignorance, boorishness (*khamstvo*), and brutality of the crowd—old problems now framed as threats to the new freedom. The danger seemed especially severe on the plebeian outskirts of towns and cities, where observers saw too little political consciousness, but a great deal of "confusion" and "ignorance." What the residents of such districts needed, one journalist argued in May, was not more help in "organizing street meetings," of which there were plenty, but good lessons on "what freedom is and how it should be understood."[81] A correspondent for the Menshevik *Workers' Paper* (*Rabochaia gazeta*) described his impressions of a mass meeting in Kronstadt, a town and naval base on an island near Petrograd: people who had "only recently been slaves" were dreaming of a world without rich and poor, without human suffering, and without war—naive dreams mixed with desires for "harsh and merciless vengeance." But how will these "simple" people react, he wondered, "when they realize that they still cannot see the shores of this kingdom," that the path ahead is still long and hard and full of "terrible storms, defeats, and disappointments"?[82]

One of the most disturbing forms of street violence in 1917, and evidence of how lower-class citizens experienced and responded to crime, was *samosud*—literally, self-made law or trial, but usually translated as mob justice. A rural phenomenon with a long history, directed especially against thieves and others seen to threaten the cohesion and livelihood of a village community, its place in the city grew dramatically in 1917 in response to the massive rise in street crime and the ineffectiveness of police and judicial authorities, though now, in place of punitive violence grounded in traditional village norms and organized by the peasant commune, an urban street *samosud* of 1917 was an act by motley plebeian crowds who came together spontaneously for this one purpose and then vanished.

Acts of "street justice" (the less judgmental translation of *samosud* I will use) typically began with a suspected thief being caught and beaten by a crowd, an on-the-spot debate over further punishment, refusal to hand the suspect over to the police if they arrived, and then a brutal beating or execution. This "judgment of the street" (*sud ulitsy*), as some called it, was invariably harsh, for the street, it was said, knows "no other action than beating to death."[83] Spontaneous street trials increased in both frequency and ferocity during course of 1917, becoming daily news by midsummer—"not exceptional, unique cases but everyday occurrences." Many ordinary city dwellers (*obyvateli*), journalists believed, fully supported the crowd, for they too deplored and feared the rise of crime.[84] By early fall, the movement expanded to punish shopkeepers thought to be hoarding bread or food; and when Jewish shopkeepers were targets, these could expand into anti-Semitic pogroms.[85]

Soviets joined their authoritative voices to many others warning that mob justice violated the proper meaning of freedom and undermined the revolution.[86] Left-leaning journalists declared *samosud* to be part of a pattern of growing public barbarity: "People have become embittered and cruel," an essayist in the *Kopeck Gazette* argued in September, "extremely on-edge (*nervny*) as a result of the harsh conditions of life."[87] Some spoke of a deep "rage" stimulating *samosud* and other public violence.[88] Liberal and socialist critics alike worried that these acts of "savage retribution" (*dikaia rasprava*, a term also used to describe the mob violence of "black hundreds") were a sign of a something dark and deep in the popular spirit. Maxim Gorky, looking back on 1917 from December, warned about the danger that street justice posed to the revolution, including to the "proletariat in power." He described a typical case from earlier in the year: a crowd in Petrograd caught a thief at a public market, beat him, and then held a vote whether to drown him in a nearby canal or to shoot him; drowning was chosen but the thief managed to swim out and crawl up the shore, so he was shot. "This is how the democracy tries its sinners," he sarcastically added, using the common term for the revolutionary urban masses allied with the radical left. But this street mentality was the polar opposite of the proper spirit of proletarian revolution, Gorky argued, which should "change the bestial character of everyday Russian life" (*zverinyi russkii byt*), and bring the light of "justice, reason, and beauty" into the "darkness of the people's life."[89]

We might interpret this violence differently—with a historian's backward look, without the anxieties and fears of those who lived through this experience, and with as little as possible of their particular prejudices and purposes. The historian Tsuyoshi Hasegawa has argued that the violence of the plebeian crowd reflected the disintegration of social order and bonds of community. Even momentary solidarity as a mob, he argues, was only a fleeting moment of unity in the normal state of fragmentation and alienation. The crowd's actions may have expressed anger and rage, and may have achieved brief feelings of empowerment, but these were acts of passion more than purpose and did little to overcome societal dissolution or their own alienation.[90] Contemporaries read the "mood" of the street as "ugly," especially during the upheavals and freedoms of 1917. But violent street rage, whether against those with privilege or against thieves and hooligans, was not about reason or beauty. We can also not read these acts as simple "resistance" to authority, much less solidarity with the revolutionary cause. Still, even crime can embody a vaguely conscious desire for justice, though laden with social distrust, anger, uncertainty, and fear. And all of this should be part of our understanding of what revolution meant on the street.

Industrial workers were expected by Marxist activists to be more conscious, disciplined, and rational than the ordinary plebeian "crowd." Workers did often act in 1917 as Marxists expected and hoped. May Day celebrations across the empire seemed to exemplify the discipline and positive mood of the urban working class. Huge marches brought together workers from every occupation and profession, every political affiliation, every national, religious, and ethnic group, all "now united into one brotherly family under the common banner of socialism."[91] In factories, workers held well-run workplace meetings; used trade unions and factory committees to increase collective oversight and supervision (known as "workers' control") over everyday workplace decisions, such as fines and work rules, and sometimes over hiring and firing; and using, when necessary, organized and disciplined strike actions to improve wages and working conditions and defend gains. At the same time, working-class discipline could be rough. Workers brought their own version of street justice to the factories, seizing the most hated foremen and managers, forcing them into wheel barrows, dumping waste on their heads, shouting at them about their abuses, and carting them into the streets. Sometimes these factory *samosuds* were less ritualized: it was enough to beat these bosses, perhaps severely, even fatally.

In the streets, workers too were growing frustrated and angry in the face of worsening food shortages, rising prices, and factories closing because of lack of supplies or fuel, and employers who began to fight back against "anarchy" in labor relations: breaking labor agreements, refusing new demands, and declaring lockouts before workers declared strikes. Some industrialists openly hoped that "the bony hand of hunger" might be a salutary influence on workers.[92] In turn, workers were beginning to feel that workplace struggles were not the solution to the everyday problems they and their families faced. The proletariat was becoming more and more like the "crowd," as workers took to the streets in groups to search for hidden storehouses of food, often assaulting suspected speculators and hoarders. By late summer, such "street actions" outnumbered strikes and other factory-based struggles.[93] Liberals and socialists appealed to workers to show moderation, "responsibility," and consideration of "the common good." But these pleas were increasingly falling on deaf ears, or at least on disenchanted and impatient minds.[94]

By summer, the mood on the working-class street was distrust to the point of hatred of almost everyone with power and status. "Class consciousness" may be one way to define this, and class vocabulary was certainly ubiquitous in workers' statements, though their language of class was as much emotional as analytical. Words like bourgeois, capitalist, and imperialist were used freely to reproach elites for selfishness and egoism—indeed, these sins seemed to define those social categories. Hence, these class terms were applied not only to industrialists and other owners of the means of production, but to anyone judged to be opposed to workers' interests. "Bourgeois" became an especially disparaging term, and was widely used to brand as enemies everyone with privilege, everyone who opposed workers' struggles, and even political leaders who had made promises after February that were not realized. By the fall, the otherness of this broadly defined "bourgeoisie" had magnified: now they were nothing less than "enemies of the people," "traitors," and "betrayers" of Russia, the revolution, and freedom.[95] Talk of radical difference between "us" and "them," "masses" and "elites" (*nizy* and *verkhy*, literally those "below" and those "above"), was increasingly pervasive and insistent.

Russian workers in 1917 knew the vocabulary of the Marxist intelligentsia and readily spoke of their own "class consciousness" and the need to fight the "counter-revolutionary imperialist bourgeoisie." And growing numbers of workers embraced Bolshevik radicalism as the only means to end "the democracy's policy of appeasing" the bourgeois government.[96] But beneath these learned vocabularies were rougher and more emotional formulations, as we see in the following "Letter to All Citizens" from the workers of the huge Putilov metal plant in Petrograd, written in the aftermath of the July days:

We are dying here, in hopeless alienation from the joys we desire, from the comfort and culture that is enjoyed not far from us...by the rich, "educated" minority. Where is justice? Where are the results of the blood and the lives of our brothers who fell in the revolution? Where is the new life...? Citizens: our renewed life cannot wait. The logic of the events that have taken place pushes the revolutionary people onto the streets and onward....Citizens: Take an honest look at the black, smoking chimneys rising up from the earth. There, at their foot, creating for you things of value that you need, are people just like you, suffering and tormented in bondage (*nevolia*) to the most complete and fierce exploitation. Class consciousness is slowly maturing there. Hatred is building up in their hearts, and the sweet conditions of another life for all mankind are being written lovingly on their bloody banner.[97]

Moderates on the left vehemently criticized the Bolsheviks for encouraging "revolution in the street" with seductive slogans that took advantage of the mood of the crowd.[98] But everyone shared a desire for some way out of the present predicament. Here is the "Wanderer," who regularly condemned the Bolsheviks for their deceptive promises and divisive behavior, writing just days before the Bolshevik insurrection:

No matter how many speeches have been heard...these have done nothing to halt the fateful disintegration. Events, having moved in only one ominous direction, will inevitably come to their logical and unavoidable conclusion. And yet. And yet! The heart of man is weak, and, despite what his mind tells him, he believes in hope, and avidly seeks it. And it is precisely in words and speeches he believes, though these have lost all value. Every morning, the man in the street (*obyvatel'*)—and, after all, we are all still only men in the street, who for all the freedoms now feel only one clearly: the freedom to be robbed every day and every hour—every morning the man in the street plunges himself into reports on meetings of countless Soviets, Committees, and Congresses and seeks something to grasp onto that will calm his exhausted and desperate spirit.[99]

For many, the Bolshevik slogan "All Power to the Soviets" was just such a hope. Critics judged this faith the result of the tragic encounter between popular desperation and Bolshevik deceit. For better or worse, however, this had become the choice in the street. Or as Victor Shklovsky cynically mused, "Russia invented the Bolsheviks as a motivation for desertion and plunder; the Bolsheviks are not guilty of having been dreamed."[100]

The Soviet Street

In the first months after the Bolsheviks came to power, non-communist newspapers described the mood on the street as far from celebratory. Most citizens, including workers, harbored "dark," "sorrowful," "melancholy" (*tosklivo*), "anxious," "confused," and "frightened" feelings about the present and the future.[101] It seemed that "the country is on its last legs . . . Total disintegration. We have slid to the bottom. There is nowhere further to go."[102] Newspapers described a nightmarish, almost dystopic, scene. Violence and crime, and the economic and social disintegration that fueled these, were dominant themes. People feared going into the streets, it was said, for thieves were running amok, gangs of boys were robbing passersby with impunity, and criminals "felt free" since they no longer had to worry about the police.[103] A reporter wandering the streets of Petrograd found absolutely "no authority and no order, no law or justice anywhere."[104] In Moscow, street fighting in early November between officer cadets and revolutionary Red Guards was described by *News for Everyone* as a "wild and mad bacchanalia" of lethal violence and "devastation."[105] And once the fighting was over, the "masters" of the city seemed to be not the victorious Soviet government or the Bolshevik party but the criminal denizens of "dark Moscow," who were waging a war "against ordinary citizens (*obyvateli*)."[106] Journalists intensified their old argument that the revolution had invigorated the "Asiatic" brutalities of the "dark masses," whose idea of "freedom" was too often little more than license unrestrained by reason or morality.[107] The word *bezobrazie*—usually translated as ugliness, deformity, or outrage, for it meant extreme disorder marked by moral disgrace and physical disgust—was common in writing about the chaos in the streets in the final months of 1917. As one reporter put it typically, "complete freedom for *bezobrazie*" now reigned in the Russian streets.[108]

Wine riots, often called "pogroms," were an especially disturbing expression of the mentality of "the crowd"—which Bolsheviks perceived as no less a threat to the revolution than their pre-October opponents had judged the threat posed by the crowd. Part of the "duty" of the revolutionary Red Guards, they declared, was to "struggle with drunkenness so as not to allow liberty and revolution to drown in wine."[109] The Bolshevik commander of the Petrograd garrison recalled a wild and drunken "orgy" in the weeks following the October revolution, as "crowds of ruffians, mostly soldiers, broke into wine cellars ... The whole city was infected by the drinking madness."[110] In provincial towns, it was often worse. A report in mid-November, for example, from Sarapul (a commercial, manufacturing, and administrative center in Kazan province) declared that "the city is tense. The crowd, inspired by rabble rousers, smashed the wine depot. ... Drunken bands are threatening shops and stores. There is a mass of fires in the city, which firemen cannot extinguish. 'Bolshevist' soldiers organize mob justice against officers. Many residents have quit their apartments and fled to who knows where. ... The general picture is dismal. Complete terror."[111]

The Russian writer Ivan Bunin—drifting politically from modest sympathy for the left to active support for the anti-Bolshevik Whites—wandered the streets of Moscow in early 1918 listening to what he would call the "savage, hysterical, and drunken ... 'music of the Revolution.'"[112] He recorded his impressions in a diary. At first, it seemed that "something remarkable is happening: almost everyone is unusually happy for some reason—no matter whom you meet on the street, you see a simply radiant face." But a few were already terrified, about the prospects for everyday survival but also about the meaning and direction of these times. "Good sir, tell me what's going on!" an old woman pleaded after stopping him in the street, "just where are we heading?"[113] Such anxiety quickly spread across elite society. For men and women like Bunin, it was not only the physical fear of crime that made it terrible to go out into the streets, but the mood in public life: "With every fiber of my being," a friend said to him in mid-March 1918, "I now avoid going out on the street unless I really have to. And not at all from fear that someone is going to mug me, but merely because of the faces that I see out there now."[114]

The street was judged and experienced not only as the realm of disorder and deformity, of *bezobrazie*, but also the "kingdom of the darkest need"—a perception that might bring us closer to the experience of the everyday person on the street, the *obyvatel'* (man in the street), the ones whose faces seemed so unbearable to Bunin's friend. In the early months of 1918, before the remaining non-soviet newspapers and magazines were shut down, journalists described the desperation of the urban crowd, whose presence and temper defined the street: the unemployed, the homeless, beggars, orphans, hooligans, drunks, criminals, speculators, prostitutes, and people desperately searching for food and fuel. The dominant mood in the street, they felt, was "fear of tomorrow."[115] Even street clocks, one reporter sardonically mused, pointed to dysfunction and disorder: all of Moscow's clocks told different times, and none the real time, suggesting that "the new times have sent us a new time—time as a question."[116] Convinced revolutionaries held on to the promise of "the future...which makes the present bearable."[117] But most people, it seems, found the *bezobrazie* of time in the present too hard to ignore or to soften with thoughts of the future.

During the civil war, city streets were even more the realm of refugees and the homeless (many of them children), beggars and criminals, and people selling or bartering their belongings for food. People ripped down fences and even parts of houses for fuel. Infectious diseases, especially typhus, were fostered and spread by failing sanitation combined with malnutrition. The brute struggle to survive was the defining everyday experience for most people. Many fled the city and its desperate streets. By 1920, Petrograd had lost more than two-thirds of its 1917 population and Moscow had lost half. Russia was being "deurbanized"—a decent scholar's word for a devastating experience. People with means fled abroad or (depending on their politics) moved to areas of the country controlled by the White armies. More troubling to Marxist revolutionaries was the disintegration of the urban working class, their social base. To be sure, many workers joined the Red Army or the government. But many more fled back home to the countryside, "running away from hunger" as Lenin admitted in 1921.[118] For those who remained in the dying cities, working-class lives were transformed by the work of survival. Time and energy were turned away from unions, soviets, and parties, and refocused on finding food. Activists complained of the loss of "civic mood" among workers and "fatigue" with politics. If workers were engaged in collective pursuits at all, this was more likely to be in their neighborhoods, especially organizing to fight street crime. Workers with jobs were working less: absenteeism reached unprecedented levels as workers could not do their jobs because of illness or, most often, they took time away from work to sell whatever they could in city markets or travel into the nearby countryside to buy or trade for food. Indeed, many workers spent more time as petty traders in the semi-legal and illegal markets than at their industrial jobs. Within their factories, workers appropriated shop materials and used working hours to manufacture objects to barter for food: metalworkers, for example, made candlesticks, hatchets, crowbars, and simple stoves—or simply stole things like nails and building materials. Women were in especially painful straits: if from the privileged classes they were denied government rations; if from the working class and fortunate enough to have jobs, they toiled for long hours at low wages before devoting their nights to the search for food and fuel. The typical worker, one newspaper concluded, was metamorphosing from a proletarian into an *obyvatel'*—the ordinary city dweller, the "man in the street." And the Marxist view of the consciousness of the *obyvatel'* was not far from the truth: "to hell with all [the parties]," the typical *obyvatel'* was said to say, "whoever gives me bread will suit me fine."[119]

Summarizing the grim evidence, historians have described urban public life during the civil war years as "social chaos," "primitivization," and "brutalization."[120] The revolutionary "leap from the kingdom of necessity to the kingdom of freedom" seems to have led first through the depths of a new and darker realm of necessity. Revolutionaries might embrace necessity as the flow of historical progress, as the destruction of the old that must precede creation of the new. The writer and activist Victor Serge recalled such thinking in a novel based on his personal experiences during the revolution and civil war: "The world must be made over. For this: conquer, hold on, survive at any cost.... We are but the instruments of a necessity which carries us along, drags us forward, lifts us up, and which will doubtless pass over our dead bodies.... The three magic words: it is necessary."[121] Most people found such faith difficult. On the political right, these conditions nurtured fury and hatred and the search for language strong enough to express it. In a diary entry in May 1919, for example, Bunin found suitable words in the historian Sergei Solovyov's description of Russia's bloody and devastating "Time of Troubles" during the seventeenth century: "The spirit of materialism, of unrestrained will, of coarse self-interest wafted destructively over Rus'... The hands of the righteous were paralyzed, and those of evil men were untied to commit all kinds of atrocities.... Crowds of outcasts, the scum of society, devastated their own homes under the banners of the leaders, impostors, hypocrites: under the guise of leading degenerates, criminals, and ambitious people."[122]

The street was a space also for fantasy and mythmaking. The first anniversary of the October revolution took place on 7 November 1918 (the Soviet government had decreed in January that Russia leap ahead thirteen days to join "with almost all cultured nations in counting time" by the Gregorian calendar). On that day, the residents of Moscow, the political capital since March, "awoke early to the sounds of singing in the streets."[123] This was the start of a nationwide celebration that covered the Soviet urban landscape with banners, flags, painted panels, huge canvasses, and giant sculptural decorations. Red was the dominant color, to symbolize revolution, sacrifice, beauty, and salvation. Gigantic paintings, many of them icon-like in style, of workers and peasants dominated the visual imagery along with symbolic rising suns and personifications (usually female) of freedom and revolution, sometimes winged and usually in classical dress. Avant-garde artists remade old streets, buildings, and statues with huge, brightly colored geometric constructions. Marches, outdoor performances, fireworks, and the unveiling of new (but temporary) revolutionary monuments added to the festive atmosphere. An enthusiastic participant recalled the mood as "universal exultation and the unmediated feeling of joy.... This was not the celebration of an anniversary, not the memory of effort and sacrifice, not the rapture of coming victory and creativity, but the joyful greeting of revolution, the happy laughter of the great masses that made the day of the Overturn great." And nothing less than the whole of human history, which had "predetermined" this revolution across the centuries, inspired the people's festive delight.[124] Insistent joyfulness would remain the hallmark of official street festivals even during the darkest days of the civil war, especially on May Day, which typically included popular carnivals, fireworks, and professionally designed and orchestrated mass spectacles. And if the real hardships of the time were hinted at, they were transfigured, though symbolism and scripted performances, into stories about the death of the old and birth of the new.[125]

The street was a place for protest, too. We can interpret much of what ordinary urban dwellers were doing every day to survive as expressions of discontent, disenchantment, even resistance. We can interpret common behaviors such as absenteeism from work and lack of diligence on the job as an implicit rejection of the appeals of the new regime to sacrifice for the revolution and help restore the economy. Pilfering factory property for personal use or for illegal sale or barter can be seen as an implicit rejection of the insistence that this was the workers' collective property to be used for the common good. And we can interpret these everyday acts as refusal by actual workers to conform to official claims about how "proletarians" were supposed to think and feel. Of course, there were also acts of unambiguous protest, though relatively rare, not least because they were so dangerous.

Labor protests reveal something of how workers experienced and judged life in the months and years after October.[126] Waves of strikes broke out in the late spring and early summer of 1918, especially in Petrograd. Deteriorating economic conditions fueled these protests: supplies of food and other necessities had continued to shrink since October while unemployment continued to rise—60 percent of Petrograd's workers were reported to be out of work in the first months of 1918. Appeals to workers to keep in mind the historic significance of the revolution, their own historic role as proletarians, the bright future ahead, and the need for solidarity and patience seemed to have little effect. Hunger was often stronger than ideology, especially given that neither the greater bargaining power of trade unions and factory committees after October nor state support for "workers' control" did much to resolve the economic crisis. Frustrated and disappointed, workers began to act openly and politically.

Gorky's *New Life* newspaper (before silenced in early July) described the "mood" on the working-class street in the spring and early summer of 1918 as "troubled" and "tense." Raucous meetings erupted around factories. An old working-class cry was heard again: "we cannot live like this any longer" (*tak dal'she zhit' nel'zia*).[127] As in the past, repression aroused more protest and a more politicized movement. When guards shot into a crowd of men and women who had gathered outside the local soviet in one of Petrograd's industrial districts to complain about shortages of food and jobs, larger rallies and strikes erupted, often including demands for new elections to all soviets and to reconvene the Constituent Assembly, and huge crowds gathered at a funeral for the fallen. An "Extraordinary Assembly of Factory Delegates" in Petrograd, organized by opposition socialist parties as a type of counter-soviet, approved plans for a citywide general strike for 2 July 1918. The slogans chosen were "Down with the death penalty! Down with shooting and civil war! Long live the Constituent Assembly! Long live freedom of speech and assembly! Long live the freedom to strike!"[128] The government had no intention of allowing such a strike, of course, which it viewed as a criminal political conspiracy of anti-Bolshevik parties rather than an authentic expression of proletarian discontent, and declared participation or support to be a criminal offence, arrested organizers, dispersed meetings, and, just in case, set up machine-gun nests on 2 July at key points in Moscow and Petrograd. No strike occurred. To reinforce their success, the government made every effort to prevent further public expressions of opposition or discontent. More opposition leaders were arrested, the remaining non-Bolshevik newspapers and magazines were closed, and a number of anti-regime suspects were executed.

Historians have debated whether these strikes and protests were motivated by economic or political discontent. But this was not a distinction that protesting workers found useful. Complaints about economic suffering could not be separated from discontent with those who held political and economic power; and political disappointment with the regime encouraged workers to take to the streets to protest economic problems. The authorities underscored the political significance of worker protests, even when workers insisted that their concerns were only economic, by using force to "liquidate" these "criminal" disorders: mass firings, arrests and summary imprisonment, and execution of ringleaders.

Protests and strikes continued sporadically during the civil war years, and with the same mix of reasons and demands: shortage of food, inadequate rations (and against privileged rations for communists and other elites), and excesses in workplace discipline. Mass meetings, marches to the local soviet, and strikes became increasingly common, especially by workers employed in the larger state-run factories of Moscow and Petrograd, but also in Ivanovo-Voznesensk, Nizhny-Novgorod, Saratov, Samara, Kharkov, Kazan, and elsewhere. Some of the biggest strikes were by metal and transport workers, who experienced most fully the policy of "militarizing" labor and production during the civil war, and among bakers and printers, who had histories of strong trade unions, shop-floor autonomy, and political independence.

Explicit politics were muted. Demands for "bread for our children" and cries of "we are starving" were safer and more likely to be heard sympathetically than complaints about the failures of the workers' government to care for workers' interests. Besides, hunger was real and overwhelming. On the other hand, widespread demands to increase food rations brought questions of state policy to the fore. Workers also tended to frame economic complaints as part of their larger disappointment with the new regime, including that the Bolsheviks had "deceived" the people. As one group of women workers put it bluntly: "You told us that there would be plenty, but the opposite is true."[129] As time passed, these everyday frustrations became more political. During a strike wave in Petrograd in March 1919, for example, striking workers at the enormous Putilov factory approved a resolution, possibly drafted by Left SRs, declaring that the only way to overcome deepening hunger was to end the dictatorship by the Bolshevik Central Committee, which had betrayed the ideals of the "October revolution," and establish a true "people's" government through freely elected worker and peasant soviets.[130] Following another wave of protests in June 1920, a correspondent for the party newspaper *Pravda* recognized that a "tense atmosphere" of frustration and anger continued to fester among workers, and worried that more was to come.[131]

During the winter of 1920–1, especially February into early March, massive labor protests erupted in Moscow, Petrograd, Saratov, Ekaterinoslav, and elsewhere.[132] Workers participated in mass meetings in factories, approved resolutions criticizing the party and the government, stopped work, and marched in the streets—demonstrations that sometimes became even larger protests against the violence used to suppress these marches. The immediate incitements were economic: factories silent and homes cold due to fuel shortages, women queuing overnight hoping to buy bread (and often getting nothing or bread of awful quality), hungry workers and soldiers begging on the streets. The suffering was compounded by a large reduction in January 1921 of the official bread ration in a number of industrial cities, including Petrograd and Moscow. The policy of forcibly "requisitioning" food supplies from peasants, along with roadblocks preventing urban workers from independently buying or bartering with peasants, failed to bring adequate supplies to the city; and since many workers had family connections in villages, the policy itself added to workers' anger. With the threat of White victory gone, the risks of protest seemed less.

As the fourth anniversary of the February revolution approached, growing numbers of workers in Moscow held mass meetings and passed resolutions demanding a restoration of free trade, an end to privileged rationing, limits on the workplace authority of managers and specialists, and, sometimes, restoration of civil liberties and of the Constituent Assembly. Mensheviks and SRs, as these last demands may reflect, were increasingly involved. Street demonstrations and strikes culminated in a march of 10,000 Moscow workers on 23 February. The government responded with some minor reforms of food policy, but chiefly by declaring martial law in the city and arresting leaders. The movement had spread to Petrograd by 22 February, with mass meetings in factories and on the streets, often accompanied by strikes and marches. Metalworkers—whom Marxists traditionally viewed as the most advanced group of proletarians—played the leading role, as they did in Moscow. Crowds moved through the streets calling on other workers and soldiers to join them. Protesters demanded the restoration of free trade in produce and goods (especially the end to roadblocks), the abolition of forced grain requisitioning, "free labor" (an end to militarization and other forms of labor compulsion), and no more "privileged rations" for communists and other special categories of people. There were also scattered demands for new and free elections to the soviets; freedom of speech, press, and assembly for workers and socialists; release of political prisoners; an end to "bureaucratism" and the new "Soviet bourgeoisie";[133] and (less common) restoration of the Constituent Assembly. Menshevik and SR proclamations for "freedom" and against Bolshevik power found support, while Bolshevik speakers were regularly shouted down. The Menshevik Fedor Dan was impressed by the "exceptional daring" with which workers now criticized the Bolshevik regime. Some "expansive people," he noted, found a feeling of "February 1917 in the air."[134]

The government responded quickly and characteristically with a mixture of reforms, especially higher food rations for workers and soldiers, and martial law—using the Cheka (the political police) and other special forces rather than regular troops, who were proving unreliable for suppressing a working-class street movement. In Saratov a large strike broke out in early March among skilled metalworkers. At mass meetings, as Donald Raleigh has described, "workers tongue-lashed the Communists." When regional party leaders tried to calm discontent by holding open elections to a commission to look into the actions of economic authorities and the Cheka, workers elected only a handful of Communists. The new commission demanded open elections to the soviets, freedom for political prisoners, independent unions, and the restoration of freedom of speech, the press, and assembly. The local party leadership accused the commission of "counter-revolution" and "hooliganism," shut it down, arrested the leaders (sentencing some to death), and declared martial law.[135]

The "mood" on the street had again become a political question. At the party congress in March 1921, Lenin warned that with the economy and society in shambles the popular "mood" had become "undoubtedly more dangerous than Denikin, Yudenich, and Kolchak [the main White Army commanders] put together."[136] Lenin, of course, had always been skeptical about the "spontaneous" mentality of workers without the guidance of more "conscious" leadership. In his defining programmatic statement for Bolshevism, the 1902 pamphlet *What is to Be Done?*, Lenin warned that left to themselves workers would never get beyond narrow-minded "trade-union consciousness," which would lead ultimately to "ideological enslavement" to "bourgeois ideology." In 1921, he emphasized the deep "petty-bourgeois anarchist elements" in the mentality of workers.[137] The general consensus among the party leadership was that the labor upheavals of 1920–1 demonstrated the "backwardness" of what remained of the working class—the conscious proletariat, it seemed, had been replaced by an undisciplined, irrational, and ignorant "crowd." That workers worried about forced grain requisitioning, they said, proved that these were only "semi-peasant worker masses." Such workers, officials argued, tended toward "hooliganism"—the well-worn term used so often over the years to dismiss social unrest as irrational disorderliness—and were susceptible to manipulation by counter-revolutionary Mensheviks, SRs, and anarchists.

The huge meeting of representatives of metalworkers' unions from across Moscow province in February 1921 has often been seen as evidence of popular ideas and moods at that moment. Observers recorded that delegates heckled and shouted at Bolshevik speakers, even at Lev Kamenev, the head of the Moscow Soviet and a member of the ruling Communist Party politburo. A *New York Times* reporter claimed that Lenin himself appeared at the meeting (there are doubts about this) and rhetorically asked workers whether they wanted to see a return of the old tsarist regime. The jeering response was "Let come who may—whites, black, or devils themselves—just you clear out."[138] The Bolshevik Commissar of Food, who attended this meeting, drew dark conclusions about workers' mentality. The main "feeling and will" among even the politically "advanced" metalworkers—"the steel spine of the proletarian revolution"—was alienation from those who held power in their name. "The workers are tired of privileges," he wrote in *Pravda*, "they don't want inequality in anything, and above all not in food rations." The heart of their worldview could be seen, he observed, in their language of "'us' and 'you,'" 'masses' and 'elites.'" Workers' speeches, the commissar concluded, revealed the "complete break between the masses and the party, the masses and the unions."[139]

Historians, echoing the judgment of Mensheviks and other oppositionists, have tended to view this movement as revolutionary, even heroic. The historian Orlando Figes, for example, compared the movement of early 1921 to the protests of 1918–20: "whereas earlier strikes had been a means of bargaining with the regime, those of 1921 were a last desperate bid to overthrow it."[140] In the most detailed scholarly study of these strikes, Jonathan Aves described a revolutionary and democratic movement for "greater popular participation," rooted in the "resilient" traditions of working-class self-organization and the popular energies released by the revolution.[141]

But we should be cautious not to romanticize these protests and not be afraid to acknowledge what was long evident in the history of urban working-class life and protest: that the ideological myth of the rational and disciplined proletariat was a simplistic and optimistic idealization that obscured the complex experiences, needs, ideas, and emotions of lower-class people. Popular slogans of the street like "Down with Communists and Jews" remind us of traditions of plebian class distrust and hostility that were quite different from the ideals of socialist and democratic struggle. That the Bolshevik authorities used arguments about worker "backwardness," "exhaustion," and "demoralization" to justify repression and centralization of power, to advance the necessity of rule "in the name of" the proletariat rather than by the proletariat itself, does not make these arguments untrue. The Menshevik Fedor Dan noted how different the labor movement of 1921 was from that of 1917: "Before us were a mass of workers who were shattered, disorganized, and exhausted by four years of suffering and deprivation, who had experienced the painful collapse of their illusions, lost all confidence in their own strength, and lacked any clear political goals."[142] The revolution of the street had come to an end. The revolution now belonged to the party and the state.

Notes

1. Nikolai Gogol, "Nevsky Prospect" (1835).
2. The Russian words, denoting more than any single English word can capture, were *poshlyi*, *bezobraznyi*, *nepristoinyi*, *urodlivyi*, and *razvratnyi*. I discuss experiences and interpretations of the modern city in Mark D. Steinberg, *Petersburg Fin de Siècle* (New Haven, 2011). The scholarly

literature on Russian urbanization and city life is quite rich, including Joseph Bradley, *Muzhik and Muscovite: Urbanization in Late Imperial Russia* (Berkeley, CA, 1985); Michael F. Hamm (ed.), *The City in Late-Imperial Russia* (Bloomington, IN, 1986); Daniel Brower, *The Russian City between Tradition and Modernity, 1850–1900* (Berkeley, CA, 1990); Catriona Kelly and David Shepherd (eds), *Constructing Culture in the Age of Revolution: 1881–1940* (Oxford, 1998), part 2; Richard Stites, *Russian Popular Culture* (Cambridge, 1992), ch. 1; Louise McReynolds, *Russia at Play: Leisure Activities at the End of the Tsarist Era* (Ithaca, NY, 2002); Roshanna Sylvester, *Tales of Old Odessa: Crime and Civility in a City of Thieves* (DeKalb, IL, 2005); Jeff Sahadeo, *Russian Colonial Society in Tashkent, 1865–1923* (Bloomington, IN, 2007); Natan N. Meier, *Kiev, Jewish Metropolis: A History, 1859–1914* (Bloomington, IN, 2010).

3. I. V. Lebedev, "Mertvye tsvety," *Malen'kaia gazeta,* 5/22 September 1914, 1.

4. e.g V. Tr-ov, "Nasha ulitsa," *Gazeta-kopeika,* 14 August 1908, 3–4; 22 August 1908, 3; 24 August 1908, 2–3.

5. "Nashi zadachi, nadezhdy, i pozhelaniia," *Novoe vremia,* 1 January 1909, 2.

6. O. Gridina, "Zverinye nravy," *Gazeta-kopeika,* 14 May 1910, 3.

7. S. Liubosh, "Griaznaia volna," *Sovremennoe slovo,* 1910/811 (7 April): 1; Evgenii Sosuntsov, "Sovremennyi antinomizm," *Tserkovnyi vestnik,* 1914/21 (22 May): 626–7. See also Sylvester, *Tales of Old Odessa,* ch. 4.

8. Barbara Alpern Engel, *Between Fields and the City: Women, Work, and Family in Russia, 1861–1914* (Cambridge, 1994); Engel, *Women in Russia, 1700–2000* (Cambridge, 2004); Engel, *Breaking the Ties that Bound: The Politics of Marital Strife in Late Imperial Russia* (Ithaca, NY, 2011); Laura Engelstein, *Keys to Happiness: Sex and the Search for Modernity in Fin-de-Siècle Russia* (Ithaca, NY, 1992); Laurie Bernstein, *Sonia's Daughters: Prostitutes and their Regulation in Imperial Russia* (Berkeley, CA, 1995); Rochelle Ruth Ruthchild, *Equality and Revolution: Women's Rights in the Russian Empire, 1905–1917* (Pittsburgh, PA, 2010).

9. E. A. Oliunina, "The Tailoring Trade in Moscow and the Villages of Moscow and Riazan Provinces: Material on the History of the Domestic Industry in Russia," in Victoria Bonnell (ed.), *The Russian Worker: Life and Labor under the Tsarist Regime* (Berkeley, CA, 1983), 153–83 (quotation p. 172). See also Rose Glickman, *Russian Factory Women: Workplace and Society, 1880–1914* (Berkeley, CA, 1984), 61–5.

10. Quoted Glickman, *Russian Factory Women,* 145.

11. Ibid. 60–1.

12. Ibid. 63–4; Bernstein, *Sonia's Daughters*, 107–19.
13. V. Pr., "Ulichnyi nakhal," *Gazeta-kopeika*, 3 July 1909, 3.
14. Vadim, "Krasnaia Shapochka," *Gazeta-kopeika*, 14 July 1913, 4.
15. V. Nedesheva, *Nevskii prospekt* (St Petersburg, 1906), 3–11.
16. Ol'ga Gridina, "Obyknovennaia istoriia," *Gazeta-kopeika*, 4 October 1910, 3; "Po baryshu—chest'," *Gazeta-kopeika*, 5 October 1910, 3–5; "Est' zhizn', kotoraia…," *Gazeta-kopeika*, 6 October 1910, 3.
17. Ol'ga Gridina, "Gorod-obmanshchik," *Gazeta-kopeika*, 24 December 1913, 3, and "Rokovaia oshibka," *Gazeta-Kopeika*, 13 March 1910, 3.
18. Key studies of the working-class experience, though focused more on the workplace and organized struggles than on everyday working-class life, include Leopold Haimson, "The Problem of Social Stability in Urban Russia, 1905–1917," *Slavic Review*, 23/4 (December 1964): 619–42; Reginald Zelnik, "Russian Bebels," *Russian Review*, 35/3 and 4 (July and October 1976); Victoria Bonnell, *Roots of Rebellion: Workers' Politics and Organizations in St. Petersburg and Moscow, 1900–1914* (Berkeley, CA, 1983); Reginald Zelnik (ed.), *A Radical Worker in Tsarist Russia: The Autobiography of Semen Ivanovich Kanatchikov* (Stanford, CA, 1986); Tim McDaniel, *Autocracy, Capitalism, and Revolution in Russia* (Berkeley, CA, 1988); Glickman, *Russian Factory Women*; Charters Wynn, *Workers, Strikes and Pogroms: The Donbas-Dnepr Bend in Late Imperial Russia, 1870–1905* (Princeton, 1992).
19. Steinberg, *Petersburg Fin de Siècle*, 179–97.
20. Arnol'dov, "Svidrigailovy," *Gazeta-kopeika*, 28 February 1909, 4; S. Liubosh, "Griznaia volna," *Sovremennoe slovo*, 1910/811 (7 April): 1.
21. V. P. Ruadze, *K sudu!… Gomoseksual'nyi Peterburg* (St Petersburg, 1908), 113.
22. Skitalets, "Ozverenie," *Gazeta-kopeika*, 16 January 1913, 3.
23. Dmitrii Zhbankov, "Itogi travmaticheskoi epidemii za noiabr'-dekabr' 1909," *Rech'*, 14 January 1910, 2. See also Louise McReynolds, *Murder Most Russian: True Crime and Punishment in Late Imperial Russia* (Ithaca, NY, 2013).
24. Among the few historians who have emphasized this everyday violence, see especially McReynolds, *Murder Most Russian*; Steinberg, *Petersburg Fin de Siècle;* Ilya Gersimov, "The Subalterns Speak Out: Urban Plebeian Society in Late Imperial Russia" and Mark Steinberg, "Blood in the Air: Everyday Violence in the Experience of the Petersburg Poor, 1905–1917," in Hans-Christian Petersen (ed.), *Spaces of the Poor: Perspectives of Cultural Sciences on Urban Slum Areas and their Inhabitants* (Bielefeld, 2013), 47–70, 97–120.

25. See Joan Neuberger, *Hooliganism: Crime, Culture, and Power in St. Petersburg, 1900–1914* (Berkeley, CA, 1993).

26. "Zhizn' za 14 kopeek," *Peterburgskii listok,* 5 January 1912, 3.

27. "Omut zhizni: khuligany," *Gazeta-kopeika,* 21 June 1908, 3; "Podvigi ulichnykh grabitelei," *Peterburgskii listok,* 2 August 1910, 3.

28. See my *Petersburg Fin de Siècle.*

29. "Detskii sud," *Peterburgskii listok,* 11 January 1910, 1.

30. Vas. Nemirovich-Danchenko, "Zhizn' deshevo! (ocherki epedimii otchaianiia)," *Zaprosy zhizni,* 1910/10 (7 March): 581–90; Stepan Filenkin, "Deshevaia zhizn'," *Gazeta-kopeika,* 23 August 1911, 3.

31. Ol'ga Gridina, "Noveishie geroi," *Gazeta-kopeika,* 5 December 1913, 3.

32. N. Valentinov, "Gorod i gorozhane," *Novyi zhurnal dlia vsekh,* 1910/20 (June): 91–6.

33. Neuberger, *Hooliganism,* esp. 13–14, 66–7.

34. See Franz Fanon, *The Wretched of the Earth,* tr. Richard Philcox (New York, 2004); James C. Scott, *Domination and the Arts of Resistance: Hidden Transcripts* (New Haven, 1992); Sarah Ahmed, *The Cultural Politics of Emotion* (New York, 2004); Sianne Ngai, *Ugly Feelings* (Cambridge, MA, 2005); Slavoj Žižek, *Violence* (New York, 2008).

35. P. Zaikin, "Petersburgskie skvernoslovie," *Gazeta-kopeika,* 3 February 1909, 3.

36. V. Novitskii, "Zver'—v chelovek," *Peterburgskaia gazeta,* 6 April 1909, 1; K. Barantsevich, "Zhazhdushchie silnykh oshchushchenii," *Slovo,* 2 February 1909, 2.

37. I. Loginov, "V gorode," *Sbornik proletarskii pisatalei,* ed. M. Gor'kii, A. Serebrov, and A. Chapygin (Petrograd, 1917), 174.

38. M. Kalinin, review of *Sbornik proletarskikh pisatelei* (Moscow, 1914) in *Rabochii,* 23 June 1914, 2.

39. M. Artamonov, "Taet," *Metallist,* 4/41 (1 April 1914): 5–6.

40. Quoted from many examples in Mark Steinberg, *Proletarian Imagination: Self, Modernity, and the Sacred in Russia, 1910–1925* (Ithaca, NY, 2002), 153–60.

41. K. Mirov, "V 'Russkom Manchestere'," *Russkoe slovo,* 14 June 1905, 3.

42. Aleksandr Rossov, "Katastrofa," *Russkoe slovo,* 10 June 1905, 1.

43. From references to the crowd in the newspaper *Russkoe slovo* during 1905, e.g. Ia. Usmovich, "D'iavol'skii zamysel," *Russkoe slovo,* 24 October 1905, 1.

44. These examples are based on my reading of the high-culture journal *Satirikon* (1908–9) and the popular *Listok-kopeika* (1909–10). The

definition of satire is from Vladimir Dal's nineteenth-century dictionary <http://dic.academic.ru/contents.nsf/ushakov> [accessed 2 August 2016]. See also Jeffrey Brooks, "Marvelous Destruction: The Left-Leaning Satirical Magazines of 1905–1907," *Experiment: A Journal of Russian Culture,* 19 (2013): 24–62. A collection of these satirical magazines can be found at <http://digitallibrary.usc.edu/cdm/landingpage/collection/p15799coll1>. [accessed 26 August 2016]

45. The best accounts of the "days of freedom" are Abraham Ascher, *The Revolution of 1905,* i (Stanford, CA, 1988), ch. 10; Laura Engelstein, *Moscow, 1905: Working-Class Organization and Political Conflict* (Stanford, CA, 1982), ch. 8; Gerald D. Surh, *1905 in St. Petersburg: Labor, Society, and Revolution* (Stanford, CA, 1989), ch. 8; Sidney Harcave, *The Russian Revolution of 1905* (London, 1964), ch. 7.

46. *Russkie vedomosti,* 21 October 1905, 1.

47. P. A. Garvi, *Vospominaniia sotsialdemokrata: stati o zhizni i deiatelnosti P. A. Garvi* (New York, 1945), 587–8.

48. Engelstein, *Moscow, 1905,* 140–2; Ascher, *Revolution of 1905,* i. 262–5; *Russkie vedomosti,* 21 October 1905, 1. On the phenomenon and symbolics of "Red Funerals," see Thomas Trice, "The 'Body Politic': Russian Funerals and the Politics of Representation" (Ph.D. Dissertation, U. Illinois, 1998), ch. 6.

49. *Russkie Vedomosti,* 22 October 1905, 1.

50. Ascher, *Revolution of 1905,* i. 253–67; Harcave, *Russian Revolution of 1905,* 203–7; Engelstein, *Moscow, 1905,* 139–43; Surh, *1905 in St. Petersburg,* 353–4; Neuberger, *Hooliganism,* 91–3.

51. See especially Robert Weinberg, *The Revolution of 1905 in Odessa* (Bloomington, IN, 1993), ch. 7.

52. Sergei Iablonovskii, "Svet i teni: Zhupel'," *Russkoe slovo,* 11 March 1905, 3; Sviashchennik G. Petrov, "Potrebnoe mest'," *Russkoe slovo,* 21 October 1905, 1.

53. Belevskii, "Chernye sotni," *Russkoe slovo,* 20 October 1905, 1; Aleksandr Rossov, "Agoniia," *Russkoe slovo,* 20 October 1905, 1.

54. G. Khrustalev-Nosar', "Istoriia Soveta Rabochikh Deputatov (do 26 noiabria 1905 g.)," in *Istoriia Soveta Rabochikh Deputatov g. S.-Peterburga* (St Petersburg, 1906), 91–8. See also Leon Trotsky, *1905* (Harmondsworth, 1971), 154–5.

55. Engelstein, *Moscow, 1905,* 143–4; Ascher, *Revolution of 1905,* i. 291–3, 304–5.

56. Ascher, *Revolution of 1905*, i. 313.
57. Engelstein, *Moscow, 1905,* 188–9; Ascher, *Revolution of 1905*, i. 313.
58. Ascher, *Revolution of 1905*, i. 321.
59. P. N. Miliukov, *Vospominaniia, 1859–1917,* 2 vols. (Moscow, 1990), i. 349.
60. Ascher, *Revolution of 1905*, i. 304–30; Engelstein, *Moscow, 1905,* 187–225; Harcave, *Russian Revolution of 1905,* 229–43.
61. "Otrezvlenie naroda," *Malen'kaia gazeta,* 23 September 1914, 1.
62. From reports in *Malen'kaia gazeta* in October 1914.
63. Figes, *A People's Tragedy,* 300.
64. N. Kholmskii, "Voina i detskaia prestupnost'," *Malen'kaia gazeta,* 19 October 1914, 4.
65. "Delo s doneseniiami i telefonnymi soobshcheniiami P.O.O. ob obshchestvennom dvizhenii," 2 January–26 February 1917, GARF, f. 111, op. 1, d. 669, l. 1–386 (quotation 37); Major General Globachev (head of the Petrograd Okhrana), "Dopolnenie k doneseniiu (sovershenno-sektretno)," 26 January 1917, GARF, f. 111, op. 1, d. 669, l. 112–13. See also Tsuyoshi Hasegawa, *The February Revolution: Petrograd, 1917* (Seattle, 1981), 201.
66. e.g. "Na ulitsakh Moskvy v eti nezabyvaemye dni," *Ezhednevnaia Gazeta-Kopeika,* 5 March 1917, 3; "Soldaty idut . . . ," *Ezhednevnaia Gazeta-Kopeika,* 6 March 1917, 3. See Orlando Figes and Boris Kolonitskii, *Interpreting the Russian Revolution: The Language and Symbols of 1917* (New Haven, 1999), 34, 42, 44–8; and Mark Steinberg, *Voices of Revolution, 1917* (New Haven, 2001), 59–63.
67. *Izvestiia soveta rabochikh i soldatskikh deputatov,* 22–4 March 1917; *Novoe vremia,* 25 March (7 April) 1917. See also Trice, "Body Politic," 279–86; Figes and Kolonitskii, *Interpreting,* 46–8, 75.
68. Victor Shklovsky, *A Sentimental Journey: Memoirs, 1917–1922,* tr. Richard Sheldon (Ithaca, NY, 1970; originally publ. Moscow, 1922), 11, 13, 16.
69. Such incidents are described in almost every memoir of 1917. For a summary, drawing on these accounts, see Figes, *A People's Tragedy,* 315–21.
70. Ruthchild, *Equality and Revolution,* 218–23; Chatterjee, *Celebrating Women,* 44–56.
71. *Izvestiia Petrogradskogo Soveta rabochikh deputatov,* 1 (28 February 1917): 2.
72. According to Nikolai Sukhanov's recollections of a conversation. N. N. Sukhanov, *The Russian Revolution, 1917: A Personal Memoir* (Princeton, 1984), 96. Gorky would later say much the same in his columns, "Untimely Thoughts," in his newspaper *New Life* (*Novaia Zhizn'.*)
73. Sukhanov, *Russian Revolution,* 96.

74. Leon Trotsky, *History of the Russian Revolution*, tr. Max Eastman (Chicago, 2008; orig. 1932), 98.
75. Figes, *A People's Tragedy*, 319 (quotations); Figes and Kolonitskii, *Interpreting*, ch. 2. See also Hasegawa, *February Revolution*, 289.
76. e.g. P.V. "Prava bez obiazannostei," *Gazeta dlia vsekh*, 1 June 1917, 2; Krasnoe pero, "Zerkalo stolitsy," *Gazeta dlia vsekh*, 1 June 1917, 3; Emigrant, "Kham," *Gazeta-kopeika*, 11 August 1917, 4. See discussions of press coverage in Chapter 3 of this volume.
77. For additional evidence from newspapers, see Tsuyoshi Hasegawa, "Crime, Police, and Mob Justice in Petrograd during the Russian Revolutions of 1917," in Charles E. Timberlake (ed.), *Religious and Secular Forces in Late Tsarist Russia* (Seattle, 1992), 241–71; "Crime, Police, and Samosudy in Petrograd in the Russian Revolution: The Subalterns and Sociological Theories of Anomie and Crowd Psychology" (unpublished conference paper), esp. 7–11; and his forthcoming book, tentatively titled *The Crowd in the Russian Revolution: Crime, Police, and Mob Justice in Petrograd, 1917–1918*.
78. Skitalets, "Poslednee dokazetel'stvo," *Gazeta-kopeika*, 23 June 1917, 3.
79. e.g. *Gazeta dlia vsekh*, 26 May 1917, 1–2. On the ubiquity of talk about economic crisis in the provincial press, see Donald Raleigh, *Revolution on the Volga: 1917 in Saratov* (Ithaca, NY, 1986), chs. 4–5; Sarah Badcock, *Politics and the People in Revolutionary Russia: A Provincial History* (Cambridge, 2007), ch. 8.
80. "Strashno, no ne beznadezhno," *Gazeta dlia vsekh*, 26 May 1917, 2; *Russkiia vedomosti*, 24 August 1917, 1.
81. "Chto nuzhno okrainom," *Gazeta dlia vsekh*, 25 May 1917, 4.
82. "Na Kronshtadtskom mitinge," *Gazeta dlia vsekh*, 25 May 1917, 1.
83. "Sud ulitsy," *Gazeta dlia vsekh*, 30 May 1917, p. 4.
84. Iu. Volin, "Samosud," *Gazeta-kopeika*, 25 June 1917, 6.
85. In addition to newspaper sources, see Hasegawa, "Crime, Police, and Mob Justice in Petrograd," 258–64, and his recent conference paper "Crime, Police, and Samosudy in Petrograd in the Russian Revolution."
86. "Bud'te chelovechny!," *Gazeta dlia vsekh*, 31 May 1917, 3.
87. Vad. Belov, "Opasnoe legkomyslie," *Gazeta-kopeika*, 8 September 1917, 2.
88. I. Ivanov, "Pechal'no," *Gazeta dlia vsekh*, 3 June 1917, 3.
89. Maksim Gor'kii, "Nesvoevremmenye mysli," *Novaia zhizn'*, 7 (20) December 1917, 1.
90. Hasegawa, "Crime, Police, and Mob Justice in Petrograd," 258–64; "Crime, Police, and Samosudy in Petrograd in the Russian Revolution."

91. "Svetlyi den'," *Gazeta-kopeika*, 20 April 1917, 3.
92. *Rech'*, 4 August 1917, 2; *Izvestiia*, 8 August 1917, 2.
93. Diane P. Koenker and William G. Rosenberg, *Strikes and Revolution*, 258–61.
94. Ibid., ch. 9; S. A. Smith, *Red Petrograd: Revolution in the Factories, 1917–1918* (Cambridge, 1983), 116–19; Diane P. Koenker, *Moscow Workers and the 1917 Revolution* (Princeton, 1981), ch. 8.
95. See the excellent discussion in B. I. Kolonitskii, "Antiburzhuaznaia propaganda i 'antiburzhuaznoe' soznanie," in V. Iu. Cherniaev et al. (eds), *Anatomiia Revoliutsii* (St Petersburg, 1994), esp. 195–7.
96. Resolution from a meeting of workers, on 27 July 1917, at twenty-seven small enterprises in the Peterhof district of Petrograd, published in the Bolshevik paper *Rabochii i soldat*, 4 August 1917, 8–9.
97. "Pis'mo Putilovtsev ko vsem grazhdanam (v poiasnenie 3, 4, 5-go iiulia)," *Novaia zhizn'*, 15 July 1917, 3. See also Steinberg, *Voices of Revolution*, 187–90.
98. *Gazeta-kopeika*, 29 July 1917, 1–3.
99. Skitalets, "Posledniaia solominka," *Gazeta dlia vsekh*, 15 October 1917, 3.
100. Shklovsky, *Sentimental Journey*, 60.
101. e.g. "Pesn' Goria (nabrosok)," *Gazeta dlia vsekh*, 12 November 1917, 3; Nikolai R-ov, "I tsvety i slezy," *Gazeta dlia vsekh*, 15 November 1917, 4; Oko, "Pliaska na vul'kane," *Gazeta dlia vsekh*, 16 November 1917, 2. On workers, in particular, see Skorpion, "Pobory bez kontsa" *Gazeta dlia vsekh*, 16 November 1917, 4; Meteor, "Po zavodam i fabrikam," *Gazeta dlia vsekh*, 24 November 1917, 3.
102. Maior Palkin, "Katimsia...," *Gazeta dlia vsekh*, 15 November 1917, 4.
103. Anskii, "Perezhytye uzhasy," *Gazeta dlia vsekh*, 8 November 1917, 3; Nabliudatel', "Kto-zhe nas zashchitit'?" *Gazeta dlia vsekh*, 14 November 1917, 2; Fugas, "'Rukavishnikovtsy,'" *Gazeta dlia vsekh*, 8 November 1917, 2; Aramis, "Volchata," 9 November 1917, 3; "Oblava na Khritrovke," *Gazeta dlia vsekh*, 8 November 1917, 2.
104. Oko, "Pliaska na vul'kane," *Gazeta dlia vsekh*, 16 November 1917, 2, and 18 November 1917, 2.
105. From reports in *Gazeta dlia vsekh* on 8–10 November 1917. See also Koenker, *Moscow Workers*, ch. 9; Eduard M. Dune, *Notes of a Red Guard*, tr. and ed. Diane P. Koenker and S. A. Smith (Urbana, IL, 1993), 58–73.
106. "Vo vlasti grabitelei," *Gazeta dlia vsekh*, 17 November 1917, 3.
107. e.g. Maior Palkin, "Dusha vopiet k nebu," *Gazeta dlia vsekh*, 10 November 1917, 3.

108. Fugas, "'Rukavishnikovtsy,'" *Gazeta dlia vsekh*, 8 November 1917, 2.
109. Mark Lawrence Schrad, *Vodka Politics: Alcohol, Autocracy, and the Secret History of the Russian State* (Oxford, 2014), 204.
110. V. A. Antonov-Ovseenko, quoted in Isaac Deutscher, *The Prophet Armed: Trotsky, 1879–1921* (New York, 1965), 323–3.
111. "Matushka-provintsiia," *Gazeta dlia vsekh*, 16 November 1917, p. 4.
112. Quoted in the introduction to Ivan Bunin, *Cursed Days: Diary of a Revolution*, tr. and ed. Thomas Gaiton Marullo (Chicago, 1998), 8.
113. Ibid. 27–8.
114. Ibid. 68–9.
115. Such stories can be found daily in *Gazeta dlia vsekh* from January through June 1918, when the paper was shut, e.g. I. Pavlov, "V lapakh goloda," *Gazeta dlia vsekh*, (25 January 1918), 3 (quotations); Nikolai Reshchikov, "Gorod sprut," *Gazeta dlia vsekh*, 17 January 1918, 3; Kr. "Gde strashnee vsego?" *Gazeta dlia vsekh*, 2 February 1918, 2; "Vopli goloda," *Gazeta dlia vsekh*, 2 May 1918, 1; M. "Net prosveta," *Gazeta dlia vsekh* 10 May 1918, 1; "Tsar'-golod," *Gazeta dlia vsekh*, 23 May 1918, 3; M. Anin, "I ona vse plachet," *Gazeta dlia vsekh*, 26 May 1918, 4.
116. "Gde 'vernoe vremia'?" *Gazeta dlia vsekh*, 23 March 1918, 3; Tetia Olia, "Malen'kii fel'eton: Chasy s voprosom," *Gazeta dlia vsekh*, 6 May 1918, 2.
117. Victor Serge, *Conquered City* (New York, 2011: orig. 1932), 17. Similar to the sentiments and mood conveyed in this novel, Serge titles the chapter on the civil war years in his *Memoirs of a Revolutionary, 1901–1941*, tr. Peter Sedgwick (Oxford, 1963), "Anguish and Enthusiasm."
118. Diane P. Koenker, "Urbanization and Deurbanization in the Russian Revolution and Civil War," in Diane P. Koenker, William G. Rosenberg, and Ronald Grigor Suny (eds), *Party, State, and Society in the Russian Civil War: Explorations in Social History* (Bloomington, IN, 1989), 81–95; Daniel Brower, "'The City in Danger': The Civil War and the Russian Urban Population," in Koenker et al., *Party, State, and Society*, 61–5; William J. Chase, *Workers, Society, and the Soviet State: Labor and Life in Moscow, 1918–1929* (Urbana, IL, 1987), 33–8.
119. Koenker, "Urbanization and Deurbanization," 96–9; Brower, "City in Danger," 58–80 (quotations about the *obyvatel'* on p. 59 from *Krasnyi put' zheleznodorozhnika*, 12 June 1919). See also Donald J. Raleigh, *Experiencing Russia's Civil War: Politics, Society, and Revolutionary Culture in Saratov, 1917–1922* (Princeton, 2002), 63–76; David Mandel, *The Petrograd Workers and the Soviet Seizure of Power* (London, 1984), 390–1; Lewis

Siegelbaum, *Soviet State and Society between Revolutions, 1918–1929* (Cambridge, 1992), 26–34; Kevin Murphy, *Revolution and Counterrevolution: Class Struggle in a Moscow Metal Factory* (Chicago, 2007), 69–73.

120. Raleigh, *Experiencing Russia's Civil War*, ch. 6. See also Chase, *Workers, Society, and the Soviet State*, ch. 1; Koenker, "Urbanization and Deurbanization," 81–104; Murphy, *Revolution and Counterrevolution*, 62–74.

121. Serge, *Conquered City*, 37, 197.

122. Bunin, *Cursed Days*, 148–9.

123. James Von Geldern, *Bolshevik Festivals, 1917–1920* (Berkeley, CA, 1993), 95.

124. Semen Rodov, "Prazdnik ery," *Gorn*, 2–3 (1919): 122.

125. In addition to von Geldern, *Bolshevik Festivals,* see Richard Stites, *Revolutionary Dreams: Utopian Vision and Experimental Life in the Russian Revolution* (Oxford, 1989), ch. 4.

126. The following discussion of workers' protests during 1918–20 is based on William G. Rosenberg, "Russian Labor and Bolshevik Power after October," discussion by Moshe Lewin and Vladimir Brovkin, *Slavic Review,* 44/2 (Summer 1985): 213–56; Mary McAuley, *Bread and Justice: State and Society in Petrograd* (Oxford, 1991), ch. 12; Vladimir M. Brovkin, *Behind the Front Lines of the Civil War: Political Parties and Social Movements in Russia, 1918–1922* (Princeton, 1994), chs. 2 and 8; Jonathan Aves, *Workers Against Lenin: Labour Protest and the Bolshevik Dictatorship* (London, 1996); Diane Koenker, *Republic of Labor: Russian Printers and Soviet Socialism, 1918–1930* (Ithaca, NY, 2005), 62–70; Alexander Rabinowitch, *The Bolsheviks in Power: The First Year of Soviet Rule in Petrograd* (Bloomington, IN, 2007), 233–59; Mandel, *Petrograd Workers and Soviet Seizure*, ch. 8.

127. *Novaia zhizn'*, 30 May 1918, 3.

128. Quoted in Aleksandr Rabinovich (Alexander Rabinowitch), "Bolsheviki, nizy i sovetskaia vlast: Petrograd, fevral'-iiul' 1918," *Anatomiia revoliutsii* (St Petersburg, 1994), 130.

129. Quoted in Elizabeth Wood, *The Baba and the Comrade: Gender and Politics in Revolutionary Russia* (Bloomington, IN, 1997), 43.

130. TsGA SPb (Central State Archive of St Petersburg), fond 1000, opis 3, delo. 302, listy 3–40b, cited and discussed in Alexander Rabinowitch, "The Bolsheviks Survive: Government and Crises in Civil War Petrograd (Some Preliminary Findings)," unpublished conference paper, June 2016 (part of his important work-in-progress on Petrograd and Bolshevism during the Civil War).

131. I. Burdachev, "Paiki i tariff," *Pravda,* 4 September 1920, 1. See also Aves, *Workers against Lenin,* 80.

132. The history of these strikes and protests is documented and discussed in Chase, *Workers, Society, and the Soviet State,* 48–56; Richard Sakwa, *Soviet Communists in Power: A Study of Moscow during the Civil War, 1918–21* (London, 1988), 243–7; McAuley, *Bread and Justice,* 404–11; Siegelbaum, *Soviet State and Society,* 76–7; Brovkin, *Behind the Front Lines,* 389–94; Aves, *Workers Against Lenin;* Figes, *A People's Tragedy,* 758–60. See also the contemporary account by Fedor Dan, *Dva goda skitanii (1919–1921)* (Berlin, 1922), 104–9.

133. McAuley *Bread and Justice,* 407, quotes these phrases from a resolution adopted at the Arsenal Works in Petrograd, published in the metalworkers' newspaper *Makhovik,* 26 February 1921, 2.

134. Dan, *Dva goda skitanii,* 106.

135. Raleigh, *Experiencing Russia's Civil War,* 387–90.

136. V. I. Lenin at the 10th Party Congress, 8 March 1921, in Lenin, *Polnoe sobranie sochineniii,* xliii (Moscow, 1970), 24.

137. Ibid.; V. I. Lenin, *What is to Be Done?* (1902) in Robert C. Tucker (ed.), *The Lenin Anthology* (New York, 1975), 23–31.

138. *New York Times,* 3 March 1921, 1. Many historians have quoted this gem, while also raising questions about its veracity.

139. A. Vyshinskii, "Uroki odnoi konferentsii," *Pravda,* 8 February 1921, 1.

140. Figes, *A People's Tragedy,* 758–60.

141. Aves, *Workers Against Lenin,* 186–7 and passim.

142. Dan, *Dva goda skitanii,* 111.

CHAPTER 6
WOMEN AND REVOLUTION
IN THE VILLAGE

Educated Russians across the political spectrum worried about the lives and mentalities of the Russian people—the *narod* in the often used Russian word that signified both "the nation" and "the people," especially the common folk. Since the nineteenth century, left-leaning intellectuals, journalists, writers, and artists looked with hope to the Russian common people as possessing an innate spirit of justice and community, most visible in the traditions of the peasant commune. Conservatives also idealized the rural folk, but according to different values and desires: the common folk were imbued with an innate faith in autocracy and the Orthodox Church.[1] Nicholas II was typical in his belief that the "true Russian people" were united under their tsar by a natural bond of love and loyalty, by a spiritual political "communion." When the revolution in 1905 suggested this communion might be breaking down, Nicholas blamed intellectuals, Jews, and other "bad people," alien to the true spirit of the nation and the people, for leading the "good, virtuous, and kind people (*narod*)" astray.[2] There was also a hard demographic and economic reality stimulating concern: nearly 90 percent of the Russian population on the eve of World War I were "peasants" (according to the legal definition, which included recent migrants to cities and rural factories, though the vast majority of peasants lived in villages and worked in small-scale agriculture).[3] Journalists, physicians, economists, government officials, clergy, and political activists of all stripes made the common folk an object of study, argument, reform, and mobilization.

They judged the condition of the people as defining and shaping the condition of the nation, and ultimately its fate, but disagreed intensely about their conclusions: peasants were a conservative community resistant to everything new (which could be judged as good or bad) or a natural force for justice and perhaps revolution, they were proof of the benefits of modern capitalism or proof of its harm, they showed why Russia needs the strong hand of absolutist monarchy or why Russia needs modern citizenship, rights, and democracy.

Historians have questioned these simplifications in recent years, reading the evidence of peasant life (including the claims of non-peasant observers) against the grain of past prejudices and agendas, recovering peasant experience separate from the myths about them. Scholars have closely examined economic relationships, family lives, religion, literacy and education, songs and rituals, relations with the state and landlords, resistance and rebellion, and many other questions. Among the most important insights is the fallacy of imagining (as many contemporaries did) a distinct and separate "peasant world," a "world apart" based on "tradition" and "authenticity," isolated from outside cultural influences and resistant to all change. Also, it made a great deal of difference whether a "peasant" was an independent working farmer (and the size and economic situation of his farm), a day laborer, a village craftsman, a migrant to the city, or a great many other variants and combinations, including where they lived geographically. It mattered no less whether this peasant was a male head of household, his wife, a subordinate son or daughter-in-law, a widow, an orphan, or many other distinctions of status based on age, gender, and family situation.[4]

Peasants left little written record about how they experienced their own lives or thought about their own place in history, especially in times not broken open by revolution. Scholars have uncovered some nineteenth-century peasant letters to family members.[5] There are scattered memoirs by peasants who became urban workers, though especially if they later participated in the revolution.[6] And there are rare oral histories.[7] Of course, we cannot read these texts as "representative" of "authentic" peasant experience: they were expressions of experience, to be sure, but of a complex experience (like all experience) shaped by the purposes of writing and the ideas communicated and the distinctiveness of the individuals inspired to write. We have vastly greater evidence from times of upheaval and revolution, especially 1905–7 and 1917–21, when rural people sent huge numbers of letters, petitions, and resolutions to people with power. These, too, must be interpreted with caution. We know little or nothing, for example, about who wrote texts signed by groups of peasants, much less how individuals understood the words they assented to. What did it mean even that they represented themselves as "peasants," with no indication of the huge range of what this might mean in terms of their everyday lives. When peasants wrote, their words were shaped by a wide range of available languages of expression, ranging from folklore and religion to formal education and reading, and by strategic considerations of why they were writing and to whom. They wrote mainly to persuade, and so kept their readers in mind. Retelling the history of peasant experience, therefore, requires not only hearing their own voices but reading this evidence (as well as what those who wrote about peasants said) "against the grain": untangling the meanings in their choices of words and stories; comparing words and practices; recognizing subjectivity and intent; and, not least, remembering that there was no typical "peasant," but a multitude of peasants whose experiences, positions in the community, and points of view differed in so many possible ways.

One of the most important differences was gender. It is still common in history writing to treat men as "normative," to assume, unintentionally, that the evidence we have about men's experiences, perspectives, actions, and voices (which is most of the evidence) tells us about both men and women within a particular social group. In Russian history, it remains common to treat the histories of male peasants as the history of "peasants" and to view what men said and did during 1905–7 or 1917–21 as the history of "peasant revolution." This chapter asks what attention to women's particular experience of revolution in the village, including the experience of gender itself—the constructed, contested, and changing ways people thought about what it meant to be a "woman" or a "man," which often colored how they experienced history and imagined change[8]—might do to our usual stories of peasants and revolution. Though limited sources make any answers inadequate and unsettled, I ask how histories of women and gender make the history of the

Russian revolution look different. Of course, gender difference was not an absolute divide. Experiences based on age, labor, and migration could cut across gender. And, not least, women's actions were often rooted in identities, grievances, and solidarities they shared with their families or the whole peasant community. But these are the sort of complications we need to keep in mind as we look for experience in all its rich complexity.

Peasant Lives

By the early 1900s, many educated Russians were leaving behind the old romanticizations of the peasantry to dwell instead on the dangers of rural "backwardness." Agricultural practices were condemned for being attached to tradition and custom rather than reason and innovation. Peasant religion was criticized as lacking true spiritual feeling, as little more than habits and rituals, and as filled with primitive, superstitious, and false (even "pagan") understandings of Orthodox belief and practice. Peasant family life was portrayed as brutally patriarchal, tolerating not only the domineering power of the older male head of household but also customs of domestic violence against wives and children and even sexual abuse of daughters-in-law. The peasant commune, ruled by the periodic gathering of household heads (mostly older men), was criticized not only for allegedly standing in the way of modern methods of agricultural practice but for inculcating in peasants a spirit of compulsion and conformity, for suppressing the individual. Violence was said to be endemic to village life, evident in regular beatings of wives and children but also in traditions of bloody battles between young men of neighboring villages. Not least, drunkenness during religious holidays was deemed a sadly characteristic sign of a debased culture. Rather than using holidays "to rest and exchange ideas," an urban newspaper critic wrote in 1903, with typical hyperbole, peasants exhaust themselves in celebrations that bring economic harm to the village and the family: "there are localities where holidays stretch out for weeks on end. These weeks are non-stop debauchery and drunkenness. One village goes to another and tries to outdo the other with 'treating,' with the amount of offered beer, vodka, and mead. The result is lost time, lost money and strength, numerous fights, and often murders and court proceedings."

The worst part, this reporter added, is that peasants viewed all this as obligation and duty to the point that a peasant who might prefer to work will be punished by the village community.[9]

Women were viewed with particular concern in this world of rural "darkness." Journalists, doctors, jurists, ethnographers, teachers, clergy, reformers, and revolutionaries all worried about the mentality of the Russian *baba*—an often-heard term that could simply mean a woman from the peasantry, but was usually tinged with implications about her backwardness. Even in the midst of the 1917 revolution, when talk of gender equality and women's rights had become common, many liberals and socialists worried about women's baneful influence on the new freedom. A feminist journalist reported in May that a male friend warned her that "if you want to restore the monarchy, just give women the vote."[10] In the Bolshevik newspaper the *Working Woman (Rabotnitsa)*, an essayist described what "everyone" knows: that peasants are "the darkest mass" of the Russian people, unable to understand what is happening around them until they have been "taught" by city life, and women are the most backward of all.[11]

This backwardness, in the view of most writers on the liberal and socialist left, was a product of systemic victimization not intrinsic nature. If anything, women were idealized as natural pillars of tradition and morality: more likely than men to be modest in manners, chaste before marriage, sober, and devoted to family and community. Women were also judged to be more devout in religious practice and pious in faith, though many on the left considered this a fault. But tradition had other dark sides, liberals and radicals insisted: a patriarchal world of "slavery" for women and girls, marked by cultural misogyny, endemic violence against wives and children, backbreaking toil, and lack of any decision-making power for women in the village assembly. The encroachments of modern life added new reasons to worry. The morally corrosive effects of city ways and consumer culture were seen as especially likely to harm women's weak and susceptible natures. New ideas and products were said to stimulate women's vanity, individualism, and desire. And given women's role in the family economy and the potential power of their sexuality, observers worried that peasant women might have an unhealthy influence over their men.[12]

Historians have generally agreed with contemporaries about one thing, however differently they have described and valued this: community was a central experience and value in peasant lives, affecting almost every relationship. And women played a key role in fostering and defending community. Most famously, the village "commune" (known as the *obshchina* or *mir*), which was controlled by the heads of households who came together in regular assemblies (the *skhod*), remained a powerful influence. Economically, village communes held collective title to peasant lands (though not to the large estates where many peasants rented land or worked for wages) and made the major decisions about land use—what work should to be done in each field (which was the responsibility of extended-family households, the other key collectivity of everyday social and economic life), when to do it, and by what methods. By tradition in many parts of Russia, the commune periodically redistributed land holdings among peasant families on the basis of hands to work and mouths to feed—though this was becoming less and less regular practice by the early 1900s. The commune also carried out a wide range of administrative functions: tax collection, military recruitment, granting or refusing permission to work away from the village, investigating and punishing petty crimes and misdemeanors, maintaining roads and bridges and the local church or chapel, dealing with outsiders (especially the government and the church), and caring for needy members of the community. As many of these functions suggest, the commune was not only part of the way peasants ruled themselves but also of how government ruled peasants—indeed, it was officially supported for this reason and many of its functions were the result of government mandates.

Community did not mean equality. Difference and hierarchy shaped the communities of household and village. While the populist left often viewed peasants as practicing a sort of primitive communism of collective land tenure, peasants' understanding of property was communal only to a degree. While peasants believed that land "belonged" to those who worked it (hence the problem with landlord land), in practice this meant control by the extended families that worked scattered strips of land in multiple fields (the government's reforms of 1906 tried to encourage the formation of unified farmsteads but with limited success). In this arrangement, the commune was a necessary mediator, but de facto family property was the implied foundation of the village economy. Even the old tradition of redistributing land and collectively coordinating its use, scholars have shown, resulted more from the practical recognition that cooperation was necessary to survive than from abstract notions of equality and collectivism. And as repartition became less common, and peasant families became more involved in commercial markets, many peasants considered their land de facto private property. There were also important social fissures within the village: peasant households with greater economic success, which often translated into greater influence in the village community; not least, hierarchies of age and gender such that the old ruled over the young and men ruled over women.[13]

In the patriarchal world of the village, women's place was reinforced by an arsenal of differentiating structures and norms—though these could vary by region and local tradition. A married woman traditionally covered her hair to signify her subordination to her husband. But she was also subordinate to others: she was expected to move into the household of her husband's extended family, where her position was initially among the lowest. She was especially likely to suffer under the distrustful authority of her mother-in-law (though, in time, she could become a ruling mother-in-law herself) and sometimes from sexual abuse by her father-in-law when her husband was away in the army or working outside the village (a custom that also reminded sons of their low position). When husbands were at home, they felt it their duty and right to forcefully regulate the behavior of subordinate family members—disciplinary beatings of women and children (including adult sons) were accepted as both culturally proper and conducive to the unity of a large extended family. The status of women in peasant society was echoed in well-known peasant proverbs: "a hen is not a bird, and a woman (*baba*) is not a person" "a *baba* is long on hair and short on brains," or "the more you beat your wife, the tastier the soup will be." The greatest insult to a male peasant was to suggest that he had become a *baba*—that he was womanly in character. Church and state reinforced these attitudes and structures at every turn, although extreme cases of brutality against women, which brought wives to court against their husbands, often resulted in support for the woman's side. But the excessive violence in these cases reminds us that inequality and physical discipline were normal and legal. Many women, divorce petitions reveal, believed that beatings were sometimes deserved.[14] Male heads of household were expected to represent their families at the communal assemblies where the most important economic and administrative decisions were made; the rare exception was when a woman was temporarily head of a household due to her husband's death or absence. Rural district courts (*volostnye sud'i*), which resolved most civil disputes among peasants, were usually led by judges chosen from among male heads of household.

A woman's place in the family and the community was not inconsequential, however. Not only would the communal and domestic economy not function without her contributions, but women found a measure of "agency" and power, historians argue, in their separate but significant role, especially as guardians of hearth and community. Wives managed the domestic economy, ran everyday life in the household, and taught their children the ways of the community. While men were working the family strips of land, women were responsible for the house, the kitchen garden, and small animals. Women made the family's clothes and engaged in a variety of crafts producing products for sale or in factory out-work, adding to the household income. During the peak time of the harvest, women would join their menfolk in the fields, though normally assigned special women's tasks. As women grew older, many exercised power outside the home: as matchmakers, midwives, or healers, and, together with other women, as enforcers of village moral codes against women judged guilty of immoral behavior or of violating communal rules. Women traditionally played particularly large roles in the religious life of their families and communities. The historian Christine Worobec has summarized all of this evidence of women's place in village life: "marriage and the responsibilities of wife, mother, and in-law that accompanied that stage of life endowed women with respect and status within the Russian peasant community." As a consequence, women "both coveted and feared marriage" for they were both "victims" and "actors" in the patriarchal world of the village. They tolerated patriarchy, even sustained it, because it gave them a measure of authority and protection, a place of value and worth. But they also understood the

177

limitations and brutalities of this traditional order.[15] Worth and subordination, marginality and importance, beatings and protection could be and were all combined and mixed.

Peasant lives and experiences were changing dramatically as peasants became more entangled with Russia's economic, social, and cultural transformations in the late nineteenth and early twentieth centuries. Schooling and self-education expanded, as did the availability of literature, magazines, and newspapers, both secular and religious, directed at common people. Only a minority of peasants were literate at the start of the new century, and women were less likely than men to have learned to read and write, but the numbers were growing. According to the 1897 census, 25 percent of male peasants and 10 percent of female peasants in European Russia could read. However, literacy was higher, and growing faster, in regions with urban or industrial centers, especially where many peasant men and women worked away from the village. In Moscow province, for example, 40 percent of male villagers and 26 percent of women were literate. The young were more literate than the old thanks to increased schooling, though schools were more common in villages near cities and boys were more likely than girls to be allowed to attend and finish. Literate culture reached beyond those who could read, of course: newspapers, magazines, and books were regularly read aloud in homes or village taverns. We cannot know for sure how this expanding print culture shaped peasants' experiences and imagination. But it certainly exposed a great many of them, men and women, to new ideas—for example, about the individual, material success, religion, science, and the meaning of being Russian—and to information about other places and times. Perhaps these encounters stimulated new thoughts about what might be possible. And perhaps, as scholars of literacy have often argued, the very act of being able to read encouraged many of them to feel a sense of self-esteem that made the ordinary deprivations, hardships, and humiliations of lower-class life more difficult to bear.[16]

Peasants were also encountering a larger world as millions took to the road to work as migrant agricultural laborers, in rural factories, and in the urban economy; to trade goods and start small businesses; to go on pilgrimages. Even a temporary migrant experience could be transformative, and not only for the migrant. The physician and writer Dmitry Zhbankov observed that peasant-workers moving between village and city had "a powerful influence on the entire life of the rural population, on its economic and social conditions, family relations, development, habits, customs, and health."[17] The most famous male peasant-worker, Semen Kanatchikov (thanks to his exceptionally influential memoir), recalled experiencing his move as a young man from his native village to Moscow, where his father brought him to work, as liberation from "the monotony of village life" and from the family's patriarchal "despotism." The bustling vitality, abundance of goods, and crowds of hurrying strangers in the city "terrified" and "delighted" him.[18]

Women experienced this mobile world in growing numbers. They were typically unmarried, widowed, or soldiers' wives, though a growing number of women left their villages to join their husbands in the city. Although some women looked to the work outside the village as a permanent escape and place of opportunity, most expected that their time away would be temporary—they left (as did most young men) with the agreement of their family heads and communities in order to benefit their kin and the village through urban work, and most returned, as planned, to marry and settle down. Still, many women found that their intentions, expectations, and attitudes were changed by this experience. Their wage contributions to the family gave them greater status or at least greater self-esteem. On the other hand, many peasants viewed a woman returned from the city as morally damaged: traditionalists said that factory life "spoiled" women such that no amount of beatings will make her as compliant as before she worked outside the home.[19] Indeed, women who spent time in the liminal space "between the fields and the city" (the title of an excellent book on the subject) often found it difficult to accept the old ways and values. Not that the new was rosy. Women had more than their fair share of humiliations as migrants: "it's hard to make it in the village," a woman working in a small tailoring shop told an activist, "but it's no easier here. There's nothing but poverty and grief wherever we are."[20] But women's experiences away, including earning their own wages, made many feel more independent and important, raising questions in their mind about how men and society treated them. Village women who had worked in the city, it was observed at the time, were "distinguished by a livelier speech, greater independence, and a more obstinate character."[21]

But even women who did not leave the village found themselves playing bigger roles in their families and communities. Married men usually left their wives behind in the village and returned infrequently. Their wives found themselves, in the words of a peasant song, "neither maiden nor widow," and burdened with additional physical labor, including in the fields. But marriage to a migrant worker had benefits, too. Migrants sent home cash, which could be used to buy goods. The wives and families of migrants were likely to eat and dress better. But the intangible changes were just as important. "In men's absence," Barbara Engel has argued, "women worked harder, but breathed more freely." Marriage to a migrant gave women "great control over their own lives," a larger voice in the village, and often a greater sense of self-worth and confidence.[22]

The physical changes in peasant life were considerable. Men and women who had been to the city, but also many who had not, began wearing urban-style clothing, which might be bought in city shops or sewn in the village on the model of pictures in magazines, along with wristwatches, cosmetics, jewelry, and new hairstyles. Clergy led the way in chastising such fashions as unchristian foppery. But peasants saw no reason why they could not be both pious and enjoy new styles and goods. Modern consumer objects found a growing presence in rural homes, including factory-made furniture and clocks. Personal photographs became increasingly popular. Even folksongs began to feature new things with new words, such as "galoshes" rather than traditional boots, or "dresses" rather than the traditional sarafan. Material changes, scholars have often shown, can both reflect and change attitudes. Historians of the Russian peasantry have seen in these objects and choices evidence of new attitudes toward the individual, public display, and success. Folksongs, again, reflected these inward changes, as peasant men and women sang more often about the value of individual feelings, the idea that men and women should choose their own partners out of attraction and love rather than leave the choice to parents, and their hopes for a freer and more prosperous life.[23]

New experiences, ideas, desires, and expectations were transforming the village world. This was a revolution in everyday lives that framed and shaped the political revolutions to come. The traditional hierarchies of power in rural communities meant that these changes provided opportunities to men more than to women: men were more likely to become literate, to leave the village for work, to have cash to purchase new things. But women's lives were changing, and when they did, the effects were even more dramatic and unsettling.

Rebellions

Historians continue to debate the reasons for peasant rebellion. Land and poverty have been at the center of this debate, not least because peasants themselves insisted they needed more land if they were to survive and improve their lives. Economists at the time, and historians since, have argued about the extent of rural poverty, whether economic conditions were improving, and whether more land would have materially improved peasant lives. Leaving aside these objective measures, most would agree that peasants felt themselves to be poor and believed that more land would help them overcome poverty. But peasants also felt that they *deserved* the land: like peasants in much of the world, they believed that land belongs by moral right to the people who work it with their own hands (even if possession was through organized peasant communities responsible for regulating its use in the best interests of all). The settlement that had abolished serfdom in the middle of the nineteenth century had left peasants with only part of the lands they worked (and often not the best lands), requiring them to pay rent or work for wages on land that was designated by the state to be the legal property of others, including non-toiling landowners, the church, and the government itself. While there were important changes in the years following—including peasant communes purchasing a great deal of the land originally deeded to nobles and evidence that aggregate peasant poverty gradually diminished—the fundamental experience of "land hunger" persisted. Whether or not the traditional peasant dream of "black repartition," when all the land would be gathered up by a loving monarch or by peasant revolution and returned to the peasantry as a whole, persisted outside the imagination of populist radicals, the realities of peasant need and popular notions of rights and justice led peasants, when opportunity arose, to demand that land be given to those who work it, or not to ask but take it.[24]

When peasants acted on these discontents and desires, they generally avoided direct confrontations with authorities, preferring anonymous, subtle, everyday forms of resistance: stealing and vandalizing landlord property (fires set in the dead of night were a favorite weapon); poaching game or cutting wood in state or private forests; home brewing and distilling (often women's work) in violation of the state liquor monopoly; avoiding recruitment into the army with feigned illness or self-mutilation; deliberately "misunderstanding" laws in ways that worked in their favor; pretending to be ignorant or stupid when in court; and similar "weapons of the weak" common to peasant resistance everywhere.[25] Less common, but more frightening to authorities, were "disturbances" (*volneniia*), which usually meant groups of peasants confronting landlords or government representatives with complaints or demands, which could become violent if the state acted violently to silence them. Disturbances usually began with collective petitions organized by the commune, often in response to some change from above that peasants believed threatened their economic lives or traditions. Indeed, until 1905, peasant disturbances tended to be local and conservative, a response to a threat to peasants' always precarious livelihood rather than a bold gamble to overturn the status quo and change their world.

Women's participation in peasant resistance and protest reveals much about women's place in the community: the differences and discriminations they faced but also the deep solidarities of identity and interest uniting men and women. Police reports about peasant disturbances in the late 1800s describe women acting alongside men in fighting efforts to confiscate land, collect unpaid taxes, or redraw boundary lines in favor of landlords. By tradition, women often stood out in front, protecting crowds with their own bodies (sometimes, for more effect, with their children in their arms or visibly pregnant) but also throwing rocks at police and soldiers and brandishing sticks, rakes, shovels, axes, and pitchforks. Sometimes women were sent ahead to confront authorities. This role for women, especially mothers, was partly tactical: women were less likely to be physically attacked than crowds of men only. But it also reflected their role as gendered symbols of community. As Engel has suggested, we see in these protests a "language of resistance," expressed with bodies, that reveal ways that peasant life "empowered" women but also limited them. What power and influence women had came from the very same customary roles that subordinated and marginalized them: their position as defenders of "family and community."[26]

The revolution of 1905 was something new.[27] Thousands of local rural uprisings occurred between 1905 and 1907. Unlike past disturbances, peasants rarely justified their actions by complaining that landlords had failed to uphold obligations or that there was some immediate threat to their livelihood. Political events in the cities—strikes, demonstrations, government concessions—raised expectations for change, encouraging peasants to take greater risks to address their needs and wants. Collective attacks on landlords' estates were the defining event. Crowds of peasants, usually after a decision by the village-wide communal assembly at which women and children were often allowed to be present, would invade estate lands, cart away stored hay and grain (for redistribution managed by the commune), seize and divide livestock and poultry, damage buildings, and destroy debt records. Peasant communities would cut firewood in state or private forests (to which many landlords had restricted peasant access in order to harvest lumber for new industrial and commercial purposes) and graze their animals on private meadows and pastures. Agricultural strikes were common in areas where large numbers of peasants worked for wages. Landlords and their families were rarely harmed physically—a reasoned restraint since that would have surely brought down even more chilling state violence against the peasant movement than occurred. But peasants did not hesitate to destroy property and buildings, often with arson. These acts, of course, had practical as well as symbolic value: if one could frighten landlords to flee from their estates, peasants could claim their lands.

Women often joined their brothers, husbands, fathers, and sons in these actions. Contemporary accounts are contradictory about the role of women: some pronounced women to be a conservative and restraining force; some judged women passive actors but "more bitter than the men"; some blamed women for "inciting" violence.[28] Historians have found that women were more likely to be involved in certain types of actions. They took an active part in seizures of hay and grain. They were frequently the first to invade forests for wood and estate orchards to pick fruit, often with the help of their children. And while women tended to

avoid arson and the destruction of property, they were regularly seen
dragging useful things home from ransacked estate houses, especially
tools, clothing, and furniture.[29] As in the past, women felt empowered to
act boldly by their traditional role as protectors of family and
community—or, at least, justified their boldness through this traditional
role. A secret report by the governor of Oryol province in 1906 described
what happened when local authorities, backed by soldiers, tried to
convince the assembled village community to return grain they had
confiscated the night before from a local estate. "The entire village,
including women and even babes in arms, was at the meeting." When
a local police official ordered the women to stand apart from the men,
"they began such a forced wailing that it was impossible to speak." After
the assembly agreed to return the grain on the following day, so as to
avoid legal action against them, the men were prepared to return to their
homes as the authorities demanded. "But the women unexpectedly
started up their earlier howling, shoved their children forward, got
down on their knees, beat themselves on the chest, and shouted:
'There is nothing to eat, but he made a fortune; we didn't steal, but as
a whole community decided to take the grain so we wouldn't die of
hunger; take, take us all, beat us, kill us and kill our children.'" The
official was impressed with their "fervor" but also found it all "learned,
insincere." The women could not be made to stop shouting until the
soldiers and police left.[30]

In looking for the motives for peasant rebellion in 1905–7, historians
usually begin with the obvious fact of economic deprivation, which
peasant actions were often explicitly aimed at correcting: inadequate
landholdings, restricted access to meadows and forests, high rents, low
wages for agricultural workers, and lack of money to buy consumer
goods, but also grievances distinct to different regions of the country
and even to individual villages. What turned these endemic discontents
into open action, however, were events outside the village, especially the
disastrous Russo-Japanese War which caused the suffering, maiming,
and death of so many young peasant men (and returning soldiers after
the war ended in late 1905 were often leaders in the most violent
actions); news of Bloody Sunday and unrest in the cities; the tsar's
promises in February and especially in October to establish national

representation and guarantee basic freedoms; and elections in 1906 to the new Duma, where male peasant representation was given a large place by a government that believed peasants were loyal to the political order. Young peasant men who had lived outside the village were often the leaders of village actions and most likely to be attracted to the All-Russian Peasant Union, a political organization established with the support of populist intellectuals during the summer of 1905.

Petitions to the government, especially during 1906 when peasants bombarded their elected representatives to the new State Duma with telegrams, petitions, and instructions, reveal something of the experiences, attitudes, and motives of peasants in the revolution. These were almost always statements from communities: written by the more literate members of a village or hired scribes, read aloud at a communal assembly, revised collectively, and approved by the gathered heads of household. Obviously, the content and wording of these texts were mediated by the influence of leaders and of ideas about what needed to be said to win the sympathy of the authorities they were writing to. Hence, petitions typically began with gratitude to the tsar for his concern about the common people, or to the Duma for its devotion to improving the life of the people. Most tried to demonstrate humility and deference in appealing for help. Particular demands were usually framed against a melodramatic narrative of peasant suffering and desperation. These were deliberate framings. As the Oryol governor noted in the report just quoted, the manner of protest was often "learned." He even doubted that protesting peasants were as hungry as they claimed, since the "harvest was decent." They were motivated, he implied, by something more than immediate necessity—an important insight.[31] Peasants often included in their petitions demands to abolish capital punishment, grant amnesty to political prisoners, provide free and universal public education to all, replace indirect taxes with an income tax, and other political reforms, indicating an awareness of the larger political environment. Indeed, these echo, often word for word, the programs of the major political parties, though these endorsements tell us little about how peasants understood these goals. Even the universal demand for "land," which was clearly the most important, had "many potential meanings," as Andrew Verner argued in his study of peasant petitions. The demand for land "served as a symbol, code-word and signifier for a whole complex of concerns that lurked out of view, just below the surface."[32]

One of these concerns was "freedom," which everyone spoke of. Quotations from a few of the many petitions to the Duma in 1906 suggest something of its meaning in the village:

Forty-five years have elapsed since we were given "Freedom," but our life has changed little for the better.... All the best land that surrounds our home village, into which our fathers and grandfathers poured their sweat and blood (indeed where we now do the same), went to the squire. We were given the land that was sandy, stony, and at a significant distance from the village.... Thus the lack of sufficient land and lack of free access to our fields forces us year after year—from the very moment "Freedom" was proclaimed—to lease the squire's land at a very high price.... Such a dependent status, with no rights whatsoever, has reduced us to poverty and ruin.[33]

The land, like air, water, and sunshine is a gift of God, and no one may dispose of it at will or exploit it. God created the world and gave human beings full control; [but] God created neither nobles nor peasants; we are all God's children... Are we peasants really only his stepsons, and the nobles his sons? This is a gross injustice. Whoever works the land should have as much of it as he and his family cultivate.

Here in our native country, we are not sure that tomorrow we will not be plundered and our property will not be burned, we are not confident that tomorrow our wives and children will not be violated by ferocious Cossacks and their commanders. We see and hear about the outrages that are committed all around us. We hear the moans of the villages that are starving in 150 districts. We hear the weeping of fathers and children who have lost their kin. Our hearts are lacerated from these moans and tears; we are in no condition to endure this any longer. Our craving for a better life, the yearning to end these groans, impel us in despair to rise up against our sworn enemy, who does not want to understand our pain.[34]

That these are *men* of the land addressing *men* of power was sometimes explicit, as here, and almost always assumed. These men were angry about the indignity of their social subordination, and justified their anger as a violation of the sacred law that all men are created equal—and I use "men" here not as a generic for "people," but as gendered in their minds. Subordination and deprivation was an insult to their masculinity as well as their humanity. These men were sure that if more communal land came into the hands of their communes, ruled by male heads of household, their economic condition would improve and they could better fulfill their roles as men. They justified this desire with another sacred law: that the land is God's, who gives it to those who will work it themselves. This argument too was gendered. Holding and working the land was the work of families not individuals; and families were properly male-led hierarchies. Indeed, as in the appeals above, peasant men were often anxious about conditions that undermined their ability to be effective breadwinners and protectors of their wives and daughters, the justification for their position in the family hierarchy.

This is not to say that most women did not agree. And not only because women "live in the same huts as their husbands," as an observer noted,[35] but because, we have seen, they identified with their communities and found an important if subordinate place there. But women could also bring a different perspective to the revolution in the village. The patterns of women's participation in collective protest—more likely to seize food and fodder and other useful things than to burn down mansions—may have reflected, as Engel has argued, women's traditional focus on defending family and community, even "a gender-related system of values that led them to refrain from some activities while plunging into others."[36] Women's activism, as in the past, was both inspired and constrained by their role in household and village. But there are signs of women thinking outside traditional values and challenging the inequalities that marked women as different and inferior. The establishment of the Duma without women's suffrage and representation provoked protests: "Before," a group of peasant women from Tver province wrote to their Duma deputy, "although men might sometimes beat us, still we resolved matters together. Now, by contrast, they say, 'You are not our comrades,' because only men can vote and be elected to the Duma. . . . Our affairs are mutual, so let them also ask us women how to resolve them." When a Duma deputy claimed that women were not interested in politics, a group of fifty-five peasant women signed a letter telling this deputy that he was "wrong to say that the peasant woman doesn't want rights. Did he ask us? We, the babas of the Voronezh district, Voronezh province, understand that we need rights and land just as men do."[37] These sorts of petitions were rare, but they are signs of change that would continue. Ideas about the natural equality and rights of "man" could apply to women too.

Experiencing War: Soldiers and Wives

The Great War brought catastrophic suffering and loss to peasant lives. Hundreds of thousands of Russian soldiers, mostly peasants, were crippled or dead within months. To cope with the incessant losses of fighting men at the front, the machinery for mobilizing soldiers unrelentingly ground away at the rural population, as did economic pressures squeezing needed resources out of people already living near subsistence. Direct evidence of peasant attitudes toward the war is limited before 1917, when their words poured forth in torrents, but it seems clear that peasants were intensely aware of the war (though rumors were a major source of information) and viewed this upheaval with a mixture of patriotism, concern about everyday survival, and suspicion of people in authority.[38] The mood of peasant recruits is telling. According to reports, their attitudes ranged from patriotic enthusiasm to opposition to the war on principle, though neither extreme was common in the early years of the war. Rather, the "typical mood" among mobilized peasants was hesitant, skeptical, and fatalistic. As the historian Allan Wildman concluded in his important study of the Russian military during the war, recruits "regarded the war as a fruitless venture of the upper classes for which they would have to pay." Inclined toward neither patriotic enthusiasm nor active dissent, the mood of peasant recruits combined hatred and fear of the German aggressors with anxiety, suspicion, and passivity before what they could not control. On occasion, recruits rioted, especially during the first mass mobilizations in July and August 1914, though these were partly sparked by a wartime alcohol ban, which interfered with the custom of recruits getting drunk on their induction day, often at village expense, or by failures to deliver promised subsidies to families when breadwinners were drafted. In a few cases, mobilized reservists on the road to dispatch points plundered local estates and tried to incite local peasants to join them. A growing number of men deserted, especially as the war dragged on, but even in the early months the War Minister acknowledged that half a million men deserted in the first year of war.[39]

The army was a man's world. Like other combatant nations, Russia used notions of masculinity to inspire men to fight.[40] This model of what it means to be a man—which would take a beating in the horrors of the war—was tied up with ideas about Russia as a nation even before the war made manliness a matter of national survival. In his study of military conscription and mobilization, Joshua Sanborn describes how the government and the military looked for every opportunity to inculcate in Russian boys of all classes the physical virtues of "health, strength, hardiness, and dexterity," and the moral virtues of courage (*muzhestvo*, a word constructed in Russian on the foundation of what is "male" or *muzhskoi*), boldness, a "hard" will, discipline, duty, and heroic self-sacrifice.[41] During the war itself, patriotic journalists lauded not only the exceptional bravery and endurance of Russian peasant fighting men, but their manly stoicism in the face even of certain injury or death.[42] This military ethos was also built on a belief that it was a man's natural duty to defend the lives and honor of their women and families. We see these ideas in many resolutions from soldiers just after the February revolution. In April 1917, for example, the men of an infantry division at the front wrote the following appeal to the Minister of War:

Back home in Russia we have our wives and children and fathers, our mothers in their old age are suffering without bread or clothing, since everything has become hard and impossible, and they write us plaintive, tearful letters here at the front. Why is it they're crying? Because they, our fathers, are old men, they cannot get a crust of bread for themselves; they are old, but the children are small, and our wives cannot cultivate the land we left behind, which at the present time is overgrown and full of weeds, desolate, and they are suffering without bread.[43]

This story was as much a calculated use of traditional ideas to legitimate their appeals as a straightforward reflection of real conditions or even their real thoughts and feelings. But the presence and power of these gendered values for thinking about men and women in war is clear.

In contrast to the image of weeping and helpless women, many peasant women participated directly in the war effort, often in jobs previously supposed to be man's work: working in industry (including traditionally male-dominated industries like metals) and transport after great numbers of men were drafted; doing much of the farm work, including heavy tasks formerly reserved for men; and directly supporting military units as cooks, supply clerks, laborers, and drivers (and sometimes nurses, though few peasant women had the training to become nurses).

Challenging traditions of women's place even more dramatically, hundreds of women enlisted in fighting units by masquerading as men: showing up at recruitment offices with their hair cut short, in men's clothing, with roughened voices, and a manly bearing. Most of these women were immediately unmasked and turned away; some succeeded in passing as men until wounded and treated; some units accepted these women even after discovering their sex. These women did not try to decouple soldiering and masculinity, but to have their adherence to the codes of masculinity accepted. The most famous example was Maria Bochkareva, a former peasant whose enlistment was eventually approved by the tsar himself, after both her mother and the army insisted that a "baba" had no place in combat. Bochkareva had no desire to upset gender norms. Her aim was to show that as an individual she deserved equal treatment because she could personally conform to the standards of being a man. Before the war, she recalled in her memoir, when she worked at a construction site (also unusual), her boss exclaimed to the men, "Look at this baba! She will have us men learning from her pretty soon. She should wear trousers." When war broke out, Maria's mother warned her that if she joined the army the men would make a prostitute of her. Indeed, the men in her regiment assumed that was her purpose in joining up, so she had to prove otherwise by fighting them off with her fists. After "many additional trials," she was "found to be a comrade, and not a woman, by the men." On the eve of their deployment to the front, her comrades even invited Bochkareva to join them on a visit to a brothel. She agreed, for this would help her "learn the soldier's life, so that I will understand his soul better." When she was authorized by the Provisional Government in the spring of 1917 to establish a "Women's Battalion of Death," the women who joined were required to crop their hair and dress and behave like men.[44]

Russia was unique in the number of women who wanted to fight and who succeeded. In addition to those who managed to enter the army in disguise, military authorities agreed in 1915, as an exception during this national crisis, to accept a limited number of petitions from women to enlist "as regular troops." In 1917, the Provisional Government established special women's battalions. As many as 6,000 women joined. They became soldiers for many reasons: patriotism, of course, but also a desire to break free of their everyday lives. Although most fighting men were opposed in principle to women in combat, journalists' accounts, aimed at stimulating patriotism at home and a fighting spirit in the army, described women soldiers as enthusiastic, disciplined, brave, and ready for sacrifice—even more so than many men. The historian Laurie Stoff has pointed to a number of reasons that Russia was unique in the number of women who wanted to serve in the military, including many of the sources of women's independence and strength within a strongly patriarchal society that we have noted: traditions of women's labor in the village; a less developed culture of domesticity and sexual puritanism; Russian cultural traditions admiring strong women, especially village traditions valuing peasant women for their strength and endurance; historical precedents of women soldiers; and economic and social changes that brought women into new roles. In 1917, the state endorsed equal rights and duties for all citizens, including women. But this radical vision may not have been the main motive behind the government encouraging the formation of women's battalions—a more important consideration was grounded in traditional gender norms: "shaming" men, with women's heroism in combat, into embracing their proper masculine duty to defend their homeland.[45]

Most peasant women experienced the war at home. But there, too, the rhetorical image of the helpless and sorrowing woman was a stereotype and exaggeration. The loss of manpower in the countryside was profound: between 1914 and 1917, nearly half of all able-bodied working-age peasant men were called to service, many never to return. In many provinces, more than 40 percent of peasant households lacked male workers by 1917. The result was a dramatic "feminization" of agricultural work. Contemporaries estimated that by 1916 women outnumbered men in farm work two to one.[46] Newspapers regularly featured articles from local correspondents describing (and usually admiring) women's readiness and ability to add to their existing labors and responsibilities much of the heavy field work on the farm that had traditionally been men's work, including plowing, mowing with a scythe, chopping firewood, and hauling manure (though correspondents noted that old men sometimes laughed mockingly at the sight of a woman with an axe in her belt or behind a plow). Near the front, local peasant women were recruited to help dig trenches and build fortifications. A liberal feminist, Elena Gal'perin-Ginzburg, one of Russia's first women jurists, in a book on peasant-women and the war published in 1916 by the League for Equal Rights for Women, quoted from press reports from the countryside: "How changed is the external appearance of the village! No men are to be seen at all. Now everywhere you see women, teenagers, and girls—working in the fields and in the threshing barns, hauling produce in carts, seated on horseback, and on the road.... Not only have women now become the head of the household but more and more of the local economy is managed by women, whose energies seem inexhaustible. A real women's kingdom (*zhenskoe tsarstvo*)." Everywhere "babas have replaced their husbands who have gone off to war: they plow and they sow and when the time comes they mow and reap and thresh," doing work that before the war was done only by men. Acting as heads of households, women represented their families in the assemblies of the peasant commune, to the point that some communal assemblies had become "almost exclusively women's assemblies."[47] Of course, these women faced considerable obstacles: not only the resistance and mockery of men, which could be ignored, but shortages of seed, the breakdown of markets and transport, the lack of agricultural equipment, and no labor for hire.[48]

Soldiers' wives, known in Russian as *soldatki* (a feminized diminutive of "soldier" or *soldat*), were a political force in the village during the war and in the revolution to come—empowered by state recognition of their special status and rights, by their numbers (in many villages, most of the married women were wives of soldiers), and by worsening material conditions that threatened the survival of their families and communities. Before the war, *soldatki* had been among the most marginalized members of the rural community—pitied as victims of fate, disdained as economic parasites who depended on the charity of relatives and of the village community until their husbands returned, and suspected of being sexually loose and dangerous as all women were traditionally presumed to be without men to control them. Their situation improved in 1912 when the government created a monthly food allowance for soldiers' wives and children. After the war broke out, the government established a special commission for "the Care of Soldiers' Families and of the Families of the Wounded and the Dead." Millions of rubles were spent on financial and food aid, supported by an empire-wide network of soldiers' aid societies that collected private donations. But the needs of such enormous numbers of wives and children, especially when prices of food and other necessities were rising rapidly, were difficult to meet.

Soldiers' wives mobilized to demand their "rights." Individually and collectively, they sent a mass of petitions and letters to government officials demanding that allowances be paid (many were late or missed); that payments be increased to match rising prices; that additional benefits be added, such as fuel, tax relief, housing; that the government prevent the village commune from taking away their land or increasing their taxes; that the government supply prisoners of war to work as agricultural laborers; and that their own men be allowed return home during harvest. The tone of their appeals could be submissive, emphasizing, in the style of traditional supplication, women's helplessness and desperation: "we peasant women . . . have been left alone as *soldatki* with small children ever since 1914 when our husbands were taken to the great All-Russian war to defend our dear Fatherland. Given our extreme poverty, we are not in a position to provide for our family" and "lack the strength to farm our land." Without help from the "most kind and gracious" (*mnogomilostivoe*, a traditional phrase in appeals to greater powers) relief committee "we will be forced to die of starvation."[49] Other appeals, by contrast, suggested not only an awareness of their legal rights (which some *soldatki* turned to the courts to enforce) but a sense of entitlement and justice, justified both by their traditional status as wives and mothers and by their sacrifice for the national struggle to defend "sacred Mother Russia."[50]

These women did not limit their efforts to words of supplication or protest. Soldiers' wives played a leading role in the "subsistence riots" that broke out in many Russian towns, variously called "hunger riots," "pogroms," and "baba riots" (*bab'i bunty*). *Soldatki* mobbed shops or market stalls where prices were judged unfairly high, suggesting an implicit moral economy of fair business practices. A typical case comes from a market town in Perm province in 1915. About 200 *soldatki* from nearby villages, in town to collect their government subsidies, began talking about high prices. The crowd began moving from shop to shop demanding that the merchants lower their prices to a level the women decided was "fair." If a merchant resisted, as most did at first, the women started dragging away sacks of flour or other food products, which usually convinced the shop owner to back down. Sometimes women did more than use threats of seizure as a way to enforce just prices: they simply took and divided the products they needed. Protests by soldiers' wives could be destructive and punitive: smashing shops and trading stalls of merchants who offended them. When police intervened, women often fought back with rakes, sticks, rocks, and fists. *Soldatki* repeatedly insisted that they were "entitled to justice." And not merely as women due protection by a patriarchal society and state, and not only as mothers, but as the wives of men fighting for their country and thus as women doing their part. Peasant wives judged the government to have failed in its responsibilities, even siding with "speculators." The typical attitude, summarized in a report by the governor of Moscow province in November 1916, was that "they are slaughtering our husbands and sons at the front, while at home they want to do us in with hunger." As Engel observed in her study of these riots, the widespread polarization of Russian society between "us" and "them" had become for soldiers' wives "a matter of life and death."[51]

Revolution in the Village: A Collective Portrait

Abstract ideas like "freedom" and "citizenship" pervaded the deluge of petitions and appeals from villages between February and October 1917. "Glory be to you, oh Lord," a peasant from Perm province wrote in a typical letter to the Soviet newspaper *Izvestiia* at the end of March, "We have lived to see the Great Joy. We have lived to see complete Freedom.... Now we are free citizens ... and we can express all our thoughts freely, and we can defend our interests for the good of the homeland and the entire people."[52] But how peasants understood freedom and citizenship—or misunderstood these and other political categories, as many contemporaries thought—has long been debated by historians.[53] Like most people, peasants fleshed out these vague notions with everything they felt they needed and desired. The result was a vision of freedom much bigger than simply the liberty to speak and act without repression. Echoing national politics, peasant communities endorsed the standard list of political demands, often with the new political vocabulary: especially "freedom of speech, assembly, unions, and strikes, and the inviolability of the person" and a representative government based on elections with "universal, direct, equal, and secret" suffrage. But few peasants stopped here. For what value could such rights have, peasants repeatedly asked, if they did not help rural communities thrive? How could freedom mean the end of "tyranny" and the coming of "joy" and "happiness" if peasants did not, for example, get the education and knowledge needed for success in a modernizing world and could not control their own local economic and social lives? Above all, how could peasants speak of freedom until all the land belonged to peasant communities to distribute "to those who labor on it"?

Land in these appeals was much more than an economic resource or a commodity. "There is no tender word the peasant would not apply to the land," declared a village committee in June. The land is "mother, benefactress. The beloved land gives us food and drink, shoes and clothing. Because our peasantry is accustomed to regarding the Land as the community's Land, the call for 'Land and Liberty' arose among us."[54] "The land we share is our mother," explained a peasant man from central Russia in August.

She feeds us; she gives us shelter; she makes us happy and lovingly warms us; from the moment of our birth until we take our final rest in eternal sleep on her maternal breast, she is constantly cherishing us with her tender embraces. And now, despite this, people are talking about selling her. . . . But selling land created by the Heavenly Creator is a barbaric absurdity. The principal error here lies in the crude and monstrous assertion that the land, which God gave to all people so that they could feed themselves, could be anyone's private property. This is just as much an act of violence as slavery.[55]

If God and Christ were assumed by most peasant believers to be male divinities—and the source of their natural right to the land, which was greater than secular laws and authorities—the land itself was a sacred female, a maternal divinity, older than Christianity (drawing on the Slavic folkloric myth of "moist mother earth"), and much closer to everyday life.

The peasant revolution was not limited to words.[56] In the spring, while waiting for the Provisional Government to pass promised land reform legislation, peasant communities, men and women, marched on local manor houses or government offices with demands to lower rents for land use and establish "fair" prices for seed, livestock, and agricultural tools. The crowds often reinforced their demands by carrying pitchforks, axes, shovels, scythes, and sometimes guns. On occasion, threats turned into attacks on manor houses and seizures of land. As the planting and mowing season began in April and May, the government continued to appeal for patience, arguing that land redistributions must wait until the election of a Constituent Assembly, which alone could legitimately redistribute property. But most peasants did not believe that they could afford economically to wait. Nor did they believe that they were morally obliged to wait, since the only just outcome was clear. So, peasant communities began to take what they believed they needed and had a right to, by tradition and now that they had become "free citizens." This stage of the peasant revolution was less destructive and more deliberate. Crowds acted, as in 1905–7, with the endorsement of village communes or of new peasant committees or assemblies at the district (volost) level. These collectives authorized land reform by direct action: seizure and cultivation of private, state, and church lands, including erasing the distinctions by pulling out boundary markers separating the lands owned by peasant communities from other lands; reintegration of lands given to peasants who had separated from the commune following the government's post-1905 effort (the Stolypin reforms) to create a class of "strong and sober" peasant landholders, who were despised as "kulaks" by most peasants; declaring all woods, meadows, and other traditional common lands open to collective peasant use. Landowners complained vehemently to local and national officials about these encroachments on the rights of private property. But the government had little effective power to stop these peasant actions. And peasants could see that the new government lacked the will or power to address their economic needs. One may argue that the Provisional Government, across the vast expanses of rural Russia, proved itself (to use a more recent term) a "failed state."

An even greater failure, with greater consequences, was the government's inability to make peasants produce and deliver sufficient supplies of grain and other food products for Russia's increasingly desperate town-dwellers, industrial workers, and soldiers. Historians have judged this "food crisis" the chief reason for the Provisional Government's collapse. As Peter Gatrell put it, "feeding Russia" during wartime was the "Achilles' heel" of both the tsarist and provisional governments (and would threaten the Bolsheviks in turn). The Provisional Government tried to resolve the situation by transforming tsarist price controls into a full-fledged state monopoly over the ownership and distribution of grain. Administrative weakness and the breakdown of transportation networks undermined this effort. But a large part of the problem was the actions of peasants, who were cultivating less land and withholding produce from the market. From the peasant's point of view, these were rational actions in the face of the economic crisis. Shortages and high prices of manu-factured goods, and low prices for grain set by the government, made it sensible for peasants to store rather than sell grain (or sell it to better paying black-market traders, which fueled inflation) or to grow only what was needed for their own family's subsistence. In addition, some of the reduction of land under the plow was a result of shortages of farm equipment, draft animals, and labor for hire. What urban elites some-times viewed as an unpatriotic peasant "grain strike" was more about survival than protest.[57]

Immediately on coming to power in October, the Bolsheviks endorsed peasant land seizures, abolished landlords' property rights, and recommended that the coming Constituent Assembly "abolish forever the right to private ownership of land" (from the "Decree on Land" approved 26 October at the Soviet congress). This was the program of the Social Revolutionary Party, Lenin acknowledged in a speech to the congress, but "what does it matter," he asked, who wrote the words since this is what peasants have carried out with their own hands and "as a democratic government we cannot ignore the resolutions of the lower strata of the people." At the same time—after all, Lenin was never one to make a "fetish," as he would say, of democracy or even of the expressed desires of the lower strata of the people, for they might lack full "consciousness"—he made it clear that Bolshevik endorsement of the peasant revolution was not their final decision. "Life is the best teacher," he commented, and peasants and the government will learn through practice what path is best—adding, slyly, that "we trust that the peasantry will make the right choice."[58] If peasants did not choose right, and the long-standing Marxist distrust of peasants as petit-bourgeois gives us reason to suspect that this "trust" was tentative at best, the Bolshevik leaders were more than ready for the new party-state to do what was necessary.

The outbreak of civil war in 1918 increased tensions between the regime and peasant communities. The embattled state needed to solve the food supply problem, which had worsened since October. Indeed, it was seriously harming the whole economy as workers left their factories almost daily to barter with local peasants for food. The Bolsheviks were sharply aware of the failings of past governments on this front. So, they launched a "battle for grain," with armed detachments of workers and communists sent into villages to compel peasants to sell grain at fixed low prices and forcibly seize "surplus" grain from "kulak grain hoarders" and "speculators." Convinced that there was a class of poor peasants ready to wage class war against a rural kulak bourgeoisie, "committees of the poor" (*kombedy*) were mobilized to aid in the seizure of grain from their more prosperous neighbors (though members of *kombedy* were often not peasant smallholders but landless laborers or village craftsmen). In 1919, this rough system of forced requisitioning was replaced by a more regularized but still compulsory grain and food levy, again enforced by armed brigades. The committees of the poor were abolished as both hated and ineffective. As the historian Lars Lih summarized the politics of this "retreat," the Bolsheviks "were anxious not to irritate the peasants any more than was absolutely necessary," while still taking more from peasants than they could afford to sacrifice.[59] In response to these many assaults, peasant communities hid grain and food supplies, further reduced production, complained to higher authorities (hoping that perhaps local authorities had overstepped what the higher-ups wanted), and periodically attacked food brigades.[60]

A revolution in village politics accompanied the revolution on the land. Historians have argued that "the peasants' concept of liberty (*volia*) meant the freedom of the village from all external powers—especially the tsarist state and the landowning gentry—and the peasants' right to rule themselves according to their own moral norms."[61] This argument is mostly true, though it underestimates the extent to which peasant communities continued to demand positive benefits from the tsarist government and then from the "worker-peasant" state. In any case, the question of *how* peasants wanted to "rule themselves" requires us to look more closely. The village commune and its assemblies remained the main authority in the village. Indeed, their power grew as tsarist-era agencies of the state in the countryside were dismantled. But every tradition was contested in these times. The rule of village patriarchs was challenged by younger men, by peasants with experience in urban or industrial work, and especially by peasant-soldiers home on leave or who had taken advantage of the political and military disorder to desert—and not only to escape the war but also so as not to miss out on their part of the revolution on the land. Village patriarchs were pressured to open communal assemblies to the entire village, allowing a voice to younger men, returned soldiers, the "rural intelligentsia" (especially school teachers), and (to a much lesser extent) women. The power of the village commune itself was challenged by a plethora of new peasant "commit-tees" and "assemblies," led mostly by these younger men. At the district (volost) level, these new bodies increasingly acted like local governments, including authorizing land seizures. After October, the revolution in rural politics deepened, but also became more disorderly—"anarchic," many said—as the Soviet government promoted new institutions of rural "democracy": village and district-level soviets; "committees of the poor" (*kombedy*); cells of the Bolshevik party; branches of the Cheka; and a few early collective farms. Again, young men dominated these new political institutions. Occasional violence against Soviet offices and representatives in the countryside, mostly around matters of land and produce, but also over such cultural matters as repression of the clergy, reminded the new regime that peasants were, at best, ambivalent allies for their vision of revolution.

The continuing flood of peasant petitions, letters, and appeals after October suggests the contradictoriness of peasant views. Many peasants seemed to view Soviet power hopefully as a forceful means to exterminate the old, crush "enemies of the people," restore the economy, stamp out crime, and bring about a "just" society without poverty, debt, ignorance, or indignity. But peasants also resented outside interference in local affairs. And when aggrieved, peasants knew how to voice resentments in words as well as in actions. As one peasant man wrote in a letter to the Bolshevik leaders in January 1918, even before peasants experienced the full force of state violence and compulsion during the civil war, the new rulers were nothing but "plunderers, rapists, destroyers, usurpers, oppressors of mother Russia" (this vocabulary is polite compared to what some wrote) entirely to blame for all the "hungry and cold," for stifling freedom, and starting a "fire" that was consuming the whole Russian nation.[62]

The Woman's Side

Where were women in the revolution in the village? Partly, they were acting in solidarity with their communities, as they often had in the past, at least in the traditional gendered roles of women and mothers defending family and community. But they were also shoved aside in a striking manner, especially given women's wartime role in the rural economy and village governance. This was a national pattern, including in cities. Although the revolution started on Women's Day, this turned out ironically to be "the only day of the revolution during which women dominated the urban space and set the political agenda," in the words of the historian Choi Chatterjee.[63] Neglect and suspicion of women by male activists, reinforced by the tendency of many women to defer to male authority, made women a rare presence in government or even in grassroots institutions in 1917. Very few women, for example, were members of factory committees or trade union leaderships, even in industries, such as textiles, where women formed a large part of the labor force.[64] Maria Kutsko, a munitions worker in Petrograd, complained

that some men in her factory insisted that, after their men returned from
the war, women would properly return to their homes and kitchens,
where they could best do their duty and "beautify the lives of men."[65] In
the villages, where traditional views of gender were even stronger, the
"democratization" of peasant politics meant the rise to power of new
men. The men who challenged the rule of the traditional village patriarchs were not challenging patriarchy itself. New rural organizations, the
various "soviets" and "committees," were as male-dominated as the old
communal assemblies. Although women in large numbers had been
doing "men's work" in the fields and representing their families in the
communal assembly when their men were away in the army, rural
politics was remasculinized by the revolution even though many men
never returned and many who did were severely disabled. Men in
the village were divided by age, experience, ideology, and economic
status, and they disagreed on many things during the revolution. But
they agreed on one thing: the place of women was not in politics.
Notwithstanding the national rhetoric about equality, in practice and
in everyday understanding, citizenship and freedom meant one thing for
women and another for men.[66]

Women may have accepted the return of male-dominated politics as
unavoidable, perhaps even natural and proper, but they were also
snubbed when they did try to participate. Few women stood as candidates for elected positions in the countryside, but the few who did were
not likely to be elected. Men generally opposed women's participation in
elections, including by keeping women ill-informed about when and
where these were taking place. Most peasant women probably shared
their community's attitudes toward gender. Many women may have
agreed, for example, with the common view that women's special
wartime role in the village economy and politics was a temporary
necessity while men were away. Even some socialist activists saw
women as proxies for their missing men: "if their husbands remain at
the front for the nation and the victory of the revolution and freedom," a
Socialist Revolutionary from Vyatka province argued in October 1917,
"then their wives in the village are obliged to fight for land, by casting
their votes for the candidates of the working people."[67] It was widely
assumed that women would step back into more traditional roles when

their men returned. Even when peasant women were politically active, they drew on traditional attitudes about gender as well as emerging new beliefs about the rights and duties of individuals as citizens regardless of gender. Most often, it seems, village women continued to feel most empowered and moved to act in public life by their identities as mothers, sisters, and daughters and by a traditional female role of self-sacrifice in defense of family and community. They were also not given much choice—not by the men rising to power in the revolution nor by the dire economic conditions that kept women preoccupied with ensuring their family's survival.

Of course, much of what I have just said is the speculation of historians. The voices of peasant women in the archive are rare. We cannot know whether or not women took part in the many gatherings that drafted and approved collective appeals—we assume they often did—or what role they may have played if they were present. Their voices heard at the time are lost to us. When reading in the archives thousands of letters and appeals, I found only a handful identified as from peasant or even working-class women. One of these was an appeal published in Maxim Gorky's *New Life* (*Novaia zhizn'*) newspaper in May 1917 from the "Smolensk Initiative Group of Women-Mothers."

Enough blood. Enough of this horrible bloodshed, which is utterly pointless for working people. Enough of sacrificing our sons to the capitalists' inflamed greed. We don't need any annexations or indemnities. Better to preserve our sons for the good of working people the world over. Let them apply all their efforts not to a fratricidal war but to the cause of peace and the brotherhood of all peoples. And let us, Russian women-mothers, be proud knowing that we were the first to extend our brotherly (*bratskaia*) hand to all mothers the world over.[68]

We know nothing about the authors, though they are presumably living in the city of Smolensk rather than in the countryside. As for any public appeal, we cannot assume that these words are an unmediated expression of the authors' deepest thoughts and feelings. But it is not unreasonable, given what we know about the history of women and gender in rural Russia, to suggest that many women, including peasant women, did find motherhood a powerful source of public legitimacy and moral authority.

Of course, as can be seen, this was a legitimacy that authorized women to make political demands as mothers defending sons. It may be that these women were using an argument they thought would be listened to. But it is likely that, like so many women, they had internalized the traditional belief that politics is men's work and women's role is to protect and promote them.

The Bolshevik party after coming to power made women's emancipation and equality a matter of policy. Decrees required equal pay for equal work, established the right for rural women to participate equally in peasant assemblies and be heads of households, and stipulated that all laws must be applied "without distinction of sex." During the civil war, the Soviet government organized military training for both girls and boys, welcomed women volunteers into the Red Army (though mostly in support roles), and briefly considered conscripting women. A special Women's Bureau (Zhenotdel) of the Communist Party was formed in 1919, tasked with raising women's consciousness of their rights and mobilizing women to participate in public life.

But these efforts to establish civic equality did not mean challenging gender norms. On the contrary, as Elizabeth Wood has shown, during the civil war women were officially lauded in familiar gendered terms: for "warming" fighting men with special "red presents" (such as hand-sewed linens and underwear), for their "deep love" for the heroes of the army, for extending special "care" and comfort to the Red Army soldier who "is defending you and your children," and for creating the right mood back home that would make men ashamed not to be fighting at the front. As Wood concludes, women were continually "characterized by certain stereotypical qualities—tender hearts, caring hands, sharp eyes." The militarized atmosphere of the civil war was yet another trend reinforcing gender traditions. The oath sworn by new recruits was in a male voice: "I, a son of the laboring people, citizen of the Soviet Republic, take on the calling of warrior in the Worker and Peasant Army." In public appeals to women, their heroism was to be helpmates to these warriors: "Proletarian Woman! The Red Army Soldier is defending you and your children. Ease his life. Organize care for him."[69]

The Bolshevik revolution and the civil war reestablished and advanced men's power in the village. As soldiers returned in large numbers in early

1918, the traditional household division of labor was fully restored as was male leadership of the community. Women stepped back from public roles. Women voted, for example, at much lower rates in elections to village soviets in 1919 than they had in local elections in 1917. Party leaders tried to offer an alternative vision of women's equal participation in public life, enabled by communal kitchens, laundries, and child care that would ease the lot of women and give them time for a larger civic role. But activists were rare sights in villages, especially rural areas distant from urban centers. And when they did appear, notably during a national campaign in 1920 to increase women's involvement in the revolution, they found peasant women suspicious of their efforts to overturn traditional ways and (rumor had it) to take their children away. "Many women among us are against organizing," a peasant woman was quoted in a local newspaper. "Women say to those who have joined that the *baba* needs to be in the home and not wander off to public meetings."[70] The backwardness of women and the need to educate and emancipate them were regular themes in letters and reports about lower-class women in the press. Beatrice Farnsworth has estimated that no more than a few thousand peasant women were "touched by the political culture of the Revolution in its first years." Of course, even modest moves by village women toward new roles and relationships, such as learning to read or sending their daughters to school, were often fiercely opposed by peasant men.[71]

In the vast archive of letters and petitions from the population that the Soviet government received during the revolution and civil war, a special collection was categorized at the time as "anti-soviet" and "anti-Bolshevik" (kept off-limits to historians until the late 1980s). Peasants wrote many of these. The authors, overwhelmingly men, directed a great deal of anger and hatred at the new Bolshevik leaders, accusing them of being traitors, German spies, Jews, and enemies of Christ, of crucifying Russia, deliberately starving the people by seizing their grain, enriching themselves at the people's expense, destroying religion, and killing only for the sake of killing.[72] Among the few texts by women is one long, handwritten letter sent in March 1918 to "gentlemen commissars." The author spoke boldly to power in terms women had often used in the past: as mothers defending community and family. It is "hunger that forces us women to write to you this letter," the author began and then embarked on a lengthy and feverish complaint. The unknown author may have been living in a town rather than a village, judging by her central concern with the lack of bread. But her sensibility can stand, in ways that are both steeped in tradition and powerfully bold, for large numbers of lower-class women in these early Soviet years.

You now enjoy the same blissful life as Nicholas Romanov did.... We working folk... don't need your lordly apartments with soft furniture and carpets, or fancy curtains and balconies, we just need bread and only bread.... This letter is being written to you by thousands of women, this is the scream of mothers hearing the crying of their children asking for bread. Woe to you if we women come to you carrying our children asking for bread and you raise your hand and shoot us.... For us mothers it is all the same what sort of government is set up. Whether it is Nicholas Romanov or Lenin and Co., we are only asking for bread, bread and nothing more.... Understand that women will do anything necessary for the sake of their children, even go to the guillotine, and take with them their hungry children. Woe to those who do not hear us.[73]

Catastrophe and Upheaval, 1920–1

Historians have found it difficult to craft a vocabulary strong enough to convey the experience of the "life in catastrophe" that overwhelmed Soviet Russia, especially rural Russia, toward the end of the civil war, as the historian Igor Narsky called it.[74] Seven years of war emaciated the country. The death or crippling of multitudes of working-aged men, the calamitous drop in the number of livestock and work horses, dire shortages of functioning farm equipment, massive grain requisitioning by force and often at gunpoint, and a ruined market were bad enough. On top of this, in 1919 and 1920, drought and extreme cold degraded rich farmlands into arid deserts and destroyed what little grain reserves remained in peasant hands. Histories of rural life in the final months of the civil war are chronicles of death and debility by hunger and disease. Many survivors took to the road as refugees, scouring the empire for food or better land, or turning to crime and highway banditry. Gangs of homeless and destitute children roamed the country. Numerous families resettled in Siberia or Russian Asia, including a great many households led by women in the place of dead or absent men. To say, as one observer of these years did, that "every revolution is a process of disintegration of the old society and culture" is true enough but banal, Narsky argued, in the face of the unprecedented disaster that befell Russia. It is even more blandly inadequate when we ask what "disintegration" meant as experience.[75] The same may be said of "crisis" and other historians' words. And detailed descriptions and statistics can be numbing. As the writer Victor Shklovsky commented in his civil war diary, "I keep describing misery and more misery. I am sick of it."[76]

Locating responsibility for this rural catastrophe is no easier. Most historians agree that the devastations caused by nature paled beside the damage inflicted by people in power, by a succession of governments and armies determined to squeeze all they could from a mobilized population. Because the Bolsheviks continued their policy of forced grain requisitioning in the face of growing evidence that a famine was likely, and even raised levies higher, their responsibility has appeared especially great. Certainly, that is how it seemed to many peasants, judging by letters sent in the summer of 1920 to family members in the Red Army.

Dear Son, Here they have flayed us from head to foot: they have taken everything: grain, cattle, fabric, butter, eggs....

Life is complete disorder, people have been tormented by these cursed communists, who chase you away from cutting wood in the Urals, take away your cattle. Almost everyone tries to go to Kazan to find bread, but the communists will knock you down and rob you on the road....

There is disorder everywhere in the countryside. Soldiers came and took away our young calf and levied very high taxes. If there is a pound of grain in the barn, they take half a pound. We don't know how we'll live. Things are very bad. And it's impossible to say anything, or they'll arrest you. They also took away our potatoes and eggs. Petya, this government is very bad.[77]

The Cheka—the security police charged with discovering and suppressing opposition to the revolution—was attentive to the "mood" of the population. By the fall of 1919, Cheka agents reported rising unease and discontent among peasants, often connected to the lack of food and excess requisitioning. By the summer of 1920, reports like this became more urgent. Agents described the mood among "the wide masses of non-proletarian and even semi-proletarian elements" to be "embittered and hostile" and warned that local "uprisings, disturbances, and rebellions are completely possible and even almost unavoidable." Even peasant communists were reported to feel "deceived." On the other hand, agents noted, lack of strong peasant organization, the absence of any unity across the country, and few modern weapons in peasant hands would make a successful uprising unlikely, especially if the government acted with sufficient force.[78]

Peasant rebellions broke out in the fall of 1920 as the White threat to the peasant revolution waned and Bolshevik grain requisitioning intensified. Dozens of major uprisings, often lasting for months, occurred across the former empire, from the Ukrainian steppe into western Siberia, from the central agricultural provinces into the Caucasus.[79] These often began as localized attacks on brigades trying to collect grain levies, escalating when government forces arrived to suppress the disturbances, and expanding as other villages responded to calls to join the fight. In many areas, peasant communities established new soviets and militias without communists. Many uprisings benefitted from leadership by experienced political activists, ranging from anarchists to Socialist Revolutionaries (typically Left SRs) to disillusioned communists. Some upheavals began as mutinies among peasant soldiers in the Red Army or were started by bands of deserters from both the White and Red armies. In a number of areas, peasants were able to occupy towns and resist military forces sent to suppress them. Some of these peasant armies had earlier taken shape in 1918–19 behind the lines of the main battles between Reds and Whites. Often dubbed "Green" armies, these were independent peasant forces determined to defend their understanding of the revolution against anyone who threatened rural autonomy and local peasant power—which usually meant first against the Whites (in alliance with the Red Army when necessary) and then against the Red victors.

Many rebel leaders had once been associated with Soviet power. The leader of the uprising in Tambov province, Alexander Antonov, was a member of the Left-SR party who had served as a local Soviet police official. Nestor Makhno, a leader of the movement in Ukraine, had once attached his independent anti-White army to the Red Army. Alexander Sapozhkov, the peasant leader of a large rebel army in the Volga region, had served in important posts in both the Red Army and the regional soviet administration. While leaders like these brought political and military experience, the rebellions were rooted in village structures of organization, especially communal assemblies, which debated and endorsed most actions. Fighters were mostly local peasants armed with axes and pitchforks until they could seize guns. The Communist leadership and press, and later Soviet historians, classified these peasant rebels as "bandits," a term often used to dismiss acts of violent dissent. Their sweeping use of the term does not mean that banditry was not part of this history—and not only Robin-Hood-style "social banditry" on behalf of the poor, but also bands of brigands and criminals robbing and killing for their own interests, though often driven to this by desperate economic conditions. The distinction between rebels and criminals is too simple a dichotomy given the realities of the day. Peasant anger could take many forms.

When peasant rebels voiced motives and goals, we see patterns across the variety of movements. The influence of the Socialist Revolutionary party, both as legacy from the past and involvement of activists in the present, was one linking element. Political programs by organizations like the "Union of the Laboring Peasantry" during the Tambov uprising in late 1920 clearly echoed SR arguments and vocabulary when calling for armed partisan struggle against the "hated" regime that had "brought the country to poverty, ruin, and shame," and especially in their positive program: "political equality for all citizens, not divided by class"; new elections to a Constituent Assembly that would exclude deputies who "do not carry out the will of the people" (*volia naroda*); freedom of speech, conscience, press, unions, and assembly; socialization of all the land, as decreed by the former Constituent Assembly; nationalization of large-scale industry, but also freedom for small capital and artisanal production; price controls for manufactured products; consumer co-operatives for essential produce; workers' control in industry; free education; and self-determination for peoples of the former Russian empire.[80] Sapozhkov's "Army of Truth" (Armiia "Pravda") issued proclamations against "false-communists" and "commissars" for abandoning "the poor, insulted, and oppressed peasantry and working population," and blamed this on the influence of "former bourgeois, landlords, generals, police, and other similar bastards, who have attached themselves like leeches to the body of the Russian people and begun mercilessly to suck its blood."[81] The slogans of peasant rebellions were often variations on the theme of "Soviet Power without Communists," sometimes elaborated into colorful (and confused) versions like "Long Live the Bolsheviks! Death to the Communists!" Peasant rebels insisted they were for "Soviet power," which had endorsed the peasant's land revolution and popular power, but against the "commissarocracy" of "Communist usurpers" who seized grain, interfered with local peasant self-governance, constricted political freedom, and brought the country to ruin. In the words of one of many songs recorded among insurgent peasants: "They rob the town and burn the village / And beat both young and old. / No mercy shown for age or sex / Or for the altars of the Lord. / They brought instead of freedom / Terror, slavery, and oppression. / The whole tormented people / Are waiting with bated breath. / The fateful hour has struck. / A thunder is heard across Russia: / To arms, fellows / We die for freedom."[82]

Actions also revealed goals and sentiments. The value of local autonomy was expressed in peasant violence against the government's power locally: expelling and killing officials, destroying government buildings, and cutting lines of communication. Violence also expressed a desire for vengeance and punishment. Crowds not only attacked and burned offices, police stations, courts, and schools, but targeted individuals with often furious brutality. Unlike the restrained physical treatment of landlords during 1917, Communists were treated as vermin or devils to exterminate. Orlando Figes has summarized the carnage: "Thousands of Bolsheviks were brutally murdered. Many were the victims of gruesome (and symbolic) tortures: ears, tongues and eyes were cut out; limbs, heads and genitals were cut off; stomachs were sliced open and stuffed with wheat; crosses were branded on foreheads and torsos; Communists were nailed to trees, burned alive, drowned under ice, buried up to their necks and eaten by dogs or rats, while crowds of peasants watched and shouted."[83] Collective violence could be quite celebratory, a sort of bloody and fiery festival of liberty: when peasant armies took over local towns they were often accompanied by singing (and sometimes music from bands or even hand-cranked gramophones), drinking, colorful banners and ribbons, and constant shouting. Peasant anger took many forms.

Women are scarcely mentioned in the histories of these rebellions, not least because they were marginalized in the rising of men and the atmosphere of violent masculinity. But women were there. When local resistance was the work of communities, women were often part of the crowd, sometimes, by old tradition, with babies in their arms. A local government official in Tambov complained that insurgent "peasants let children and women go ahead of them in order to advance under their cover against [requisitioning] detachments."[84] When resistance became war by partisan armies, women helped to deliver food and information, scouted enemy territories, and sometimes, though rarely, were arrested or killed in action. More often in these documents, peasant women are victims of the communists: raped, whipped with lashes for their association with "bandits," held as "hostages" to put pressure on male peasants, and sometimes executed.[85] When women are mentioned in rebel statements, they are most likely to appear as loved ones to be defended or survivors who would remember a fighter's sacrificial courage, as in a poem aimed at mobilizing "brother-fighters" by the rebel leader Antonov himself: "Your father, mother, brother, wife, children, and sister are left behind, / Your descendants will long remember and honor you / Will exalt you with honor and glory / When they begin to live victorious."[86] This was a man's revolution.

Communist propaganda—at the time a term lacking the pejorative connotations it has now, but meaning communications aimed at deepening people's knowledge and raising their consciousness about big questions of life and history—insisted that gender equality was a major goal of the revolution. However, in the face of crises that threatened the very survival of Bolshevik power, the practical work of advancing women became a less pressing priority. Worse, the rising tide of propaganda produced by the regime tended to reinforce traditional ideas about gender.[87] Calls to support the Red Army, we have seen, portrayed men as masculine heroes and women as helping with love, tenderness, care, and support. Political posters tended to depict the revolution in masculine form. There was a brief moment when the revolution was visualized as a woman, adapting imagery from European and American revolutionary traditions mixed with religious imagery: as in the giant bas-relief by Sergei Konenkov mounted in 1918 on the Kremlin wall in Moscow, facing Red Square, representing the revolution (the word, in Russian, is feminine) as an enormous female figure with wings, dressed in classical gown, with one breast bared, holding a palm frond (traditional symbol of righteousness, victory, martyrdom, and resurrection), standing upon the crushed symbols of violence and repression, the sun rising at her back.[88] But after the civil war began, the dominant symbol of the cause became the male worker, usually a blacksmith—archaic in relation to actual industry but allegorically expressive and widely understandable as a symbol of the strong and masculine worker forging a new world.[89] When women entered this picture at all, they were usually auxiliaries—as in the 1920 poster (Figure 6) of the woman as blacksmith's helper (a job no women actually held, so entirely metaphoric).[90]

In a very widely distributed poster of 1920, "What the October Revolution Gave the Woman Worker and the Peasant Women" (Figure 7) the revolution is again personified as a woman, and not a winged angel-like abstraction but a strong woman of work, perhaps even a blacksmith herself—for she is wearing a blacksmith's apron and holds a symbolic hammer. But she is not here to work. She is the revolution as maternal benefactress. Dressed in symbolic red, standing on a rock labeled "the land to the peasant and the factories to the worker," she shows women what they have been "given." With an extended arm, her palm turned softly and generously upward, she gestures toward a sunlit utopian palace where the Soviet of Workers' and Peasants' Deputies houses a maternity home, a preschool, a school for adults, a library, a dining hall, and a working-woman's club. On the lower left we see the women who will benefit from these institutions: mothers in dresses and kerchiefs with their children in tow.

Lurking behind these sunny images, however one might worry about their gendered conventions and inequalities, is a darker image of the woman as danger to the revolution, as symbol of backwardness and counter-revolution. The peasant *baba*—visually signified by headscarf, Russian blouse, and aproned skirt, perhaps with a child at her side—remained a

Figure 6. Nikolai Kogout, "With weapons we defeated the enemy, with labor we will win bread. Everyone to work, comrades." Poster, 1920. Public domain. Courtesy of Victoria Bonnell.

Figure 7. "What the October Revolution Gave the Woman Worker and the Peasant Woman." Poster, 1920. Public domain. Courtesy of Victoria Bonnell.

figure of anxiety for many urban revolutionaries. Consider this image from 1920, the famous poster-cartoon (Figure 8) by Mikhail Cheremnykh and Vladimir Mayakovsky of the "baba who sells bagels in the bazaar." Produced by the Russian Telegraph Agency (ROSTA) to be displayed in public windows, these cartoons told instructive stories with simple pictures and captions. In this one, a Red Army soldier off to the front in Poland asks the "baba" in the marketplace for a free bagel. She refuses, shrieking at him, "What the hell is the Republic to me?" In other frames we learn that her ignorant selfishness helps the "ferocious" Poles crush the "skinny" men of the Red Army. But she pays a price: when the Polish army occupies her town, a Polish officer comes across this "stupid baba" in the marketplace and devours not only her entire stock of bagels but the woman herself.[91]

Figure 8. Vladimir Mayakovsky and Mikhail Cheremnykh, ROSTA Window No. 241, 1920. Public domain.

In this increasingly masculinized revolution in a still patriarchal culture and society, the image of the ignorant baba resonated with many Russians, including socialists and feminists hoping to transform society and the culture. As did positive images of women as sources of nurture, support, tenderness, and care. But these were not settled questions, by any means. And there would be fights ahead, as there had been in the past, to promote women as human equals: "beautifying life," as the factory worker Maria Kutsko put it in June 1917, turning a cliché about women on its head, "not only at home by the stove" but in "working hand in hand" with men in the factories and in the world to "improve our common working lives, to make this life beautiful, pure, and bright for ourselves, for our children, and for the whole working class. This, it seems to me, is the real beauty and meaning of life."[92]

Notes

1. Cathy A. Frierson, *Peasant Icons: Representations of Rural People in Late Nineteenth-Century Russia* (Oxford, 1993).
2. Mark D. Steinberg and Vladimir M. Khrustalev, *The Fall of the Romanovs: Political Dreams and Personal Struggles in a Time of Revolution* (New Haven, 1995), 16–23 (the quotations are from Nicholas II).
3. *Statisticheskii ezhegodnik Rossii, 1914* (Petrograd, 1915), 1.
4. Examples in English include Ben Eklof, *Russian Peasant Schools: Officialdom, Village Culture, and Popular Pedagogy, 1861–1914* (Berkeley, CA, 1986); Ben Eklof and Stephen Frank (eds), *The World of the Russian Peasant: Post-Emancipation Culture and Society* (Boston, 1990); Esther Kingston-Mann and Timothy Mixter (eds), *Peasant Economy, Culture, and Politics of European Russia, 1800–1921* (Princeton, 1991); Christine Worobec, *Peasant Russia: Family and Community in the Post-Emancipation Period* (Princeton, 1991); Stephen Frank and Mark Steinberg (eds), *Cultures in Flux: Lower Class Values, Practices and Resistance in Late Imperial Russia* (Princeton, 1994), 34–53; Jeffrey Burds, *Peasant Dreams and Market Politics: Labor Migration and the Russian Village, 1861–1905* (Pittsburgh, PA, 1998); Stephen Frank, *Crime, Cultural Conflict, and Justice in Rural Russia, 1856–1914* (Berkeley, CA, 1999); David Moon, *The Russian Peasantry, 1600–1930: The World the Peasants Made* (London, 1999); Boris Mironov (with Ben Eklof), *The Social History of Imperial Russia, 1700–1917* (Boulder, CO, 2000); Chris Chulos,

Converging Worlds: Religion and Community in Peasant Russia, 1861–1917 (DeKalb, IL, 2003); Jane Burbank, *Russian Peasants Go to Court: Legal Culture in the Countryside, 1905–1917* (Bloomington, IN, 2004); Corinne Gaudin, *Ruling Peasants: Village and State in Late Imperial Russia* (DeKalb, IL, 2007); S. A. Smith, "'Moral Economy' and Peasant Revolution in Russia, 1861–1918," *Revolutionary Russia*, 24/2 (December 2011): 143–71; Christine D. Worobec, "Russian Peasant Women's Culture: Three Voices," in Wendy Rosslyn and Alessandra Tosi (eds), *Women in Nineteenth-Century Russia: Lives and Culture* (Cambridge, 2012), esp. 43–4.

5. For examples in translation, see Olga T. Yokoyama, *Russian Peasant Letters: Life and Times of a Nineteenth-Century Family* (Wiesbaden, 2010).

6. The most famous, especially in translation, is by Semen Kanatchikov. See Reginald Zelnik (ed.), *A Radical Worker in Tsarist Russia: The Autobiography of Semen Ivanovich Kanatchikov* (Stanford, CA, 1986).

7. Notably, Barbara Alpern Engel and Anastasia Posadskaya-Venderbeck (eds), *A Revolution of their own: Voices of Women in Soviet History* (Boulder, CO, 1998).

8. See especially Joan Wallach Scott, *Gender and the Politics of History* (New York, 1988); Barbara Alpern Engel, *Women in Russia, 1700–2000* (Cambridge, 2004), introduction.

9. Vl. B., "O derevenskikh prazdnikakh," *Novoe vremia*, 30 April 1903, 4. See also Stephen Frank, "Confronting the Domestic Other: Rural Popular Culture and its Enemies in Fin-de-Siècle Russia," in Frank and Steinberg, *Cultures in Flux*, 74–107; Frierson, *Peasant Icons*, chs. 6–7.

10. Mariia Ancharova, "Zhenshchiny i uchreditel'noe sobranie," *Zhenskoe delo*, 9 (1 May 1917), 1.

11. A. U. "O krest'ianakh i o zemle," *Rabotnitsa*, 5 (14 June 1917), 3.

12. Frierson, *Peasant Icons*, ch. 8.

13. In addition to the works already cited in this chapter, see David A. J. Macey, *Government and Peasant in Russia, 1861–1906* (DeKalb, IL, 1987); Roger Bartlett (ed.), *Land Commune and Peasant Community in Russia* (London, 1990); Judith Pallot, *Land Reform in Russia, 1906–1917: Peasant Responses to Stolypin's Project of Rural Transformation* (Oxford, 1999); David Kerans, *Mind and Labor on the Farm in Black-Earth Russia, 1861–1914* (Budapest, 2001).

14. Worobec, *Peasant Russia*; Rose Glickman, *Russian Factory Women: Workplace and Society* (Berkeley, CA, 1984), ch. 2; Beatrice Farnsworth and Lynn Viola (eds), *Russian Peasant Women* (New York, 1992); Barbara Alpern Engel, *Between Fields and the City: Women, Work, and Family in Russia,*

1861–1914 (Cambridge, 1995), ch. 1; Engel, *Breaking the Ties that Bound; The Politics of Marital Strife in Late Imperial Russia* (Ithaca, NY, 2011), esp. ch. 4.

15. Christine Worobec, "Victims or Actors? Russian Peasant Women and Patriarchy," in Kingston-Mann and Mixter, *Peasant Economy, Culture, and Politics*, 177–206.

16. On literacy, schooling, and reading, see Jeffrey Brooks, *When Russia Learned to Read: Literacy and Popular Culture, 1861–1917* (Princeton, 1985), ch. 1; Eklof, *Russian Peasant Schools*; A. G. Rashin, *Naselenie Rossii za 100 let (1811–1913): Statisticheskii ocherk* (Moscow, 1956); *Pervaia vseobshchaia perepis' naseleniia Rossiiskoi Imperii 1897 g.*, xxiv: Moscow province (St Petersburg, 1905); *Chislennost' i sostav rabochikh v Rossii na osnovanii dannykh pervoi vseobshchei perepisi naseleniia Rossiiskoi Imperii 1897 g.* (St Petersburg, 1906).

17. Quoted from an essay by Zhbankov in the doctor's journal *Vrach* (1895) by Jeffrey Burds, "The Social Control of Peasant Labor in Russia," in Kingston-Mann and Mixter., *Peasant Economy, Culture, and Politics*, 55.

18. Zelnik (ed.), *A Radical Worker in Tsarist Russia*, 1–8.

19. Engel, *Between Fields and the City*, 117–25.

20. E. A. Oliunina, "The Tailoring Trade in Moscow and the Villages of Moscow and Riazan Provinces: Material on the History of the Domestic Industry in Russia," in Victoria Bonnell (ed.), *The Russian Worker: Life and Labor under the Tsarist Regime* (Berkeley, CA, 1983), 172.

21. Quoted by Engel, *Between Fields and the City*, 82.

22. Ibid. 41–53.

23. In addition to sources cited so far in this chapter, see Robert Rothstein, "Death of the Folk Song?," in Frank and Steinberg, *Cultures in Flux*, 108–20; Eklof, *Russian Peasant Schools*; Jeffrey Burds, *Peasant Dreams*; Jane Burbank, *Russian Peasants Go to Court*.

24. For an overview of peasant resistance and protest, especially before 1905, see Moon, *Russian Peasantry*, ch. 7.

25. The phrase is from James C. Scott, *Weapons of the Weak: Everyday Forms of Peasant Resistance* (New Haven, 1985).

26. Barbara Alpern Engel, "Women, Men, and Languages of Peasant Resistance, 1870–1907," in Frank and Steinberg, *Cultures in Flux*, 34, 37–43; Robin Bisha, Jehanne Gheith, Christine Holden, and William Wagner (eds), *Russian Women, 1698–1917: Experience and Expression: An Anthology of Sources* (Bloomington, IN, 2002), 339–43.

27. The following draws especially on Abraham Ascher, *The Revolution of 1905*, i. *Russia in Disarray* (Stanford, CA, 1988), 161–4; ii. *Authority Restored* (Stanford, CA, 1992), 111–28; Maureen Perrie, "The Russian Peasant Movement in 1905–7," in Eklof and Frank, *World of the Russian Peasant*, 193–218. For a recent study, see Burton Richard Miller, *Rural Unrest during the First Russian Revolution: Kursk Province, 1905–1906* (Budapest, 2013).

28. *Agrarnoe dvizhenie v Rossii v 1905–1906 gg.* (St Petersburg, 1908), quoted by Engel, "Women, Men, and Languages of Peasant Resistance," 45n.; Perrie, "Russian Peasant Movement," 208.

29. Engel, "Women, Men, and Languages of Peasant Resistance," 44–50; Perrie, "Russian Peasant Movement," 208.

30. "Secret Report of 5 August 1906 of the Oryol Governor to the Department of Police," *1905: Materialy i dokumenty: Agrarnoe dvizhenie v 1905–1907 gg.*, i. 1st edn. S. Dubrovskii and B. Grave (Moscow, 1925), 216–18, tr. Christine Worobec in Bisha et al., *Russian Women, 1698–1917*, 343–5.

31. Ibid. 344.

32. Andrew Verner, "Discursive Strategies in the 1905 Revolution: Peasant Petitions from Vladimir Province," *Russian Review*, 54/1 (January 1995): 65–90 (quotations pp. 69, 88); Abraham Ascher, *The Revolution of 1905*, ii. 119–22; Gregory Freeze, *From Supplication to Revolution: A Documentary Social History of Imperial Russia* (Oxford, 1988), 274–85.

33. Quoted Freeze, *From Supplication to Revolution*, 281–2.

34. Quoted Ascher, *The Revolution of 1905*, ii. 120.

35. Quoted in Perrie, "Russian Peasant Movement," 208.

36. Engel, "Women, Men, and Languages of Peasant Resistance," 44–50 (quote p. 45).

37. Quoted ibid. 50–1.

38. e.g. Corinne Gaudin, "Rural Echoes of World War I: War Talk in the Russian Village," *Jahrbücher für Geschichte Osteuropas*, NS 56/3 (2008), 391–414; Mark Baker, "Rampaging Soldatki, Cowering Police, Bazaar Riots and Moral Economy: The Social Impact of the Great War in Kharkiv Province," *Canadian-American Slavic Studies*, 35/2–3 (2001), 137–55.

39. Allan Wildman, *The End of the Russian Imperial Army*, i. *The Old Army and the Soldiers' Revolt (March–April 1917)* (Princeton, 1980), ch. 3 (quotation pp. 77–8); Joshua A. Sanborn, *Drafting the Russian Nation: Military Conscription, Total War, and Mass Politics, 1905–1925* (DeKalb, IL, 2003), ch. 1.

40. Karen Petrone, *The Great War in Russian Memory* (Bloomington, IN, 2011), ch. 3.

41. Sanborn, *Drafting the Russian Nation*, 132–46.
42. Petrone, *The Great War*, 82–5.
43. Letter to the Minister of War from soldiers of the 64th Infantry Division at the front, 13 April 1917, RGVIA, f. 2003/c, op. 2, d. 118, ll. 251–550b., in Steinberg, *Voices of Revolution*, 118.
44. Maria Botchkareva (as set down by Isaac Don Levine) *Yashka: My Life as a Peasant, Officer, and Exile* (New York, 1919), quotations on pp. 28, 80, 81–2; Bessie Beatty, *The Red Heart of Russia* (New York, 1918), ch. 5.
45. Sanborn, *Drafting the Russian Nation*, 146–53; Melissa Stockdale, "'My Death for the Motherland is Happiness': Women, Patriotism, and Soldiering in Russia's Great War, 1914–1917," *American Historical Review*, 109/1 (February 2004), 78–116; Laurie S. Stoff, *They Fought for the Motherland: Russia's Women Soldiers in World War I and the Revolution* (Lawrence, KS, 2006).
46. Peter Gatrell, *Russia's First World War: A Social and Economic History* (Harlow, 2005), 156.
47. Quoted Elena Gal'perin, *Zhenshchina-krest'ianka v nyneshnei voine i reforma volostnogo samoupravleniia* (Moscow, 1916), 2, 9.
48. Alfred Meyer, "The Impact of World War I on Russian Women's Lives," in Barbara Clements, Barbara Engel, and Christine Worobec (eds), *Russian Women: Accommodation, Resistance, Transformation* (Berkeley, CA, 1991), 213–15; Aaron B. Retish, *Russia's Peasants in Revolution and Civil War: Citizenship, Identity, and the Creation of the Soviet State, 1914–1922* (Cambridge, 2008), 45–9; Engel, *Women in Russia*, 128–33; Gal'perin, *Zhenshchina-krest'ianka*, esp. 1–11.
49. Quoted in Emily E. Pyle, "Peasant Strategies for Obtaining State Aid: A Study of Petitions during World War I," *Russian History*, 24/1–2 (Spring–Summer 1997), 56–7.
50. Beatrice Farnsworth, "The Soldatka: Folklore and the Court Record," *Slavic Review* 49/1 (Spring 1990): 58–73; Barbara Alpern Engel, "Not by Bread Alone: Subsistence Riots in Russia during World War I," *Journal of Modern History*, 69/4 (December 1997), 696–721 (esp. 708–10); Emily E. Pyle, "Peasant Strategies for Obtaining State Aid: A Study of Petitions during World War I," *Russian History*, 24/1–2 (Spring–Summer 1997), 56–7 (quotation); Baker, "Rampaging Soldatki," 142–9; Sarah Badcock, *Politics and the People in Revolutionary Russia: A Provincial History* (Cambridge, 2007), 164–80; Retish, *Russia's Peasants*, 49–51, 107–8, 155–6; Gaudin, "Rural Echoes of World War I," 413.

51. Engel, "Not by Bread Alone," 696–721 (quotations pp. 712, 717). See also Choi Chatterjee, *Celebrating Women: Gender, Festival, and Bolshevik Ideology, 1910–1939* (Pittsburgh, PA, 2002), 46.

52. Letter to *Izvestiia* from the peasant Nikolai Burakov, Perm province, 30 March 1917, GARF, f. 1244, op. 2, d. 5, l. 3–30b., in *Steinberg, Voices of Revolution,* 128–9.

53. In addition to the studies listed in n.56, see Orlando Figes and Boris Kolonitskii, *Interpreting the Russian Revolution: The Language and Symbols of 1917* (New Haven and London, 1999), ch. 5 ("The Language of Revolution in the Village").

54. "Protocol of a meeting of the Sadki village committee," 8 June 1917, GARF, f. 6978, op. 1, d. 244, ll. 50–500b., in *Steinberg, Voices of Revolution,* 142–3.

55. "Man and the Land," letter-essay by Semen Martynov, a peasant from Oryol province, August 1917, GARF, f. 1778, op. 1, d. 234, ll. 88–89ob., in *Steinberg, Voices of Revolution,* 242–5.

56. The major studies of the peasant revolution from 1917 through 1921 are Donald Raleigh, *Revolution on the Volga: 1917 in Saratov* (Ithaca, NY, 1986) and *Experiencing Russia's Civil War: Politics, Society, and Revolutionary Culture in Saratov, 1917–1922* (Princeton, 2002); Orlando Figes, *Peasant Russia, Civil War: The Volga Countryside in Revolution, 1917–1921* (Oxford, 1989); Retish, *Russia's Peasants;* and Badcock, *Politics and the People.*

57. Lars Lih, *Bread and Authority in Russia, 1914–1921* (Berkeley, CA, 1990), chs. 3–5; Gatrell, *Russia's First World War,* ch. 7; Retish, *Russia's Peasants,* 98–105; Badcock, *Politics and the People,* ch. 8.

58. James Bunyan and H. H. Fisher (eds), *The Bolshevik Revolution, 1917–1918: Documents and Materials* (Stanford, CA, 1961; 1st edn 1934), 128–32.

59. Lih, *Bread and Authority,* 172.

60. On the Bolshevik procurement campaigns, see especially Figes, *Peasant Russia, Civil War,* 249–67; Lih, *Bread and Authority,* chs. 6–7; Raleigh, *Experiencing Russia's Civil War,* 301–20; Retish, *Russia's Peasants,* 164–75.

61. Figes, "The Peasantry," 546. See also Orlando Figes, *A People's Tragedy: The Russian Revolution, 1891–1924* (Harmondsworth, 1996), 98–101.

62. "Letter to the Bolshevik leaders from a peasant, Oryol province, 10 January 1918," GARF, f. 1235, op. 140, d. 8, ll. 154–155ob, in Steinberg, *Voices of Revolution,* 302–3.

63. Chatterjee, *Celebrating Women,* 58.

64. Diane P. Koenker and William G. Rosenberg, *Strikes and Revolution in Russia, 1917* (Princeton, 1989), 314–16.

65. Letter from Maria Kutsko, a worker at the Petrograd Munitions Factory, *Rabotnitsa,* 25 June 1917, 14.

66. Badcock, *Politics and the People,* 105–8, 168; Retish, *Russia's Peasants,* 47–54, 117, 122–3, 128. For the larger context of the persistence of gender structures as women's role changed during wartime, see Margaret Randolph Higonnet, Jane Jenson, Sonya Michel, and Margaret Collins Weitz (eds), *Behind the Lines: Gender and the Two World Wars* (New Haven, 1987).

67. *Narodnoe delo,* 29 October 1917, 3, quoted in Retish, *Russia's Peasants,* 122.

68. "To All Russian Women-Mothers" from the Smolensk Initiative Group of Women-Mothers, *Novaia zhizn',* 5/18 May 1917, 4, in Steinberg, *Voices of Revolution,* 98.

69. Elizabeth A. Wood, *The Baba and the Comrade: Gender and Politics in Revolutionary Russia* (Bloomington, IN, 1997), 49–67; Engel, *Women in Russia,* 140–6; *Sobraniia uzakonenii i rasporiazhenii rabochego i krest'ianskogo pravitel'stva,* no. 33, 27 (14) April 1918, no. 446 (the oath).

70. *Viatskaia zhizn',* 13 May 1920, 3, quoted in Retish, *Russia's Peasants,* 227. See Figes, *Peasant Russia,* 206–8; Retish, *Russia's Peasants,* 203, 227–8, 263.

71. Beatrice Farnsworth, "Village Women Experience the Revolution," in Farnsworth and Viola, *Russian Peasant Women,* 145–60.

72. GARF, f. 1235, op. 140 (formerly *sektretnyi chast'*).

73. GARF, f. 1235, op. 140, d. 10, l. 158–1590b.

74. Igor' Narskii, *Zhizn' v katastrofe: Budni naseleniia Urala v 1917–1922 gg.* (Moscow, 2001), esp. 261–306. See also Figes, *Peasant Russia,* 267–73; Raleigh, *Experiencing Russia's Civil War,* ch. 6; Retish, *Russia's Peasants,* 239–53.

75. Narskii, *Zhizn' v katastrofe,* 122 (responding to a line by Nikolai Berdiaev).

76. Viktor Shklovsky, *A Sentimental Journey: Memoirs 1917–1922* (Ithaca, NY, 1970), 113.

77. Peasant letters from August 1920, quoted from archive sources in Narskii, *Zhizn' v katastrofe,* 281.

78. Narskii, *Zhizn' v katastrofe,* 306–13. This evidence concerns the Ural region, the focus of Narskii's research, though would surely apply elsewhere.

79. The following discussion is based especially on Figes, *Peasant Russia,* ch. 7; Figes, *A People's Tragedy,* 753–8; Raleigh, *Experiencing Russia's Civil War,* 382–7; Narskii, *Zhizn' v katastrofe,* 313–20; Vladimir M. Brovkin, *Behind the Front Lines of the Civil War: Political Parties and Social Movements in Russia, 1918–1922* (Princeton, 1994), chs. 9–11; *"Antonovshchina":*

Krest'ianskoe vosstanie v Tambovskoi oblasti v 1920–1921 gg.: Dokumenty, materialy, vospominaniia (Tambov, 2007).

80. "Programma Soiuza trudovogo krest'ianstvo," in *"Antonovshchina,"* 223–4.

81. Iu. Iu. Anshakova, "Armiia 'Pravdy' Nachdiva Sapozhkova," *Izvestiia Samarskogo nauchnogo tsentra Rossiiskoi akademii nauk*, 8/3 (2006), esp. 777.

82. RGVA, f. 235, op. 1, d. 29, ll. 72–72ob, in *"Antonovshchina,"* appendix 3.

83. Figes, *People's Tragedy*, 757, and *Peasant Russia*, 346.

84. *"Antonovshchina,"* 111.

85. Ibid. 16–18, 111, 127, 135, 138, 190, 346–7, 379, 380. See also scattered references to women's involvement in Erik Landis, *Bandits and Partisans: The Antonov Movement in the Russian Civil War* (Pittsburgh, PA, 2008), e.g. 135–6.

86. RGVA, f. 9., op. 28, d. 661, ll. 42–42ob., *"Antonovshchina,"* appendix 2.

87. Richard Stites, *The Women's Liberation Movement in Russia: Feminism, Nihilism, and Bolshevism, 1860–1920* (Princeton, 1978), 317–28; Victoria E. Bonnell, *Iconography of Power: Soviet Political Posters under Lenin and Stalin* (Berkeley, CA, 1997), chs. 1–2. Wood, *The Baba and the Comrade*, chs. 2–4; Engel, *Women in Russia*, 139–40; Figes and Kolonitsky, *Interpreting the Russian Revolution*, 110.

88. See Mikhail Guerman, *Art of the October Revolution* (Leningrad, 1979), illustrations pp. 179, 180, 182, 282.

89. Bonnell, *Iconography of Power*, 23–4.

90. Nikolai Kogout, "With weapons we defeated the enemy, with labor we will win bread. Everyone to work, comrades" (1920). See Bonnell, *Iconography of Power*, 23, 75–6.

91. ROSTA window #241 (1920). For these and other civil war era posters of peasant and worker women (along with a great many more images of heroic men), see Guerman, *Art of the October Revolution*, illustrations pp. 41–2, 44, 51, 64, 75 (a 1926 poster misdated 1920), 82, 84, 98; and Bonnell, *Iconography of Power*, figures 1.1, 1.4, 2.9, 2.10, 2.13–14, plate 2.

92. Letter from Maria Kutsko, a worker at the Petrograd Munitions Factory, *Rabotnitsa*, 25 June 1917, 14.

CHAPTER 7
OVERCOMING EMPIRE

When Emperor Nicholas II was crowned in Moscow in 1896, he ceremonially entered the city on a white stallion surrounded by symbols of the multi-ethnic, multi-national, and multi-confessional empire he believed he united. The *New Times* (*Novoe vremia*) newspaper gushed with Russian national and imperial pride at the great "diversity of peoples" on display in the mass procession hailing the new tsar, with representatives from "every locality of the empire . . . dressed in their local costumes. What a collection of hats, caftans, shoes! What variety of human appearance! What richness of types!"[1] Territorial expansion was a hallmark of Russia's history, as was the increasing ethnic diversity that expansion brought. When Nicholas II took the imperial throne, his subjects spoke nearly one hundred native languages and embraced a huge variety of religious beliefs and practices. Indeed, to the dismay of some, "Russians" were no longer the majority: in the 1897 census (the first census of the entire population of the Russian empire), which measured ethnicity by native language, more than 55 percent of the population declared their mother tongue to be a language other than Russian. This included neighboring Slavic languages like Ukrainian, Belarusian, and Polish, but also Turkic, Baltic, Caucasian, Germanic and other language groups.[2] Some of these non-Russians looked to histories of once having their own states or even regional empires, such as the Poles. Others were beginning to discover and invent themselves as modern nations, such as Ukrainians and Turkestani Muslims. But these were complicated times for identity and belonging: a growing number of people felt that the old categories of identity like nation, ethnicity, or religion were too rigid and simple to define their place in a changing, and increasingly cosmopolitan, world.[3]

Russian elites could romanticize imperial diversity—perhaps in answer to their growing anxieties about how to ensure Russia's unity and stability amidst all this heterogeneity. This was partly the traditional pleasure of heroic conquest, reinforced with the modern belief that Russia was participating in the great European mission of spreading "civilization." But there was a growing argument about Russia's approach to empire as different from European imperialism and colonialism, as more virtuous, as a uniquely positive embrace of diversity. The Russian empire, these idealists (or apologists, depending on one's point of view) insisted, was "not built on the bones of trampled nations" and did not rule its subjects with colonial self-interest and greed.[4] Unlike Western European colonizers, one of Nicholas II's advisors on Asia argued, who "feed on the sweat and blood" of their subjects, "holding, as far as they can, millions of suffering two-legged beings in economic slavery," all the while declaring that they are bringing culture, progress, and Christian values to supposedly backward peoples, Russians bring to their imperial subjects only "true moral support, unselfish help, and real unity on the basis of mutual interest." Partly because Russian expansion was across land rather than overseas, but mostly because Russia's spirit of empire was thought to be different, a stark contrast could be established: Western European colonialists are always strangers and exiles in their colonies, while Russian settlers always feel "at home" (*rodnoi, rodstvennym*).[5] By no means was this meant to erase national, ethnic, or religious difference, much less hierarchy. This was an argument not about democratic integration and assimilation, and certainly not about equality, but about imperial unity and stability—an imperialist cosmopolitanism, one might paradoxically call it.

The February revolution dramatically altered the Russian imperial terrain by making the "self-determination of peoples" the new guiding principle. In practice, the liberals who directed the new Provisional Government worried that unleashed national liberation movements threatened the common cause of the Russian revolution. In a report in May 1917 to the congress of the left-liberal Constitutional Democratic

(Kadet) party, Paul Miliukov, then foreign minister in the Provisional Government, expressed the dominant liberal view: while we recognize the principle of "local autonomy," the overriding principle must be "the unity of the Russian State." Socialists were more supportive of national struggles, but not much. The Congress of Soviets in June 1917, for example, endorsed the right to "political autonomy" for all the peoples of the empire, even to the point of independence and secession, and criticized the Provisional Government for a lack of "vigorous action" to "satisfy the demands of the nationalities," but also warned against actions that "disunite the forces of the revolution, give rise to endless disputes within every national group and, by setting off one national group against other groups, reduce the scope of the revolution, undermining the economic and military strength of Russia, and thereby lessen the possibility of consolidating free Russia."[6] The imperial myth of the great "diversity of peoples" united in common cause found new life in the revolution. Later, in Stalin's time, this would evolve into the ideal of the Soviet Union as built out of the "friendship of peoples."

The Bolsheviks initially approached the question of empire in a disruptive spirit: encourage the empire's subject peoples to rebel against Russian domination, unleash minority nationalisms to unmask hypocrisy about unity in diversity, support national movements to further the disintegration of the old order (including the new liberal order emerging after the fall of autocracy). After they came to power, the Bolsheviks initially continued to focus on unmaking the empire: one of the government's first decrees, signed by Lenin as head of state and Stalin as Commissar of Nationality Affairs, affirmed the "equality and sovereignty of the peoples of Russia; the right of the peoples of Russia to free self-determination, including the right to separate and form an independent state; abolition of each and every privilege and limitation based on nationality or national religion; free development of the national minorities and ethnographic groups inhabiting the territory of Russia."[7] The Bolsheviks embraced and justified nationalism among non-Russians as a force to overcome the past, including the "Great Russian chauvinism" that had sustained imperial inequalities. But, as a matter of ideological conviction, the Bolsheviks also viewed nationalism as a historic stage to be overcome by economic, political, and cultural progress. As Lenin argued on the eve of the war, in his essay "On the Right of Nations to Self-Determination," revolutionary Marxists faced a "two-sided task": recognize the rights and struggles of nations in their fight against imperial domination, including the right to secession, while at the same time advancing the "struggle against nationalism of every kind," "defending the unity of the proletarian struggle and proletarian organizations...despite bourgeois inclinations toward national insularity."[8] The Bolsheviks worried that nationalism would lead people into the arms of national bourgeoisies whose talk of national unity masked their deep need to stop revolution against social inequality and oppression.

This created a dilemma. How to encourage ethnic and national anti-imperialism, to fight against the oppressive relationships and mentalities of empire, and to ally with national activists who also wanted to transform their societies, without strengthening ideologies and movements that rejected the primacy of class solidarity and struggle? How to allow the "free development" of national, ethnic, and religious institutions and identities without these sustaining ethnic and national divisions, prejudice, and discrimination? How to accept the "right to separation" as a political principle while building a diverse and inclusive socialist society on the ruins of the Russian empire? Stalin, as the chief administrator of Soviet nationalities policy, tended to answer complexity with simplicity, to address problems with formulas, and to treat declarations as achievements. Typical was his announcement to the party congress in 1921 that "under the Soviet regime in Russia and in the republics connected to Russia [many of which, he knew, had been established with Red Army intervention, including in his own native Georgia] there are no longer ruling nations or nations without rights, no metropole or colonies, no exploiters or exploited." In a word, "national oppression has been abolished." All that remained of the "national question" was to overcome "backwardness" so that less advanced peoples can "catch up with central Russia."[9]

This chapter looks at the thorny history of anti-imperial revolution through three individuals: Mahmud Khoja Behbudi, a Muslim activist in Central Asia; Volodymyr Vynnychenko, a Ukrainian political leader and writer; and the enigmatic Jewish author Isaac Babel. Of course, no selection of individuals or stories can represent the variety of ways people experienced and challenged imperial difference. So, these are "telling" stories, each in its own way revealing of larger histories, but not archetypal stories. Partly, this is the nature of all history writing, of all attempts to describe patterns in a diverse and complex reality. But unavoidable selectivity is magnified when we turn to the history of peoples kept on the margins of the traditional national narrative. Recent scholarship has done a great deal in recent years to bring out of the shadows this history of empire and imperial experience. Still, there are limitations built into the historical record—which is one of the reasons (though not the only one) that women and commoners, the margins of the margin as it were, are relatively invisible in these histories.

The complex multiplicity of Russia's imperial history has been a major theme in recent scholarship: the Russian empire as a complex and vital world of inconsistency, change, and uncertainty, a "strange hybrid," even a mass of "polyvalence" and "asymmetry." This was partly a consequence of the different times when different peoples were brought into the empire, of varied attitudes and policies toward different ethnicities and religions, and the diversity of on-the-ground relationships. This story was so complex that even ruling political elites found it difficult to describe the nature of their own empire. As one official complained in 1904, there seemed to be no way to define the "multiple particularities of Russian imperial life . . . In our life there's chaos, a muddle of conceptions and relations; in local areas you can't figure anything out."[10] This "muddle of conceptions and relations" was especially evident in the *experience* of empire. To say the obvious: the actual lived experiences and practices of ethnic and national belonging did not fit the myth, promoted by nationalists, that one's identity is a fixed and natural essence. The everyday encounter with belonging and distance—the experience of "difference" that was at the heart of "identity"—was unstable, varied, volatile. Difference could be enjoyed, celebrated, and accommodated, or experienced as a danger and a problem. Difference could nurture alienation, prejudice, exclusion, inequality, domination, and violence, but also discovery, negotiation, ambiguity, and opportunity, including new definitions of self and community. Empire changed almost everything and everyone it touched, but not in ways that were predetermined or predictable.

We could revel in this motley diversity. As we have emphasized throughout this book, this is part of the truth of the past that we sometimes lose sight of. But history is a story of patterns. And the three men whose stories shape this chapter, for all their differences, had much in common with one another and with many other people of empire (especially other educated men like themselves) in a time of change and revolution. For one, the encounters that shaped them extended beyond the borders of their communities, native regions, and the empire. All three were wanderers, exiles, and cosmopolitans. Their personal histories were transnational and even global as well as tied to national experience and struggle. All three were intensely concerned with the condition and fate of their own "nations," and strong critics of the inequalities, injustices, and exclusions that their people suffered. But they were not nationalists, at least not easy ones. In different ways, they linked the liberation of their people to bigger changes in the world. Indeed, all three rejected an uncritical embrace of their own ethnic, national, and religious "traditions," finding what was accepted as normal in their communities to be limited, harmful, and unsustainable. This went deeper than political argument. All three men were troubled and torn in their affiliations and commitments. Their ethnic or national identities were undermined by hybridities and uncertainties. Their desire for recognition for their own people was colored by a desire that their own people recognize their common humanity with others. And their ideological commitments were darkened by doubt and pessimism. Yet, they were also political dreamers, utopians even, seeking to remake life into what it should be, or at least believing that it was their obligation to speak out about the harm people suffered in the world as it was. Perhaps this is also why all three expressed themselves through fiction, finding in literature an expressive space to explore the complex experiences of darkness and possibility in the world.

Modernist Islam in Colonial Central Asia

Although Russian elites tended to view Muslims as a single group, and Muslim nation-builders tried to create a sense of common identity and purpose, these were stories imposed on enormous diversity. Nearly fourteen million Muslims lived in the Russian empire at the turn of the century, the largest group of non-Orthodox subjects, shaped by varied experiences of settlement, migration, conversion to Islam, and Russian conquest. Islam as an ethnicity or a nationality had to be invented and constructed, which the imperial state and Muslim activists tried to do for different reasons. "Turkestan" was even more an invention—an administrative territory that brought together, following the nineteenth-century Russian conquest of Central Asia, a diverse array of nomadic and settled peoples, with a variety of cultures and languages, across a vast region that includes today's Kazakhstan, Uzbekistan, Turkmenistan, Kyrgyzstan, and Tajikistan. Most historians now recognize the comparability of Russian rule in Central Asia to European colonialism: in the "Orientalist" assumptions about indigenous peoples and cultures; in the conflicting goals of ensuring political stability while promoting a disruptive "civilizing mission"; and, especially, in the enormous distance between rulers and ruled in matters of power, culture, and everyday social experience. At the same time, historians debate the extent to which native peoples were treated as absolute alien "others" or included as subjects in a complex and even mutually beneficial relationship in which indigenous peoples enjoyed an autonomous sphere of their own and certain types of power.

European colonialism was certainly on the minds of Turkestan's Russian rulers as they sought to build a modern society in the region, to bring "progress" to the "East," which included economic "development" (especially cotton production), railroad lines, integration into Russian and European trade networks, settlers with new skills, European architecture and city planning, improved sanitation systems, and Russian-style schools for natives. At the same time, the government favored a policy of limited interference with traditional Islamic practices and relied administratively on existing religious, cultural, and social institutions and elites. This restraint was partly a result of the administrative weakness of the central state. But the government also feared that interference with religious traditions and institutions would inflame what they considered the natural "fanaticism" of Muslims. The ultimate goal was to remake Muslim societies along Russian and European lines. Many Russian leaders hoped that Islam would simply decay in the face of

Russian and European modernity. But few Russians doubted that Islam was anything other than a "backward" and "alien" religion that could never be assimilated to European and Christian civilizational values. These beliefs sustained practices that amounted to a type of apartheid in the Muslim lands of the Russian empire.[11]

Mahmud Khoja Behbudi (transliterated also as Mahmudxo'ja Behbudiy, 1874–1919) was one of the most prominent Central Asian "Jadids"— Muslim intellectuals, mostly educated young men, whose efforts to reform education (the term "Jadid" comes from the "new method," or *usul-i jadid*, schools they promoted and organized) challenged entrenched assumptions, values, practices, and institutions within Muslim culture and society. Like many Jadids, Behbudi had a traditional background. His father was a *qazi*, an elected judge responsible for *sharia*, or Islamic law, in a village near Samarkand (Samarqand in modern Uzbek).[12] He received a traditional Islamic education, evidently first at home and then at a madrasa secondary school. After his father's death, Behbudi worked as a scribe for an uncle, also a *qazi*, and later became a *qazi* himself, in time reaching the high status of *mufti*, making him a member of the local cultural and legal native elite (Figure 9). He joined Turkestan's native economic elite as well: by 1913, he owned agricultural land, a grain trading business, and two homes in Samarkand (choosing, in a deliberate boundary-crossing move, to live mainly in his home in the city's Russian district). At the same time, he was an active and outspoken journalist, author, playwright, bookseller, philanthropist, and civic organizer. He wrote newspaper and magazine essays; prepared school books and primers for "new method" schools; drafted a proposal on Turkestan autonomy and religious reform that he submitted to the Muslim deputies of the new State Duma after 1905 and later delivered to a Russian state official on an inspection tour of Turkestan; organized a "Muslim reading room" in Samarkand in 1908; wrote a play that, when eventually staged in 1914, was the first work of modern theater performed in a Central Asian language; founded a weekly magazine, the *Mirror* (*Ayina* or *Oyina*, 1913–15), which was the first periodical in Turkestan in a local language and an important forum for reformist ideas; and opened and ran a bookstore in Samarkand, which stocked materials from all over the Muslim world on a wide range of secular and religious subjects. Behbudi's high social position, solid religious credentials, and

Figure 9. Mahmud Khoja Behbudi. Public domain. Courtesy of Adeeb Khalid.

demonstrated commitment to Muslim civic life and reform made him a respected and influential leader of the emerging national movement in late-imperial Central Asia.

In the freer and more hopeful conditions after the overthrow of the autocracy, Behbudi founded the newspaper *Liberty* (*Hurriyat*) and was selected by the Samarkand Executive Committee of the Provisional Government to be one of two representatives of the majority Muslim population. Behbudi accepted, though also understood that this paltry representation underscored the limits of the revolution in Central Asia, which began in a Russian settler community that did not want the majority indigenous population to have its proper share of power or even an equal part. After 1917, Behbudi worked above all for this democratic goal. In April, he was a delegate at the First Congress of the Muslims of Turkestan, held in Tashkent, a city that had become an epicenter not only of the revolution among Russians in Central Asia but also of popular mobilization among Muslims, who, to the Russians' surprise and worry, came together at unprecedented mass meetings and formed their own liberationist organizations. At this Muslim congress, Behbudi argued for the territorial autonomy of Turkestan within a federative democratic Russian state, a principle endorsed by the majority. After Bolshevik-led soviets came to power in October, Behbudi was elected chairman of the soviet of the old city (the Muslim district) of Samarkand and played a leading role in the most important move toward Muslim self-determination in Central Asia, the proclamation in late November of an Autonomous Turkestan at the fourth regional congress of Turkestan Muslims, held in the town of Kokand. Behbudi was elected to the ruling council of the "Provisional Government of Autonomous Turkestan," often called the Kokand Autonomy. Worried about Bolshevik intentions, the new government sought allies to protect them. Emissaries were sent to discuss cooperation with the anti-communist movement forming in the Russian south and with the Ottoman empire, moves that only worsened their relations with the Soviet government. Behbudi tried to secure international support for Turkestan's autonomy at an anticipated postwar peace conference that was expected to decide the new national boundaries that would replace the fallen empires. Autonomous Turkestan lasted only a few months: in February 1918, the Tashkent soviet sent armed forces to Kokand and violently overthrew the government. Behbudi was killed the following year in mysterious circumstances. Evidently on his way to the Peace Conference in Versailles, he was arrested while traveling through the independent territory of Bukhara, possibly suspected by supporters of the emir of Bukhara of being involved in the struggle between conservative forces on the side of emir and liberal and radical forces led by Jadids and communists. Behbudi was imprisoned in the town of Karshi (Qarshi), tortured, and killed. In 1923, the Soviet government would honor his memory by renaming the town Behbudi.

The men we call "Jadids" called themselves "progressives" or "the enlightened," for their signature effort to reform education was part of a sweeping vision of radical change, of cultural revolution. And though they avoided the perilous terrain of formal politics before 1917, their work was deeply political. They challenged the local authority of traditional elites, especially the religious law establishment, the *ulama*, whose authority was backed by the imperial state. Indeed, that the Jadids were mostly young men challenging the older men of the *ulama* was reflected in the dismissive term "youth" that their opponents often used, though Jadids would sometimes embrace the term themselves, proud of their challenge to the old, in every sense. These youthful intellectuals criticized not only existing institutions and authorities but also the consciousness and identity of Russia's Muslims, including about what it means to be a Muslim in the empire and in the world. They challenged traditional assumptions about the incompatibility of religious belief and modern scientific knowledge. They challenged limits set by the imperial state on the extent of Muslims' civic and political participation, but also Muslim elites' denigration of popular opinion. "Modernity" was a central ideal and practice. This meant actively engaging the larger world, secular print culture, and the emerging public sphere for assembly and discussion. Not least, modernity meant actively engaging with new attitudes, especially the claims of reason and science as forms of knowledge, growing belief in the human capacity to understand and solve the problems of the world, new views of time as "progress" and so a new awareness of "backwardness," new conceptions of "the nation," and faith in the possibility and value of renewal and change. In many respects, Jadidism was a movement for what would later be called "cultural revolution," with implications for almost every aspect of life. And like most cultural revolutionaries, Jadids felt a mixture of alienation, even disdain, for their own people as they presently were and a driving passion to uplift and transform them and the world around them.[13]

Travel was a personally transformative experience for Behbudi and others like him. At the age of 25, in 1899, he boarded the Transcaspian Railway in Samarkand for a journey to Transcaucasia in the Russian empire, Istanbul, Cairo, and Mecca. The ostensible purpose was religious: making the hajj pilgrimage to Mecca, an experience he shared with many other Jadidists.[14] But travel also brought Behbudi into contact with a changing world, especially a changing Muslim world, and with the porousness and fluidity of connections and boundaries in a world otherwise still dominated by nation-states and empires. Among all the many places travelling Jadids encountered, from Afghanistan to the Middle East, Ottoman Istanbul was perhaps the most important experience. The vital cosmopolitanism of Istanbul stirred many educated young Muslims, including Behbudi. In Istanbul (though also in Cairo), he encountered new developments in education and culture, a lively Muslim press, and activists advancing cultural reforms. Returning to Samarkand, Behbudi immediately subscribed to a newspaper published by the Crimean Tatar Ismail Bey Gasprinsky, the founder of Jadidism in the Russian empire, and began to contribute his own essays to Turkestan's main Turkic-language newspaper, the state-controlled *Turkestan District News*. Like many others, Behbudi was becoming a "Muslim cosmopolitan."[15]

Travel, along with a great deal of reading (which was also a form of world encounter), encouraged unflattering comparisons between colonial Turkestan and conditions and mentalities elsewhere in Russia and abroad. In the mirror of these larger worlds, Behbudi began to see and experience in new ways his own local world and the imperial world in which it was enmeshed. Travel stimulated his fascination with modern geography, transnational connections, and change. When he eventually opened his own bookstore, he stocked a wide range of maps and atlases, for he saw the political implications of geographic knowledge: the separations and connections among peoples are artifacts of history and so could be changed again. The world's modern empires, Behbudi concluded, had conquered the world by knowing it. The time had come for conquered nations to use this same knowledge for their liberation.

In the vocabulary Behbudi and other Jadid reformers continually used, they were on a mission to "awaken" their fellow Central Asian Muslims "from the sleep of ignorance," which would be replaced by the "knowledge" that would bring a place in the modern world. Hence, their preoccupation with education and culture. Their first line of attack was to promote an alternative method of schooling to the traditional Islamic maktabs and madrasas. Influenced by Ottoman education, by Gasprinsky's "new method" schools in the Crimea, and by Russian government schools for Central Asian natives (which some Jadids had attended), they were convinced of the necessity to teach true literacy to children, beyond the traditional focus on rote reading of sacred texts. Jadid schools included religious instruction, sacred history, Quran recitation, and prayer, but pupils were encouraged to "understand" the meanings of sacred words and acts, not merely repeat them. In addition, the curriculum included science, arithmetic, geography, literature, and history, including the world history of Muslims from ancient times to the present—a topic about which Behbudi wrote a textbook. Even the arrangement of the classroom—students in rows on benches ("like Russians," a traditionalist critic complained) rather than in a circle on the floor—sought to bring to education a new modern ethos of order, reason, and progress, a changed physical experience that would inspire mental change.[16]

Ethics and morality were part of these lessons—and the moral message was specific and explicit: cultural knowledge was more important than material wealth, truth and generosity were virtues, wastefulness and disorder were sins, and all these values were linked to the highest virtue of all: love of "nation."[17] Jadid writings about matters other than education were also preoccupied with ethics and morality. Munawwar Qari (1878–1931), a leader of the Tashkent Jadids who was closely associated with Behbudi, summarized Jadid views in an essay he published in 1906 in his newspaper, the *Sun*:

All our acts and actions, our ways, our words, our schools and seminaries, our methods of teaching, our morals are corrupt. If we continue in this way for another five or ten years, we are in danger of being dispersed and effaced under the oppression of developed nations.... O coreligionists, O compatriots! Let's be just and compare our situation with that of other, advanced, nations. Let's secure the future of our coming generations and save them from becoming slaves and servants of others. The Europeans, taking advantage of our negligence and ignorance, took our government from our hands and are gradually taking over our crafts and trades.[18]

At stake in moral education, Behbudi believed, was nothing less than the survival of Muslims in modern society. But survival opened up richer possibilities: a new free life defined by "progress" (*taraqqi*, another favorite term). Behbudi constantly wrote of the signs of "decline," "disorder," and "chaos" among Muslims, which, he warned, threatened national extinction. It was urgent that Muslims harness modern European culture to the cause of Muslim salvation and progress.

In his magazine, the *Mirror*—for it held up a mirror to Muslim society in order to admonish and inspire—Behbudi worried aloud about Muslim backwardness and decline. After visiting Palestine in

1914, he described "the melancholy contrast" between the "elegant" and "heavenly" garden and church of a Russian Orthodox monastery near Hebron and the "slovenly Muslims resembling nomads and their poverty-stricken houses" just outside, or the "brilliant" domes and crosses of Jerusalem with the "slovenly" and "rusting" Muslim religious buildings.[19] He regularly wrote reproachful accounts of public immorality, including the evils of alcohol and prostitution brought by colonizing Russians to Central Asia. But he was even more harsh in condemning the evils associated with "traditional" ways, such as extravagant feasts and evening entertainments featuring dancing boys (*bachas*) in female dress who were sometimes also abused sexually by adult males. And this all mattered politically: because of "debased" traditions, Muslims were demeaned and defeated by more advanced cultures.[20] Cultural revolution, he implied, would become political revolution.

As a playwright, Behbudi dramatized the inevitable path leading from ignorance to immorality to death, and the path of salvation through knowledge and morality. *The Patricide* (*Padarkush*)—written in 1911, published in 1913 after difficulties with the censor, and staged across Central Asia in 1914—was both a personal morality tale and a national allegory. Indeed, it was subtitled a "national tragedy." It tells the story of a rich man (named simply "Bai," from the Turkic word for a person of power, status, and wealth—hence a translator rendered this as "Mr Rich") who refuses to send his son Tashmurad to school. Against arguments in favor of schooling by both a traditional religious teacher (a mullah) and a progressive Muslim "intellectual," the rich father reminds them both that in this world "men honor the wealthy man more than the learned man." After all, the father points out, his own illiteracy did not prevent him from becoming a successful and respected "magnate." The mullah advocates education as a religious duty. The intellectual (satirized slightly with his Russian-style overcoat and cane, cigarette, disinclination to sit on the floor, sprinkling Russian words in his Uzbek vocabulary, and long-winded speeches) advocates education as "necessary for the nation." The son's fate in the play is meant to show the wages of ignorance. Tashmurad falls in with a group of debauched young men. One evening, while drinking at a local tavern, his friends decide to arrange a visit from a Russian prostitute named Liza. Lacking the 15 rubles and carriage fare she will demand, they hatch a plot to break into the father's strongbox. When Tashmurad's father awakens and screams, he is stabbed to death by the leader of the gang. The moral of the story is clear: ignorance leads to drunkenness, lust, greed, and murder. "You became a victim of backwardness," the mullah tells the rich man's wife as her husband lay dying on the floor and as her son awaits arrest. The intellectual offers a more radical lesson, a political message grounded in the history of empire and a vision for overcoming it: "The developed peoples of the world achieved progress through knowledge; the colonized and declining peoples are this way because of their lack of knowledge." Russia occupies a contradictory role in this play: symbolized by a Russian prostitute bringing temptation and moral danger, but also serving as a source of modern knowledge, order, and progress—though misused by Russia to oppress others.[21]

The idea of "progress" (*taraqqi*) was central to the Jadids' vision of overcoming empire. Like many liberals and socialists, Jadids believed that the world was in a modern "new age" defined by constant change and improvement and they embraced it. Their definition of progress included the development of science, technology, and the economy. But the deeper ethos of this ideology was a very modern faith in human agency, a belief that human beings, armed with human knowledge and skill, can overcome any obstacle and move history forward toward the new and the better. This conviction rejected both the skepticism about modern progress that was spreading among educated Russians and Europeans and the traditional religious understanding of history as a narrative of divine control and intervention. And because this vision of progress gave a leading role in history to men educated in modern knowledge like themselves, it challenged the social and cultural authority of the *ulama* to lead Central Asian Muslims. No less, it challenged the colonial dichotomy of native and Russian, for progress was for everyone equally and universal in its forms. Recognizing the logic of the modern world was a matter of national and religious survival, Jadids argued. Even more, this logic posed a radical challenge to many distinctions and inequalities in the present world, especially in the world of empire.[22]

The idea of a rising "nation" was central to this challenge to empire. Most historians today recognize that nations are historically constructed: they are "imagined communities" not natural and essential ones, they are always works-in-progress, the result of ongoing human efforts to define, imagine, and construct both connections and differences, especially in relation to "others." When Behbudi and other Jadids used the term "nation" (*millat*), which they often did, their meanings were varied but invariably challenged imperial norms. In contrast to the ethno-linguistic categories applied to them by the Russian government—such as Uzbek, Tajik, Sart, Turkic, or Kyrgyz—Jadids offered a new and embracing vision of a "Muslim nation," though the boundaries and connections were still emerging and shifting. When Jadids spoke of the "Muslim nation" (or the "Muslim language," a term they also used) they might mean the Muslims of Turkestan, all the Muslims in the Russian empire (in 1915 Behbudi wrote that "we Muslims constitute the second largest nation in the Russian empire"), all Turkic peoples, or the worldwide community of Muslims.[23] But mostly they defined their nation as bounded by the Russian empire. In 1914, Behbudi advised readers of his paper the *Mirror* how to answer perplexed outsiders who could not figure out "what should we call you if we can't call you Sart," which was the common but pejorative term for urban Turkic-speakers in Central Asia.[24] One possible answer reflected new "scientific" categories of ethnicity: you might say you are an Uzbek or a Tajik, for example. But Behbudi preferred a larger identity: when outsiders complain that they cannot distinguish among the various "Turks, Arabs, and Persians" in the region, embrace that and tell them we are the "Muslims of Turkestan."[25] Behbudi's complex and heterodox view of the Muslim nation can be seen in his argument, in an earlier article in the *Mirror*, that the Muslims of Turkestan need to be fluent in four languages: Turkic (the native language of the majority Uzbek population), Persian or Farsi (the language of Tajiks, of the madrasas of Samarkand and Bukhara, and of a great deal of modern literature written in the region), Arabic (the language of Islam), and Russian (to participate in the larger imperial polity).[26] One thing was stable and clear in all these variations on the theme of national identity: they were subversive of older ways of thinking about being Muslim in the empire.

Politically, Behbudi and other Jadids wanted a sort of post-imperial empire: inclusion as full and equal citizens, including democratic power over their own lives, that would overcome imperial relationships without dismantling imperial borders. The 1905 revolution offered a rare opportunity to express such desires out loud. The status quo had been that Central Asian Muslims were allowed limited self-government in their own separate sphere. In the new atmosphere of possibility after the October Manifesto, which promised equal rights and electoral representation to all subjects of the empire, reformers demanded much more. Behbudi drafted a program for change and sent it to the "Muslim Faction" of deputies in the new State Duma.[27] Turkestan, he argued, must become a self-governing state within the Russian empire, ruled by a legislature formed on the basis of an equal franchise for all residents, thus giving the Muslim majority predominant power. No less important, this new Muslim-majority state would be a force for progress, especially for cultural reform, including overcoming religious "superstition." To lead this modernizing effort, he proposed a special ministry responsible for "spiritual and internal affairs"—covering education, law, and religious institutions—to be led by individuals, like himself, "acquainted with sharia and the present era."[28]

Recognition and inclusion required that Central Asians navigate the elusive line between assimilation and distinction, between Russification and preserving national-cultural identity. Muslims must learn the Russian language and Russian ways, he believed, without losing the differences that defined them as a distinct and worthy nation. In Behbudi's 1911 play *The Patricide,* the "enlightened Muslim intellectual" is ridiculed for his exaggerated copying of Russian-ness but not for his deeper embrace of Russian and European cultures. In the play, he argues that, after an educated boy learns "the religion and language of our own nation," he must then go to a Russian school and perhaps a Russian university to study modern and useful fields like medicine, law, engineering, pedagogy, economics, agriculture, commerce, or physics. And then "it is imperative to become a real companion to the homeland and state of Russia. And it is necessary to enter civil service, so that the homeland (*watan*) and nation (*millat*) of Islam may be served according to our way of life and the needs of our age."[29] The ambiguity in this statement was characteristic of Behbudi's thinking: the need to combine "our way of life" and the needs of "our age" (or "sharia and the present era," as he wrote in his Duma proposal), to serve both the Russian empire and the Muslim nation. Indeed, Behbudi's use of the word "homeland" seemed to refer to both the Muslim nation of Turkestan and the Russian empire.[30]

But this imperial homeland must be a new type of empire, a post-colonial empire of citizens. In Behbudi's public speeches and in his essays in the *Mirror*, he insisted that the Muslim elite educate its youth to become "judges, lawyers, engineers, teachers, the supporters and servants of the community, i.e., deputies to the State Duma, technicians to reform our workshops, people who have studied the science of commerce to help us in commercial establishments and banks," as well as to "develop people who, in city dumas and in the zemstvos [institutions of local self-government] to be introduced in the future for the Russian homeland, would work for the true faith of Islam, for the weak and the poor."[31] However ambiguous, compromised, and assimilationist these arguments may have been, they also radically challenged the actual place and experience of Muslims in the Russian empire. Indeed, the very ambiguity in how "homeland" was defined disrupted the traditional exclusions, binaries, and hierarchies of empire. The Russian empire was not actually a polity of citizens, least of all for its non-Russian subjects, and certainly not a democratic federation of free and self-governing states in common union for the benefit of all. But Jadids were determined to believe this was not impossible.

When Russia entered the World War, Behbudi and other Jadids saw an opportunity to take their fight against discrimination and exclusion to a new level, more public and political than any time since the brief opening of 1905–7. Most Jadids supported the war effort: a patriotic stance that can be seen as both a compromise with the imperial state and a challenge to it. Behbudi was a leader in organizing fund-raising efforts in support of the war. He underscored his patriotic reasoning tersely: "the Russian state is home for us Russian Muslims"—but to say so was also to demand that Muslims be treated as family. Even after Ottoman Turkey entered the war on the side of Germany in November 1914, Behbudi insisted that "our common religion and common race cannot hinder our friendship with Russia."[32] He dated this Russian-Muslim "friendship" back "fifty years"—perhaps a surprising way to describe the experience of Central Asians after the conquest, but a sign of the complex path along which Jadids were seeking inclusion and equality. When a huge anti-draft rebellion broke out among Central Asians in 1916, after the government ended the traditional military exemption for natives (for the army desperately needed bodies), Jadids were not sympathetic to the rebels' cause. Behbudi, typically, saw the exemption as a sign of colonial discrimination and exclusion and therefore its abolition as a step toward opening the mainstream of Russian imperial life to Muslims as equal citizens.[33]

The 1917 revolution in Turkestan unfolded in this complex colonial world. As elsewhere on the empire's diverse peripheries, the class polarizations and ideologies that dominated the story of 1917 in the center were altered by the complex geographies of nationality and religion. In Central Asian capitals like Tashkent, the radicalized workers and soldiers who established soviets were mainly Russians and showed little interest in the native lower classes of the countryside and small towns or even in the residents of their own city's Muslim district—indeed, if they thought about the natives at all, most Russians worried about losing their many privileges if freedom and democracy meant majority rule. On the other hand, Muslims were far from united: traditional religious elites, merchants, reformist Jadids, and lower-class Muslims were divided (including among themselves between, for example, moderates and radicals or rural and urban) over what "freedom" and "equality" meant.

The huge range of civic and political organizations formed in 1917 embodied these many divisions. There were local executive committees, established mainly by liberal elites, loyal to the new Provisional Government (inviting a few elite and modern Muslims, including Behbudi, to represent the majority population); soviets established by Russian workers and soldiers (including many who had been sent to the region to suppress the uprising in 1916); an artisans' Soviet of Muslim Workers' Deputies; a new "Society of the Ulama" that tried to extend into modern politics the power of the traditional religious-legal establishment; leftist "shura" councils, typically led by Jadid intellectuals, that tried to unite the many new political organizations among Muslims in the cause of radical change; a succession of Turkestan-wide Muslim congresses;

varied political parties; and a profusion of publications. This revolutionary institutional landscape was further complicated by groups based in the imperial center, such as the Central Bureau of Russian Muslims and the All-Russian Muslim Congress, which also tried to influence how the revolution unfolded in Central Asia. There was a great deal of mutual suspicion among groups vying to represent, define, and direct the revolution locally. The *ulama* elite, in particular, continued to fear and despise the intellectual "youth," whom they accused of being a "tribe of hypocrites and innovationists" threatening the true faith and proper authority.[34]

The coming of Bolshevik power was a mixed blessing for the Jadids. In November 1917, Russian soldiers in Tashkent seized control of the city in the name of the new Soviet government. The Society of the Ulama responded in strongly nationalist terms, protesting the very idea that "a handful of immigrant soldiers, workers, and peasants who are ignorant of the way of life of the Muslims of Turkestan" should have any right to govern the region.[35] Behbudi and other Jadids responded by establishing, without *ulama* participation, an autonomous Muslim government for Turkestan in Kokand, which, unlike Tashkent, had no large Russian settler community or strong institutions of power representing the empire's political center. Their declaration that Turkestan was "territorially autonomous in union with a Federated Democratic Russian Republic" was justified as expressing "the will of the peoples inhabiting Turkestan toward self-determination according to the principles proclaimed by the Great Russian Revolution." The details, it was said, would be worked out by a "Turkestan Constituent Assembly"—not the All-Russian Constituent Assembly, it should be noted. The Kokand government promised that "the rights of national minorities inhabiting Turkestan will be fully protected"—putting the Russian settler community, including those claiming to represent Soviet power in Central Asia, in their democratic place as "minorities" with rights.[36] As we have seen, this government was overthrown by Bolshevik armed forces after only a few months. But this was only part of an increasingly chaotic and violent environment: growing economic desperation, especially in rural areas, reaching the point of famine by the end of 1917 and lasting into 1920;

armed conflicts over food supplies; and a so-called "basmachi" (bandit) revolt in rural areas against both Soviet rule and urban Muslims, indeed against all who challenged traditional ways.[37]

The Bolshevik revolution had a lot to offer Jadids and other progressive Muslim intellectuals, not least because many had become frustrated with the unresponsiveness of the Muslim masses to their modernizing efforts and with the increasingly entrenched position of traditional elites. The communist state was viewed by many Jadids as a powerful potential ally. After all, the Bolsheviks were committed to a cultural revolution very similar to their own: a thoroughgoing effort to overcome popular ignorance though modern enlightenment and education. The new government was also prepared to back native intellectuals against both the old elites of the *ulama* and against Russian settlers who opposed Soviet power. The revolution seemed to offer inclusion as equals in the mainstream of a modern society. And Bolshevik anti-colonialism was appealing. Stalin, as Commissar of Nationality Affairs, insisted in his 1919 statement on "Our Tasks in the East," that the government's goal was to "eradicate all the restrictions . . . that prevent the peoples of the East from developing the maximum independent activity on the path to liberation from the survivals of medievalism and national oppression."[38] These were not empty words: Jadids found many opportunities to enjoy power and influence in revolutionary Turkestan: in the press, in cultural life, in education, in government.[39]

When Behbudi was murdered in 1919 by forces of the emir of Bukhara, he was evidently suspected of being on the side of the Communist-Jadid alliance with which the emir's government was in conflict. We do not know much about Behbudi's views of the Soviet government or of Muslim communists, though he had always leaned more liberal than socialist. But even if he might have eventually agreed to work with the Soviet government, as many other Jadids did, his primary commitment was always to liberating the Muslims of Turkestan—his "nation"—from the oppressions and inequalities of empire. This would have made his relationship with the new Russian rulers uneasy at best, especially as the central state became increasingly intrusive in Central Asia. Most Jadids, even on the left, were too heterodox in their mixing of socialism and nationalism, and in their insistence that the liberation of nations was at least as important as class struggle in history, for their relationship to Soviet power to be smooth or long-lasting.

I expect Behbudi might have agreed with the views of Abdurrauf Fitrat in 1919, who praised Lenin's determination to "awaken and unite" the peoples of the East, but warned that Russian Bolsheviks might fall back into old colonialist habits and try to "paint the East in the colors of communism by force," rather than taking "account of the point of view of the East and its own intuition."[40] Behbudi knew Fitrat well: in the spring of 1917, when Fitrat, a Jadid from Bukhara, fled from the emir, he went to Samarkand and became a regular contributor to Behbudi's newspaper *Liberty* (*Hurriyat*) and its editor in August. After 1923, when the Soviet government purged Fitrat and other anti-colonial Jadids from the government in Bukhara, in which Fitrat had been a leader since 1920, he turned away from politics, devoting himself to the study of Uzbek language, literature, and music. But politics found him: during 1937–8, he was arrested and shot along with many former Jadids accused of Turkic nationalism. Behbudi would likely have been among them had he been alive. Instead, all the Stalinist government could do was erase the memory of Behbudi's struggles by removing his name from the town where had been tortured and killed. As elsewhere in Soviet Union, overcoming empire remained unfinished business.

"All-Sided Liberation": Making a Ukrainian Revolution

The emergence of Ukraine as a modern nation vividly illustrates how nations are purposeful social constructions, histories unfolding amidst great diversity, discontinuity, and change, out of which national activists try to construct coherent, stable, and usable narratives about space and time—geography and history—and enact these in political life.[41] Russian officials and much of Russian society viewed Ukrainians not as a separate nation, much less an equal one, but as a minor branch (along with Belarusians) of the "All-Russian" nation, to use a term increasingly viewed by Ukrainian activists as an imperialist category that denied Ukrainians their own national history, culture, and rights. For most Russians, Ukrainians were "Little Russians" (*Malorossy* or *Malorusy*, where the prefix "malo-" meant lesser or minor) and their language (and, by extension, their culture) a "dialect" of the Great Russian language. The geographic term "Ukraine" meant, to most Russians, just what it literally said: a "borderland," a "frontier," the edge of something else. The lands where most Ukrainian speakers lived was indeed a borderland in an important sense: a place of moving peoples, shifting borders, and the diversity and instability this produced. And Ukraine's borderland position was underscored, and further complicated, by imperial boundaries that had many Ukrainians, and lands with majority Ukrainian-speaking populations, across the border in the Austro-Hungarian empire, especially in eastern Galicia. In turn, Ukraine was home to many other peoples, some with local privilege and power, some even more marginalized. Large minorities of Russians, Jews, Poles, Germans, Tatars, and others lived in the nine majority-Ukrainian provinces of the Russian empire, mostly in the cities and towns where native Ukrainians were a minority (most "Little Russian" speakers lived in the countryside and worked in agriculture). In the Ukrainian "capital" of Kiev (Kyiv in Ukrainian), for example, Ukrainians comprised 22 percent of the population (based on 1897 census data of natively spoken languages), compared to 53 percent Russians, 13 percent Jews, and 7 percent Poles. In the port city of Odessa (Odesa), only a tenth of the population reported Ukrainian to be their native language.[42]

A national "cultural reawakening" was well underway among Ukrainian elites in the early decades of the twentieth century. European ideas about the nation as a people's deep and natural essence, preserved in folk traditions, inspired many educated Ukrainians, though often quite Russified or Polonized themselves, to discover the "authentic" Ukrainian national identity in the culture and language of the peasantry. These "Ukrainophiles," as they were sometimes called (with more than a hint of derision), worked to recover and restore the suppressed and forgotten identity of Ukraine as a "nation."[43] All national identities, of course, are stories about history. And the most influential author of this new narrative of Ukrainian national history was the historian Mykhailo Hrushevsky (1866–1934).[44] In 1894, he became a professor of east European and Ukrainian history at Lviv University in Austrian Galicia, an important center for the growing Ukrainian national movement, for the Austro-Hungarian monarchy gave more latitude to Ukrainians, including allowing teaching and publishing in Ukrainian, which was forbidden in the Russian empire. Hrushevsky was sharply conscious of his political tasks in Lviv: to train a new generation of young Ukrainian scholars who could advance the cause of national liberation and use the greater freedom in Galicia to build Ukrainian cultural, scholarly, and political institutions for all of Ukraine. No less, his task was to construct a history that could overcome the Russian imperial narrative. Ukrainian national development, he insisted, resulted not from the efforts of elites or state institutions but from the history of the common people, especially their economic, cultural, and spiritual life. Only through the study of the people's history, Hrushevsky insisted in his inaugural lecture, could one see that Ukraine already existed as a nation in essence though not yet in political form. In his teaching, public lectures, essays in magazines and newspapers, and scholarly writings (especially his influential *History of Ukraine-Rus*), Hrushevsky reiterated this clear lesson: there is a continuous history of a single nation across centuries of changing borders and foreign rule, reaching from medieval Kievan Rus, through the seventeenth-century Cossack state (*hetmanate*), and persisting to the present.[45]

The revolution of 1905 created unprecedented opportunities for anti-imperial and national movements. In Ukrainian cities, as in towns across the empire, there was an explosion of meetings, demonstrations, strikes, publications, and organizations. Nationalists found unprecedented opportunities to be heard and eager audiences for their message. Hrushevsky was able to publish widely in the Russian empire in both Ukrainian and Russian. His message was direct and insistent: Ukraine was a historical and ethnic nation with a natural right to autonomy. This lesson was directed as much at Russians as Ukrainians and helped put the "Ukrainian question" on the agenda of Russian liberals and socialists, who began to recognize that the liberation of Russia must include overcoming the legacies of imperial rule.[46] As "an 'empire of peoples' (*imperiia narodov*) among whom the ruling nationality are only a minority," Hrushevsky argued, Russia cannot be "free or successful" until the peoples that constitute the empire enjoy their own "free and unfettered existence." Indeed, he insisted, until Russia was transformed into "a free union of peoples, its complete renewal, its full liberation from the dark remnants of the past, remains unimaginable."[47]

In 1917, after the tsar was overthrown, Hrushevsky returned to Kiev, where he was elected president of the Ukrainian Central Rada (council), which soon became a proto-parliament for the emerging Ukrainian nation-state. Hrushevsky's political position was like that of most anti-imperial activists in Ukraine and across the Russian empire at that moment: not secession but "autonomy," a "free Ukraine in a free Russia." But he also shared the widespread conviction that if Russians resisted demands for autonomy, independence would be the only possible course. "The flag of independent Ukraine remains folded," he warned, but would be unfurled if "all-Russian centralists" remained deaf to the just demand of the empire's national minorities.[48]

Hrushevsky's vice-president in the Central Rada was Volodymyr Vynnychenko (1880–1951).[49] Unlike the well-born professor-president, Vynnychenko (Figure 10) was the son of peasants who had migrated to the town of Yelisavetgrad (Yelysavethrad) in central Ukraine. He studied

Figure 10. Volodymyr Vynnychenko, 1920. Public domain.

at a local gymnasium, thanks to financial support from his older brother, who worked as a printing worker in the city, but was expelled before graduating, evidently for writing politically tinged satirical verses. Wandering from job to job across southern Ukraine, he continued to study on his own, and was able to earn a diploma by examination, which allowed him to enter the university in Kiev in 1900 to study law. Like many students in Kiev, politics interested him more than his studies. He joined the underground Revolutionary Ukrainian Party (RUP), recently established by students in Kharkov (Kharkiv) in 1900, which has been described as the "first Ukrainian political party in the Russian empire."[50] Ideologically, the RUP combined socialism with the cause of national identity and liberation, though the balance between socialism and nationalism would become a point of growing contention, especially as the party's rather vague populism evolved into a more ideologically rigorous Marxism. In 1902, Vynnychenko was arrested for taking part in student demonstrations, for which he was expelled from the university and drafted into the Russian army. After briefly enduring army life, he fled across the border to Galicia, where he joined the foreign branch of the RUP, occasionally smuggling revolutionary texts back across the border with the help of a fake passport, though he was caught in 1903 and imprisoned for more than a year.

Vynnychenko's political awakening arose, by his own account, at the intersection of social and national experience and feeling. Writing in his diary in 1919, he recalled that "from the time the landowner Bodisko beat my father on his estate, fooled him, exploited him, chased him from his plot into the field, where I was tending livestock, from that moment I already took into my soul the seed of hatred for social exploitation, for Bodiskos of all types."[51] Other youthful experiences added feelings of *national* humiliation and anger to these social emotions. He recalled, for example, how, as a gymnasium student, teachers and other students ("young gentlemen") treated him as a "little muzhik" (peasant) and a "little khokhol" (a derisive term for Ukrainian).[52] Whether or not these stories of social and national insult and awakening were literally true— Vynnychenko, after all, was a fiction writer and these diary recollections were composed many years later in revolutionary times—they fit a narrative of experience we know to be true for many people across the empire.

The revolution in 1905 opened new opportunities for political activism, but also deepened a tension plaguing Ukrainian socialists and other national and social activists across the empire: what should be the proper balance and relationship between fighting for the cultural and political freedom of one's nation or ethnic group, and fighting for the political and social transformation of the whole of Russia into a free, equal, and inclusive democratic polity? A significant minority of the Revolutionary Ukrainian Party answered this question in an orthodox Marxist way, condemning nationalism as a "bourgeois" deviation and organizing a Ukrainian section of the empire-wide Russian Social Democratic Workers' Party (RSDWP). Vynnychenko and the majority of RUP members answered differently: one cannot subordinate, and thus efface, the national cause to the larger political and social struggle against autocracy and social inequality—the two depend on one another. Insisting they were Marxists, they refused to join the "All-Russian" party, establishing instead an independent party, the Ukrainian Social Democratic Workers' Party (USDWP), with Vynnychenko as party leader.[53]

In 1906, Vynnychenko was arrested. When released on bail, he fled to Western Europe before his trial. During the next few years, he wandered in exile, living in the émigré capital of Geneva, on the Italian island of Capri (where Maxim Gorky's villa was a gathering place for émigré revolutionaries and writers), and in Paris, Zurich, Florence, and Lviv. In Paris, he met Rosalia Lifshits, a Russian-Jewish medical student, whom he married in 1911. One biographer has called this marriage a "political act" as much as a personal one: a "demonstrative symbolic statement," in the face of widespread Ukrainian anti-Semitism, about a vision of a Ukraine where national and religious prejudice would be overcome, where diversity would be a virtue of the liberated nation.[54] Vynnychenko periodically crossed the border illegally into Russia, especially to meet with his publishers, for during his long exile he flourished as a writer, producing a great many stories, plays, and novels in Ukrainian and in his own Russian translations. He became "Ukraine's most acclaimed author" of the time.[55] Soon, alongside Hrushevsky, he would become one of Ukraine's most important political leaders. These roles were not separate: as we shall see, his views on questions of nation, empire, and revolution were closely entwined with his literary vision.

The upheavals of 1917 drew Vynnychenko back to the Russian empire and politics. In Kiev he became a leader of the independent Ukrainian Social Democratic Workers' Party and editor of the party's newspaper, the *Workers' Gazette* (*Robitnycha hazeta*). He was elected to the Ukrainian Central Rada as one of two vice-presidents and chaired its executive committee. In May, he led the Rada's delegation to Petrograd to negotiate with the Provisional Government for Ukrainian autonomy. Like Hrushevsky, he believed that national liberation would come through transforming the Russian empire into a democratic federation of autonomous nation-states. This was a view shared by most national activists across the empire: national freedom through democratic federalism not nationalist fragmentation. But both the liberals who led the new Russian government in Petrograd and the socialist leaders of the Petrograd Soviet were unwilling to grant autonomy before a decision by the All-Russian Constituent Assembly. As we have noted, this reluctance ran deeper than a formalistic attachment to a decision by a properly elected body. Russian liberals and socialists viewed national liberation movements as a potential distraction from the common cause, the "All-Russian" cause, of revolution and freedom.

Running out of patience, and increasingly skeptical about the professed support in Petrograd for autonomy and self-determination, in June 1917 the Ukrainian Central Rada unilaterally proclaimed Ukrainian autonomy and named Vynnychenko chairman of the executive committee of the new Ukrainian government, known as the General Secretariat—making him effectively the first president of the first autonomous Ukraine. In the wake of the October revolution, the Central Rada, in a proclamation Vynnychenko helped draft, proclaimed an autonomous "Ukrainian People's Republic" within a new "federated Russia of equal and free peoples."

Tensions between the Rada and the Soviet government arose immediately. At the beginning of December, the Bolshevik leadership issued a public manifesto addressed to the Central Rada. The Soviet government "once again" affirmed "the right to self-determination to all nations oppressed by tsarism and the Great Russian bourgeoisie, up to and including the right of these nations to secede from Russia," but also emphasized, as in the past, that this right must conform to "the interests of the unity and fraternal union of the working and exploited masses in the struggle for socialism." The Soviet government declared support, in principle, for the right of "the Ukrainian People's Republic ... to completely separate from Russia or to enter into an agreement with the Russian Republic on federal or similar relations between them." The problem was the Central Rada: "We accuse the Rada of conducting, while hiding behind national phrases, a duplicitous (*dvusmyslennaia*) bourgeois policy, which was already expressed in the Rada's non-recognition of the soviets and of Soviet power in Ukraine," and was now even more evident in the Rada's support for the emerging Kadet and Cossack front in the Don and Kuban regions of Ukraine against Soviet power in Russia and in the Rada's efforts to disarm workers' Red Guards and Soviet troops. "This duplicitous policy has made it impossible for us to recognize the Rada as the authoritative representative of the laboring and exploited masses of the Ukrainian Republic." Rather, the Rada had "betrayed the revolution." Further charges and demands concluded with an ultimatum: if anti-Soviet actions do not cease in forty-eight hours, the Soviet government will consider "the Rada to be in a state of open war against Soviet power in Russia and in Ukraine."[56]

When Bolshevik Red Guards attempted to install a Soviet government in Kiev in January 1918, the Central Rada answered by proclaiming the Ukrainian People's Republic an "independent, free, and sovereign state of the Ukrainian people, dependent on no one." Vynnychenko and other leaders saw no choice but to declare independence once the Soviet government in Petrograd, in the words of a proclamation that Vynnychenko helped draft, started a "fratricidal war" against Ukraine in order to bring the "free Ukrainian republic under their power." The General Secretariat became the Council of People's Ministers (*Rada Narodnykh Ministriv*) and Vynnychenko was named prime minister and minister of internal affairs.

Ukrainian independence was short-lived. A right-wing coup in April backed by German military forces pushed Vynnychenko out of power and into the opposition, though when the defeated Germans left Kiev in December, the People's Republic was restored with Vynnychenko as chairman of a new executive body known as the Directory. When the Red Army entered Kiev in February 1919, he stepped aside for Symon

Petliura, whose military background and more conservative politics were thought to be better suited to the tasks of armed resistance against Soviet Russia and procuring aid from Western countries, though Vynnychenko personally considered Petliura's politics abhorrent. Following Soviet victory in 1920 in the "Ukrainian civil war" (a messy affair involving battles between Whites, Reds, independent Cossacks, and the Ukrainian Directory), Vynnychenko travelled to Moscow to seek an agreement with the Bolshevik government about the future of Ukraine. Frustrated by Bolshevik unwillingness to compromise with Ukrainian desires for recognition and autonomy, Vynnychenko left again for Western countries in dismay and defeat. He would spend the next thirty years in exile, until his death in 1951. As an émigré, he tried to navigate a political position combining criticism of Soviet nationalities policy with support for the revolution and Soviet power. He helped organize a foreign branch of the Ukrainian Communist Party and was a regular contributor to its newspaper the *New Age* (*Nova droba*), published in Vienna in 1920–1. But he grew increasingly disenchanted with the politics of both the Soviet state and Ukrainian émigrés. And both grew more hostile to him: the Bolsheviks distrusted him as a nationalist and Ukrainian nationalists distrusted him for his unrepentant socialism.

Categories like nationalism and socialism, however, are rather too simple to capture the shape and texture of Vynnychenko's vision of emancipation. His literary work suggests something of these richer and more elusive depths.[57] Vynnychenko's earliest stories were largely realistic descriptions of the social lives of Ukrainian peasants, workers, hobos, criminals, students, and revolutionaries, often based on his own encounters as he wandered around Ukraine. After he fled the Russian empire in 1906 to avoid prison and Siberia, his writings took a different turn. In the West, he experienced the life of an émigré and exile, a wanderer in a strange land. As for many intellectuals and activists—including the three individuals considered in this chapter—Vynnychenko's encounter with this different world helped him see stories of home in new ways, rethink their meanings, and imagine new possibilities.

Not surprisingly, nostalgia imbues many of Vynnychenko's stories, whether set in Ukraine or among Ukrainian exiles in the West, often expressed through intimate sensory memories from childhood: "the wet scent of rain and young grass from the Dnieper [river region]," the warm and expansive steppe that shapes "blood and soul," the taste and smell of "buckwheat filled varenyky [dumplings]," "the scent of humidity," a "dreamy pink sky."[58] The idealization of lost places and times, of course, is often part of the construction of national feeling. Vynnychenko sometimes imagined returning home, though he knew this would mean certain arrest and exile deep into the Russian interior. To return to Ukraine, he wrote in a letter in 1909, meant "signing my own death sentence. After my first arrest I will commit suicide."[59]

Vynnychenko's feelings for the nation were not only nostalgic: he demanded respect and recognition for Ukraine and Ukrainians. In 1913, he published in Russian an "Open Letter to Russian Writers" that criticized the "unconscious" tendency in a great deal of Russian literature to stereotype ethnic others. The Ukrainian characters who appear in Russian literature, he argued, are much like the stereotypes of Jews and Armenians that Russians also have "a weakness for." They are "one-sided" figures at best, brought in for local color, not real human beings with real human experiences and subjectivities. "Always and everywhere [in Russian literature] the 'khokhol' is a little stupid, a little cunning, a little lazy, melancholic and sometimes good-natured." These stereotypes are "shameful" not only for Ukrainians whose equal humanity is not recognized but for Russian writers themselves and Russian literature.[60] During the war, which brought fronts of fighting and occupation onto Ukrainian lands, Vynnychenko rhetorically wondered why our "brother" Russians show little concern with the suffering of Ukrainians? Why does "the love among Ukrainians for their own nation (*narod*) and sorrow for its fate elicit...wrath, indignation, and feelings of spite, or, at best, sarcasm or indifference?" The answer, he argued (writing in Russian, so again addressing Russians as much as Ukrainians), is that Ukrainians are becoming strong and aware as a nation, and "they fear us." But nothing can stop the development of Ukrainian "conscious-ness," he declared, which is already manifest in its intelligentsia. "Just as you cannot stop the formation of clouds, arising from the earth and returning to it, so it is impossible to stop the formation of a nationally conscious stratum in a people. We emerge from the raw earth, from the soil, from the depths of our nation, and we again return to it, and we again arise."[61]

For all his nostalgia for home and his feelings of proud unity with the rising Ukrainian nation, Vynnychenko could not help feeling alienation from his own people as they actually were. This was partly the result of attacks against him for translating his works into Russian, though this is what allowed him a readership big enough to make a living as an author—indeed it made him the mostly widely read Ukrainian author since Nikolai Gogol. Nationalist critics declared translation to be a "betrayal" of the cause and labeled him a "slave of All-Russian culture," even a half-Ukrainian and half-Russian "literary hermaphrodite."[62] As late as January 1917, he worried that if he returned to Ukraine "people will spit in my face on the streets" for this alleged infidelity to national purity. "I wished for foreign lands, exile, prison, anything but my native land."[63] But the alienation went deeper than this experience of rejection. As we have seen for Behbudi and many Jadids (and will see for Isaac Babel, too), Vynnychenko could not reconcile himself with given realities, with social values as they were, with what was accepted by most people as normal and natural. We see this strongly in his literature, which Mykola Soroka, the leading scholar of Vynnychenko's fiction, described as Vynnychenko's "moral laboratory" for analyzing alternative "possibilities" for how to live in the world.[64]

Ukrainian critics at the time judged Vynnychenko's stylistic shift from realistic descriptions of everyday life among the Ukrainian people to a literature of ideas as an unfortunate effect of Vynnychenko's exile from the Ukrainian land. But we can interpret this shift as an intellectual and political choice: a turn from describing reality as it was to imagining a possible new reality. And like other reformers and radicals across the empire, Vynnychenko believed that it was not enough to change structures of power. Liberation, a true overcoming of empire, demanded deep changes in people's mentalities and values, in their moral and spiritual lives, in their selves. A true revolution needed to be, Vynnychenko insisted, all-sided, all-embracing, universal liberation (*vsebichne vyzvolennia*)—an interdependent unity of national, cultural, political, social, moral, and spiritual liberation.[65] To explore and promote this vision, he examined in his fiction questions of sexuality, emotion, will, and character. Ultimately, the point was to ask the most important question: how to realize a fully human and fully free personality, especially in the face of the crushing conditions and legacies of unfreedom?

Vynnychenko called this construction of the new, free person "honesty with oneself"—a phrase, a slogan even, that he used repeatedly, most famously in a novel published in 1910 with this as its title. "Honesty with oneself" meant overcoming "disharmony" and lack of "integration" between ideas and emotions, surfaces and depths, the political and the personal. Vynnychenko was especially concerned with the lack of intellectual and emotional "honesty with oneself" among revolutionaries. The revolutionaries in his stories, especially the men, are all too often immoral and hypocritical: they lie, mistreat women, and neglect their families, while insisting on their superior ethics. The hero of the novel *Honesty with Oneself* is an artist and revolutionary named Myron Kupchenko who advocates "free love" and physical pleasure without shame. Outraged party leaders decide to put Myron on trial for his open sexual life, though they themselves secretly visit brothels. Vynnychenko demanded a "new morality," an argument voiced by a number of different characters. This new morality would break through the old dichotomies of politics and everyday life, and mind and body, which Vynnychenko portrayed as false divisions that lead only to illness and death—often suicide—and undermine the cause of true revolution.[66]

These ideas took a more nationalist turn in his 1916 novel *I Want!* (*Khochu!*). The hero, a Russified Ukrainian poet named Andrii Khalepa, whose main goal in life is sexual pleasure, which he justifies philosophically as following Nietzsche's ideas of the superior man, shoots himself out of disenchantment with the world and disgust with his own life. While recovering from his failed suicide, friends mention that "Khalepa is an old Ukrainian name" of ancient Cossack origin. This discovery of nation and history becomes his personal salvation. The lost freedoms, dignity, and autonomy of the Cossacks, suppressed by the expanding imperial Russian state, was one of the most important legends inspiring the modern consciousness of Ukrainian nationhood and the need to fight for its liberation.[67] Khalepa embraces this history in moral, psychological, and spiritual terms, as a way to free his own inward personality, to overcome failure and suffering, and find a new life. He contrasts "these laughing, mighty, boisterous people," his new-found ancestors, with his own persona as "a wretched intellectual." In this "forgotten" national history, he finds the vitality he lost but desperately needs, a path to a new person whose mind and body are united, whose emotions give real power to words, whose life has purpose entwined with others. In this individual morality tale, of course, is a vision of how a nation can be redeemed.[68]

Back in Kiev in 1917 as a political leader of the revolution, Vynnychenko turned his pen to explicitly political writing. He drafted the first of the Central Rada's political declarations known as "Universals" (the historical term that the Cossack states of the seventeenth and eighteenth centuries had used for policy declarations) and participated in writing the three Universals to follow.[69] The First Universal, in June 1917, defined national "freedom" in the context of a transformed Russia. "Let there be a free Ukraine. Let the Ukrainian people have the right to order their own life on their own land, without separating from the whole of Russia or breaking with the Russian state." The idea of a "free Ukraine" *within* a "federated Russia of equal and free peoples" (in the words of the Third Universal in November) was a persistent ideal (and not only in Ukraine, as we have seen), but clashed with the unwillingness of Russian leaders in Petrograd to agree to autonomy (at least before a decision by the Constituent Assembly) and with growing desires for complete independence.

Vynnychenko insisted, as did others fighting to overcome the damaging effects of imperial domination, that neither autonomy nor independence would be true liberation unless there was a thoroughgoing transformation of Ukrainian society and life. The necessity of social revolution within the national revolution was most explicit in the Third Universal, which proclaimed that, in order to "create order and build a new life" in the Ukrainian People's Republic, all land would be the property of the laboring population and transferred to those who worked it, all workers would enjoy an eight-hour workday, and the state would control all production in order to address both workers' demands and the economic crisis. Above all, Ukraine was to enjoy all the "freedoms won by the all-Russian revolution: freedom of speech, the press, religion, assembly, unions, strikes, the inviolability of the person and one's home, and the right and possibility of using local languages in relations with all institutions." At least in these hopeful early months of revolution, a transformed "All-Russian" ideal, a unifying category that had been viewed by nationalists as suppressing the separate identities and freedoms of Ukrainians, now seemed a source of liberating power.

By 1920, Vynnychenko recognized that most of his ideas had been overwhelmed by political facts on the ground, but also by a deeper failure to overcome the inward legacies of empire. The Ukrainian cause lay mostly in ruins. He blamed this on the failure to achieve "all-sided liberation," to achieve psychological "integration" and "honesty with oneself." He saw the symptoms of this in the hypocrisy of the "Russian democratic intelligentsia," especially around the national question. He described their intellectual and emotional failings in *Rebirth of a Nation (Vidrodzhennia natsii)*, his account of the Ukrainian revolution, written in exile in Prague and published in 1920:

They recognized whatever was best and most progressive with their brain, with their mind. Intellectually, the Russian intelligentsia always fought, even to the point of fanaticism, for progress, equality, and liberty.... But in real, everyday, and especially emotional, life, they were still imbued to the marrow of their bones with Russia's darkness, brutality, violence, and disorder, both physical and moral.... The same applied to the Ukrainian question. In their studies, in the newspapers, in their speeches you heard sincere words about the equality of all peoples, about the equality of the Ukrainian nation, about its rights. But in the kitchen, in everyday life—there was the bayonet, the fist, the slap in the face of the old servant woman [Ukraine] for offending the privileges and tastes of the "barin" [lord]. And they were sincere in both situations. The intellect lives one life, the emotions another. But there is neither connection nor wholeness.[70]

The Ukrainian intelligentsia also failed the test of "all-sided liberation." This had an immediate and practical side: the one-sided focus of the Central Rada on peasants, who were overwhelmingly Ukrainian, and neglect of urban workers, who were more ethnically mixed. As a consequence, most workers in Ukraine turned to the Bolsheviks. But there was also a deeper and bigger one-sidedness: not understanding that national liberation without "social and economic liberation" would lead to failure. What was the value, Vynnychenko asked, in creating a Ukraine that was a state "like that of other people" (*iak u liudei*)? The point of the Ukrainian revolution was to achieve freedom from empire that was new and different, to reject what was accepted as normal, to overcome not only an empire but the nation that empire had shaped. Vynnychenko blamed the bourgeoisie, who were unable to see what freedom from empire truly required, who were inspired mainly by "greed," "egoism," lack of "desire to work," and "eternal debauchery," all of which produced a "false and harmful understanding of the revolution and freedom." In a truly liberated Ukraine, there would be no such class.[71]

Vynnychenko also denounced Soviet nationality policy. On the one hand, he embraced the social cause and global impact of the All-Russian revolution. "The fate of the rebirth and liberation of Ukraine," he argued in his conclusions to *Rebirth of a Nation*, "depends on the global struggle between socialism and capitalism," and in this the Russian revolution and Soviet power played a positive role. "Soviet Russia... has truly given Europe a real example of a social miracle, which fills the revolutionary and vital elements with delight and chills the parasitic, criminal, and corrupt elements with deadly fear."[72] But appreciating this achievement only strengthened Vynnychenko's dismay and frustration that Soviet leaders fell back so easily into one-sided chauvinistic habits—proof again of the deep disharmony in the mentality of the Russian intelligentsia, especially when it came to relations between the peoples of the Russian empire.

A revealing expression of Vynnychenko's persistent critique of the imperial mentality of the Russian radical intelligentsia, which Soviet power did not lessen, can be seen in his famous "open letter" to Maxim Gorky in 1928. Vynnychenko had long admired Gorky, spent time with him and other Russian revolutionaries at Gorky's house in Italy, and had much in common with him: Gorky, too, was a writer from the provincial lower classes, a wanderer and observer of plebian life, an independent socialist who continually insisted on the need for cultural and moral revolution if the political and social revolution was to succeed, a critic of hypocrisy, and a champion of "honesty." So when Gorky dismissed the Ukrainian language in 1928 as only a "dialect" of Russian, Vynnychenko could not be silent. In this word "dialect," Vynnychenko wrote (in Ukrainian), there is "a whole political-national worldview. It contains a whole history of mutual relations between two Slavic peoples.

In it is much suffering, violence, and evil, citizen Gorky. The origins of this word lay in the whole history of imperialist-colonial policies of Russian tsarism in Ukraine." How could Gorky not understand this, as one of the first to "boldly tear away the fig leaf of silence which the Russian intelligentsia has so often covered the zoological nakedness of tsarist despotism concerning the Ukrainian question?" How could Gorky allow himself to repeat the "colonial crap (*hydoty*) of tsarist imperialism" that Ukrainian is not a language? Coming from a "spokesman for Russian proletarian culture" this was especially "disgraceful."[73]

Vynnychenko's insistence on sweeping multidimensional change, especially his refusal to separate the national and social revolutions, or the Ukrainian and Russian revolutions, deepened his alienation from others. Rejected by the Bolsheviks as a nationalist and by Ukrainian nationalists as a communist, he continued to find that many people wanted to "spit in [his] face on the street," as he had put it in January 1917. This remained a danger even after his death. A Ukrainian émigré historian, for example, chastised Vynnychenko for being a dangerous "social utopian" whose disdain for statehood "like that of other people" without "total liberation" contributed to Ukraine again falling into "total national and social servitude" to Russia.[74] Other critics have been even less restrained, mocking Vynnychenko, for example, as "the illegitimate offspring of Karl Marx and a good-looking and sexy Ukrainian village wench."[75]

Like many of his own literary characters, Vynnychenko did not find this hybrid life easy, or happy, or even certain. He wrote the following in his diary in June 1920, while in Moscow trying, and failing, to convince Lenin and the Bolsheviks of his vision of the Ukrainian revolution and to find a place for himself in the emerging revolutionary world. "Again I face the same tragedy that has been tearing me apart for almost two years. To join with the Russian Bolsheviks is to smother my nation, and myself, with my own hands. To join with the Petliura forces, with reaction, is to smother the revolution, my own self, and everything I think to be good for humanity."[76] In December, on the eve of his departure for another long period of exile in the West, he elaborated on his painful relationship with Russian communists in a letter addressed to the Central Committee of the Russian Communist Party, but never sent. Communism, he argued, was better than socialism because it possessed the "more transformative" understanding that to liberate humanity one must overcome "binariness, inconsistency, and dishonesty with oneself and others." The trouble was that Russian communist leaders were not, in fact, "honest with themselves," for they failed to see their own "Russian nationalism." To be sure, this nationalism was not stated in programs or resolutions. It was not even believed in their own rational minds, which reviled Russian nationalism as backward. But as a "sensibility," Russian national chauvinism had been "imbibed with their mother's milk" and remained deep within their consciousness: "It is in your blood, in the way you think and feel," Vynnychenko wrote. Bolsheviks may think they have rejected the conservative idea of Russia "great, united, and indivisible," the notorious slogan of the White Armies. But "honesty with oneself" would reveal that even this despised idea was a sensibility they still had not overcome.[77]

Perhaps Vynnychenko was a "utopian," determined, against all odds and all criticisms, to hold together values others kept apart, to embody the harmony of seeming opposites—including nationalism and cosmopolitanism—to realize the impossible "all-sided liberation." Perhaps he understood this. In March 1920, the newspaper of the foreign branch of the Ukrainian Communist Party, the *New Age* (*Nova doba*, published in Vienna), featured an unsigned essay by Vynnychenko on "Utopia and Reality" (*Utopiia i diisnyst'*). All "sober-minded" people of influence in Russia and Ukraine, he noted, say that "world revolution is a utopia, a dreamer's fantasy, an impish invention by extremist-fantasists." But these sober-minded realists are wrong about what is real and what is utopian, for the old world will soon come tumbling down, and it will "fall with a great thundering noise under the indelicate blows of 'fantasist' proletarians." For "the only living, true reality at the present time," he concluded, "is the Great World Revolution." The triumph of this revolution is "the only, inevitable, and necessary reality." Trying to deny this "is a truly criminal and stupid utopia, a hopeless fantasy." If utopia, as we will argue in the next chapter, is not a synonym for the impossible but a vision that reveals the bankruptcy of imagination that cannot see beyond the world as it is, then Vynnychenko and his "fantasist-communists" and "fantasist-proletarians" were indeed utopians in the positive sense of questioning what is real and possible.[78]

Cosmopolitan Journeys: Jews, Empire, and Revolution

The stereotypical image of Russian Jews living in a distinctive world of tradition—and, less nostalgically, of discrimination, victimization, and poverty—echoed the view of many non-Jews at the time, including the tsar and most officials of the Russian state, that Jews were inexorably "alien," impossible to integrate, even into an empire that claimed to embrace its great "diversity of peoples" and "richness of types." Distinctiveness was partly the product of policy. Legal restrictions on residence meant that the vast majority of Russia's Jews lived in small towns (*shtetls*) within the "Pale of Settlement" on the western frontiers of the Russian empire. Legal restrictions on occupation and landholding meant that Jews worked mainly as shopkeepers, peddlers, traders, and artisans. While most Jews living in the Pale did, indeed, try to have as little as possible to do with their Slavic Christian neighbors, the Jewish world was fractured, contested, and changing. Religion, culture, politics, and class divided Jews from one another and from any simple story about tradition or change. The Jewish "community" of the Russian empire included Orthodox and Hasidic Jews, "enlightened" followers of the Haskalah, Marxists favoring an autonomous Jewish socialist labor movement (the General Jewish Labor Bund of Lithuania, Poland, and Russia, founded in 1897), Marxists who believed that only a united "All-Russian" struggle would end the oppression of Jews, Zionists who saw salvation only in a separate Jewish nation-state, and many other differences of opinion and strategy. The boundaries were often blurred: religious Jews, for example, could be attracted to secular ideologies and secular radicals could embrace prayer and mysticism. Most important, Jewish life was outgrowing the shtetl, as an increasing number of Jews were able to live in cosmopolitan cities like Vilna, Kiev, Odessa, Moscow, and St Petersburg. It was becoming less and less possible to speak of Jewish life as ghettoized and tradition-bound. Indeed, growing anti-Jewish violence may have been less a timeless response to Jewish "otherness" than a reaction to the increasing visibility of Jews in public life, especially in times of rapid social change and political upheaval.

Jews began to participate in the secular world more than ever—and to explore different ways of being Jewish—as educational restrictions lessened, job restrictions weakened (especially in the professions), and political activism, both alongside Russians and in the separate cause of Jewish liberation, grew. Spaces of public life outside of school, work, and politics, especially cultural, charitable, professional organizations, and the press, were no less important to Jewish involvement in the Russian imperial world. In journalism, for example, a variety of new publications for Jewish audiences arose, even before the liberalization of censorship laws in 1905, the most influential of these based on the Russian imperial capital, such as the Yiddish-language newspaper the *Friend* (*Der fraynd*, 1903–12) and the Russian-language Zionist magazine *Jewish Life* (*Evreiskaia zhizn'*, 1904–7). Many Russian publications, such as the influential liberal newspaper *Speech* (*Rech'*, St Petersburg, 1906–17) and the mass-circulation *Kopeck Gazette* (*Gazeta-Kopeika*, St Petersburg, 1908–17), had Jewish correspondents, columnists, editors, and publishers. To apply the controversial term "assimilation" to all of this would terribly oversimplify even the most secular and integrated practices. The involvement of Jews in the non-Jewish world was rarely a way to vanish as a member of a distinctive ethnic and religious group, even were this possible in the face of a widespread prejudice and discrimination. Rather, this was a complex and shifting path of participation, engagement, and adaptation—a typical imperial story.[79]

Odessa was a consummate imperial city, a cosmopolitan city.[80] Historically, it was the capstone of Russia's imperial expansion to the south, founded in the eighteenth century after the region was conquered in a war with Turkey. It quickly became Russia's finest example of imperial cosmopolitanism, a port city that attracted immigrants from across the empire and abroad. A British visitor in the 1870s thought that "if I had suddenly been set down in the middle of the city, in ignorance of its name and position, I should have been puzzled to say what country I was in. There is nothing national about Odessa."[81] An Italian traveler in 1913 concurred, commenting not only on the diversity of peoples but the instability of boundaries and intensity of mixing: Odessa, he felt, was not so much an international city, with distinctive national and ethnic districts, as an "a-national, Esperanto city."[82] The 1897 census (measuring ethnicity by native language) found that half the population were Russians, a third were Yiddish-speaking Jews, nearly a tenth were

Ukrainians (the majority population outside the city), along with smaller but significant numbers of Poles, Germans, Greeks, Tatars, Armenians, and others.[83] Cosmopolitanism is an overused and disputed term. But to the extent that it tries to capture and interpret the experience of living in spaces of great human diversity, of daily encounters with difference (encounters that include coexistence and mutual influence but also friction and conflict), and complicates histories that neglect or marginalize these stories, the idea speaks a great deal about Odessa and the Russian imperial experience.[84]

Odessa had a distinctive reputation, influenced not least by the work of the many writers who were born or lived there, including a great many Jewish writers. Odessa, in this account, was a bourgeois world of business and opportunity dominated by a large and respectable middle class, but also a "looking-glass world" where every middle-class value was subverted. Odessa was a city of industrious merchants and a "city of thieves," a global economic capital and a frontier town, respectable and irreverent, sophisticated and seedy, a "fabled land of gold, abundance, and sin, where the unlikely seems natural and the implausible is expected to happen."[85] If the imperial capital of St Petersburg, by reputation, symbolized Russia looking outward toward Western Europe and modernity, and Moscow represented a national gaze directed inward toward native traditions, Odessa looked every which way, and with a vision that was fractured, overlapping, and blurred, marked by identities and attachments that were constantly shifting, blended, and mixed. The revolution stirred new chaos into this brew, as the city changed hands repeatedly between 1917 and 1920, with local authority held in turn by the Ukrainian Central Rada, Bolshevik Red Guards, Austrian troops, the White Army, French troops, and the Red Army.

Odessa was also a "Jewish city." With its reputation, especially during the boom years of the late nineteenth century, as a "Russian Eldorado" where even the poorest shtetl Jew could strike it rich and escape discrimination and violence, Odessa was a magnet for Jewish migrants. In reality, the vast majority of Odessa's Jews worked as small shopkeepers, sales clerks, peddlers, or workers. Most earned modest incomes and many were destitute. But Jews also owned or operated most of the city's artisanal workshops, industrial enterprises, and trade and commercial establishments. Many of Odessa's doctors and journalists were Jews. This middle class supported Jewish schools, theaters, and publications, sustaining a thriving Jewish civic life. Odessa Jews might be religious or secular, political or not, and in many different ways. In Odessa, Jewish modernity was on display as nowhere else, traditional boundaries were constantly crossed and confused, and new possibilities seemed open. Odessa, one influential historian of Russian Jews called it, was the "anti-shtetl."[86]

Isaac Babel (1894–1940) was born in Odessa in 1894, though his family moved when he was a small child eastward along the Black Sea to the port city of Nikolayev (Mykolaiv in Ukrainian) for a business opportunity (Figure 11).[87] This move enabled the Babel family, who also changed their name from the more shtetl-sounding Bobel, to rise into the middle class. They moved back to Odessa in 1906, now able to

Figure 11. Isaac Babel, 1920. Public domain.

afford a fine apartment in a "respectable" neighborhood in the city center. Isaac was enrolled at the age of 11 (having studied previously at home) in the Nicholas I Commercial School, a place, he would later recall, where "the sons of foreign merchants, children of Jewish brokers, Poles of exalted lineage, Old Believers, and many overgrown billiards players" all studied together. During breaks, the students would go slumming to "the piers at the port, or to Greek coffee houses to play billiards, or to the Moldavanka [the neighborhood where Babel's family had lived when he was born, famous for its Jewish poor, thieves, and gangsters] to drink cheap Bessarabian wine in cellars."[88]

Like many imperial subjects, Babel's life became more and more one of movement. He went to Kiev in 1911 to study at the Institute of Finance and Business Studies, moving with the school to Saratov when it was evacuated during World War I (he managed to avoid the draft, initially through his student status and then, when even many students were recruited, possibly due to poor health). He also began to write fiction, on the Jewish experience. In 1916, he was able to move to Petrograd (where Jews needed special exemptions to reside) to study law at a private university, but also to be closer to the center of the Russian world of letters. He shopped his first stories around to a number of publishers without success until he met Maxim Gorky, who encouraged him and published a few stories. Gorky also advised, Babel later claimed, that he "go out into the world of people" (*v liudi*), to learn about life if he really wanted to be a writer. So,

for seven years, from 1917 through 1924, I went out into the world of people: I served as a soldier on the Romanian front, in the Cheka [the political police], in the People's Commissariat of Enlightenment, in food requisitioning expeditions in 1918, in the Northern Army against Yudenich, in the First Cavalry Army, in the Odessa regional executive committee, in the Seventh Soviet Printing House in Odessa, and as a reporter in Petersburg, Tiflis, and elsewhere. Only by 1923, had I learned to express my thoughts clearly and succinctly. Then I really began to write.[89]

Perhaps that is what happened. Babel mixed fact and fiction in all his writings, including in this commissioned autobiographic sketch written in the 1920s. Scholars have questioned a number of details. But the general truth is not in doubt: in "the world of people," specifically the bloody and disorderly world of revolution and civil war, Babel found his material and his voice as a writer. One might doubt his ideological commitment to the political struggles he participated in. But there is no doubt about his commitment to telling stories and to seeking the "truth" about life that literature so often makes possible. He became one of the Soviet Union's most celebrated authors, though as cultural repression grew during the 1930s his life became more and more difficult. During the Great Terror, like so many Soviet cultural figures, he was arrested and executed. He was cleared of all charges only after Stalin's death.

Babel's relationship to being a Jew was complex but not unusual. The school he attended was more secular than others his parents might have chosen but at home they required him to study, he recalled, "Hebrew, the Bible, and Talmud until the age of sixteen."[90] Babel knew Yiddish. Indeed, scholars have noted how deeply his Russian writing resonated with Yiddish style and tradition.[91] But like many striving or successful Jewish families, the Babels embraced Russian language, literature, and culture—out of real attachment and pleasure, and as a path of integration and participation into "civilization."[92] This pattern had become a tradition among Odessa's middle-class Jews. The famous Zionist Vladimir Jabotinsky (Zhabotinskii in Russian), for example, who was born in Odessa in 1880, grew up in a family that spoke Russian at home, loved Russian literature, and had little involvement with Jewish belief or ritual. Young Jabotinsky attended an elite Russian gymnasium and then went to Western Europe to study and work as a journalist for Odessa newspapers, dreaming of a career as a Russian man of letters.[93] Similarly, during Babel's Kiev years, he spent much of his free time with a Jewish family of even more cosmopolitan and cultured inclinations than his own. Music, art, and literature defined their existence. Babel also fell in love in this family with a young woman he would later marry.

For all his reach toward Russian and European culture, Babel was drawn as a writer toward the Jewish experience. His first published tale, "Old Shloyme" (1913), was about a poor 86-year-old shtetl Jew. In a sentimental tone, the story raised issues almost never seen before in Russian writing, even by Jews: anti-Jewish laws, conversion as a means to avoid discrimination, and the loss and rediscovery of Jewish identity. Though "old Shloyme" is not a religious man, indeed in his younger days he was thought to be an atheist, he is overwhelmed by the "boundlessness of the disaster" that his son wants "to leave his people for a new God" in order to avoid eviction from their home, to abandon forever "the God of an oppressed and suffering people." He hangs himself.[94] We see in this story Babel's sense of Jewish life as physically embodied in places, smells, and tastes. This was developed more fully in the second story (unpublished during Babel's lifetime), "At Grandmother's," a remembrance of childhood filled with sensual memories of Odessa streets, aromas, language, and food—including grandmother's Sabbath "gefilte fish with horseradish (a dish worth embracing Judaism for)."[95]

Babel found in journalism a way to earn needed money, but also to experience and observe diverse social worlds, including the scattered Jewish worlds of the Russian empire. He was especially attracted to the feuilleton, the observational sketch of everyday city life, as an ideal medium to develop his powers of observation, to experience everyday life, and to voice feelings and ideas. In 1916, after moving to Petrograd, he published three feuilletons under the heading "Leaves from My Notebook" (*Moi listki*). The first two are set in the capital, in the world of writers and readers. In one, among the assortment of different people he sees in the Public Library is a sleeping Jew, "an immutable feature of every public library in the Russian Empire... Where he is from, nobody knows. Whether he has a residence permit or not, nobody knows. ... In his face is a terrible, ineradicable weariness, almost madness. A martyr to books—a distinct, Jewish, indomitable martyr." The second sketch describes writers waiting to see a magazine editor, hoping to get published. The "most doleful" of these solicitants, his eyes filled with both tiredness and "fanatical striving toward something," is a Jew from Lithuania who had been "wounded during a pogrom in one of the southern towns" and wounded again fighting in the French Foreign Legion during the present war. The last piece in this trilogy turns to Odessa, as a counterpoint to these melancholy sketches of sadness and failure. "The typical Odessan," Babel declared, "is the exact opposite of the typical Petrogradian." Every Russian reader knew that the northern capital is a world of cold and fog and melancholy moods. Odessa brings to Russia "lightness and sunshine." To be sure, the southern city is full of "fat and funny bourgeois," "pimply and skinny dreamers, inventors, and brokers," and hopelessly impractical *luftmenschen* (Yiddish for people who seem to live on air), not to mention factory workers and "a very poor, crowded, and suffering Jewish ghetto." And yet, it will be from this Odessa that salvation will come. There is no "real, joyful, clear description of the sun" in Russian literature, Babel insisted. No wonder Russians have been drawn for centuries "to the south, the sea, and the sun ... For they feel the need to freshen the blood. We are being stifled. The literary Messiah, for which we have waited so long and fruitlessly, will arrive from there—from the sun-drenched steppes washed by the sea."[96] In these claims, Babel managed to rework a history of imperial expansion toward the south into a promise of coming redemption, of cultural and spiritual revolution.

Babel's experience as an observer of everyday life took a darker direction in 1918, when he wandered the streets of the revolutionary capital as a columnist for Gorky's independent socialist newspaper, the *New Life*. His sketches, under the heading "Diary" (*Dnevnik*), were harsh in detail and depressing in mood. Hunger, "poverty and wretchedness," murder, executions, suicide, child abuse, corruption, and chaos were his main themes, as they were in daily news reports—a dark lament softened only by what seemed to be Babel's resigned acceptance. "Every day people stab one another, throw one another off bridges into the black Neva, hemorrhage from hapless or wretched childbirth. That's how it was. That's how it is now." Mostly, he let his characters reflect on what this all meant. In a "godforsaken" provincial railway station, for example, he overheard this conversation: in response to a merchant who expressed contempt for popular drunkenness, "a bearded muzhik [peasant] said roughly: 'our people is a people that drinks. Our eyes need to be murky (*mutnyi*) ... Take a look,' the muzhik said, pointing at a field. 'Black and endless ... You see the murk (*mut'*)? The people's eyes have to be like that too—murky.'"[97] There seemed little evidence in the everyday life of ordinary people that a revolution had taken place at all, at least not what the revolution people needed or desired. For the pregnant women in a new "maternity palace," the subject of another diary sketch, the experience of the aftermath of overthrowing the tsar and the bourgeoisie was mainly "standing in lines outside food stores; factory sirens calling their husbands to defend the revolution; the heavy anxiety of war and the convulsions of revolution leading them to no one knows where." For those not yet born, Babel suggested, "at some point or other we should make a revolution. Taking up rifles and shooting at one another is perhaps, sometimes, not a bad thing to do. But that's still not the whole revolution. Who knows, perhaps it is not the revolution at all."[98]

Babel was drawn more and more deeply into this uncertain revolution, especially at its imperial margins, including "taking up rifles and shooting at one another." In his autobiographical sketch, Babel reported that he fought on the Romanian front in 1917, worked for the Cheka in 1918, participated in the defense of Petrograd against the Whites in 1919, and participated in armed food requisitioning detachments to the Volga region. But his deepest and most sustained encounter with the violence of revolution came in 1920, while serving as a reporter during the Polish-Soviet War, assigned by the Russian Telegraph Agency to Semyon Budyonny's First Cavalry Army, comprised mostly of Cossacks from the Don and Kuban river regions of the south. As an embedded war correspondent (we might call him today), Babel experienced the revolution at the borders of collapsing empires—Russia and Austro-Hungary. (And it was experience he was after, thinking of writing projects he had in mind.) On one side of this battle were Polish forces led by Józef Piłsudski (backed by Ukrainian forces led by Symon Petliura and at times supported by France, England, and the United States), who launched the war to extend the borders of the new Polish state to the east, limit the spread of Bolshevism, win Ukrainian "independence" under Poland's guidance, and lay the foundations for a grand federation under Polish rule that would stretch from the Baltic Sea to the Black Sea. On the other side were the Bolsheviks, who opposed Poland's eastward expansion, but also saw opportunity: an invasion to overthrow Piłsudski's conservative nationalist regime that would inspire a Polish workers' uprising, which would ignite proletarian revolution across in Germany and then spread across Europe and the world.

Babel's articles in the First Cavalry Army's broadsheet *Red Cavalryman* (*Krasnyi kavalerist*) were partisan and unambiguous. He signed his essay

"K. Lyutov," from the name on the identity papers he was given (Kirill Vasilievich Lyutov) by the Odessa authorities for this assignment. Perhaps, he wished to mask his Jewish background. But he also may have intended the symbolic gesture: his fictive new name, from the Russian *liutyi,* implied fierce, merciless, even cruel, almost the opposite of what we know of Babel's personality, but a persona he sometimes tried to adopt. When Babel later turned these experiences into the fiction of the *Red Cavalry (Konarmiia)* tales, their first-person narrator bore the name Lyutov as well. This does not mean, of course, that either of these "Lyutovs" expressed Babel's experiences and views in a direct or simple way. Rather, these two Lyutovs remind us of the interplay of facts, interpretations, and imagination evident in both journalism and literature—and, for that matter, in experience itself.

The *Red Cavalryman* articles were typical propagandistic pieces of hyperbolic outrage and determination, with good and evil clearly marked and distinct. Red heroes were "unwavering" fighters ready to lay down their lives "for the cause of the oppressed." The Polish army was a savage force defending only the interests of the *pany* (rich landowners) and, no doubt because they knew they were doomed, had become "crazed" monsters perpetrating the most savage brutalities, not least against the Jews, whom they viewed as "dumb beasts" not even worth shooting: rape, knifing, and torture were thought more suitable and carried out in horrific ways, all "to the accompaniment of jokes about communism and Yid commissars." The Polish enemies were nothing but "rabid dogs" who deserved to be crushed and killed: "Finish them off, Red Army fighters! Stamp down harder on the rising lids of their rancid coffins!"[99]

Such moral and political clarity was absent from Babel's diary—a writer's diary, with numerous notes to himself about things to remember in order to write about later.[100] Compared to his later fiction, his diary is less artful in its prose and more raw in its subjectivity. But we see the same concerns—revolution, violence, the past and the future, and the experience of Jews in this history—and the same ambiguous judgments. Riding with Budyonny's cavalry took Babel through the heart of the East European Jewish borderlands. His encounter was full of thoughts and emotions, not least about own identity as a Jew and as a willing participant in revolution. As a rule, Babel was guarded about his own

Jewishness, not least among the swaggering Cossack cavalrymen with whom he now lived and rode. When faced with their brutalities and abuses, "I keep quiet, because I'm a Russian" (24 July). The backwardness and weakness of Jews repelled him. But he also recognized feelings of kinship, perhaps precisely because this Jewish world was "dying and decaying" (3 June). When he first encountered the "synagogue buildings and ancient architecture" of Zhitomir (an old city in northwestern Ukraine with large populations of Poles and Jews, the scene of major pogroms in 1905 and again in 1919 and 1920), he commented "how all this touches my soul." Although these Jews were "pathetic" and "feeble," especially in the face of violence against them, Babel felt that he was among "my own people," and when "they think I am Russian, my soul is laid bare" (3–5 June). Wandering around Jewish "ghettos," surrounded by ruins and by "lanky, silent, long bearded" Jews, so unlike the Odessa type, he still insisted that they were "my own kind—they understand me" (21 July). Babel regularly forayed away from the company of Red Cossack warriors he had been assigned to cover, to spend time with local Jews: a synagogue caretaker, a half-starved intellectual, a tsaddik (revered holy man). Sabbath evening prayers in a Hasidic synagogue in Dubno in western Ukraine, though he was surrounded by the city's "most repulsive-looking" Jews, prompted Babel's reflection that "a quiet evening in a synagogue always has an irresistible effect on me" (23 July).

The catastrophe of diasporic Jewish life was fully on display in these battle-scarred borderlands. Too many people still despised Jewish difference. And the revolution, at least as enacted by Red Army Cossacks, changed nothing. "The same old story, the Jews are plundered, bewilderment, they look to Soviet power as savior; suddenly shrieks, whips, Yids" (11 July). Babel saw a direct historical line connecting anti-Jewish massacres during the Cossack uprising against Polish rule in the seventeenth-century to the anti-Jewish attitudes and violence of the present: "Khmelnytsky, now Budyonny, the unfortunate Jewish population, everything repeats, now that whole history—Poles, Cossacks, Jews—is repeating with striking precision, the only thing new is communism" (18 July). And he traced this historical line still further back: during the night of Tisha B'av, the festival lamenting the destruction of the Temple, the foundational Jewish catastrophe, a "dejected and angry" old woman recalled "the terrible words of the prophets: they will eat dung, the maidens will be defiled, the menfolk killed, Israel subjugated." Babel seemed to agree: "outside the window, Demidovka [a poor town to the west of Dubno], night, Cossacks, everything just as it had been when the Temple was destroyed" (24 July). But Jewish lamenting was a mark also of Jewish weakness: when Cossacks looted a synagogue—they even "tossed out the Torah scrolls and took the velvet coverings for saddle cloths"—"the Jews smile obsequiously. That's religion" (29 August).

But what answer could there have been? What could save Jews, and the collapsing world, from catastrophe? For Zionists like Babel's fellow Odessan Vladimir Jabotinsky, the only possible answer was a post-imperial world where every nation lived separately on its own lands, without the "blending and mixing" of peoples, without cosmopolitan diversity, integration, or "assimilation" (a condition Jabotinsky knew well from his own upbringing), a new redeemed condition that would begin when Jews overcame their national dispersal and returned to a renewed Land of Israel.[101] For Babel, like most Russian Jews, the fight could be nowhere else than where Jews already lived. He hoped "revolution will do some good" in overcoming all the "filth, apathy, hopelessness of Russian life" (28 July). Personally, he served as both propagandist and comforting angel when reassuring "these tormented people" (24 July), suffering at the hands of both anti-Bolshevik Poles and communist Cossacks, that "everything is changing for the better," that "miraculous things are happening in Russia—express trains, free food for children, theaters, the International." His listeners responded with "delight and distrust." But his own thoughts were ambivalent: "you'll have your sky filled with diamonds [from the final lines of Chekhov's play *Uncle Vanya*], everything will be turned upside down, everyone uprooted yet again, I feel sorry for them" (23 July). He knew he could "enthrall" these suffering people with his "fairytales about Bolshevism" (24 July). He just could not enthrall himself. The inability to overcome uncertainty haunted his strongest convictions. In this, of course, he was not alone.

Babel's doubts partly reflected his skepticism about violence as a way to overcome the afflictions of the world. Sometimes his thoughts about violence were as bleakly negative as his *Red Cavalryman* articles were heroically positive. After his first experience in battle, he wrote that this was simply "Hell. Our way of bringing freedom—horrible" (18 August). More often, he was torn. Pondering the "many-layered" character of these Red cavalrymen—"petty looting, bravado, professionalism, revolutionary spirit, savage cruelty"—he thought of the revolution: "we're the vanguard, but of what? The population awaits saviors, Jews their freedom—and in ride the Kuban Cossacks" (21 July). But his reflections also led him into a deeper and more murky terrain. Babel repeatedly used the word *toská* as an explanation and sign of what he could not explain. The Russian word is elusive in meaning: the usual translations as melancholy, mourning, anguish, sorrow, longing, or nostalgia capture only parts of it. At one time used mainly to speak of feelings about one's inner personal life, by Babel's time *toska* had become a way to comment about the experience of living in modern society. Witnessing the devastation in Brody, the most important Jewish city in Austrian east Galicia—synagogues destroyed, homes and stores looted, nothing to eat, and Red Army Cossacks in the streets—he felt around him "unbearable *toska*, people and souls crushed" (30 July). The melancholy was mostly his own. He continually asked himself, "Why this *toska* that I can't get over?" Perhaps it was because he was "far from home." But homesickness had a political context: "because we destroy, move like a whirlwind, like lava, hated by everyone, life shattering into pieces, I am at a huge never-ending service for the dead" (6 August). How could one not feel "*toska* for the fate of the revolution?" (23–4 August). Death, it seemed, was often stronger than the new life. The emerging new world, he feared, was "stillborn."[102]

Babel began in the early 1920s to interpret through fiction the encounters he had described in his 1920 diary, which would become his famous *Red Cavalry* collection.[103] In 1924, the first three stories appeared in the influential journal *Red Virgin Soil* (*Krasnaia nov'*). In his diary entry of 3 June, Babel had described wandering around Zhitomir in the wake of a pogrom—"carried out first by Poles and then, of course, by Cossacks"—discovering an "indescribable" little shop owned by "a little Jew, a philosopher." The shopkeeper's philosophy: "they all say they are fighting for truth (*pravda*) and they all plunder. If only there were a government that was good." In the fictionalized version, the old man is given a name, Gedali. His cramped little shop, we are told, was filled with dead flowers, skulls, and other "treasures" of the past, and "a gentle aroma of decay" enveloped everything. As the sun set on a Sabbath eve, stirring in the narrator a "dense sadness of memories," the old man expounded his philosophy. "Yes, I hail the revolution, yes, I hail her," he told his visitor, "but it hides from Gedali and sends ahead of itself nothing but shooting." Gedali admitted to being pleased that the revolution was beating the "Pole, the vicious dog," for Poles were guilty of terrible violence against the Jews, including blinding Gedali himself. "That's wonderful, that's revolution!" But then the revolution turned and stole from Jews and threatened to shoot them. Why? Because that is what revolution does. The narrator agreed: the revolution "'cannot not shoot,' I tell the old man, 'because that is what she is—revolution.'" But Gedali was reluctant to accept this simple moral symmetry:

the Pole shot because he was the counterrevolution; you shoot because you are the revolution. But the revolution is happiness (*udovol'stvie* [which also suggests pleasure and satisfaction]). And happiness does not love orphans in the house. Good deeds are done by the good person. The revolution is the good deed of good people. But good people do not kill. Which means the revolution is being made by bad people.... And so, all of us learned people fall upon our faces and cry aloud, "woe to us, where is the sweet revolution?"

If there was hope, Gedali concluded, it was for a new "International of good people. I want every soul to be accounted for and given the highest grade rations. Here, soul, eat, go ahead, find happiness in life."[104]

On the Sabbath, in another story, Gedali took our narrator to the house of a Hasidic rebbe, whom he found sitting at a table in a stone room that felt "like a morgue." The rebbe was surrounded by "liars and men possessed by devils." Praying in a corner were "broad-shouldered Jews who resembled fishermen or apostles." Standing by a wall was "a youth with the face of Spinoza, with the mighty forehead of Spinoza, with the sickly face of a nun. He was smoking, and quivering, like a fugitive brought back to prison after a chase." This was the rebbe's son, Ilya (Elijah), the narrator was told, "an accursed son, a wicked son, a disobedient son." The narrator was glad to leave this death-like world for his revolutionary mobile home, "the agit-train of the First Cavalry Army, where awaited me the sparkle of hundreds of lights, the enchanted brilliance of the radio station, the insistent rolling of the printing presses, and my unfinished article for the *Red Cavalryman* newspaper."[105]

The narrator met the rebbe's son a few months later. In his diary entry on 12 September 1920, which was Rosh Hashanah eve, Babel had described a panicked retreat: as their train left the station "wounded men with distorted faces jumped into a railroad car, a political officer, panting, his trousers fallen down, a Jew with a delicate, translucent face." As fiction, this political officer was the rebbe's son. As the "typhoid-ridden peasant horde" tried to board the fleeing train, the narrator tossed the crowd some leaflets written by Trotsky, having run out of potatoes to throw: "but only one of them stretched out a dirty, dead hand for a leaflet. And I recognized Ilya, the son of the Zhitomir rebbe ... a prince who had lost his trousers and been broken in two by a soldier's knapsack." He pulled him into the carriage and discovered that he was a communist. Indeed, he was already in the party when they first met in that morgue-like home, but Ilya hesitated to leave his mother. When attached to a Red Army regiment that lacked enough weapons, he experienced the disaster that brought him to this train. Gathering together Ilya's belongings, which had fallen out of his small trunk, the narrator noticed "the mandates of a political agitator and the mementos of a Jewish poet. Portraits of Lenin and Maimonides lay side by side. The gnarled steel of Lenin's skull and the pale silk of the Maimonides portrait. A strand of female hair had been placed in a book of the resolutions of the Sixth Party Congress." As the young man lay dying, "pages of the *Song of Songs* and revolver cartridges drizzled on me in a sad, sparse rain .... a sad rain of sunset washing the dust from my hair." And when the rebbe's son died, "I, barely able to accommodate the storms of my imagination within my ancient body, received my brother's last breath."[106]

Babel was indeed kin to this hybrid communist Jew, agitator poet, and advocate of steel and silk. Violence and death were as central to Babel's reflections as they were ubiquitous in the life of the revolution and in the question of ways to be Jewish. Activists, ranging from Zionists to socialists to ambivalent revolutionaries like Babel, despaired of the weak, obsequious, and passive Jewish type associated with the shtetl—just as Behbudi decried the moral and intellectual backwardness of traditional Muslims and Vynnychenko rejected a Ukrainianness that had not yet overcome values nurtured in conditions of imperial oppression. Babel, in his civil war writings, juxtaposed Jewish fragility and decay with the virility and fertility of Russians, Ukrainians, Cossacks, and Poles. A Cossack who was insulted and morally injured, for example, sought bloody vengeance. An insulted and injured Jew would only lament, talk, and write.[107] But Babel resisted this simple dichotomy by seeking an alternative, more vital, type of Jew. Zionists like Jabotinsky offered the virile Jew of heroic combat and manual labor. Babel's "Lyutov" offered a Bolshevik version: a spectacled Jew on horseback, riding with Cossacks into battle, telling old Jewish philosophers like Gedali that the revolution must be "eaten with gunpowder" and "seasoned with the finest blood," and embracing the vital modernity of trains, electricity, and revolution.

Babel knew another Jewish answer, of course: the Odessa Jew. In Petrograd in 1916, we saw, he looked to the sunny and funny spirit of Odessa's Jewish dreamers, jokesters, inventors, and brokers. In his 1920 diary, he contrasted the "lanky, silent, long-bearded" Jews of Poland and Ukraine with the "fat and jovial" Jews of Odessa (21 July). He developed this further when working his civil war notes into fiction: "Lifeless Jewish shtetls... A synagogue crouches on the barren earth, eyeless and battered, enmeshed in a warren of hovels... Narrow-shouldered Jews linger sadly at the crossroads. In one's memory flares up the image of southern Jews—jovial, paunchy, bubbling like cheap wine." To be sure, in the lives of the shtetl Jews of the Pale of Settlement there was a "dark grandeur" born of "grief." But there was no "warm pulse of blood" in their bodies.[108] Babel developed this contrast still further in his popular "Odessa stories" of the early 1920s. Here was the life-affirming alternative to the bloodless grandeur of suffering: a Dionysian (or Rabelaisian) Jewish spirit of feasting, sensuality, money, and laughter. Here was the vital Jewish street, populated by secular and iconoclastic Jews, Jewish tricksters and gangsters, and Jewish pleasure.

Most of these tales featured Benya Krik the gangster. In the most famous story, "How it was Done in Odessa," the narrator and an old man sat on a cemetery wall. While gazing at this landscape of the dead, the narrator asked how Benya Krik became the Jewish "king" of Odessa. "Well then," he was told,

> forget for a time that you have glasses on your nose and autumn in your heart. Forget that you start fights from behind your writing desk and stutter when you are among people. Imagine for a moment that you fight in public squares and stutter only on paper. You are a tiger, a lion, a cat. You can spend the night with a Russian woman, and the Russian woman will be satisfied. You are twenty-five years old. If the sky and the earth had rings attached to them, you would grab these rings and pull the sky down to earth.

This was the sort of man Benya Krik was, a new Jew who boldly wore cream-colored pants, a chocolate jacket, and raspberry red boots—a proud and unafraid Jew, an audacious man of the world who had overcome every injury of diaspora and empire. Krik knew all about Jewish exile and suffering: it seemed to him that God made "a mistake when he settled the Jews in Russia so they could be tormented as if they were in hell." But he was going to fight and play not mourn, and live in a fecund (and funny) Jewish world of song, love, sex, and birth.[109]

These were stories from the past. And like almost everything else Babel wrote, the "dense sadness of memory" blended with visions of living heroically in the new. Fighting and shouting in the public square about a revolution for happiness and pleasure, or simply embracing pleasure, contended and mixed with the need to mourn all the loss, failure, and disenchantment. Babel could ride bravely alongside Red Cossacks without, as it were, losing the glasses of knowledge on his nose or the melancholy in his heart. For perhaps these were not contradictory perspectives. Perhaps these were part of a unifying and transcending vision in which salvation required one to grasp the power of all dimensions of human experience, including what conventional wisdom viewed as opposites. Or perhaps this was something like what Walter Benjamin, the German-Jewish radical thinker, suggested in his reflections on history and salvation in 1940, amidst another catastrophe for Jews and the world, that there is insight in the traditional Jewish belief that the path into the future is found not by "inquiring into the future" itself, but along the dialectical path of "remembrance" in the present. Indeed, if one could "grasp the constellation" that is the intersection of past, present, and future one could see that "every second was the small gateway in time through which the Messiah might enter."[110]

To overcome the oppressive legacies of an imperial past and the limits of the revolutionary present, to build a path out of the world as it was, and as it is, toward the world as it ought to be, Behbudi, Vynnychenko, and Babel believed that nothing less than deep revolutions in culture, morality, and spirit could save their peoples and all people. This was a cultural revolution that should not overthrow difference and diversity or reject the essential dialogues between "our way of life" and the needs of "our age," Behbudi insisted, but must realize the potentials of this entire cosmopolitan mix. This was a revolution not limited to any one aspect of human experience or need, for only "all-sided liberation," Vynnychenko warned, would be liberation at all. Even what seemed like contradictions—violence and happiness, loss and redemption, mourning and laughing—must be united in this revolution, Babel showed, if the truth that can make one free was to be grasped. In different ways, all three reached toward a revolutionary knowledge that might open that "small gateway" through which the darkness of inequality, exclusion, and violence could be overcome.

Notes

1. *Novoe vremia*, 11 May 1896, 1–2. See also Richard Wortman, *Scenarios of Power: Myth and Ceremony in Russian Monarchy*, ii (Princeton, 2000), 351.

2. N. A. Troinitskii (ed.), *Pervaia vseobshchaia perepis' naseleniia Rossiiskoi Imperii, 1897 g.*, vyp. 7 (St Petersburg, 1905), 1–9. Finland was not included in the census.

3. Influential books on the history of the Russian empire include Daniel R. Brower and Edward J. Lazzerini (eds), *Russia's Orient: Imperial Borderlands and Peoples, 1700–1917* (Bloomington, IN, 1997); Jane Burbank and David Ransel, *Imperial Russia: New Histories for the Empire* (Bloomington, IN, 1998); Adeeb Khalid, *The Politics of Muslim Cultural Reform: Jadidism in Central Asia* (Berkeley, CA, 1998); Andreas Kappeler, *The Russian Empire: A Multiethnic History*, tr. Alfred Clayton (Harlow, 2001); Robert P. Geraci, *Window on the East: National and Imperial Identities in Late Tsarist Russia*

(Ithaca, NY, 2001); David Schimmelpenninck van der Oye, *Toward the Rising Sun: Russian Ideologies of Empire and the Path of War with Japan* (DeKalb, IL, 2001); Daniel Brower, *Turkestan and the Fate of the Russian Empire* (London, 2003); Nicholas Breyfogle, *Heretics and Colonizers: Forging Russia's Empire in the South Caucasus* (Ithaca, NY, 2005); I. Gerasimov, S. Glebov, A. Kaplunovskii, M. Mogil'ner, and A. Semenov, *Novaia imperskaia istoriia postsovetskogo prostranstva* (Kazan, 2004); Robert Crews, *For Prophet and Tsar: Islam and Empire in Russia and Central Asia* (Cambridge, 2006); Jeff Sahadeo, *Russian Colonial Society in Tashkent, 1865–1923* (Bloomington, IN, 2007); Jane Burbank, Mark von Hagen, and Anatolyi Remnev (eds), *Russian Empire: Space, People, Power, 1700–1930* (Bloomington, IN, 2007); Ilya Gerasimov, Jan Kusber, and Alexander Semyonov (eds), *Empire Speaks out: Languages of Rationalization and Self-Description in the Russian Empire* (Leiden, 2009); Vera Tolz, *Russia's own Orient: The Politics of Identity and Oriental Studies in the Late Imperial and Early Soviet Periods* (Oxford, 2011); Stephen M. Norris and Willard Sunderland (eds), *Russia's People of Empire: Life Stories from Eurasia, 1500 to the Present* (Bloomington, IN, 2012); Joshua A. Sanborn, *Imperial Apocalypse: The Great War and the Destruction of the Russian Empire* (Oxford, 2014); Willard Sunderland, *The Baron's Cloak: A History of the Russian Empire in War and Revolution* (Ithaca, NY, 2014); Mustafa Tuna, *Imperial Russia's Muslims: Islam, Empire, and European Modernity, 1878–1914* (Cambridge, 2015); Elena Campbell, *The Muslim Question and Russian Imperial Governance* (Bloomington, IN, 2015); Adeeb Khalid, *Making Uzbekistan: Nation, Empire, and Revolution in the Early USSR* (Ithaca, NY, 2015).

For studies of the Soviet "empire," in addition to the books already listed that cross the 1917 divide, see especially Yuri Slezkine, *Arctic Mirrors: Russia and the Small Peoples of the North* (Ithaca, NY, 1994); Bruce Grant, *In the Soviet House of Culture: A History of Perestroikas* (Princeton, 1995); Terry Martin, *The Affirmative Action Empire: Nations and Nationalism in the Soviet Union, 1923–1939* (Ithaca, NY, 2001); Ronald Grigor Suny and Terry Martin (eds), *A State of Nations: Empire and Nation-Making in the Age of Lenin and Stalin* (Oxford, 2001); Adrienne Edgar, *Tribal Nation: The Making of Soviet Turkmenistan* (Princeton, 2004); Francine Hirsch, *Empire of Nations: Ethnographic Knowledge and the Making of the Soviet Union* (Ithaca, NY, 2005); Marianne Kamp, *The New Woman in Uzbekistan: Islam, Modernity, and Unveiling under Communism* (Seattle, 2006).

4. Nikolai Danilevsky in 1871 and Mikhail Pogodin in 1854, quoted in Mark Bassin, "Geographies of Imperial Identity," *The Cambridge History of*

Russia, ii. *Imperial Russia, 1689–1917*, ed. Dominic Lieven (Cambridge, 2006), 54, 63.

5. E. E. Ukhtomskii, *Puteshestvie na vostok ego Imperatorskogo Vysochestva Gosudaria naslednika Tsarevicha, 1890–1891*, 4 parts (St Petersburg and Leipzig, 1893), esp. pt. 3: 209, 213–14, 225, 228; pt. 4: 226–7, 242; Ukhtomskii, *K sobytiiam v Kitae: Ob otnosheniiakh Zapada i Rossii k Vostoku* (St Petersburg, 1900). See Schimmelpenninck, *Toward the Rising Sun;* Tolz, *Russia's own Orient;* Marlène Laruelle, "'The White Tsar': Romantic Imperialism in Russia's Legitimizing of Conquering the Far East," *Acta Slavica Iaponica,* 25 (2008): 113–34.

6. Both documents are translated in Robert Paul Browder and Alexander F. Kerensky, *The Russian Provisional Government, 1917: Documents,* 3 vols. (Stanford, CA, 1961), i. 317–19.

7. "Declaration of the Rights of the Peoples of Russia," 2 (15) November 1917, in *Dekrety Sovetskoi vlasti,* i (Moscow, 1957), 39–41.

8. For a translation of Lenin's essay (originally published in April–June 1914 in *Prosveshchenie*), see <https://www.marxists.org/archive/lenin/works/1914/self-det/> [accessed 26 August 2016] (the quotation is from the final paragraph).

9. I. V. Stalin, "Doklad ob ocherednyi zadachakh partii v natsional'nom voprose," *Desiatyi s"ezd Rossiiskoi kommunisticheskoi partii: Stenograficheskii otchet* (Moscow, 1921), in vol. v of Stalin's collected works, at <http://www.magister.msk.ru/library/stalin/> [accessed 26 August 2016].

10. Burbank et al., *Russian Empire,* 7, 15, 17–19, 53–4, 170, 197, 204 (quotation), 425.

11. Key works on Central Asia and on Muslims in the Russian empire, notwithstanding sometimes large differences in interpretation, include Brower and Lazzerini, *Russia's Orient;* Khalid, *Politics of Muslim Cultural Reform;* Brower, *Turkestan and the Fate of the Russian Empire;* Crews, *For Prophet and Tsar;* Sahadeo, *Russian Colonial Society in Tashkent;* Tuna, *Imperial Russia's Muslims;* Campbell, *The Muslim Question;* Khalid, *Making Uzbekistan.*

12. I use established English language spellings of place names rather than transliterate these names according to current scholarly standards from Uzbek, Ukrainian, Polish, or Russian. Readers should keep in mind that these established English spellings are not politically neutral: they tend to be adaptations from the Russian and so reflect the history of imperial rule.

13. Adeeb Khalid's work is far and away the best scholarly source for the study of Central Asian intellectuals, reformers, and politics in the pre-revolutionary, revolutionary, and Soviet years. Indeed, I rely rather heavily

on his work (I am also unable to read the original Uzbek and Tajik sources). I am also grateful to him for looking over a draft of this section.

14. On the growing importance of the hajj for Russia's Muslim subjects and the government's active involvement in supporting and regulating it, see Eileen Kane, *Russian Hajj: Empire and the Pilgrimage to Mecca* (Ithaca, NY, 2015).

15. For the use of this term in the context of British India, see Seema Alavi, *Muslim Cosmopolitanism in the Age of Empire* (Cambridge, MA, 2015).

16. Khalid, *Politics of Muslim Cultural Reform*, 161–2, 164, 168, 173, 176.

17. Ibid. 169–72.

18. "Islah ne demakdadur [What is Reform]," *Khurshid* [The Sun], 28 September 1906, in Charles Kurzman (ed.), *Modernist Islam, 1840–1940: A Sourcebook* (Oxford, 2002), 228. See also Khalid, *Politics of Muslim Cultural Reform*, 136–7.

19. Quoted from *The Mirror*, 27 November 1917, in Adeeb Khalid, "Representations of Russia in Central Asian Jadid Discourse," in Brower and Lazzerini, *Russia's Orient*, 188.

20. Khalid, *Politics of Muslim Cultural Reform*, 137–41, 146.

21. Mahmud Khoja Behbudi, *Padarkush* (Samarkand, 1913). A translation and analysis appears in Edward Allworth, "Murder as Metaphor in the First Central Asian Drama," *Ural-Altaische Jahrbuecher*, 58 (1986): 65–97. For discussion, and alternate translations of selected passages, see Khalid, *Politics of Muslim Cultural Reform*, 129–30, 144, and his "Representations of Russia," 191–5.

22. See Khalid's discussions of the concept of "progress," in *Politics of Muslim Cultural Reform*, esp. 107–13, and *Making Uzbekistan*, esp. 27–9.

23. Khalid, *Politics of Muslim Cultural Reform*, esp. 175–6, 184–90, 214.

24. On the meanings of "Sart," see Khalid, *Politics of Muslim Cultural Reform*, 199–209, and Sahadeo, *Russian Colonial Society in Tashkent*, passim.

25. Khalid, *Politics of Muslim Cultural Reform*, 174–6, 190–7, 206, 209–14 (Behbudi quotations on p. 194).

26. Khalid, *Making Uzbekistan*, 295.

27. On Muslim politics in 1905–6, see Campbell, *The Muslim Question*, ch. 6.

28. Khalid, *Making Uzbekistan*, 47–9.

29. From the translation by Allworth, "Murder as Metaphor," 87–8.

30. On Jadid meanings of homeland (*watan*), Khalid, *Politics of Muslim Cultural Reform*, 209.

31. Ibid. 217.

32. Ibid. 237–9, 241.

33. Ibid. 239–41; Sahadeo, *Russian Colonial Society in Tashkent*, 176–82.
34. From an article published in a conservative paper in June 1917, quoted in Khalid, *Making Uzbekistan*, 61.
35. Quoted ibid. 71–2.
36. Resolution of 27 November 1917, published in *Izvestiia Vremennogo pravitel'stvo Avtonomnogo Turkestana*, 13 December 1917, in *Pobeda Oktiabr'skoi revoliutsii v Uzbekistane: sbornik dokumentov*, 2 vols. (Tashkent, 1963 and 1972), ii. 27.
37. Khalid, *Politics of Muslim Cultural Reform*, 245–301, and *Making Uzbekistan*, chs. 2–3; Sahadeo, *Russian Colonial Society in Tashkent*, chap. 7; G. Safarov, *Kolonial'naia revoliutsiia: Opyt Turkestana* (Moscow, 1921); Shoshana Keller, *To Moscow, Not Mecca: The Soviet Campaign Against Islam in Central Asia, 1917–1941* (Westport, CT, 2001), ch. 2.
38. I. Stalin, "Nashi zadachi na Vostoke," *Pravda*, 2 March 1919, in I. V. Stalin, *Sochineniia*, iv (Moscow, 1947), 236–9.
39. Adeeb Khalid, *Making Uzbekistan*, and his "Nationalizing the Revolution in Central Asia: The Transformation of Jadidism, 1917-1920," in Suny and Martin, *A State of Nations*, 145–62.
40. Quoted in Khalid, "Nationalizing the Revolution," 150–1.
41. Mark von Hagen, "Does Ukraine have a History?" *Slavic Review*, 54/3 (Fall 1995): 658–73. See also Serhii Plokhy, *Unmaking Imperial Russia: Mykhailo Hrushevsky and the Writing of Ukrainian History* (Toronto, 2005), esp. 7–13; Serhy Yekelchyk, *Ukraine: Birth of a Modern Nation* (Oxford, 2007), 6–7.
42. Troinitskii (ed.), *Pervaia vseobshchaia perepis' naseleniia Rossiiskoi Imperii, 1897 g.*, table XIII (distribution of the population by native language). See also Michael Hamm, "Continuity and Change in Late Imperial Kiev," in Hamm (ed.), *The City in Late Imperial Russia* (Bloomington, IN, 1986), 92.
43. See Kappeler, *The Russian Empire*, 220–30; Yekelchyk, *Ukraine*, 39–61; Plokhy, *Unmaking Imperial Russia*, 17–21.
44. See, especially, Plokhy, *Unmaking Imperial Russia;* Thomas M. Prymak, *Mykhailo Hrushevsky: The Politics of National Culture* (Toronto, 1987).
45. Frank Sysyn, "Introduction to the *History of Ukraine-Rus',*" in Mykhailo Hrushevsky, *History of Ukraine-Rus'*, tr. Marta Skorupsky, ed. Andrzej Poppe and Frank E. Sysyn, i. (Edmonton and Toronto, 1997).
46. Plokhy, *Unmaking Imperial Russia*, 56–7.
47. M. Grushevskii, *Osvobozhdenie Rossii i ukrainskii vopros: stat'i i zametki* (St Petersburg, 1907), p. iii.
48. Quoted by Plokhy, *Unmaking Imperial Russia*, 74–5.

49. Biographical information is from a number of sources, though these are sometimes contradictory and poorly referenced. Most useful are S. Chmyr, "Vladimir Kirillovich Vinnichenko," *Politicheskie Partii Rossii, Konets XIX–pervaia tret' XX veka: Entsiklopediia* (Moscow, 1996), 113–14; Andrew Kaspryk, "Volodymyr Vynnychenko's Nietzschean Revolutionary Hero" (Ph.D. thesis, University of Illinois, Chicago, 2000); and Mykola Soroka, *Faces of Displacement: The Writings of Volodymyr Vynnychenko* (Montreal, 2012). On his role during 1917–19, see Taras Hunczak (ed.), *The Ukraine, 1917–1921: A Study in Revolution* (Cambridge, 1977), passim.

50. Paul R. Magocsi, *A History of Ukraine: The Land and its Peoples,* 2nd edn (Toronto, 2010), 402.

51. Volodymyr Vynnychenko, *Shchodennyk* [Diary], i (1911–1920), ed. Hryhory Kostiuk (Edmonton and New York, 1980), 353, quoted in Kaspryk, "Volodymyr Vynnychenko's Nietzschean Revolutionary Hero," 2–3.

52. Quoted in Ivan L. Rudnytsky, "Volodymyr Vynnychenko's Ideas in the Light of his Political Writings," in his *Essays in Modern Ukrainian History,* ed. Peter L. Rudnytsky (Edmonton, 1987), 428.

53. The programs of the RUP, the USDWP, and others are summarized in the encyclopedia *Politicheskie Partii Rossii.*

54. Kaspryk, "Volodymyr Vynnychenko's Nietzschean Revolutionary Hero," 5.

55. Soroka, *Faces of Displacement,* 15.

56. "Sovet Komissarov—Rade" (4 December 1917), *Izvestiia,* 6 December 1917, 1–2.

57. Important recent literary studies of Vynnychenko's work are Soroka, *Faces of Displacement,* and Kaspryk, "Volodymyr Vynnychenko's Nietzschean Revolutionary Hero." Because my knowledge of Ukrainian is limited, I have relied a good deal on these studies in considering Vynnychenko's fiction. I am grateful to both scholars for their work.

58. From Vynnychenko's stories "Zina" (1909), "A Mystery" (1910), and "Story about Yakim's House" (1912), discussed in Soroka, *Faces of Displacement,* 57–61, 82–93.

59. Volodymyr Panchenko, *Tvorchist Volodymyra Vynnychenka 1902–1920 rr.* (Ph. D. dissertation, Kiev University, 1998) at <http://library.kr.ua/books/panchenko> [accessed 9 August 2016], section 2.3. See Soroka, *Faces of Displacement,* 68.

60. "Otkrytoe pis'mo k russkim pisateliam," *Ukrainskaia zhizn'* (Moscow), 1913/10, in Volodymyr Vynnychenko, *Publitsystyka,* ed. Viktor Burbela (Kiev, 2002), 35–8.

61. "V chem nasha sila," *Ukrainskaia zhizn',* 1915/7, in *Publitsystyka,* 39–43.

62. Soroka, *Faces of Displacement,* 34–5, 65–7.

63. Vynnychenko, *Shchodennyk*, 23 January 1917, i. 249–50.

64. Soroka, *Faces of Displacement*, 32–3.

65. Rudnytsky, "Volodymyr Vynnychenko's Ideas," 417–36.

66. *Honesty with Oneself* (*Chesnist z soboiu*, 1910). My discussion draws on Soroka, *Faces of Displacement* (especially ch. 1) and Kaspryk, "Volodymyr Vynnychenko's Nietzschean Revolutionary Hero" (especially chs. 3 and 8). Vynnychenko elaborates his ideas in "About the Morality of the Exploiters and of the Exploited" ("Pro moral panuiuchykh i moral pryhnoblenykh"), a reply to criticism of his novel *Honesty with Oneself,* published in the journal *Nash holos* in Lviv in 1911.

67. Suppressed Cossack autonomy was a key theme in Hrushevsky's *History of Ukraine-Rus'*, but was an older and larger story. See Serhii Plokhy, *The Cossack Myth: History and Nationhood in the Age of Empires* (Cambridge, 2012).

68. Quotations from *I Want! A Novel (Khochu! Roman)* are from Kaspryk, "Volodymyr Vynnychenko's Nietzschean Revolutionary Hero," 353–6.

69. The Ukrainian-language texts of the Universals are available at <http://gska2.rada.gov.ua/site/const/> [accessed 26 August 2016] and <http://tsdea.archives.gov.ua/ua/?page=nezal_19_#U_1> [accessed 9 August 2016]. Translations: <http://www.ditext.com/hunczak/universals.html> [accessed 9 August 2016].

70. V. Vynnychenko, *Vidrodzhennia natsii*, i (Kyiv-Viden, 1920), 99–100. See also Kaspryk, "Volodymyr Vynnychenko's Nietzschean Revolutionary Hero," 7.

71. Vynnychenko, *Vidrodzhennia natsii*, i. 150.

72. Ibid. iii. 502.

73. V. Vynnychenko, "Odvertyi lyst do M. Gorkoho," first published in *Ukrains'ki visti* (Paris), 19 July 1928, 3–4 (and soon reprinted in many other Ukrainian-language publications), in Vynnychenko, *Publitsystyka,* 191–8. Discussed in Mykola Soroka, "The Russian-Ukrainian Encounter: Gorky Versus Vynnychenko," *Toronto Slavic Quarterly,* 16 (2006) at <http://sites.utoronto.ca/tsq/archive.shtml> [accessed 26 August 2016].

74. Rudnytsky, "Volodymyr Vynnychenko's Ideas," 417–36.

75. Quoted ibid. 429.

76. Vynnychenko, *Shchodennyk*, 3 June 1920, i. 433–4. See also Soroka, *Faces of Displacement*, 100.

77. "Ne u vs'omu chesny z soboiu (vyryvky z neposlanoho lista do TsK RKP)," December 1920, in Vynnychenko, *Publitsystyka,* 58–63.

78. V. Vynnychenko, "Utopiia i diisnist'," *Nova doba*, 2 (13 March 1920), 1. See Soroka, *Faces of Displacement*, 101.

79. See, especially, Steven Zipperstein, *Imagining Russian Jewry: Memory, History, Identity* (Seattle, 1999); Zvi Gitelman, *A Century of Ambivalence: The Jews of Russia and the Soviet Union, 1881 to the Present* (Bloomington, IN, 2001); Alice Stone Nakhimovsky, *Russian-Jewish Literature and Identity* (Baltimore, MD, 1992); Michael Stanislawski, *Zionism and the Fin de Siècle: Cosmopolitanism and Nationalism from Nordau to Jabotinsky* (Berkeley, CA, 2001); Benjamin Nathans, *Beyond the Pale: The Jewish Encounter with Late Imperial Russia* (Berkeley, CA, 2002), Yuri Slezkine, *The Jewish Century* (Princeton, 2004); Sarah Abrevaya Stein, *Making Jews Modern: The Yiddish and Ladino Press in the Russian and Ottoman Empires* (Bloomington, IN, 2004); Jeffrey Veidlinger, *Jewish Public Culture in the Late Russian Empire* (Bloomington, IN, 2009); Kenneth Moss, *Jewish Renaissance in the Russian Revolution* (Princeton, 2009); Eugene M. Avrutin, *Jews and the Imperial State: Identification Politics in Tsarist Russia* (Ithaca, NY, 2010); Eugene M. Avrutin and Harriet Murav, *Jews in the East European Borderlands: Essays in Honor of John Doyle Klier* (Boston, 2012).

80. The following draws on some of the vast scholarship about Odessa, its history, myths, and especially its Jewish communities. See Steven J. Zipperstein, *The Jews of Odessa: A Cultural History, 1794–1881* (Stanford, CA, 1985); Patricia Herlihy, *Odessa: A History, 1794–1914* (Cambridge, MA, 1986); Robert Weinberg, *The Revolution of 1905 in Odessa: Blood on the Steps* (Bloomington, IN, 1993); Roshanna P. Sylvester, *Tales of Old Odessa: Crime and Civility in a City of Thieves* (DeKalb, IL, 2005); Charles King, *Odessa: Genius and Death in a City of Dreams* (New York, 2011); Jarrod Tandy, *City of Rogues and Schnorrers: Russia's Jews and the Myth of Old Odessa* (Bloomington, IN, 2011); Rebecca Jane Stanton, *Isaac Babel and the Self-Invention of Odessan Modernism* (Evanston, IL, 2012).

81. Mrs [Katharine Blanche] Guthrie, *Through Russia: From St. Petersburg to Astrakhan and the Crimea* (London, 1874), ii. 284. See also King, *Odessa*, ch. 5.

82. Quoted by Herlihy, *Odessa,* 274.

83. On population, see Frederick W. Skinner, "Odessa and the Problem of Urban Modernization," in Hamm (ed.), *The City in Late Imperial Russia*, 209–18; Herlihy, *Odessa*, ch. 10; Weinberg, *The Revolution of 1905*, 1–20.

84. The literature on cosmopolitanism as a concept (variously descriptive, analytical, philosophical, and ethical) and studies of past and present cosmopolitan cities, very often port cities, is vast and rapidly growing.

85. Sylvester, *Tales of Old Odessa*, 3, 49; Stanislawski, *Zionism,* 126; Tandy, *City of Rogues and Schnorrers*, 2 (quotation), 17; Stanton, *Isaac Babel*, 26.

Grigorii Freidin, "Forma soderzhaniia: Odessa—mama Isaaka Babelia," *Neprikosnovennyi zapas*, 4/78 (2011) at <http://magazines.russ.ru/nz/2011/4/fr26.html> [accessed 26 August 2016].

86. John Klier quoted in Sylvester, *Tales of Old Odessa*, 13.

87. My discussion of Babel's biography, experiences, and writings are based on scholarly studies of his life and work and on Babel's own writings. Gregory Freidin is the most knowledgeable and insightful scholar now working on Babel, evident in a large number of essays and a forthcoming book. For example, Gregory Freidin, "Isaac Babel," *European Writers: The Twentieth Century* (New York, 1983); Freidin (ed.), *The Enigma of Isaac Babel: Biography, History, Context* (Stanford, CA, 2009). I have benefitted enormously from his insights (and not only about Babel)—and his willingness to look over a draft of this section. See also Milton Ehre, *Isaac Babel* (Boston, 1986); Nakhimovsky, *Russian-Jewish Literature and Identity*; Efraim Sicher, "The Jewishness of Babel," in his *Jews in Russian Literature After the October Revolution* (Cambridge, 1995) and his *Babel' in Context: A Study in Cultural Identity* (Boston, 2012); Harriet Murav, *Music from a Speeding Train: Jewish Literature in Post-Revolution Russia* (Stanford, CA, 2011); Stanton, *Isaac Babel and the Self-Invention of Odessan Modernism*. For Babel's works in translation, see especially *The Complete Works of Isaac Babel*, ed. Nathalie Babel, tr. Peter Constantine (New York, 2002) and *Isaac Babel's Selected Writings*, ed. Gregory Freidin, tr. Peter Constantine (New York, 2010). Both volumes also contain chronologies of Babel's life by Freidin, where he attempts to sort out the facts from Babel's partly self-invented biography. For the Russian originals, I have relied on Isaak Babel', *Sobranie sochinenii v chetyrekh tomakh* (Moscow, 2006). My quotations are based on the Russian originals, usually as checked or adapted versions of Constantine's translations.

88. Babel', "Avtobiografiia" (first published in *Pisateli: Avtobiografii i portrety sovremennykh russikh prozaikov*, Moscow, 1926), reprinted in Babel', *Sobranie sochinenii*, i. 35–6.

89. Ibid. i. 36.

90. Ibid. i. 35.

91. Sicher, "Jewishness of Babel," especially 75–9, 82–5, and *Babel' in Context*, especially ch. 2.

92. On the larger trend, including Babel's place, see Slezkine, *The Jewish Century*, ch. 3 ("Babel's First Love").

93. Joseph B. Schechtman, *Rebel and Statesman: The Vladimir Jabotinsky Story, the Early Years* (New York, 1956); Nakhimovsky, *Russian-Jewish Literature and Identity*, ch. 2; Stanislawski, *Zionism*.

94. "Staryi Shloime," *Ogni* (Kiev), 9 February 1913. Babel's authorship was not acknowledged at the time. In the following notes, Babel's works are given as titles alone, along with their date and publication details. They can be found in translation in *The Complete Works of Isaac Babel* and in Russian in Babel', *Sobranie sochinenii*.

95. "Detstvo. U babushki" (written 1915; first published 1965).

96. "Moi listki: Publichnaia biblioteka," *Zhurnal zhurnalov*, 48 (1916); "Moi listki: Deviat'," *Zhurnal zhurnalov*, 49 (1916); "Moi listki: Odessa," *Zhurnal zhurnalov*, 51 (December 1916).

97. The first quotation is from Babel's first column, "Pervaia pomoshch'" (First Aid), *Novaia zhizn'*, 9 March 1918. The second is from a piece published just after *Novaia zhizn'* was closed by the government, "Na stantsii: nabrosok s nature" (At the station: a sketch from life), *Era* (Petrograd), 13 July 1918.

98. "Dvorets materinstva" (The Palace of Motherhood), *Novaia zhizn'*, 31 March 1918.

99. *Krasnyi kavalerist*, 13 and 14 August, 17 September 1920. English translations can be found in *Complete Works*, 363–76, and *1920 Diary*, 101–8.

100. English translations of the diary include Constantine's in *Complete Works* and H. T. Willetts in Isaac Babel, *1920 Diary* (New Haven, 1995). My translations are from the Russian originals in *Sobranie sochinenii*, ii. 222–334. In the text, I cite the date of the original diary entry.

101. See Vladimir Jabotinsky's essay "On Nationalism," published in *Odessa News* (*Odesskie novosti*) on 30 January 1903, <http://ru.wikisource.org> [accessed 9 August 2016]; and his essay "Race" (Rasa) of 1913 in V. L. Zhabotinskii, *Fel'etony* (Berlin, 1922), 167–76.

102. Murav, *Music from a Speeding Train*, 24, 42.

103. In addition to the translation in *Complete Works*, 197–361, see also the excellent translation by David McDuff in Isaac Babel, *Collected Stories*, ed. Efraim Sicher (London, 1994), 91–233.

104. "Gedali," *Krasnaia nov'*, 1924/4 (June-July), in *Sobranie sochinenii*, ii. 70–4. Although "Gedali," unlike the following two stories, was written in the present tense, I have rendered "Gedali" in the past tense as well, to emphasize Babel's reworking of history and memory across these three tales and in *Red Cavalry* generally.

105. "Rabbi," *Krasnaia nov'*, 1924/1 (January–February), in *Sobranie sochinenii*, ii. 79–82.

106. "Syn Rabbi," *Krasnaia nov'*, 1924/1 (January–February), in *Sobranie sochinenii*, ii. 191–4.

107. See discussion in Nakhimovsky, *Russian-Jewish Literature and Identity*, 71, 89–96.

108. "Uchenie o tachanka" (The theory of the tachanka), *Izvestiia Odesskogo gubispolkoma*, 23 February 1923, in *Sobranie sochinenii*, ii. 87–8.

109. From "The King" (Korol', 1921) and "How it was done in Odessa" (Kak eto delalos' v Odesse, 1923), *Sobranie sochinenii*, i. 60–80. Translations in *Complete Works*, 133–54, and Babel, *Collected Stories*, 237–54. See Nakhimovsky, *Russian-Jewish Literature and Identity*, 97–102.

110. Walter Benjamin, "On the Concept of History," *Selected Writings*, 4 vols. (Cambridge, MA, 2003), iv. 397.

CHAPTER 8
UTOPIANS

As a 12-year old in the provincial Georgian city of Kutaisi during the 1905 revolution, Vladimir Mayakovsky, later Russia's most famous "futurist" writer, found thinking about revolution a lot more interesting than thinking about his school work. When his family had to move the following year to Moscow for economic reasons, he volunteered to help Marxists distribute leaflets to workers. When this landed him in prison in 1909 at the age of 16, he enjoyed "raising hell" in jail as much as he had in school and outside factory gates. Years earlier, Lev Bronstein, before becoming famous as "Trotsky," also encountered the thrill of imagining revolution while in high school in the Ukrainian provincial town of Nikolayev, to which his family had recently moved, where he met socialist exiles sent there by the government to keep them out of the main centers of radical activism. He decided, as a teenager, to make revolution his profession, leading in a few years to his own arrest and exile to Siberia at the age of 19. Alexandra Kollontai, growing up in a prosperous St Petersburg family, came to revolution as a discontented young housewife and mother, discovering in socialist books and circles a vision of radically different possibility for her own life and that of other women. The year Trotsky was arrested, she published her first book on a new type of family, the first step toward her life as a revolutionary committed to advocating a new type of love for a new type of society.

These three revolutionaries, different in so many ways despite their shared Marxism and Bolshevism, would surely have joined together to protest my title for this chapter about them. Utopia is a problem for revolutionaries, especially Marxists. If utopia means—as most people have said it does since Thomas More invented the term in his sixteenth-century book *Utopia,* a punning mixture of the Greek for "happy place" (*eutopos*) and "no place" (*outopos*)—a perfected world grounded not in observable reality but in imagination, hope, and desire, a Marxist must reject the charge that they are anything of the sort. Russian Bolsheviks were especially offended by the label, which was often hurled at them by more orthodox Marxist critics. Marxists, in theory, take a fact-based and rational view of social and economic relations, of people as they are, and of the possibilities for change. As Friedrich Engels famously declared in his influential book on different types of socialism, Marxism was "scientific" not "utopian." The problem with "utopian" socialists, Engels complained, was that their solutions to social problems arose entirely out of "the human brain," rather than evolving through careful and reasoned analysis of actual social and economic conditions. It was enough for a utopian socialist, he mocked, that socialism was "the expression of absolute truth, reason and justice, and has only to be discovered to conquer all the world by virtue of its own power."[1] Or as Trotsky would later put this when rejecting the label, utopia is inspired by faith in "miracles" rather than knowledge of "facts."

By calling Kollontai, Trotsky, and Mayakovsky "utopians" I am not trying to turn the tables on them and define their thinking, along with so many other activists in the revolution, as what they denied: ungrounded expressions of fanciful desire and wishful illusion, though there were certainly elements of this. Nor am I branding them as utopians in the negative definition that has become especially common since the Russian revolution and remains strong today: people who so believe in their impossible vision of a perfect society that they try, with terrible consequences, to force it upon the world, which is the story, often framed as "tragedy," that many historians have told about the Bolshevik revolution.[2]

We need not accept these definitions of utopia. I think we can learn something new about the experience of those who tried to make the Russian revolution if we question these conventional definitions.[3] As an alternative, I look to definitions of utopia suggested by a different group of Marxist thinkers, especially Ernst Bloch (1885–1977), Walter Benjamin (1892–1940), and Theodor Adorno (1903–1969). These philosophers were not as enamored with the nineteenth-century cult of scientific rationality as traditional Marxists and were more open to recognizing the intellectual and political value of less "rational" ways of understanding reality and possibility. No less important, they were profoundly affected by the devastating experiences of the first half of the twentieth century, including two world wars and the Russian revolution itself. Indeed, precisely because they experienced the world in such a troubled and disenchanted condition, they sought new sources for hope and of the will to change. It may say something of our own times, too, that their writings have received new attention as part of a renaissance of interest in utopia in both scholarly and public spheres. A remarkable number of writers in recent years have been arguing that, in our era of globalized capitalism, vast inequalities, economic crises, disrupted environments, and frustrated past hopes, including disappointment with the claims and results of communism, we need more than ever a new politics of utopia—not least as a method of thinking about the everyday world that will transform what we dare to try.[4]

This understanding of utopia is less a story about an idealized distant place or time (though such tales can inspire), and even less a fantasy or a blueprint with no grounding in reality, than a way of thinking and feeling about the possibility of living differently than given in the present. This attitude may be rooted in desire, but this is desire as an alternative form of knowledge, understanding, and action—in philosophical terms, an epistemology, a hermeneutics, and a praxis.[5] First, to simplify this rich body of thinking, utopia is a stance of "determined negation of that which merely is" in the name of "what should be." As Bloch put this, the "utopian impulse" is a natural urge found in all human societies to "venture beyond" the limits and inadequacies of the world as it is, beyond the "darkness of the lived moment," to discover an emerging "not-yet." Or as he more lyrically wrote in his 1918 book *Spirit of Utopia,* utopia is an impulse, deep in the human psyche, to "summon what is not, build into the blue, build ourselves into the blue, and seek there the true, the real, where the merely factual disappears." Because the merely factual, he knew, is often a world of oppression, brutality, and suffering.[6]

Second, this utopia challenges what we imagine to be possible and impossible, what we assume to be the limits of "reality." In Bloch's words again: "the ocean of possibility is much greater than our customary land of reality." Because we are located so fully in our non-utopian present, in a world of expectations shaped more by what actually is than by what might be, we naturally mistake the visionary's "not-yet" for the realist's "impossible."[7] Already in the eighteenth century, Jean-Jacques Rousseau said something similar (and is often quoted for this utopian insight): "the bounds of possibility, in moral matters, are less narrow than we imagine: it is our weaknesses, our vices, and our prejudices that confine them." This is why, he noted, slaves often "smile in mockery" at those who preach freedom.[8]

Third, utopia challenges how we think of time, especially the time of history. Instead of the conventional view of historical time as orderly, linear movement forward, as mere "progress," utopian time is what a recent scholar has called a "queer time" that disturbs the trapped linearity of "straight time," which "tells us that there is no future but the here and now of our everyday life." Queer time is utopian "open-ness" to unimagined historical possibility.[9] In 1940, during a particu-larly dark time in Europe, Walter Benjamin tried to grasp the right metaphor for describing this open conception of time. Adapting the Marxist image of revolution as a "leap from the kingdom of necessity to the kingdom of freedom," he suggested that history is always "open towards the future," that it always contains within itself the "redemp-tive" possibility for a sudden appearance of a "messianic time" that could "blast open the continuum of history," overcome a history marked mainly by "catastrophe," and allow humanity to "leap in the open air of history."[10] This leap, he argued, is also how Marxists understand revolution. Or at least, Benjamin suggested in an aside, revolution is the refusal to accept any longer the catastrophe of the present: "Marx says that revolutions are the locomotive of world history. But perhaps it is quite otherwise. Perhaps revolutions are an attempt by the passengers on this train—namely the human race—to activate the emergency brake."[11] Either way, what is essential is that revolutions disrupt assumptions that the future can only appear along the straight tracks where the present seems to be heading, and so challenge how we understand time and history in order to overcome the "state of emergency in which we live," which has become so normalized that we no longer recognize that it is an emergency at all.

Utopia is this open disruption of the now, for the sake of possibility, not a closed map of the future. It is the leap not yet the landing.

Kollontai, Trotsky, and Mayakovsky shared this type of thinking. In different ways, they refused to accept the limitations of the present in theory or practice: the "darkness" and "catastrophe" that Mayakovsky the poet colorfully called "the shit of the present." They were among many who fought against constricted assumptions about what was possible and not, against those who warned that a leap toward the kingdom of freedom was utopian. With vigorous energy and strong language, they devoted their lives to the "negation of that which merely is" in the name of "what should be." In the most practical ways they could find, they disturbed the "darkness of the lived moment" and tried to smash the barrier holding back the "ocean of possibility." Or, at least, changing metaphors again (for metaphors help our minds see what is hard to grasp in plain language), they pulled at the emergency brake. At the very least, as the Marxist literary theorist Fredric Jameson put it, they "rattled the bars" of necessity.[12] Perhaps this refusal would open the way toward a future that had simply "not yet arrived." Perhaps it was simply necessary to act "as if" the kingdom of freedom was possible. Certainly, their utopian impulses would collide with the stubbornness of the present, with the tenacious force of necessity. All three would find their dreams curtailed, their efforts to leap into the clear, free, and unpredictable open air of history grounded—though each reacted very differently. Their early critical impulse, rather than their later disappointments, is the story this chapter explores, for this was the utopian impulse so central to the experience of the Russian revolution for so many.

Alexandra Kollontai (1872–1952)

Kollontai began her fight against the world as it was given to her in intimate and gendered spheres so often dismissed by Russia's revolutionaries as secondary (Figure 12).[13] Born into an old noble family in St Petersburg, she defied the conventions of her class and her own parents' will by declaring that she would marry only "out of a great passion," which she believed she felt for an "impecunious young engineer" (and cousin) Vladimir Kollontai.[14] After a few years of marriage and

Figure 12. Alexandra Kollontai, 1910. Public Domain.

the birth of their child, she grew disenchanted—perhaps with Vladimir and their relationship, though she would later describe her feelings as arising from a growing awareness that love, domesticity, and mother-hood were not enough for a woman to enjoy the fullness of life. Vladimir judged her interest in reading, her time spent at public lectures, and her participation in underground socialist circles as "an act of personal defiance directed against him." Refusing to be constrained, she left with her young son, though she kept her married name, perhaps as a sign of independence from her family.[15] Her first public act in her new independent life was to write and publish a book on child-rearing, in which she argued, along familiar progressive lines, that parents should nurture and stimulate their children's moral and intellectual independ-ence, spirit of autonomy, and strength of will. This will not lead to egoism, as most people believed, but to a desire to uplift the whole of society: a weak-willed person "will never take courage, will not have the desire to go against predominant beliefs; he will not begin to search for new ways, he will not begin to fight for new truths, and without such a fight...humanity will never go forward and no perfection will be possible."[16] Clearly this was a story about herself. But she began to see the connection between her story and lives outside her social class: she found it increasingly difficult, she later claimed, to "lead a happy, peaceful life when the working population was so terribly enslaved."[17] When revolution erupted in St Petersburg in 1905, she was already a well-known speaker at workers' study circles and meetings of socialist activists.

Kollontai wrote two pamphlets for workers during this first Russian revolution, which described the Marxist vision of the communist future and the path to realizing it. In a communist society, she explained, "all of today's injustice and poverty" will be overcome, because production will be "for social and personal use" not private commercial gain, and the capitalist spirit of competition and egoism will be replaced by the communist spirit of cooperation and the common good. This was not a "fantasy" or an "empty dream," she insisted. On the contrary, human history proves that "the whole order of things, all human relations" can be "refashioned." But history also teaches us that refashioning the order of things requires more than the efforts of individual "people of good will." It can only occur through the collective effort of the masses of "new people": working-class people whose spirit of cooperation and equality, whose "resentment and hatred" of oppression, emerges out of the very conditions of their present lives.[18] Life itself, she argued, teaches workers the evils of inequality and oppression, and creates "unconscious, instinctive" alternative ideals, a "class psychology" that will become "the greatest weapon in the historical process."[19]

In some respects, these were standard Marxist arguments about history, class, and socialism. But we can also see Kollontai's distinctive emphasis and style: greater stress on the centrality of moral and spiritual transformation; greater weight given to emotion, psychology, and experience; greater readiness to imagine the liberated future. We see these same orientations in two articles about Marxist morality and ethics written at the same time for educated readers. Rejecting the neo-Kantian argument that there are abstract moral absolutes existing in nature itself and the Nietzschean argument that the will of exceptional individuals can create new moral norms—ideas widespread among Russian intellectuals—Kollontai emphasized the Marxist view that ethics derive from social relations and social experience. Present society is dominated, she argued, by a "bourgeois morality" that idealizes individualism and the "unrestricted expression of one's own 'I,'" softened only by "compulsory" ideas of "duty" and "obligation." However, deep within bourgeois society, the experience and interests of proletarians lead them toward a new morality, toward an ethics of "solidarity, unity, self-sacrifice, and the subordination of personal interests to the interests of the group." These proletarian values, however, only hint at the moral world to come. "In that new world, still far from us, there will no longer be a place for compulsion," there will no longer be a place for ideas like duty, because "personal desire will coincide with social imperatives." She sensed the utopian nature of her claims, but did not back away from them. Rather, she tried to show how they grew from concrete conditions: a "radical metamorphosis" of all current social and economic relationships was historically inevitable, which would produce a new economy and society based on community and solidarity, and create a "social atmosphere" in which "a higher moral type of person, now inaccessible to us," can be realized. The problem was not the idea of a morally free and transcendent "superman," but its impossibility in capitalist society: when society grows beyond competing individuals and antagonistic classes then the "new man" will be born, "the harmonious, whole, strong, and beautiful image of the true superman."[20]

For Kollontai, talk of the "new man" and the "superman" concerned women especially (of course, the Russian terms were not gendered as English usage at the time was). Her focus on women was in opposition to "bourgeois feminists," who considered charity and educational uplift enough to improve the lives of women crushed under the burden of poverty and labor. But Kollontai's position was even more at odds with her Marxist comrades in the Russian Social-Democratic Workers' Party, who believed that class struggle alone would free women. When Kollontai organized women workers during 1905–7, her work was blocked, she recalled with bitterness, by both the "party center" and "rank-and-file comrades," who reacted to her efforts with an ugly mixture of fear and contempt: fear that attention to women's needs would undermine socialist unity and contempt for work among women workers as a distraction from the main cause, as a sign of "hated feminism."[21]

But Kollontai persisted. In 1908, she organized a delegation of working women to participate in the First All-Russian Women's Congress—a feminist gathering of mostly middle-class professional women. Social-Democratic party leaders insisted that workers and socialists should boycott the congress, which Kollontai ignored. She did not disagree with the critique of these bourgeois feminists, especially their "above-class" fantasy that women of all classes should unite around the cause of democracy and suffrage. Indeed, her participation was mainly disruptive and performative. She did not expect to change the minds of the feminist majority, but considered a visible stance of dissent, which would culminate in a demonstrative walk-out of her group, to be morally important and politically instructive for working women. Her speech to the congress was typical. The trouble with you bourgeois feminists, she told them, is that you think the "woman question" arose only when "a conscious vanguard of fighters for women's emancipation spoke out openly in defense of their trampled rights and interests." But the real history of the woman question began "when millions of women were thrown into the labor market by the power of the all-mighty Moloch—capital," leading them to experience the "hellish" suffering that capitalism inflicted on working people and their families. What do feminists offer women tormented by "the triple burden of worker, homemaker, and mother?" Nothing but slogans, such as "become free in love and free in motherhood" and free of "age-old morals," that have little bearing on the realities of most women's lives. Yes, she agreed, we need political rights for women, including suffrage, but not as an end in itself, rather as "a weapon in the struggle" toward the ultimate goal: "delivering the working woman from the abyss of suffering and evil." As long as the capitalist system of producing value through exploitation exists, the working woman cannot be a "free, independent personality, a wife who chooses her husband only by the dictates of her heart, a mother who can look to the future of her children without fear." The goal of a true woman's movement, she told the congress, must be nothing less than "the all-sided emancipation" of the woman "as a person and a human being." And this will be impossible until women are freed from "the chains and slavery of capitalism."[22]

Kollontai developed the moral, emotional, and utopian sides of her vision of women's emancipation in a book she wrote for the congress, but publication was delayed when the manuscript went astray in the post on the way to Maxim Gorky in Italy, where he eventually published the book. Of course, she insisted she was neither a moralist nor a utopian: "We willingly leave everything that belongs to the realm of 'moral wish' or other ideological constructions at the complete disposal of bourgeois liberalism. For us, the emancipation of women is not a dream, not even a principle, but a concrete reality, a fact that is daily coming into being" in "real-life relationships."[23] What is "utopian" is the feminist belief that new and free forms of love, marriage, and family are possible without radically transforming the whole social system.[24]

At the same time, Kollontai's language of argument was built around a moral vision, in the utopian mode, of a radically different self and society created through the experience of struggle against the darkness of the present. Only in the future socialist world of "harmony and justice," she predicted, will women experience "the joys and charms of life" that are denied them in the present. Women who do not "feel a strong faith in the coming of a more perfect social order," suffer from their narrow view of what was real and possible: "the future of humanity must seem gray, dark, and hopeless." Yes, the path to this future will be harsh and "thorny," surrounded by "dangerous precipices" and "hungry predators." But there is no other way to reach that "alluring, flickering goal in the distance—all-sided liberation in a renewed world of labor," entry into a "new, bright temple of common labor, comradely solidarity, and joyful freedom." This future is not a fantasy or a wish, because it is produced by the conditions and experience of the present: through suffering and struggle a woman transforms herself from a "humiliated, downtrodden slave without rights" into an "independent worker, an independent personality, free in love."[25] Of course, this transformation would remain incomplete in the "gloomy" reality of the present. The ideal of "free love," promoted by radical feminists, was impossible in the present society marked by inequality, exploitation, possessiveness, and property. Until the structure of "all human relations" and the "whole psychology of humanity" has changed, there could be no true freedom in love and no true spirit of comradely relations. This would require a different human spirit. But this was not a mere fancy: one could already "catch sight of pale glimmerings" of these future attitudes and future relationships in the lives of working-class women.[26]

In the years following, Kollontai became more and more certain that the deepest human experiences of love and intimacy must be at the center of what revolution should be about. In December 1908, she fled the Russian empire in order to avoid arrest and remained abroad until 1917, working as a party activist, speaker, and writer. During these years of European exile, she experienced another disappointment in her personal life. Having fallen in love with the Menshevik economist Peter Maslov, she expected that a relationship with a comrade to whom she felt politically and intellectually close would be enriched by a similarly close and comradely emotional and sensual relationship. Instead, she found traditional male attitudes toward gender and love: unable to empathize with her feelings as a human being, he "saw in me only the feminine element which he tried to mold into a willing sounding board to his own ego," and cared sexually only for his own physical satisfaction.[27]

As Kollontai's thoughts matured about the present and future of sex, morality, and the "new woman," she wrote and published three important articles on these questions. No Russian Marxist had ever written so explicitly about gender, intimacy, or emotions, nor so strongly linked these questions to socialist revolution. (In 1918, she would republish these articles together as a book with few changes, for little had changed in her views or in conditions and attitudes.) She began with a human condition she had often experienced: loneliness. Taking up the common observation at the time that loneliness was the defining experience of modern urban life,[28] she pushed this cliché in a more radical direction: in the age of "capitalist property, class contradictions, and individualistic morality, we all live and think under the dark sign of inescapable and inevitable spiritual solitude," especially in the "crowded, alluring and carousing, noisy and shouting cities," even when among "close friends and comrades." This modern condition drives one to "grab with sick greed at the illusion of a 'congenial soul'" and be enchanted by the magic of "crafty Eros." But disenchantment is inevitable, especially for women, for a "normal woman seeks in sexual intercourse completeness and harmony; the man, reared on prostitution, overlooking the complex vibrations of love's sensations, follows only his pallid, monotone, physical inclinations." The conditions of modern capitalist existence and the way bourgeois men and women learned to love degraded the "love act" from "the ultimate accord of complex spiritual feelings and emotional experience" into something "shameful, low, and coarsely animalistic." Yet, Kollontai saw hope precisely in this "tragic" modern experience: "a longing (*toska*) for the ideal of the still unrealized future," "the fresh scent of new strivings in life, rising from the social depths."[29] These were her arguments in 1911, which she developed further in a key essay of 1913 titled "the new women."

If salvation was a "new morality" created by "new people," the fragmentary glimmerings of the new could be seen in the changing lives and mentalities of women. The harbinger of this future was the bold and independent "single woman" (*kholostaia zhenshchina*) trying to make her way outside home and family, who "possesses a self-defining inner world, lives with the interests of a whole person, is externally autonomous and internally independent." Her thoughts, emotions, and expectations are so radically new that "our grandmothers and even our mothers could not have imagined" her. The evidence for this new woman was still mainly in fiction—and Kollontai's essay is mainly a review of recent literature. But fiction is not make-believe, she insisted. These literary heroines are not "artistic fantasies" but reflections of a current reality in which the new woman is already a "real living fact." Though usually a professional woman, she might be a "poor, single, factory girl." What distinguishes her is that "she is proud of what she is, proud of her inner strength, proud that she is her own self."[30] This emerging new woman understands the harm caused by "the feminine virtues on which she had been raised over centuries—passivity, submissiveness, compliance, softness." She knows that life requires a personality defined by "action, fortitude, decisiveness, and toughness, in other words by those 'virtues' that were until now considered the property of men." Unlike her mother and grandmothers, the new woman does "does not fear life" or "hypocritically wrap herself in the faded cloak of female virtue." She "demands from fate her share of personal happiness." But "emotionality" and intimacy do not define her: she treats love and passion as only a single "dimension" of the richness of "life experiences," no longer, as for women of the past, the "essence of her life."[31]

This new woman, however, is only the embryo of the future, not the future itself. The "harsh reality" of modern capitalist existence forces women to suppress emotionality and become like men, to approach passion warily, for the woman of the past is still warring for the new woman's soul. In love, she "fears that the power of feeling might awaken in her the sleeping atavistic inclinations to become the 'sounding board' of a man, might force her to surrender her own self, to abandon her 'cause,' her calling, her life tasks." Ideally, the woman in love is "redeemed from love's servitude, and proudly and joyfully stretches to her full height." But in this world as it is she must concentrate on the "struggle against 'moral captivity,' even against outwardly free feelings. This is the rebellion of the woman of our age of transition, who has still not learned how to combine inner freedom and independence with the all-consuming power of love." This is not yet the future. The time when a woman can embrace all the "earthly pleasures" without becoming their slave is still only becoming.[32]

Kollontai claimed to find the "germ" of this future in urban working-class lives: not in "the 'cultured districts' [of the city] with their sophisticated, individualistic mentality," but in the "crowded dwellings of the workers, where, amidst the stench and terrors beget by capitalism, amidst tears and curses, living springs find a way to emerge." Kollontai knew the cruel realities of everyday life for workers and their families, including the contempt and brutality with which most working-class men treated women and the submissiveness of most women. But this, she insisted, was only the lingering presence of the old, not the "active, creative" side of workers' lives, which was leading them toward something "new," something beyond the "monogamous-possessive family" and the subordination of women. In the fight against capitalist oppression, workers discover the necessity of comradely solidarity and equality, ethical principles that touch even workers' sexual lives. This led to her boldest argument yet: sex was not a side issue in the proletarian struggle. Throughout history, "the sexual moral code is an integral part" of "the class ideology" of every rising class. For the working class, the new sexual morality is intimately connected to the struggle against capitalism and bourgeois rule: "only with the help of its new spiritual values, created in the depths . . . will this struggling class strengthen its social position; only by means of new norms and ideals can it successfully take power away from antagonistic social groups."[33]

"Life itself" led working-class women out of the home into independent work. As a result, only for a working-class woman does "the assertion of her personality (*lichnost'*) coincide with the interests of her class." Proletarians discover that the old "passive female virtues" are hindrances in the struggle for social transformation, which requires a "rebellious personality challenging every form of enslavement."[34] Or, at least, that is how it should be. The woman should be viewed as a "self-valued human being," as a "person" (*zhenshchina-lichnost'*, literally a woman-personality).[35] To realize this future, this utopian "not-yet" that challenges the present darkness with a powerful longing for the new, women will have to "fight on two fronts: against the external world and against the inclinations of her grandmothers that dwell still deeply within her."[36]

In 1917, during the first weeks after the fall of the monarchy, Kollontai became one of Lenin's staunchest allies (though she had joined the Bolshevik wing of the party only during the war) in demanding that the revolution be turned toward soviet power and socialism. Lenin, in Switzerland, entrusted her with carrying his message to party leaders in Petrograd. When Lenin himself returned to Russia, Kollontai was one of the few party leaders immediately to embrace his "April Theses." When she rose at a meeting in Petrograd to defend Lenin's call for an immediate end to the war and the transfer of all power to the soviets, "her support called forth nothing but mockery, laughter, and hubbub," according to a witness.[37] Kollontai's optimism about what was possible, which nurtured her radicalism and impatience in 1917, led her to the center of events. She was a popular speaker at meetings and rallies across the city, especially among women. She was chosen as a Bolshevik representative to the Central Executive Committee of the Petrograd Soviet. She was invited into the Bolshevik party's Central Committee. And, immediately after October, she joined the first cabinet of the new government as the People's Commissar of Public Welfare, which made her, she believed, "the first woman in history" to be member of a national government.[38]

Kollontai looked back at these early months of the young "workers' government" as a time "rich in magnificent illusions, plans, ardent initiatives to improve life, to organize the world anew, months of the real romanticism of the Revolution."[39] Possibilities seemed boundless. Ideas that had once been only "dreams" now had a government prepared to implement them. Hence the logic of reprinting her prewar essays on women, the family, and the new morality (gathered into a book titled *The New Morality and the Working Class*), and her 1914 pamphlet, *The Working Mother*, which described a future when a working woman would experience motherhood as a great joy and children would thrive:

Imagine a society . . . where everyone does the same amount of work and society in return looks after them and eases their lives. . . . Maternity will no longer be a cross to bear, for what will remain will be only its joyful aspects, only the great happiness of being a mother. . . . But isn't such society a fairytale (*skazka*)? Could such a society ever really exist? The science of economics and of the history of society and the state shows that such a society must and will come into being. However hard the rich capitalists, factory owners, landowners, and property owners fight against it, this "fairytale" will become real and true. The working class all over the world is fighting to make this dream come true.[40]

In 1918, she believed, the Soviet government was making this dream real. The "still unrealized future," as she had called it in 1911, seemed closer than ever before

In a speech to the First All-Russian Congress of Worker and Peasant Women in November 1918, Kollontai presented her vision of what she had been trying achieve as People's Commissar of Public Welfare (by then she had resigned that post in protest against the Brest-Litovsk peace treaty with Germany). She pointed to state-organized maternity homes and childcare as enabling women to work without worrying about their children or being dependent on men. And this was part of a bigger transformation in women's lives, which was itself part of a revolution of millenarian proportions: "the red flag of the social revolution . . . proclaims to us the approach of the heaven on earth to which humanity has been aspiring for centuries."[41] Of course, given the harsh economic conditions in these years and resistance to her efforts by many of her male comrades, little could be accomplished. Perhaps this was part of the reason, by Kollontai's own testimony, that she "began to long for the time" when she "wasn't a people's commissar, but an ordinary party agitator travelling around the world and dreaming of revolution."[42] Resigning from the government was likely about much more than Brest-Litovsk.

Kollontai's radical "longing" and "dreaming" had already made her a dissenter within her own party. In 1914, living in Germany, where she was active in the German Social-Democratic party, she not only rejected the party's support for the war but vigorously criticized a decadent ethos that she blamed for leading the party elites to this fateful betrayal of principles. Well before the war, she argued, "creativity had dried up" and the old "vital spirit" of "impatient movement forward" was lost. The party had become a "bureaucratic machine" that "stifled" in the masses the "vital, creative spirit of class obstinacy" (*stroptivost'*), critical thought, and "spontaneous protest."[43] After October 1917, she argued much the same about the Bolshevik party. She aligned with the "Left Communist" opposition in 1918, for which she was expelled from the party's Central Committee. And, we saw, she resigned from the government to protest the Brest-Litovsk treaty, which she considered a betrayal of the principles of international revolution. The left-wing French diplomat Jacques Sadoul described Kollontai during these struggles of 1918 as a "vestal of the revolution" who wished to "maintain in all its purity the flame of the maximalist ideal."[44]

Kollontai's most sustained and influential role as revolutionary vestal came in 1921 with her leading role in the "Workers' Opposition," at a time when she was also head of the Women's Section of the Communist Party, the Zhenotdel. Several Bolshevik trade union leaders had organized the faction toward the end of 1920 in opposition to Trotsky's proposals to continue the "militarization" of labor used to mobilize the economy during civil war and to transform trade unions into government bodies tasked with promoting economic development and educating workers in communist ideology. Trotsky believed that military-style labor discipline (and military-style punishments for indiscipline) would be useful to rebuild the shattered economy and improve workers' mentalities. When union activists warned that "you cannot build a planned economy the way the pharaohs built their pyramids"[45] and condemned these plans as a betrayal of proletarian democracy, Trotsky responded that it was sheer utopianism to think that proletarian democracy meant that that the Bolshevik party must "trust its fate" to workers no matter the changing composition and vacillating mood of that class. This was to make a "fetish of democratic principles," Trotsky declared, and to prefer fantasy to reality.[46] The Workers' Opposition rejected Trotsky's logic: it was precisely "faith" in the masses and reliance on initiative and power from below that was required if the revolution was to transform society rather than only hold power for its own sake. They were outraged by Trotsky's economic plans, and not much happier with Lenin's compromise proposal to preserve unions' independence but deprive them of them any economic power. The Workers' Opposition demanded full "control" of the economy in the hands of trade unions and other workers' institutions, all power within unions in the hands of rank-and-file workers, and the restoration of democratic elections and freedom of discussion within the ruling party. They declared their enemy to be the "enormous bureaucratic machine" that was growing at the expense of "the creative initiative and self-activity" of organized workers, who alone could overcome economic ruin and build a socialist society.[47]

Kollontai drafted a pamphlet on behalf of the Workers' Opposition in preparation for the debate on these issues that had been authorized for the tenth Party Congress, to be held in March 1921. She defended their arguments against both Trotsky's militaristic "centralism" and the compromise positions offered by Lenin and others, as growing from a richer sense of reality and possibility. She mocked the "sober" policies of state and party leaders, the "statecraft wisdom of our ruling heights," their supposedly sensible willingness to "adapt" and "compromise." "Today we might gain something with the help of your 'sober policy,'" she imagined workers saying to Lenin and Trotsky, "but let us beware lest we find ourselves on a false road that, through turns and zigzags, will imperceptibly lead us away from the future toward the debris of the past."[48] The only way to open up the world of "new possibilities," the only path for "the creation of new forms of production and life," is "freedom" for workers to "speak their creative new word." The demands of the Workers' Opposition, she argued, were based on this recognition of the necessity of "freedom," "self-activity," and "creativity" for workers. The party leadership, unfortunately, "distrusted" the very workers who ought to be the foundation of the "proletarian dictatorship." And this distrust produced two evils: "bureaucracy," which is the "direct negation of mass self-activity," and workers' "bitterness" and "alienation" from the government, which "deadens and kills the self-activity of the masses."[49]

Kollontai contrasted the deadly blight of bureaucracy to the "instinctively healthy (*stikhiino-zdorovoe*) class creativity of the workers." There is only one true Marxist answer to the key question of "to whom will our party entrust the building of the communist economy"—bureaucrats or workers? Communism cannot be achieved "by the hands of Soviet officials." "It is impossible to decree communism. It can be created only through the lived experiences and desires (*zhivym iskaniem*), even if they are sometimes mistaken, and creative effort of the working class itself." This is a "simple Marxist truth" understood by "every child in Soviet Russia." Against Trotsky's argument that the problem is not bureaucracy itself but a tendency to adopt the "bad sides of bureaucratism," Kollontai answered that there are no good sides to bureaucracy. It is an unambiguous "scourge," which "has seeped into the very marrow of our party and eaten through to soviet institutions," that treats "every new thought" as "heresy," that replaces the open exchange of opinions and initiative from below with "formal resolution of decisions handed down from above," that "restricts and limits at every step" the "vital initiative" of workers who alone can transform the economy with their "miracles of enthusiasm." The sooner the party leadership understands these truths, "the sooner we can step across that forbidden border (*zapovednyi rubezh*) beyond which humanity, freed from external economic laws, and with the rich and valuable knowledge of collective experience, will begin consciously to create the history of humanity in the communist epoch"—the sooner, she might have said, humanity can "leap from the kingdom of necessity to the kingdom of freedom."[50]

Kollontai's defense of the Workers' Opposition's refusal to accept "sober" assumptions about what was necessary and possible, even in the dark and difficult conditions at the end of the civil war, emerged from her life-long history of fighting against structures and attitudes that constricted the full development of the "person" (*lichnost'*). Socialism, she was convinced, demanded an all-encompassing transformation of everyday life (*byt*)—a cultural revolution in which public life and personal life, even the most intimate relations, are linked, where it is impossible to separate the struggle to transform the external structures of society from the struggle to transform the inward personality, including the morality and emotions at the heart of people's lived experiences.

Dismay over policy decisions at the end of the civil war did not lessen her belief that this deep and all-encompassing revolution was underway. Indeed, she wrote two of her most utopian statements after the Workers' Opposition had been suppressed and the New Economic Policy (NEP) had enshrined the ethos of adaptation and compromise and allowed so much of the old everyday life to return. In 1922, she published a short story for worker and peasant youth imagining the communal life of the future. Set during Christmas 1970, some nostalgic "veterans of the 'Great Years' of the world revolution" decide to decorate a tree and invite young people to hear their stories of 1917. In this not-so-distant future, the entire world is organized as a global federation of communes. Poverty and war have been banished; property and money are gone and crime with them; the family has been replaced by communal life; and work is for pleasure, depending on what an individual enjoys, plus two hours of work each day for the benefit of the commune. The "beautiful," healthy bodies of the young people who come to hear the elders' memories are proof of this new life. Only one thing from the old world has been preserved: the struggle for the good, for "what would life be like without struggle . . . without eternally striving forward—into the unknown, toward the unattainable," a life defined and made joyous not by "accomplishment" but only by "eternally rebellious seeking (*v vechno miatezhnom iskanii*)." For these young communards, the challenge ahead was overcoming physical nature, an even greater task than the "easy" challenge, now complete, of overcoming human injustice.[51]

She returned to the question of intimate and inward life in the revolution in a controversial essay, "Make Way for Winged Eros (Letter to Laboring Youth)," published in 1923 in the journal of the Communist Youth League (Komsomol). She described a new phase in the "civil war" between proletarian and bourgeois ideologies: the "revolution in the worldviews, emotions, and structure of soul of working humanity"—in other words, in the common expression of the time, "the struggle for the new *byt*," for new everyday practices and mentalities.[52] During the civil war, she argued, men and women were "in the grip of other emotions, of more practical passions and experiences," not least survival, and so had no time for the "riddle of love." They coupled and uncoupled, for the instincts of nature remained. But these acts took place without "great inward emotions." The conditions of revolution and civil war left neither time nor energy for anything more than the "naked instincts" of "wingless Eros." Now, however, the revolution could turn toward an even greater task: fighting the "decaying bourgeois world" on the "spiritual-cultural front." Sex and love, she argued as she had in the past, are always entwined with ideology, politics, class, and history. Bourgeois sexual morality is a mixture of possessiveness and hypocrisy, of patriarchal ownership and prostitution—a reflection of bourgeois society and values. The proletariat, by contrast, embraces a "richer and many-stringed" sexual life, for workers need very different "qualities of soul" to build the new world: not least, "sympathetic feelings of sensitivity, compassion, and empathy" for the "personality of the other." But this is only the present, not yet the future which is still unimaginable: "in the realized communist society, love, 'winged Eros,' will appear in a different, transfigured form completely unknown to us . . . Even the boldest fantasy is incapable of imagining what it will look like." All that was certain, she believed, was that the revolutionary proletarian spirit of solidarity, sympathy, and love will cause to grow on the wings of Eros "new feathers of never before seen beauty."[53]

The "utopian form," as a way of thinking and writing, has been called a "meditation on radical difference, radical otherness," on the possibilities for a life so utterly different from this one that we cannot imagine what it will be like, for "our imaginations are hostages" to the only realities we have experienced, and so we find it hard to imagine the future except as a negation of what we reject in the past and the present.[54] Kollontai acknowledged these limits, and precisely as proof not of utopian impossibility but of how "never before seen" the future will be. Kollontai also shared the utopian conviction, as she told an American reporter in 1918, that "even if we are conquered . . . we are breaking the way, abolishing old ideas," and creating a legacy that others will build with.[55] Years later, recognizing perhaps that so many of her ideals remained unrealized, she would reiterate the utopian principle that criticism and struggle is more important than "accomplishment." And even if nothing was produced beyond words and dreams, these "would come to be a historical example and help others move ahead. We worked for that time and for the future."[56]

Lev Trotsky (1879–1940)

Lev Bronstein's enthusiasm for revolution began as a high school student in Nikolayev (the same southern Ukrainian town where Isaac Babel would later live as a child), influenced by encounters with revolutionaries exiled there (Figure 13).[57] He was initially suspicious, even frightened, of

Figure 13. Lev Trotsky. Drawing by Yury Annenkov, 1922. Annenkov, *Portrety* (Petrograd, 1922). Cover of *Time Magazine*, 21 November 1927. Library of the University of Illinois, Urbana-Champaign.

the radicalism that led to their arrest and exile—he later described his temperament in those years as "bookish, abstract, and therefore skeptical of revolution" and of "socialist utopias." But "the ideas filling the air proved stronger than I, especially since in the depths of my soul I wished for nothing better than to yield to them." He feverishly devoured populist and Marxist writings, though in a manner that was "nervous, impatient, unsystematic."[58] Isaac Deutscher, who wrote the first full-length biography of Trotsky, observed that in becoming a socialist the future Trotsky "embraced a mood rather than an idea."[59]

This mood also led him initially to dislike Marxism for its totalizing claims to scientific truth and its reduction of history to economic forces, leaving little place for human spirit, will, and action.[60] The idealism and heroism of populist socialism felt richer and truer. He made this point in debating an outspoken Marxist in a Nikolayev circle he frequented, Alexandra Sokolovskaya (whom he would marry in prison when both were on their way to Siberian exile): "I can't imagine how a young girl so full of life can stand that dry, narrow, impractical stuff!" To which she replied, "I can't imagine how a person who thinks he is logical can be contented with a headful of vague, idealistic emotions!" But young Lev, in the words of an early biographer who worked in consultation with Trotsky, was too "full of fire and power and a sense of infinite impossibilities" to believe that the way to "mold future history" was to be a "cool and practical engineer." Even as Trotsky embraced the Marxist understanding of history and class, he still found the spirit of preacher, politician, and evangelist more to his taste.[61] Trotsky's fire also led him toward the life of a professional revolutionary. When a member of their group decided to return to school and finish his medical studies, Trotsky gave him a photograph of himself on which he wrote "faith without deeds is death."[62] Trotsky's own deeds, though still modest, led to his arrest in January 1898 for trying to organize local workers, two years in prison, and exile to Siberia.

In Siberia, Trotsky found work as a village correspondent and literary critic for the newspaper the *Eastern Review (Vostochnoe obozrenie)*. He chose for his nom de plume Antid Oto, a wry adaptation of the Italian for "antidote," for he fashioned himself as a radical antidote within mainstream journalism, bringing a Marxist "angle of vision" to the "'eternal' problems of life: love, death, friendship, optimism, pessimism, and so forth."[63] His 1901 essay "On Optimism, Pessimism, the Twentieth Century, and Many Other Things" is typical of his intellectual and emotional style at the time. At the age of 21, Trotsky felt ready to take up all the big questions that interested the public at the start of a new century. Since pessimism was widespread in early twentieth-century Russia,[64] he reflected on the variety of types. The most common was the "philistine pessimist" whose worldview is grounded in "experience that does not range beyond the shop counter, the office desk, and the double bed, who skeptically shakes his head and condemns the 'idealistic dreamer' with the pseudo-realistic conviction that 'there is nothing new under the sun, that the world is nothing but eternal repetition of what has already been.'" A newer type, more characteristic of decadent modern times, was the "absolute pessimist" who looks at the present as "empty and dark" and the future as uncertain. Trotsky judged this to be a "pessimism that might create a philosopher or lyric poet but not a civic fighter." Against both the narrow-minded philistine and the melancholy philosopher Trotsky offered a superior hybrid, a dialectical synthesis: the "pessimist of the present" and "optimist of the future." Only this point of view could see all the darkness of the times in which one lives and feel the "passion, faith, and fighting spirit" required to "confidently knock at the gate of history." To be sure, the new-born twentieth century seemed determined to "drive the optimist of the future into absolute pessimism and civic nirvana. 'Death to Utopia! Death to faith! Death to love! Death to hope!' thunders the twentieth century with salvoes of rifle fire and the roar of cannons. Surrender, you pathetic dreamer! Here I am, your long-awaited twentieth century, your 'future.'" But the pessimist of the present and optimist of the future has the vision and boldness to answer no less loudly that "you are only the present." Indeed, to see that the darkness of the present itself gives rise to "the forces creating the future. And what a future!... As long as I have breath, I will fight for the future, for that bright and radiant future when man, strong and beautiful, will master the drifting stream of history and direct it towards the boundless horizon of beauty, joy, and happiness!"[65]

Along with such rhetorical perorations, which reflected the style of newspaper columns (and he was a great success as a journalist) as well as his own mood, Trotsky was concerned with the practical question of how exactly to "master the drifting stream of history." So when the first contraband copies of the underground newspaper of the Russian Social Democratic Workers' Party, *The Spark* (*Iskra*) reached Trotsky in Siberia, along with Lenin's pamphlet *What is to be Done?*, he found that his vague ideas about the need for a new type of revolutionary movement were already being developed by more experienced Russian activists in European exile. "My handwritten essays, newspaper articles, and proclamations...suddenly looked small and provincial to me."[66] He decided to escape—though this meant leaving his wife and two daughters behind—and make his way to Western Europe to join this movement. Once there, he became a regular contributor to *The Spark,* though his florid rhetoric led some of the more senior Marxist leaders to doubt his seriousness and depth. Indeed, his biographer Deutscher concluded, "the distinctive mark of his early contributions to *The Spark* lies not so much in originality of ideas as in the force of the emotional current that runs through them." Trotsky's oratory, for which he would become famous in 1905 and 1917, was imbued even more with this "intensity of thought, imagination, emotion, and expression."[67] He displayed this to full effect at the second party congress in the summer of 1903, which both established the Russian Social Democratic Workers' Party on a firm footing (the first congress had ended with almost everyone's arrest) and produced a lasting schism between Bolsheviks and Mensheviks.

At the start of the congress, Trotsky was so reliable and vehement an ally of Lenin's that he was nicknamed "Lenin's cudgel."[68] But this alliance did not last long. Trotsky agreed with Lenin on the necessity of a centralized and disciplined party, but he was troubled by Lenin's maneuvering to maximize his own control over the party, and soon shifted away from Lenin and his faction of "hards," as the Bolsheviks were initially called (against the Menshevik "softs"). In a pamphlet Trotsky wrote right after the congress, he openly condemned Lenin's politics of the "iron fist" and "will to power," not least because it was predicated on Lenin's own personal "hegemony." He judged Lenin's methods as comparable to those of Maximilien Robespierre, the Jacobin architect of dictatorship and terror during the French Revolution, methods that ultimately destroyed the democratic revolution they were meant to promote: "The Paris proletariat elevated Robespierre hoping that he would raise them out of poverty. But the dictator gave them too many executions and too little bread. Robespierre fell and when he fell he pulled down the whole Mountain [the Jacobins] with him, and with it the cause of democracy altogether."[69] Trotsky elaborated these warnings even more ominously (and perhaps prophetically) the following year in a pamphlet, *Our Political Tasks,* published in Geneva in 1904. Lenin's plan to "substitute" the party organization and its "professional revolutionaries" for the movements of the working class and history will "lead to this: the party organization first 'substitutes' itself for the party as a whole; then the Central Committee substitutes itself for the party organization; and finally a 'dictator' substitutes himself for the Central Committee." This peril was rooted in Jacobinism itself: "absolute faith in the metaphysical idea" of "truth," which only an elite of leaders can fully grasp, resting on "absolute distrust for living people" and suspicion of everyone who does not agree. This was made more harmful, during the French revolution, by Jacobin "utopianism": failure to see that their "truth," an egalitarian republic based on reason and virtue, was in conflict with a system of private property and class inequality that they were unable to repudiate. This "gigantic contradiction" led to the guillotine as their only means to stay in power. Lenin was following the same path, Trotsky contended. Real revolutionary socialists, Trotsky insisted, embrace a more optimistic truth based not on abstract "revelation" from above but faith in the common people and their struggle: "This is what deeply distinguishes us from the Jacobins. Our attitude towards the elemental social forces, and therefore towards the future, is one of revolutionary confidence."[70]

These arguments evolved toward a theory of "permanent revolution," a vision more radically optimistic than even most Bolsheviks at the time were ready to accept: that proletarian power in Russia was not a distant goal after Russia overcame its backwardness but an immediate and practical task. He saw proof in the social rumblings stimulated by the Russo-Japanese War. At the end of 1904, Trotsky wrote about the fervent atmosphere surrounding the liberal "banquet campaign" of dinners, speeches, and resolutions calling on the government to grant greater civil liberties and political representation. In such an environment, he argued, "the incredible becomes real, the impossible becomes believable." The problem was that liberals by nature will not be able to sustain this. They are too timid and hypocritical to challenge the tsarist system, to believe the impossible. They were afraid even to speak the word "constitution," worrying that the masses would not understand. But "behind the fear of the word was concealed the fear of the act: fear of struggle, of the masses, of revolution." This debilitating liberal (and bourgeois) pessimism made it necessary that "the people" themselves realize the democracy that liberals wanted but dared not fight for.

Most Marxists, especially his fellow Mensheviks, considered such an argument folly if not heresy: it was historically mistaken and politically harmful for the common people to themselves make the democratic revolution that was the destined task of the bourgeoisie and the liberal intelligentsia. But war made the impossible possible, Trotsky argued. He viewed the Russo-Japanese War in terms that would apply even more to the World War a decade later: a "dreadful monster, breathing blood and fire" accompanied by "the furies of crisis, unemployment, mobilization, hunger, and death." While this initially produced in the people only "depression and despair," the experience of war changed the mood on the street from "blank despair" to "concentrated indignation." In this atmosphere, the time was ripe to start a revolution "of the street," a general strike of urban workers for peace and a Constituent Assembly.[71] This was a fair prediction of what would actually happen later in 1905 and much later, and more completely, in 1917. But in 1904 (or, for that matter, in the early months of 1917), this vision of how revolutions unfold seemed absurdly utopian even to most revolutionaries.

The movement of the street that erupted after Bloody Sunday drew Trotsky back to Russia in order to participate in a revolution that was transforming his theories into "living reality."[72] The threat of arrest, though, forced him to base his efforts not in the capital but in nearby Finland (part the Russian empire but enjoying greater freedom). Because most socialists continued to believed that the immediate task was a liberal "bourgeois democratic" revolution, Trotsky did all he could to undermine faith in the bourgeois path of legality and reform. After the tsar's manifesto on 6 August granted a consultative Duma, Trotsky chastised liberals for their inability to understand that democracy is "never achieved with the signing of a parchment. Such things take place on the streets. They are achieved through struggle."[73] During the October general strike, more living proof of his theoretical hopes, he returned to St Petersburg and was elected vice-chair of the Soviet of Workers' Deputies. He drafted resolutions, participated in decision-making, and gave numerous speeches.

Most of all, he reveled in the vitality of "the street," with its disorderly intensity and uncontrollable possibility. Such a revolution, he would later write, "is attractive like a young, passionate woman with arms flung wide, showering avid kisses on you with hot, feverish lips." He often interpreted these events in such emotional terms, and he saw emotion as a source of unprecedented possibility:

A tremendous, mysterious process was taking place in countless hearts: bonds of fear were being broken, the individual personality, having hardly had time to become conscious of itself, became dissolved in the mass, and the mass itself became dissolved in the revolutionary élan.... It rushed forward like the ocean tide whipped by a storm. Every day brought new strata of the population to their feet and gave birth to new possibilities. It was as though someone were stirring the social cauldron, right to its very bottom, with a gigantic spoon.... Everything disintegrated, everything turned to chaos. Yet at the same time within this chaos there arose a need for a new order, and elements of that order began to crystallize.[74]

If this revolution, as Lenin would later claim, was the "dress rehearsal for the revolution of 1917,"[75] Trotsky's culminating turn on its stage was when he rose to address the court at his 1906 trial, accused along with other Soviet leaders of planning an armed uprising. Trotsky converted his position as defendant into that of prosecutor, charging the government with political illegitimacy. He grounded his case in moral law (though, as a Marxist, he would not have called it that). The tsarist regime, he explained, rules through violence when it feels strong and through concessions when it feels afraid. The street, by contrast, is inspired by "conscience," "enthusiasm," and a spirit of "moral regeneration." How can the Soviet leadership be charged with planning, as the prosecutor charged, armed struggle against the existing "form of government" when there is no legitimate government.

For a long time past the government has not been supported by the nation but only by its military-police-Black Hundreds apparatus. What we have is not a national government but an automaton for mass murder.... If you tell me that the pogroms, the murders, the burnings, the rapes... are the form of government of the Russian Empire—then I will agree with the prosecution that... we were arming ourselves... against the form of government of the Russian Empire.[76]

Sitting in his prison cell, awaiting transport to Siberia, filled with the experiences of revolution, Trotsky wrote about the certainty of further revolution in Russia, which would continue until it brought the proletariat to power. This was not a utopian dream, he insisted, for "utopia" meant faith in "miracles" rather than in "facts," a vision in contradiction to the flow of history.[77] Trotsky offered a new realism that challenged how people understood reality. Although his comrades would view his jailhouse essays on the coming revolution as a work of fantasy, Trotsky refused to accept conventional ideological assumptions about what was necessary and possible, especially the long-standing Marxist view that backward Russia required a bourgeois-democratic revolution before a proletarian-socialist one could succeed. For Trotsky, it was the "ultimate utopia" to think that the proletariat, once seizing power, "would be able to limit its mission, even if it wanted to, and create a republican democratic environment for the social supremacy of the bourgeoisie." To think that workers could stop their revolution at this stage was "the worst kind of utopianism, the revolutionary utopianism of philistines."[78] Trotsky tried to cut through both the darkness of the present and ideological assumptions about history to "disclose 'possibility'" in historical conditions like none seen before.[79] He acknowledged the huge challenges, not least the need to win support from Russian peasants and to expand the revolution to Western Europe, for a Russian proletarian regime could not last long alone in a world of bourgeois enemies. But he insisted that history had created the real conditions to realize something unexpected and new: the top-heavy power of the Russian autocracy, the weakness of the Russian middle classes, and the distinctive course of Russia's industrialization, which created a large working class highly concentrated in big cities and big factories, were elements of Russian "backwardness" that paradoxically created unique opportunities for proletarian revolution. What was truly "unrealizeable" and "impossible"[80] was to imagine that this revolution could be "interrupted."[81]

In the years of repression and retreat after 1905, Trotsky continued to express such arguments about revolution with an optimism and zeal that was striking at a time when most educated Russians were depressed about prospects for even a liberal bourgeois revolution. After escaping again from Siberian exile, Trotsky settled in Vienna and devoted his energies to publishing, writing, and speech-making. Viewing words as practice, with real effects in the living world, he honed his powers of public oratory, studying speakers he found most compelling, such as the French socialist leader Jean Jaurès (1859–1914), whose "volcanic moral passion" and "gift of concentrated anger" impressed Trotsky.[82] When war broke out in August 1914, Trotsky welcomed it as a door opening to global revolution. The spectacle of the major socialist leaders and parties in Western Europe supporting their governments with as much patriotic enthusiasm as they had previously devoted to internationalism and antimilitarism shocked and depressed the remaining anti-war socialists. But Trotsky interpreted the disaster of war and the betrayal on the left optimistically. "The war of 1914," he insisted, will lead history out of its "blind alley" by making clear to everyone the utter failure of the false hopes of the past, including capitalism, imperialism, the nation-state, liberalism, and reformist socialism. This death of illusions will make the most radical visions of a new world no longer utopian: nations will free themselves from empires, colonial peoples will awaken, and the nation-state itself will be abandoned as a relic of the old world of capitalism, oppression, and war. "In the present historical circumstances the proletariat can have no interest in defending the outdated national 'Fatherland' . . . but in creating a more powerful and resilient fatherland, the republican United States of Europe, as the foundation for the United States of the World." Rejecting the "despair" that so many "revolutionary Marxists" felt at the outbreak of war and the abandonment of internationalism by the socialist parties, Trotsky countered with visionary optimism. "The epoch we are entering will be our epoch. . . . We revolutionary socialists did not want the war. But we do not fear it. . . . Amidst this hellish music of death, we preserve our clarity of thought and unclouded vision, and we feel ourselves to be the only creative force of the future."[83]

When revolution broke out in Petrograd, Trotsky was living in the Bronx in New York City (he ended up in the United States after having had fled Vienna, where he faced arrest as a subject of an enemy power, and after being expelled from France and then Spain for his anti-war politics). Even with only sketchy details from the American press, he was sure this was the "Second Russian Revolution," which would evolve uninterruptedly into socialist revolution. "What is now happening in Russia," he wrote in the émigré socialist newspaper *The New World* (*Novyi mir*) at the beginning of March 1917, "will enter history forever as one of its greatest events. Our children, grandchildren, and great grand-children will talk of these days as the beginning of a new epoch in human history. . . . The powerful avalanche of the revolution is in full swing and there is no human force that can stop it." While most socialists saw only a liberal bourgeois revolution, Trotsky saw the beginning of permanent revolution. The Provisional Government is dreaming, he declared, when it tries to call "insurgent Russia" back to order. "The Russian revolution will not stop. As it develops, it will sweep off its path the bourgeois liberals just as it is now sweeping aside tsarist reaction." And then it will "extend its hand to the proletariat of Germany and all Europe."[84] As for critics who worried about the risk of gambling success on an uprising by the German proletariat, he questioned their appreciation of the new reality: "Really, we do not need to rack our brains over so implausible (*never-oiatnyi*) a supposition. The war has transformed the whole of Europe into a powder magazine of social revolution. The Russian proletariat is now throwing a flaming torch into that powder magazine."[85]

By 1917, Trotsky was no longer as isolated as he had long been in these arguments. Most importantly, Lenin was saying much the same in March in a series of urgent "Letters from Afar" from Zurich to the party newspaper *Pravda* in Petrograd (which Kollontai brought to Petrograd on Lenin's behalf) and then after his own arrival in the capital in April. Lenin tried to convince his hesitant comrades (Trotsky was still a Menshevik, though clearly far from the center of his party) that the February revolution was the "first stage" of a bigger revolution, a "historic moment" when the proletariat should prepare to take power into their own hands and create a "revolutionary-democratic dictatorship of the proletariat and the poor peasantry." The "miracles of proletarian and popular heroism" that had made the February revolution must be turned into "miracles of proletarian and popular organization, to prepare for victory in the second stage of the revolution."[86] Most Bolsheviks resisted these arguments, worrying that Lenin had lost touch with political reality, having been away for so long, or even that he had somehow succumbed to "Trotskyism." The suspicion was not unreasonable. Lenin argued that the most immediate task was to "present a patient, systematic, and persistent explanation" of the error of continued support for the Provisional Government and to "preach" the necessity that the soviets take power. Trotsky, though formally joining the Bolshevik party only after the July Days, was already preacher-in-chief.

At mass public meetings, in essays in the press, at factory assemblies, at gatherings of sailors and soldiers, and in the revived Petrograd Soviet, Trotsky insistently made the case for the revolution's uninterruptable drive toward socialism. On his first day back in Petrograd in May, on the podium of the soviet he had co-led in 1905, he declared, much to the annoyance of the moderate Mensheviks and Socialist Revolutionaries who held sway there, that the revolution had "opened a new epoch, an epoch of blood and iron, a struggle no longer of nation against nation, but of the class of the suffering and oppressed against the ruling classes." A newspaper report of the meeting recorded "stormy applause." "I think that your next step will be to transfer all power into the hands of the workers' and soldiers' soviets," which will both "save Russia" and be the "prologue to the world revolution."[87] He acknowledged the risks. "History has given no guarantees to us, to revolutionary Russia, that we shall not be crushed, that our revolution will not be strangled by a coalition of world capital and that we will not be crucified by world imperialism." But history also guaranteed, Trotsky believed, that the revolution was impossible to stop.[88]

The mass arrests following the July Days put Trotsky back in the same prison where he had been incarcerated as a soviet leader in 1905. Released on bail in early September, as part of an effort to marshal support against Kornilov's attempt to overthrow the government, he redoubled his campaign of words against the Provisional Government and the socialists who tolerated and even participated in the government. In the weeks before the October insurrection, Trotsky seemed to be "speaking everywhere simultaneously,"[89] making the case for soviet power. But it was more than a rhetorical flourish that he continually declared that "the time for words has passed."[90] He was at the center of Bolshevik planning of an armed seizure of state power. Bolshevik dissenters warned that the party was too isolated, the masses too passive, the economic condition of the country too abysmal, and the European working class too far from revolution for a seizure of power in Russia by a minority proletarian party to lead to anything but catastrophe.[91] Things turned out less dire than skeptics feared, but this does not mean that Trotsky and other leaders of the insurrection were not risk-taking "illusionists," as even his sympathetic biographer Deutscher recognized: they "needed a world-embracing hope to accomplish the world-shaking deed."[92] The utopian principle of hope can produce daring actions, challenging the boundaries of the real and the possible. And yet, reality can exact a price for such daring. Trotsky was sure that their world-embracing hope and world-shaking deeds were in accord with the flow of history itself. Hence his famous dismissal of the Mensheviks and SRs who walked out of the soviet congress to protest the Bolshevik-led uprising: "your role is played out, go where you belong: to the trash heap of history." Once in power, needing to defend soviet power against threats from all sides, world-embracing hope would justify even more disturbing deeds.

Coercion, violence, and "terror" were key elements of Trotsky's job "arming the revolution" as Commissar of War and head of the Revolutionary Military Council, which was tasked with building and deploying a Red Army. Trotsky was not the most fervent defender of coercion and violence. As Trotsky himself had once anticipated, Lenin revealed a striking attraction to authoritarian and violent rule. In the first year after coming to power, Lenin talked explicitly and continually of the need for discipline, control, suppression, coercion, dictatorship, and terror. For good measure, he intensified the force of these nouns with suitable adjectives: iron discipline, ruthless suppression, merciless terror. And while his calls for repression were mainly aimed at "rich exploiters," he also targeted "crooks, idlers, and hooligans" and proletarians "who shirk their work."[93] Once civil war was fully underway, Lenin even more furiously demanded "merciless class terror" against every enemy of the revolution. After a peasant uprising in Penza province, for example, he advised local communists to "hang no fewer than 100 known kulaks, rich men, bloodsuckers" and seize many more as "hostages" so that "the people will see, tremble, know, shout: they are strangling and will strangle to death the bloodsucker kulaks."[94]

While dashing between military fronts in his armored command train, Trotsky took time to write a lengthy pamphlet justifying revolutionary dictatorship and violence. *Terrorism and Communism,* published in 1919, was a response to an anti-Bolshevik pamphlet of the same name by the German social-democrat Karl Kautsky, who condemned the Bolshevik revolution for trying to impose on Russia the political will of a minority class, and predicted dire consequences: dictatorship, civil war, and terror, which would end not in socialism but in "barbarism." Citing Marx, Kautsky accused the Bolsheviks of utopianism: true socialism is not a "ready-made utopia" to be imposed through "political victory," but must emerge out of a history of economic and social development.[95] Trotsky turned the tables on Kautsky, arguing that his faith that democracy could be achieved under conditions of capitalism, imperialism, and bourgeois rule was the most "pitiful, reactionary utopia." And it was "absolute utopianism" to believe that these could be overcome "imperceptibly and painlessly, without insurrections, armed conflicts, attempts at counterrevolution, and severe repression."[96]

Trotsky emphasized necessity in the turn to violence and dictatorship. If the revolution "had taken place a few months, or even a few weeks, after the establishment of the rule of the proletariat in Germany, France, in England, there can be no doubt that our revolution would have been the most 'peaceful,' the most 'bloodless' of all possible revolutions on this sinful earth." But the desperate violence of the class enemy, backed by foreign imperialists, left no choice. This had become a "life-and-death" struggle to survive. There is "in history no other way of breaking the class will of the enemy except by systematic and energetic use of violence." It works, so it is justified, for "who aims at the end cannot reject the means." Only a utopian would *not* to be willing to use repression and violence in a "life-and-death" struggle to defend the revolution.[97] Lenin had made a similar argument before the civil war began in a letter to American workers: to imagine that revolutionary class struggle will not "always, inevitably, in every country" take the form of civil war, which is "inconceivable without the most terrible destruction, without terror, without the restriction of formal democracy in the interests of this war," was to live in a "philistine utopia."[98]

But there was more to these arguments than expediency and necessity. If war is an extension of politics, and class war, according to Marxism, its most historically important expression, then the dictatorship and violence of the proletariat is not only *necessary* to overcome the resistance of the bourgeoisie, but virtuous and just: it is a dictatorship to eradicate the sources of dictatorship, class struggle to end class itself, terror to end the causes of violence. Hence, there can be no moral equivalence between the Red terror and the White terror, even when the practices are exactly the same. "The same rifles, the same cartridges in both camps. Where is the difference? There is a difference, gentlemen, and it is defined by a fundamental test: who is in power? The working class or the landlord class, Pharaohs or peasants, White Guards or the Petrograd proletariat?"[99] History makes the difference. White violence is ineffective, Trotsky believed, because terror "is helpless . . . if it is employed against a historically rising class." But Red terror works, because this is a fight against a historically doomed class that "does not want to leave the scene of operations."[100]

Trotsky tried to avoid moral arguments, but they are implicit here, not least because moral ideals are imbedded in all socialist thought. When Kautsky complained that violence is a violation of the absolute "sacredness of human life," Trotsky replied that "as long as human labor power, and consequently, life itself, remain articles of sale and purchase, of exploitation and robbery, the principle of the 'sacredness of human life' remains a shameful lie . . . To make the individual sacred we must destroy the social order that crucifies him. And this problem can only be solved by blood and iron."[101] Lenin made a similar argument in his appeal to American workers, recalling the insistence of the American Socialist leader Eugene Debs, when protesting World War I, that the only "holy and legitimate" war would be "the war against the capitalists, the war to liberate mankind from wage slavery," which is precisely what the Bolsheviks are doing, Lenin claimed.[102] As the civil war began, leaders of the Cheka, the chief arm of the "Red Terror," similarly insisted on the humanism of terror: the point was to save human lives from the class that drained the "juices of life" from the people; Red violence was "cleansing," an expression of how much "we value and love life as a sacred gift of nature."[103] In 1921, Walter Benjamin would define this as "divine violence," a moral and sacred violence to destroy the sources of violence and "deliver justice" "for the sake of the living."[104] In older terms, familiar to all these revolutionaries, these arguments echoed the religious millenarian vision of the world of evil and suffering transfigured through a bloody apocalypse and the secular variation on this theme as a revolution against injustice and oppression that must pass through a "final battle" when the "wretched of the earth" rise up and destroy the ruling class of "vultures" and "cannibals" (in the words of the nineteenth-century communist anthem, *The Internationale*). It is "utopian," so many believed, to think there is any other way to redemption and freedom "on this sinful earth."

Marxists refused the tainted label of utopianism for themselves, of course: utopians are dreamers, idealists building castles of perfection out of nothing more than desire and wish. But Trotsky also rejected the narrow-minded "philistine utopianism" that viewed the present as the best that reality will allow. At the same time, he believed that, to break through the limiting prison of present reality, people must change. Destroying old structures and changing social conditions were necessary but not enough to change the world if the human personality (*lichnost'*) remained the same. So, with the military struggles over, Trotsky turned his energies toward the world of culture and the self, to the "cultural revolution" and "struggle for the new everyday life (*novyi byt*)," which preoccupied so many Bolsheviks, like Kollontai, at the end of the civil war and at the start of allowing the return of so much of the old under the New Economic Policy (NEP).

Trotsky wrote a series of articles in the newspaper of the Communist party, *Pravda,* about the "problems of everyday life" (*voprosy byta,* which became the title of a 1923 book collecting these essays).[105] His topics included family life, reading, religion, labor, drinking, sex, and swearing. But his driving concern was how to create a new person, "to improve and 'finish' the physical and spiritual nature of man," which was the ultimate "goal of communism," the "music of the future."[106] As a "pessimist of the present" (to borrow his own youthful terminology), he saw the challenges: economic and social breakdown and a disastrously low "development of the masses," especially their "cultural level" and "political consciousness."[107] But he remained an "optimist of the future." And like all true utopians, he knew that it was impossible to imagine that future, that a vision of what is yet to be from within the walls of the present can be no more than "speculative." But he was certain that the human being of the communist future would be magnificent, physically and spiritually:

Man (*chelovek*) will put forth the goal of mastering his own feelings, raising instincts to the heights of consciousness, making them crystal clear, extending the lines of his will into hidden and secret places, and thereby raising himself to a new stage—in order to create a higher social-biological type, or, if you like, a superman.... Man will become incomparably stronger, smarter, and more subtle. His body will become more harmonized, his movements more rhythmic, his voice more musical.... The average human type will rise to the heights of an Aristotle, a Goethe, or a Marx. And above this ridge new peaks will rise.[108]

This future was not a fantasy, Trotsky insisted. There was "no doubt whatsoever," he told a group of students in 1923, that the "human being of the future, the citizen of the commune, will be a very interesting and attractive creature ... [with] a psychology very different from ours." What was "utopian," he argued, was to think that this "new human being" could "be formed first and then will create the new conditions." The task at hand must be to nurture people who can "fight for the creation of conditions out of which will grow the harmonious citizen of the commune."[109] These immediate tasks may seem modest: "step-by-step strengthening of the ground beneath our feet." But these "steps," Trotsky promised, will lead to a more heroic and transcendent movement: "what Engels called the leap from kingdom of necessity to the kingdom of freedom."[110]

Vladimir Mayakovsky (1893–1930)

"Verses and revolution somehow united in my head," Mayakovsky recalled about the effects of the readings that his older sisters kept him well-supplied with while he was in school in the Georgian provincial capital of Kutaisi—the family lived, and Mayakovsky (Figure 14) was born, in the mountain village of Bagdati (or Baghdati), which was renamed Mayakovsky from 1940 until 1990.[111] The upheavals of 1905, which were strong in Georgia, stimulated his interest in revolution all the more and made his interest in school even less. In 1906, his father, a forestry official, died from blood poisoning that resulted from accidently stabbing himself with a needle while sewing together official papers (a symbolic death for a bureaucrat?). The suddenly impoverished family sold what they could and moved to Moscow, where Vladimir entered a new school but also found work to help support the family. Moscow presented even more opportunities to become politically active. Attracted to the Russian Social-Democratic Workers' Party, especially the more radical Bolsheviks (who had also been a strong presence in Kutaisi), he volunteered to distribute underground leaflets to workers,

Figure 14. Vladimir Mayakovsky. Photograph by Alexander Rodchenko, 1924. Public domain.

which led to his arrest. In prison, he enjoyed playing the part of heroic rebel against all authority (he was a teenager, after all), ignoring police requests that he "maintain order" when not in his cell, refusing to return to his cell when it was his time to go to the latrine, and trying to rally other political prisoners against the officers. A police inspector complained of Mayakovsky's "riotous behavior." Mayakovsky took pride in this: "I raised hell (*skandalil*). They kept moving me from station to station...and finally to the Butyrka [Butyrskaya prison], solitary cell No. 103."[112]

While in prison, the mixing of "verses and revolution" in Mayakovsky's head grew stronger. He began to think about art as a revolutionary practice. By his own description, he "threw" himself into literature, starting with the new and modern and working back to the classics. Released to his mother under police surveillance, Mayakovsky later recalled his mood on emerging from prison as "agitated." He no longer saw party work as his calling: "I was faced with the prospect of an entire life writing leaflets putting forth ideas taken from books that were [politically] correct but were not the result of my own thinking." He was sure he could write better than all of the literary "greats" in which he had immersed himself because he had "the correct attitude toward the world."[113] But it was his agitated mood as much as his determination to create revolutionary art that defined this biographical moment. Victor Shklovsky, a radical literary critic who knew Mayakovsky well, described this mood as a "spiritual craving," a desire for "a new sight and hearing" that could cut through the "contradictions of his time."[114]

Mayakovsky found new comrades among an emerging group of "futurist" painters and poets. They were a diverse and eclectic group, united mainly by their desire to revolutionize art and literature in order, somehow, to revolutionize the world. They were notorious for their outrageous artistic performances—the most daring example a futurist "tour" of cities and towns across the empire during the winter of 1912–13 by Mayakovsky, the painter David Burlyuk, and the poet Vasily Kamensky. With wooden spoons or radishes in their lapels, pictures painted on their faces, and wearing top hats on their heads, they marched solemnly down the middle of the street, loudly proclaiming their most daring verses. Their performances were always sold out, if only for the promise of scandal, as the artists eccentrically drank tea on stage (or splashed it on the audience), read poems that seemed to most listeners to have no evident meaning, gave lectures denouncing all art of the past and the present except their own, and invited the audience to boo and hiss at them, shouting insults in return, which was Mayakovsky's particular specialty. Sometimes, things become so raucous—with amusement turning to anger and threats of violence from the crowd—that the police had to be called.[115] According to Kamensky, these three poets on tour were "express trains from the Future," who "shook the streets of Kharkov, Odessa, Kiev, Rostov, Baku, Tiflis, Kazan, Samara, Saratov, and smaller cities no less than an earthquake." Or, trying an even more extravagant metaphor, he proclaimed this a "triumphal march of three Poets-Prophets-Futurists, whose sun-radiating Will, wafting from their joyous youth—summoned by the anarchic sign of Modernity (*vzyvalas' anarkhicheskim znamenem Sovremennosti*)—strengthened in tens of thousands of hearts the Rebellion of the Spirit."[116]

Mayakovsky treated these aesthetic riots as political acts. If the heart of utopianism is radical negation of reality as it merely is, a determination to "rattle the bars" holding back the world of possibility, to "blast open the continuum of history," Mayakovsky practiced this with less irony than most futurists. He did not like to stay within the rules of the game of *épater les bourgeois* ("shocking the middle class"), but was increasingly inclined, as Edward Brown described in his excellent critical biography, "to deliver a real affront, deeply serious and apparently intolerable, to his audience."[117] Mayakovsky declared that he was no "madman" or "clown" entertaining bourgeois audiences with desired scandal. He was more like an angry Jeremiah railing against the world's failings, sins, and false prophets. "An hour from now," he proclaimed in a poem often read aloud to café audiences, "your flaccid fat will flow / man by man out onto the clean street / and here I have revealed to you so many boxes of verse. / That's me—spendthrift and prodigal of priceless words." He told the "crowd"—mocked as men with food stuck in their mustaches and women so heavily made up that they "peer out / like an oyster from a shell of things"—that he wanted to spit in their faces.[118]

Journalists and critics complained that the futurists had lowered art to the level of "the street" and "the crowd"—accusations that most futurists probably welcomed. "Futurism got its ideal for life from apaches [street hooligans], the dissipated, prostitutes, and other social scum," one hostile critic declared in a journal published by the Russian Orthodox Church.[119] The moral ethos of futurism, another critic concluded, was one with the motto of the whole modern age: "depravity is strength." The "futurist is a naked savage . . . in a bowler hat." Most troubling of all, he added, futurism is inspired not by a vision of any future at all, but by an apocalyptic "feeling of 'the end.'"[120] But this apocalyptic spirit could be interpreted differently. A more sympathetic writer agreed that futurism was "decadent," but saw this stance as conscious "negation of the modern present (*sovremennost'*) . . . in the name of the future."[121] In the utopian spirit, futurism was a visceral and anarchistic rejection of every conventional habit, value, and structure that stood in the way of the new. For futurists, it was right and good that the "philistine" crowd, for whom the present was the only future they could imagine, should be shocked and outraged. How else could one disrupt the dominant worldview that sees in the present only the "eternal repetition of what has already been," as Trotsky had defined the mentality of the "philistine pessimist." How else could one "leap," in Walter Benjamin's words, into the "open air of history"?[122]

Futurist books were as disruptive in form as they were in content, breaking every rule in sight.[123] A jumble of clashing typefaces and images flew across pages proclaiming an explosive end to everything old and trite, a challenging "slap in the face" to realism in art and reality itself. Books bound with burlap or printed on wallpaper samples contained fiery manifestos, "transrational" vocabularies, calculated absurdities, and every other conceivable means of refusing to be bound by the dead hand of the unimaginative present, of embracing and championing the vital chaos of the emerging new. Commercial publishers refused to print them, Mayakovsky claimed, because "the capitalist nose smelled dynamiters in us."[124] That is certainly how they wanted to be seen, as the artistic equivalent of anarchists. Mayakovsky's contributions to futurist publications between 1912 and 1914 were fully in this disruptive spirit. And so was his personal style in these years, dressed in a bright yellow loose-fitting shirt, big extravagant bow-ties, a spoon or radish in his lapel. He was purposefully outlandish, even literally so as a gesture toward another place and time. He was at war with the present, with everyday life (*byt*), and especially with philistine acceptance of convention as truth: the "filthy stigmas of Your 'Common Sense' and 'good taste'" that still rule "for now."[125]

The present, in Mayakovsky's poetry before 1917, was a dark place, and the heart of this darkness was the modern city, where people experienced so much suffering and sin: cold fog, dismal rain, and cutting winds (nature was an enemy, resisting human imagination and will), oppressive objects (smokestacks, windows, bathrooms, elevators, trams), abused bodies and spirits, devouring desire and greed, harsh laughter, sickness, death, loneliness, melancholy (*toska*), and despair.[126] Deliverance from this dark reality was brought by the anti-reality of "Vladimir Mayakovsky"—not his actual self, still bound to everyday life and ordinary time, but his persona as mythic poet, revolutionary artist, and redeeming savior.

In December 1913, which we now know to be among the final days of the final year before the old world collapsed in war and revolution (hence, 1913 has often been nostalgically romanticized), Mayakovsky staged his play *Vladimir Mayakovsky: A Tragedy* as part of a futurist theatrical event in St Petersburg by the "Union of Youth," which alternated his play with the avant-garde opera *Victory over the Sun* (which dramatized in surrealistic form the struggle by the heroic bearers of the future to overthrow the forces of the past and the present). A poet named Mayakovsky, "perhaps the last poet," appears in "the spider-web of streets" during a "beggars' holiday." He sees crippled men and madness everywhere. He sees that men and women "in the land of cities" are ruled by "soulless things" with "blocked emotions." In response, ready to die for the sins of this world, the poet prepares to "lie down / bright / in linen clothing / on the soft bed of the shit of the present / and quietly / kiss the knees of the track / as the wheel of the locomotive hugs my neck." But rather than die for the world, he decides instead to incite mass refusal any longer to accept the "shit of the present." Frustration, madness, and anger—the emotional experience of the living darkness of the present—become revolution. Even material things rebel against their slavery to "old lady time," the ultimate ruler, who had named and confined all things.

In the new world created by this revolution, the poet Mayakovsky, wearing toga and laurel wreath, is worshiped as a ruling prince. But this new world turns out to be a dystopic extension of the old: built around the exchange of money and sex, including factory-made kisses that become living beings. Plus, life is rather "dull" and "melancholy." Unable to endure this disappointing new reality, though its citizens seem not to care and bring the poet tears they feel they no longer have any use for, the poet gathers these tears in a suitcase and journeys to the farthest north where, "exhausted / in my last delirium / I will cast your tears / to the dark god of storms / at the very source of beastly faiths" (or, perhaps, "the source of the sign of the beast," as one scholar translated this ambiguous last line). The many allusions to the poet as Christ redeeming human suffering become fully explicit in this culmination. "Come unto me," the poet Mayakovsky proclaims to the world, "all who have shattered the silence / who find / the noose of our days too tight." He accepts others' pain for crucifixion on his own "cross of laughter"— an image combining radical negation, suffering, and a promise of salvation—and suggests visiting the place where "they crucified the prophet for his holiness." He declares himself ready to die in order to carry away the burden of people's tears to his own Golgotha, "leaving my soul on the spears of the city's buildings, shred by shred."[127]

Mayakovsky embraced war in 1914 for its anarchic vitality and apocalyptic possibility, an attitude shared with many avant-garde artists, for whom the image of war had already become a metaphor for the death of the old that would finally allow the birth of the new—the moment "everyone is waiting for," as another futurist wrote in the first study of Mayakovsky's poetry, "when the present will finally do away with itself and open up the lands of the men of the future."[128] Despair over the realities of the present had inspired a utopian desire for a different reality and a utopian belief in its possibility. Futurist art had long tried to blast open the measured continuum of time. Their time seemed to have come. Embracing the war effort, Mayakovsky made crude cartoon-like propaganda posters skewering (literally, in some drawings) the German and Austrian enemy accompanied by folksy, patriotic verses. He also tried to enlist, but was rejected because of his political past. A year later, after catastrophic losses in the battlefields, the army was less particular and sent Mayakovsky a draft notice. By then, Mayakovsky was less enthusiastic. With help from Maxim Gorky, who had connections, he was assigned to a military automobile school in Petrograd and so avoided the bloodshed of the front.

Mayakovsky defended his initial attraction to war in articles he published in a Moscow newspaper toward the end of 1914. "Violence in history is always a step toward perfection, toward the ideal kingdom," he declared. War redraws boundaries and remakes "human psychology." War "is not senseless murder, but a poem about the liberated and exalted soul," inspired by feelings so different from those of normal times. In these conditions, the "human essence is changing. The powerful people of the future are being born." Therefore, art must embrace the "magnificence" of war, even "ride on the gun-carriage wearing a hat of orange feathers of fire."[129] But Mayakovsky's optimistic enthusiasm was not the whole of his feelings about the war, especially when he shifted his gaze from desires and ideas to lived experience. He also wrote, in these same months, dark poems about spilled blood, death, and unbearable loss—such as a grieving mother lashing out at the "newspapers' eyes" and the hysterical patriotism of the public so at odds with her loss.[130]

During the summer of 1915, working on his deeply personal poem, "A Cloud in Trousers," Mayakovsky again envisioned a revolution entwined symbolically with the passion of Christ. In the utopian mode, Mayakovsky's Christ offered salvation from the present world of suffering, oppression, darkness, and death by means of a new truth from beyond the limits of reality and possibility as they were assumed to be.

> Beyond where man's meager vision breaks off,
> a certain year approaches
> at the head of hungry hordes,
> wearing the thorny crown of revolutions.
> I shall be, for you, its precursor;
> I am everywhere there is pain:
> in every drop of the stream of tears,
> I've nailed myself to the cross.
> Nothing can be forgiven anymore ...
> And when,
> proclaiming his coming with insurrection,
> you step out to meet the savior—
> I'll tear out my soul for you,
> stomp on it,
> to make it big!—
> and give it to you, bloodied, as a banner.[131]

In 1916, Mayakovsky started work on a pair of long poems, "War and the Universe" (*Voina i mir*) and "Man" (*Chelovek*, or Person), which suggest something of his inner struggle to make sense of the present and the future. He would later describe this as a conflict between the hope in his mind and the doubt in his spirit: "In my head 'War and the Universe' unfolded. In my heart—'Man.'"[132] The work of his head was a confident prophecy of a transformed world, of perfection born in violence, of an epic utopia. The poem begins in the present world of urban gluttony, lust, and sickness—the city as a modern Sodom, which was already a cliché in both press and literature. The soundtrack of that life, as we would say now, was the tango—indicated by lines of music interspersed in the text. (The tango had become, for the prewar Russian press, a symbol of cosmopolitan decadence.) War disrupts this world, though not as a vital and necessary devastation of the old but as the senseless bloodshed of gladiators in a pagan Coliseum. In the face of such horrors, the "angels tremble" and the gods—"Sabaoth / Buddha / Allah / Jehovah"—flee the heavens. For this and for all human suffering, the poem declares, everyone is personally guilty. The music in the text suitably changes to an Orthodox chant for the dead.

But out of this catastrophe comes a new and redeemed world. In this utopia—the first section of the poem to appear in print, published by Maxim Gorky just after the February revolution—"there will be no one to torment man. / People will be born, / real people, / much more merciful and better than god." This new and "redeemed" world arrives apocalyptically: "A whisper. / The world / unclenches its black lips. / Louder / A hurricane / roars awake," and the dead arise. Every nation brings its natural gifts to this new world for the pleasure and glory of united humanity. America brings the power of machines, Italy its warm nights, Africa the hot sun, Greece the beautiful bodies of youth, Germany philosophy, and France love. Russia "opens its heart in a fiery hymn." The very air and mood are renewed. Nature is transfigured: the sea, "so stormy yesterday / lies down by your feet / and purrs." Machines of war "sit before one's house / on the lawn / peacefully trimming the grass." And every sin, across all time, is forgiven through love: "Cain / under a tree / plays checkers with Christ." This was also a personal utopia, overcoming the darkness in Mayakovsky's life caused by his love for a woman married to a close friend: in this transformed world, he and his beloved are together.[133]

The poem "Man" responded to these dreams and promises with gloomy doubt—shifting from the utopia of hope to the utopia of radical negation, the repudiation of a reality that is impossible to accept. Money, Mayakovsky believed, is the heart of darkness of the present, as it has been for so many utopias, including Thomas More's original. Money stands for everything objective, quantifiable, and conventional, the antithesis of life, emotion, thinking, music, and poetry. "Man" is a story of the birth, experience, passion, ascension to heaven, and return to earth of the poet "Mayakovsky." The poet is "shackled" and "captive" in a world where money is king and defended by "law" and "religion." In a foaming sea of money, "geniuses, hens, horses, and violins drown. / Elephants drown. / Little things drown." Just by thinking of suicide, "Mayakovsky" ascends to heaven, physically rising from the street toward the cosmos as ordinary passersby cry out in astonishment. But the promised bliss of heaven—the archetypal closed utopia of perfection—is disappointing: it is dull, routine, and cold, a cloudland of "cleansed smoothness" where everything "is in frightfully good order / at rest / in ranks," and people lack bodies and so also lack hearts. Heaven has no need or desire for what a poet can offer. But time moves slowly in paradise, until finally, after many thousands of years, the poet Mayakovsky rouses himself and returns to earth. Surely by now, the world had become new, a true paradise? But no, nothing had changed. The passage of time had not brought happiness any more than had his passage into the place beyond time, life, and death. This was the final and worst disappointment. Mayakovsky, the "Man" of the title, realizes that there is nowhere left to go, apart from refusing to stay. Heaven and earth have failed. Space and time have left him adrift. All that remains is to wander for eternity among planets and stars, in the nowhere outside of everything.[134]

When revolution broke out in February 1917, Mayakovsky joined other soldiers from his automobile unit in the streets of Petrograd. Recording his experiences in a "poeto-chronicle," he described a millenarian moment: "Citizens! / Today, the thousand-year old 'Before' has collapsed, / Today, the whole basis of the world has been altered." And this was a cosmic millennium: "The movement of planets / the existence of states / are all subject to our will. / The land is ours. / The air is ours."[135] When the Bolsheviks came to power in October, he rushed to the party's headquarters to declare himself ready "to do anything" for "my revolution."[136] In the years ahead, he would work actively for the new government: during 1918–19 in the Fine Arts Department of the Commissariat of Enlightenment, and during 1919–21 as a designer of propaganda posters and poetic ditties for ROSTA, the state news agency. But just as he had decided in 1906 that his role in the revolution required more than "writing leaflets," he insisted after 1917 not only that art itself was a revolutionary practice but that it was the role of artists to push the new state beyond its narrow understanding of what revolution meant.

Together with his old futurist comrades Burlyuk and Kamensky, Maya-kovsky helped put together a *Futurists' Newspaper* (*Gazeta Futuristov*), published by a largely imaginary "Association of Socialist Art" that listed its address as the Poet's Café in Moscow. Only one issue appeared, in March 1918. The front page featured three manifestos, all signed or co-signed by Mayakovsky, laying out their vision of the next stage of revolution. Appropriating the Russian folk belief that the earth rested on the backs of three whales, these three futurists described the whales of the old order as "political slavery, social slavery, and spiritual slavery." February had destroyed the first whale and "October threw the bomb of social revolution underneath capital. Far on the horizon we see the fat backsides of the fleeing factory owners." All that remained was the third whale, "slavery of the Spirit. And as of old it spews out a fountain of fetid water, which is called the old art." The time had come for the next stage of revolution in which artists were the vanguard class: "We, the proletarians of art call the proletarians of factories and soil to the third revolution, bloodless but severe, the Revolution of the Spirit." The main weapon in this new revolution was a new art, radically different in form and social location. It must be a "democratic" art freed from the prison of museums, palaces, and books. It must take to the streets and be "inscribed at the crossroads of the buildings, fences, roofs, and streets of our cities and villages and on the backs of automobiles, carriages, and streetcars, and on the clothes of every citizen." It seemed enough for art, like the Bolshevik Red Guards of October 1917, to seize every public space for the world to change.[137]

Lenin and other government officials began to lose patience with the more-radical-than-everyone-else stance of artists like Mayakovsky. That these "left artists" were "unintelligible" to workers and peasants was only the surface of a deeper error: their nihilistic rejection of the entirety of the old culture at a time when the first cultural task of the revolutionary state must be to bring culture and enlightenment to the masses. Lenin described the proper approach to cultural revolution: "It is necessary to grasp all the culture that capitalism has left and build socialism from it. It is necessary to grasp all the science and technology, all the knowledge and art. With this, we will be able to build the life of a communist society."[138] But radical artists like Mayakovsky believed that cultural revolution—the third revolution, the revolution of the spirit—demanded the eradication of the shackles of the old that were restraining the world from leaping into the new. Typical was Mayakovsky's "Order to the Army of Art," which appeared in the first issue of a new weekly newspaper organized by communist artists, *Art of the Commune* (*Iskusstvo kommuny*).

> **Comrades!**
> **To the barricades!—**
> **the barricades of hearts and souls.**
> **The only true communist**
> **is one who's burnt every bridge going back.**
> **Enough marching, Futurists—**
> **it's time for a leap into the future! . . .**
> **Wipe everything old from your heart.**
> **The streets are our brushes.**
> **The squares our palettes.**
> **The days of revolution have yet to be sung**
> **by the thousand-paged**
> **book of time.**[139]

In an editorial manifesto in verse in the second issue of *Art of the Commune*, Mayakovsky added metaphors of violence to this millenarian "leap into the future." It is not enough to put only *political* enemies "up against the wall." If we truly "seek the future," we must also kill the White Guards of art: "It's time / for bullets / To whistle on museum walls. / Shoot at the old from your hundred-inch cannon-throats, / Sow death in the enemy's camp."[140]

For the first anniversary of the October revolution, Mayakovsky prepared a performance that imagined the future after the destruction of the old. Titled "Mystery-Bouffe," it was a religious mystery play in a mocking carnival spirit. Or, as Mayakovsky explained in a prologue for a version performed for delegates to the Congress of the Communist International in Moscow in June 1921, this was "mystery play for the proletariat and an *opera bouffe* for the bourgeoisie," a sacred miracle for the rising common people and a jester's mockery for the dying elite.[141] Performed across the country, the play begins as the entire planet is flooded by the waters of revolution. The last human survivors, including both the privileged "clean" and the laboring "unclean," are aboard a new Noah's ark, built by the unclean, who eventually throw the old elites overboard. Walking on water, a prophet appears (Mayakovsky performed this role, of course), who tells of a promised land. After a journey through Hell (not very frightening compared to what the unclean experienced on earth) and Heaven (too abstract and dull), they reach "the Promised Land," which appears suddenly, eschatologically: "A gigantic gate reaches across the whole stage . . . The gates swing open to reveal a city. And what a city! Huge crystalline factories and buildings tower into the sky. Trains, streetcars, and automobiles are wrapped in rainbows. In the center, a garden of stars and moons crowned by the radiant corona of the sun. Out of display windows the finest things emerge and head toward the gates, led by the bread and salt of welcome." (In the 1921 version, revised after considerable criticism, this procession of things is led by a hammer and a cycle carrying bread and salt.[142])

Time has long been at the heart of modern utopian thinking—the new and better world often located in another time rather than a distant place. But time could be as much an obstacle as a path, when stuck in its conventional steady pace. Like Trotsky and Kollontai, Mayakovsky sought to blast open the continuum of the present to make way for a new time, to stop "marching" though history, as Mayakovsky put it, in order to take a transcending "leap into the future." Time was often Mayakovsky's nemesis. Before 1917 especially, he described time as holding back the future, crushing it under the weight of everyday reality, of the "merely factual," as Bloch put it, rather than the "not-yet" of what ought to be. Time, in Mayakovsky's treatment, was a "lame icon dauber," an "old woman," a "fetter" and a "chain" yoking man to the present.[143] During the war, Mayakovsky seemed to despair of the possibility of escaping the heavy chains of time. Even after "thousands and millions" of years, he wrote in "Man," nothing on earth would be different, the "terrible avalanche of years" would bury every possibility and hope.[144] Revolution blasted apart this slow and burdened temporality, shattering in an instant the "thousand-year old 'Before.'"[145] But the old time would not step aside. So, as for the military enemy during the civil war, anything less than its extermination left open the risk of its return to power. As Mayakovsky wrote in 1919, "We / cannot just fantasize / about the new order / but have to dynamite the old... / With heat, / with burning, / with iron, / with light; / scorch, / burn, / cut, / raze!... / If it's old—kill it. / Use their skulls as ashtrays! / In a savage rout / we'll wash away the old / and thunder a new / myth across the world. / We'll kick down / the fence of time."[146]

The old time was linked to the old *byt*—the untransformed routines, habits, and conventions of everyday life, against which Trotsky and Kollontai also fought. The old *byt* embodied the past in the present, the slow and repetitive march of ordinary time. It must be destroyed for the future to appear. "Enough / of time-the-reptile's / groveling, / Enough / of time-the-mole's / digging! / ... / Time forward! / Forward my land, / let's / obliterate / the old junk!... / Stronger / my commune / strike / make that monster-*byt* / die."[147] But as Trotsky and Kollontai also found, the "monster-*byt*" refused to die. Mayakovsky worried about this in a melancholy poem he wrote toward end of 1920, as the battles of the civil war were winding down but before the major compromises of NEP. "The storms of revolution have subsided. / The Soviet muddle is covered in slime. / From behind the back of Soviet Russia / has crawled out / purring / the philistine." Karl Marx, from his portrait on the wall, "looks and looks all around, / and suddenly opens his mouth / and shouts: / 'the revolution is snared in a web of ordinariness (*obyvatel'shchina*), / of a commonplace everyday life (*obyvatel'skii byt*) more terrible than Wrangel [the White Army general].'"[148] The mole and snake of unambitious time was all that remained. Life again was fettered and chained to the present, prevented from making that desired "leap" from necessity to freedom.

Deeper into the 1920s, the era of NEP's necessary compromises with the old, Mayakovsky felt more and more that the utopian not-yet had vanished, that slow digging time had devoured possibility and hope. In 1926, he saw around him "less and less love, / and less and less daring, / and time, / with a running start, / smites me head on."[149] On 14 April 1930, Mayakovsky shot himself through the heart. Scholars have interpreted his suicide as a "refusal to bow to *byt* and time," as an "acknowledgment on his own flesh and bone of the total capitulation of the future to the might of the past."[150] Mayakovsky offered his own ambiguous explanation in a fragment of an unfinished poem he included in his suicide note: "As they say / 'the incident is closed.' / Love's boat / has smashed against *byt.*"[151] Mayakovsky was partly speaking literally about love, about his own difficult personal life. But he was also surely commenting, as were other disenchanted idealists, about the times: "love's boat" as the revolution crashing against ordinary life (*byt*), against the "merely factual" (as Bloch put it in 1918), against "necessity," against "philistine" time.

Notes

1. Frederick Engels, *Socialism: Utopian and Scientific* (1880), ch. 1 at <https://www.marxists.org/archive/marx/works/1880/soc-utop/>. [accessed 26 August 2016]

2. e.g. Mikhail Heller and Aleksandr Nekrich, *Utopia in Power: The History of the Soviet Union from 1917 to the Present* (New York, 1986); *Martin Malia, The Soviet Tragedy: A History of Socialism in Russia, 1917–1991* (New York, 1994); Richard Pipes, *Communism: A History* (New York, 2001).

3. Closer to my approach is Richard Stites, *Revolutionary Dreams: Utopian Vision and Revolutionary Life in the Russian Revolution* (Oxford, 1989) and Susan Buck-Morss, *Dreamworld and Catastrophe: The Passing of Mass Utopia in East and West* (Cambridge, MA, 2002). See also William G. Rosenberg (ed.), *Bolshevik Visions: First Phase of the Cultural Revolution in Soviet Russia* (Ann Arbor, 1990).

4. A good entry point into the growing field of utopian studies is <http://utopian-studies.org>. [accessed 12 August 2016]

5. In addition to the works cited in the following notes, see Ruth Levitas, *The Concept of Utopia* (Syracuse, NY, 1990) and *Utopia as Method: The Imaginary Reconstitution of Society* (New York, 2013); David Harvey, *Spaces of Hope*

(Berkeley, CA, 2000); Fredric Jameson, *Archaeologies of the Future: The Desire Called Utopia and Other Science Fictions* (London, 2005).

6. "Something's Missing: A Discussion between Ernst Bloch and Theodor W. Adorno on the Contradictions of Utopian Longing," in Ernst Bloch, *The Utopian Function of Art and Literature: Selected Essays*, tr. Jack Zipes and Frank Mecklenburg (Cambridge, MA, 1988), 12; Ernst Bloch, *Geist der Utopie* (Munich and Leipzig, 1918), 9; Bloch, *The Spirit of Utopia*, tr. Anthony Nassar (Stanford, CA, 2000, from the revised 1923 German edn), 3; Bloch, *The Principle of Hope*, 3 vols. (Cambridge, MA, 1995), especially i. 3–18 (Introduction) and 287–316 ("Summary/Anticipatory Composition").

7. "Something's Missing," 6; Fredric Jameson, "The Politics of Utopia," *New Left Review* 25 (January–February 2004), 46.

8. Jean-Jacques Rousseau, *Social Contract*, trans. G. D. H. Cole (London, 1913), book III, ch. 12.

9. José Esteban Muñoz, *Cruising Utopia: The Then and There of Queer Futurity* (New York, 2009), 22–5.

10. Walter Benjamin, "On the Concept of History," *Selected Writings*, 4 vols. (Cambridge, MA, 2003), iv. 389–411.

11. Benjamin, "Paralipomena to 'On the Concept of History,'" *Selected Writings*, iv. 402.

12. Jameson, *Archaeologies of the Future*, 232–3, and ch. 13 ("The Future as Disruption").

13. The main English-language biographies are Barbara Evans Clements, *Bolshevik Feminist: The Life of Aleksandra Kollontai* (Bloomington, IN, 1979); Beatrice Farnsworth, *Aleksandra Kollontai: Socialism, Feminism, and the Bolshevik Revolution* (Stanford, CA, 1980); Cathy Porter, *Alexandra Kollontai: A Biography* (London, 1980; rev. edn Chicago, 2014). For Kollontai's own account, see *The Autobiography of a Sexually Emancipated Communist Woman* (New York, 1971), and, in Russian, "Avtobiograficheskii ocherk," *Proletarskaia revoliutsiia*, 1 (1921): 261–302, and *Iz moei zhizni i raboty: gody i liudi* (Moscow, 1974). Many of Kollontai's writings are available in English in Alix Holt (ed.), *Selected Writings of Alexandra Kollontai* (New York, 1977), online at the Marxists Internet Archive <http://www.marxists.org/archive/kollonta/index.htm>, [accessed 12 August 2016], and in Russian in *Izbrannye stat'i i rechi* (Moscow, 1972). Some additional works in Russian are available as links at <http://az.lib.ru/k/kollontaj_a_m> [accessed 12 August 2016]. Works by Kollontai in this section will be cited without author.

14. *Autobiography of a Sexually Emancipated Communist Woman*, 10–11. Before the book's first publication in German in 1926, Kollontai excised from the

galleys many of the more unorthodox phrases and passages. When I quote from these deleted sections, I will indicate this in the notes.

15. Ibid. 11–12.
16. Quoted Clements, *Bolshevik Feminist*, 21.
17. *Autobiography of a Sexually Emancipated Communist Woman*, 11.
18. *Kto takie sotsial-demokraty i chego oni khotiat?* (Who are the social democrats and what do they want?, 1906), in *Izbrannye stat'i i rechi*, 32, 35–6, 42.
19. *K voprosu o klassovoi bor'be* (On the question of class struggle, 1905), in *Izbrannye stat'i i rechi*, 20–2, 25.
20. "Problemy nravstennosti s pozitivnoi tochki zreniia" (Questions of morality from the positivist point of view), *Obrazovanie*, 1905/9 (September): 77–95 (esp. 80, 94); 1905/10 (October): 92–107 (esp. 106–7); "Etika i sotsial-demokratiia" (Ethics and social democracy), *Obrazovanie*, 1906/2 (February): pt 2, 28–32 (esp. 24–7, 30). See also Clements, *Bolshevik Feminist*, 38.
21. "Towards a History of the Working Woman's Movement," in *Selected Writings*, 53. See also *Autobiography of a Sexually Emancipated Communist Woman*, 13 (passage deleted).
22. "Zhenshchina-rabotnitsa v sovremennom obshchestve" (The woman worker in contemporary [or modern] society), from *Trudy vserossiiskogo zhenskogo s"ezda* (St Petersburg, 1908), 792–801. Online at <http://levoradikal.ru/archives/264>. [accessed 26 August 2016] Much of this speech was included in the introduction to her book *Sotsial'nye osnovy zhenskogo voprosa* (The social bases of the woman question) (St Petersburg, 1909). A translation appears at <https://www.marxists.org/archive/kollonta/1908/social-basis.htm>. [accessed 26 August 2016].
23. From the introduction to *Sotsial'nye osnovy zhenskogo voprosa*, 5.
24. Ibid. 196, 198 (68–9 in the translation in *Selected Writings*).
25. Ibid. 109–10 (63–4).
26. Ibid. 196–7 (68–9). See also discussions in Clements, *Bolshevik Feminist*, 56–61; Farnsworth, *Aleksandra Kollontai*, 33–7.
27. *Autobiography of a Sexually Emancipated Communist Woman*, 22 (deleted passage); Clements, *Bolshevik Feminist*, 68–9; Porter, *Alexandra Kollontai*, 164–8.
28. e.g. M. Liberson, *Stradanie odinochestva* (St Petersburg, 1909).
29. From "Na staruiu temu" (On an old theme) and "Polovaia moral' i sotsial'naia bor'ba" (Sexual morality and the social struggle), both published in *Novaia zhizn'* in 1911 and republished as "Otnoshenie mezhdu polami i klassovaia bor'ba" (The relation between the sexes and the class struggle) and "Liubov' i novaia moral" (Love and the new morality) in *Novaia moral' i rabochii klass* (The new morality and the working class) (Moscow, 1918),

quotations pp. 40–1, 51. See also the discussion of these texts in Clements, *Bolshevik Feminist*, 69–72.

30. "Novaia zhenshchina" (The new woman), *Sovremennyi mir*, 1913/9: 151–85, as reprinted in *Novaia moral'*, 3–35 (quotations pp. 3–6). An English translation, based on the 1920 German edn of *The New Morality and the Working Class*, is included in *Autobiography of a Sexually Emancipated Communist Woman*, 51–103. See discussion in Richard Stites, *The Women's Liberation Movement in Russia: Feminism, Nihilism, and Bolshevism, 1860–1930* (Princeton, 1978), 348–50; Clements, *Bolshevik Feminist*, 73–4.

31. "Novaia zhenshchina," in *Novaia moral'*, 8–9, 17–18, 24, 30–1.

32. Ibid. 26, 29–31.

33. "Polovaia moral' i sotsial'naia bor'ba" (1911), in *Novaia moral'*, 58–61.

34. "Novaia zhenshchina," in *Novaia moral'*, 33.

35. Ibid. 17, 29.

36. Ibid. 35.

37. N. N. Sukhanov, *The Russian Revolution, 1917: A Personal Record* (Princeton, 1984), 288; Clements, *Bolshevik Feminist*, 109; Farnsworth, *Aleksandra Kollontai*, 74.

38. *Autobiography of a Sexually Emancipated Communist Woman*, 35.

39. Ibid. (She deleted the phrase "magnificent illusions" before publication.)

40. *Rabotnitsa-Mat'* (St Petersburg, 1914; reprinted repeatedly in 1917 and 1918). For an English translation see "Working Woman and Mother," *Selected Works*, 127–39 (I have adapted the translation from the Russian original).

41. *Sem'ia i kommunisticheskoe gosudarstvo* (Moscow, 1918), 23, quoted Farnsworth, *Aleksandra Kollontai*, 144.

42. Quoted Clements, *Bolshevik Feminist*, 130.

43. "Pochemu molchal proletariat Germanii v iul'skie dni?" *Kommunist* (September 1915), in *Izbrannye stat'i i rechi*, 158; Diary entry, 23 August 1914, in *Iz moei zhizni i raboty*, 161. See also *Selected Works*, 85, 99–103.

44. Jacques Sadoul, *Notes sur la revolution bolchevique* (Paris, 1919), 316. Also quoted in Clements, *Bolshevik Feminist*, 146. The original vestals were virgin priestesses tending the sacred eternal fire in ancient Rome.

45. R. Abramovich at the Third Congress of Trade Unions, in Isaac Deutscher, *The Prophet Armed: Trotsky, 1879–1921* (Oxford, 1954), 500.

46. From debates at the Tenth Party Congress, March 1921, quoted and discussed ibid. 508–10.

47. "Tezisy rabochei oppozitsii," *Pravda*, 25 January 1921, 2–3. Available in translation as "Theses of the Workers' Opposition" at, https://www.marxists.org/archive/shliapnikov/1921/workers-opposition.htm>. [accessed 26 August 2016].

48. *Rabochaia oppozitsiia* (Moscow, 1921), 15–16. An English translation was published as A. Kollontai, *The Workers' Opposition* (Chicago, 1921) and reprinted (apart from the opening section) in Holt (ed)., *Selected Writings*, 159–200. Quotations here are translated from the original Russian; for reference, I indicate in brackets the relevant pages in *Selected Writings* (in this case pp. 167–9).

49. *Rabochaia oppozitsiia*, 19, 24, 33, 38–9, 47 [171, 176, 185, 190–1, 199–200].

50. Ibid. 22, 32, 35, 38–40, 48 [174, 184, 187, 189–92, 200].

51. *Skoro (cherez 48 let)* (Omsk, 1922). Online at <http://az.lib.ru/k/kollontaj_a_m/text_0080.shtml>. [accessed 26 August 2016] For an English translation see also *Selected Works*, 232–6.

52. See Stites, *Revolutionary Dreams;* and Christina Kiaer and Eric Naiman (eds), *Everyday Life in Early Soviet Russia: Taking the Revolution Inside* (Bloomington, IN, 2006).

53. "Dorogu krylatomu Erosu! (pis'mo k trudiashcheisia molodezhi)," *Molodaia gvardia*, 1923/3 (May), 111–24 <http://az.lib.ru/k/kollontaj_a_m/text_0030.shtml>; [accessed 26 August 2016] "Make Way for Winged Eros (A Letter to Working Youth)," *Selected Works*, 276–92.

54. Quotations are from Jameson, *Archaeologies of the Future*, pp. xii–xvi (quotations).

55. Bessie Beatty, *The Red Heart of Russia* (New York, 1918), 380.

56. *Den första etappen* (Stockholm, 1945), Kollontai's Swedish-language autobiography, quoted Clements, *Bolshevik Feminist*, 147–8.

57. *Moia zhizn': opyt avtobiografii*, 2 vols. (Berlin, 1930), i. 159, 166–7; *My Life: An Attempt at an Autobiography* (New York, 1970), 135, 142–3. Biographies of Trotsky's life range from sympathetic (especially Deutscher, *The Prophet Armed*) to hostile (notably Robert Service, *Trotsky: A Biography*, London, 2009), and from factually careful to error-ridden. See also Ian D. Thatcher, *Trotsky* (London, 2003); Geoffrey Swain, *Trotsky: Profiles in Power* (London, 2006); David North, *In Defense of Leon Trotsky* (Oak Park, MI, 2010); Joshua Rubenstein, *Leon Trotsky: A Revolutionary's Life* (New Haven, 2013).

An incomplete edition of Trotsky's works was published in the Soviet Union as Lev Trotskii, *Sochineniia* (Moscow, 1925). These and other works are available at <http://www.magister.msk.ru/library/trotsky/trotsky.htm> [accessed 12 August 2016]. A selection of works is also available at <https://www.marxists.org/russkij/trotsky/index.htm> [accessed 12 August 2016]. For online English translations, see <http://www.marxists.org/archive/trotsky/index.htm> [accessed 12 August 2016] (English). Quotations from Trotsky's writings here are adjustments of existing translations based on the original Russian text—and cited without author.

58. *Moia zhizn'*, i. 120–2; *My Life*, 98–9.

59. Deutscher, *The Prophet Armed*, 23.

60. *Moia zhizn'*, i. 122; *My Life*, 99.

61. Max Eastman, *Leon Trotsky: The Portrait of a Youth* (New York, 1925), 52–3.

62. G. A. Ziv, *Trotskii: kharakteristika (po lichnym vospominaniiam)* (New York, 1921), 19.

63. *Moia zhizn'*, i. 151; *My Life*, 127.

64. See Chapter 2 in this volume.

65. "O pessimizme, optimizme, XX stoletii i mnogom drugom," *Vostochnoe obozrenie*, 17 February 1901, at <http://www.magister.msk.ru/library/trotsky/trotl457.htm>. [accessed 26 August 2016] See also Deutscher, *The Prophet Armed*, 53–4 (I have used some of his translation).

66. *Moia zhizn'*, i. 157; *My Life*, 132.

67. Deutscher, *The Prophet Armed*, 67, 69.

68. Krupskaia, *Memories*, 99.

69. *Vtoroi s"ezd Ross. Sots.-Dem. Rabochei Partii: otchet sibirskoi delegatsii* (Geneva, 1903), quotations 11–13, 20, 28–9. For an online transcription of an incomplete English translation, see <https://www.marxists.org/archive/trotsky/1903/xx/siberian.htm>. [accessed 26 August 2016]

70. *Nashi politicheskie zadachi* (Geneva, 1904), in *L. D. Trotsky o Partii v 1904* (Moscow, 1928), 127, 185–7. See Deutscher, *The Prophet Armed*, 88–90. For an English translation of *Our Political Tasks*, see <https://www.marxists.org/archive/trotsky/1904/tasks/index.htm> [accessed 26 August 2016].

71. *Sochineniia*, ii/1 (Moscow, 1925), 3–53. For an English translation of parts of this brochure, see Leon Trotzky [*sic*], *Our Revolution: Essays on Working-Class and International Revolution, 1904–1917*, ed. and tr. Moissaye J. Olgin (New York, 1918), 29–44. See also Deutscher, *The Prophet Armed*, 108–12.

72. *Sochineniia*, ii/1. 54–70 ("Chto zhe dal'she," writing in Munich 20 January/ 2 February 1905). Translation in Trotzky, *Our Revolution*, 51–61 (titled "The Events in Petersburg").

73. *Sochineniia*, ii/1. 198 ("Open Letter to Professor P. N. Miliukov," August 1905).

74. Leon Trotsky, *1905* (Harmondsworth, 1971), 212. This book was written in Vienna in 1908–9 and first published in German.

75. *Moia zhizn'*, i. 213; *My Life*, 186. This image was evidently first used by Lenin in 1920 in his pamphlet on "Left-Wing Communism: An Infantile Disorder."

76. Trotsky, *1905*, 398–414. The Russian text is in *Sochineniia*, ii/2 (Moscow, 1927), 163–78.

77. "Itogi i perspektivy: dvizhushchie sily revoliutsii," in L. D. Trotskii, *K istorii russkoi revoliutsii* (Moscow, 1990; based on a 1919 edn of the banned 1906 original). Translated as "Prospects of a Labor Dictatorship," in Trotzky, *Our Revolution*. For comments on utopia, see Trotzky, *Our Revolution*, 106, 113, 127, 129–32, 177.

78. "Itogi i perspektivy," 101, 105–6.

79. Ibid. 84.

80. Ibid. 99.

81. Ibid. 104. Although he would later call this vision a theory of "permanent revolution" (*permanentnaia revoliutsiia*), in 1906 he used the term "uninterrupted revolution" (*nepreryvnaia revoliutsiia*). See the discussion of this work in Baruch Knei-Paz, *The Social and Political Thought of Leon Trotsky* (Oxford, 1978), 64–87, 110–14, 120–44, 152–3.

82. "Zhan Zhores," *Kievskaia mysl*, 17 July 1915, in *Sochineniia*, viii (Moscow, 1926), 20–33.

83. Collected into a pamphlet, *War and the International*, this was published first in German in 1914 and in English in 1918 (as *The Bolsheviki and World Peace*). My quotations are translated from a reprint of the German edn, *Der Krieg und die Internationale* (Chicago, 1918), pp. v, viii, 83–5. See also Isaac Deutscher (ed.), *The Age of Permanent Revolution: A Trotsky Anthology* (New York, 1964), 71–9.

84. "Revoliutsiia v Rossii," *Novyi mir*, 16 (3) March 1917; "Dva litsa," *Novyi mir*, 17 (4) March 1917, in *Sochineniia*, iii/1 (Moscow, [1924]), 5–7, 11.

85. "Ot kogo i kak zashchishchat revoliutsiiu," *Novyi mir*, 21 (8) March 1917, in *Sochineniia*, iii/1. 17–20. See Deutscher, *The Prophet Armed*, 245.

86. Lenin, "Letters from Afar" (7–25 March 1917) and "April Theses" (as published in *Pravda*, 7 April 1917), in V. I. Lenin, *Izbrannye proizvedeniia*, 4 vols. (Moscow, 1988), ii. 116–31. English translations of Lenin's works can be found at <https://www.marxists.org/archive/lenin/works/index.htm> [accessed 26 August 2016]

87. Speech to the Petrograd Soviet, 5 May 1917, in *Izvestiia*, 7 May 1917, 3.

88. Speech at First All-Russian Congress of Soviets, 9 June 1917, Trotsky, *Sochineniia*, iii/1. 131.

89. See Sukhanov, *The Russian Revolution*, 578.

90. e.g. in the resolution he wrote for the Petrograd garrison, 21 October 1917, *Rabochii put' [Pravda]*, 4 November (22 October) 1917, 12–13 (Trotsky identified as author in *Sochineniia*, iii/2).

91. Views summarized by Lenin, "Letter to Comrades" (17 October 1917), at <https://www.marxists.org/archive/lenin/works/1917/oct/17.htm>. [accessed

26 August 2016] See also "Iu. Kamenev o 'vystuplenii,'" *Novaia zhizn'*, 18
October 1917, 3.

92. Deutscher, *The Prophet Armed*, 293.

93. See especially Lenin's essays "How to Organize Competition" (December
1917) and "The Immediate Tasks of Soviet Power" (April 1918).

94. Lenin, "Telegram to Penza Communists" (11 August 1918), in Richard
Pipes (ed.), *The Unknown Lenin: From the Secret Archive* (New Haven,
1998), 50–2 (including photo of original text). See also James Ryan,
Lenin's Terror: The Ideological Origins of Early State Violence (New York,
2012), 106–13.

95. For an English translation, Karl Kautsky, *Terrorism and Communism:
A Contribution to the Natural History of Revolution* (London, 1920),
quotation 92.

96. *The Defense of Terrorism (Terrorism and Communism): A Reply to Karl
Kautsky* (London, 1921), 36, 64 (see also 13). Pages cited here and in what
follows are from this first English translation, checked against the Russian
original, *Terrorizm i kommunizm* (Petrograd, 1920), reprinted in *Sochineniia*, xii (Moscow, [1925]), 9–180 and at <http://www.magister.msk.ru/
library/trotsky/trotlo33.htm>. [accessed 26 August 2016]

97. *Defense of Terrorism*, 22, 52, 55–8.

98. Lenin, "Letter to American Workers" (first published in Russian in
Pravda, 22 August 1918). Lenin, *Polnoe sobranie sochinenii*, 5th edn
(Moscow, 1969), xxxvii, quotations pp. 57–8. For an English translation
(the letter was published in the US in December 1918), see <https://www.
marxists.org/archive/lenin/works/1918/aug/20.htm>. [accessed 26 August
2016]

99. *Defense of Terrorism*, 159.

100. Ibid. 55–6.

101. Ibid. 59–60.

102. Lenin, "Letter to American Workers."

103. Quotations from Cheka leaders in publications dated September and
November 1918, in Ryan, *Lenin's Terror*, 114–15.

104. Walter Benjamin, "Critique of Violence" (1921), in Benjamin, *Selected
Writings*, ed. Michael Jennings et al., 4 vols. (Cambridge, MA,
1996–2003), i. 248–50.

105. *Voprosy byta* (Moscow, 1923); Leon Trotsky, *Problems of Everyday Life*
(New York, 1973). The Russian text is online at <http://www.magister.
msk.ru/library/trotsky/trotl910.htm>. [accessed 26 August 2016]

106. "Neskol'ko slov o vospitanii cheloveka," in *Voprosy byta*, online at <http://www.magister.msk.ru/library/trotsky/trotl933.htm>. [accessed 26 August 2016] For a translation, see "A Few Words on How to Raise a Human Being," in Trotsky, *Problems of Everyday Life*, 140.

107. Speech to Tsekran (Transport workers' union), 2 December 1920, in *Sochineniia*, xv (Moscow, 1927), 422.

108. *Literatura i revoliutsiia* (Moscow, 1991; orig. 1923), 196–7. For an English translation, see <http://www.marxists.org/archive/trotsky/1924/lit_revo/cho8.htm> [accessed 26 August 2016].

109. "Tasks of Communist Education" (Speech at the Communist University, 18 June 1923), in *Sochineniia*, xxi (Moscow, 1927), 327–8.

110. "Ot staroi sem'i—k novoi" (From the old family toward the new), *Pravda*, 13 July 1923, 2.

111. "Ia sam" (1922), in V. V. Maiakovskii, *Izbrannye sochineniia v dvukh tomakh* (Moscow, 1981), i. 35–50 (quotations pp. 38, 40). The complete works in Russian are *Polnoe sobranie sochinenii v trinadtsati tomakh* (Moscow, 1955–61), available in the Fundamental Digital Library at <http://feb-web.ru/feb/mayakovsky/default.asp?/feb/mayakovsky/texts/mso/mso.html> [accessed 12 August 2016]. Translations of selected works include *The Bedbug and Selected Poetry*, ed. Patricia Blake, tr. Max Hayward and George Reavey (Bloomington, IN, 1960), and *Selected Poems*, tr. James H. McGavran III (Evanston, IL, 2013).

    Major biographical and literary studies in English of Mayakovsky include Edward Brown, *Mayakovsky: A Poet in the Revolution* (Princeton, 1973); Bengt Jangfeldt, *Majakovskij and Futurism, 1917–1921* (Stockholm, 1976); Jangfeldt, *Mayakovsky: A Biography*, tr. from Swedish by Harry Watson (Chicago, 2014); Victor Terras, *Vladimir Mayakovsky* (Boston, 1983). On "futurism," see especially Vladimir Markov, *Russian Futurism: A History* (Berkeley, CA, 1968; reprinted Washington, DC, 2006); Marjorie Perloff, *The Futurist Moment: Avant-Garde, Avant Guerre, and the Language of Rupture* (Chicago, 2003); Nina Gurianova, *The Aesthetics of Anarchy: Art and Ideology in the Early Russian Avant-Garde* (Berkeley, CA, 2012).

112. "Ia sam," 41.

113. Ibid. 41–2.

114. "O Maiakovskom" (1940), in Viktor Shklovskii, *Zhili-Byli: vospominaniia, memuarnye zapisi, povesti i vremeni, s kontsa XIX v po 1962 g.* (Moscow, 1964), 216–17.

115. Markov, *Russian Futurism,* 132–8; Brown, *Mayakovsky,* 43–6.

116. Vasilii Kamenskii, *Ego-moia: biografiia velikogo futurista* (Moscow, 1918), 131.

117. Brown, *Mayakovsky,* 91.

118. "Nate!" (Take that!, 1913), *Izbrannye sochineniia,* i. 61, as translated in *Selected Poems,* 46.

119. Evgenii Sosuntsov, "Sovremennyi antinomizm," *Tserkovnyi vestnik,* 21 (22 May 1914): 626–7.

120. [No author], "Futurizm," *Tserkovnyi vestnik,* 27 (3 July 1914): 825–6.

121. Genrikh Tastevin, *Futurizm (na puti k novomy simvolizmu)* (Moscow, 1914), 30–2, 78. See also Joan Neuberger, "Culture Besieged: Hooliganism and Futurism," in Stephen Frank and Mark Steinberg (eds), *Cultures in Flux: Lower-Class Values, Practices, and Resistance in Late Imperial Russia* (Princeton, 1994), 185–203.

122. On anarchy, art, and Russian futurism, see Gurianova, *Aesthetics of Anarchy,* ch. 1.

123. Ibid., ch. 6.

124. "Ia sam," 45.

125. D. Burliuk, Aleksandr Kruchenykh, V. Maiakovskii, and Viktor Khlebnikov, "Poshchechina obshchestvennomu vkusu" (Slap in the Face of Public Taste, the opening manifesto of the 1912 almanac of the same name), in *Manifesty i programmy russkikh futuristov,* ed. Vladimir Markov (Munich, 1967), 50–1.

126. See especially "Noch'" (Night) (1912), "Utro" (Morning) (1912), "Iz ulitsy v ulitsu" (From Street to Street) (1913), "Koe-chto pro Peterburg" (Something about Petersburg) (1913), "Ulichnoe" (Of the Street) (1913), "Ia" (Me) (1913), "Liubov'" (Love) (1913), and "Shumiki, Shumy, Shumishchi" (loosely translatable as Noisekins, Noises, and Noisings) (1913).

127. "Vladimir Maiakovskii: Tragediia," in *Izbrannye sochineniia,* ii. 7–23. For Paul Schmidt's translation, see <http://ustheater.blogspot.com/2010/08/vladimir-mayakovsky-vladimir-mayakovsky.html> [accessed 26 August 2016].

128. Gurianova, *Aesthetics of Anarchy,* ch. 7. The quotation is from A. Kruchenykh, *Stikhi Maiakovskogo* (Moscow, 1914), quoted Gurianova, *Aesthetics of Anarchy,* 167.

129. "Shtatskaia shrapnel'" (Civic shrapnel), a series of three essays published in *Nov'* in November 1914, in *Polnoe sobranie sochinenii,* i. 302–10; "Budetliane" (People of the Future), *Nov',* 14 December 1914 in *Polnoe sobranie sochinenii,* i. 329–32.

130. Notably, "War is Declared" and "Mama and the Evening Killed by the Germans."
131. "Oblako v shtanakh," *Polnoe sobranie sochinenii,* i. 185, 409. In 1918, Mayakovsky revised the phrase "a certain year" (kotoryi to god) to "1916." See also Brown, *Mayakovsky,* 115.
132. "Ia sam," 46.
133. "Voina i mir" (1915–16), *Izbrannye sochineniia,* ii. 51–79. With a variation on the middle letter in the word "mir"—prerevolutionary Russian had two letters that are now rendered simply as "i" in both modern Russian and in transliteration—"Voina i mir" would be translated as "War and Peace," thus evoking, with irony, Lev Tolstoy's great epic.
134. "Chelovek" (1916–17), *Izbrannye sochineniia,* ii. 80–105.
135. "Revoliutsiia: poetokhronika" (17 April 1917), *Izbrannye sochineniia,* i. 95–101.
136. "Ia sam," 47.
137. These manifestos, "Decree No. 1 on the Democratization of the Arts," "Manifesto of the Flying Federation of Futurists," and the only one signed by Mayakovsky alone, and the only one included in his collected works, "Open Letter to Workers," are quoted and discussed in Jangfeldt, *Majakovskij and Futurism,* 18–23.
138. V. I. Lenin, "Successes and Difficulties of Soviet Power" (1919), in *Polnoe sobranie sochinenii,* 5th edn, xxxviii (Moscow, 1969), 55. On Lenin's "anti-iconoclasm" see also Stites, *Revolutionary Dreams,* 76–8.
139. "Prikaz po armii iskusstva," *Iskusstvo kommuny,* 7 December 1918, in *Izbrannye sochineniia,* i. 106–7.
140. "Radovat'sia rano" (It's too early to rejoice), *Iskusstvo kommuny,* 15 December 1918, in *Izbrannye sochineniia,* i. 108.
141. *Polnoe sobranie sochinenii,* ii. 357.
142. "Misteriia-Buff," *Polnoe sobranie sochinenii,* ii. 231, 235, 346.
143. From "A Few Words about Myself" (1913), "Vladimir Mayakovsky" (1913), and "Man" (1916–17).
144. "Chelovek," *Izbrannye sochineniia,* ii. 95.
145. "Revoliutsiia: poetokhronika" (17 April 1917), *Izbrannye sochineniia,* i. 97.
146. "150,000,000" (1919–20), *Izbrannye sochineniia,* ii. 112–13.
147. "Zastrel'shchiki" (Instigators, 1929), *Polnoe sobranie sochinenii,* x. 87 and "Marsh vremeni" (March of time) from *Bania* (The bathhouse, 1919–30), *Izbrannye sochineniia,* ii. 523–4.
148. "O driane" (1920–1), *Polnoe sobranie sochinenii,* ii. 73–5, 498.

149. "Razgovor s fininspektorom o poezii" (Conversation with the tax collector about poetry, 1926), *Izbrannye sochineniia*, i. 279–86.

150. Lawrence Stahlberger, *The Symbolic System of Mayakovsky* (The Hague, 1964), 135; R. D. B. Thompson, "Mayakovsky and his Time Imagery," *Slavonic and East European Review* 48/2 (April 1970): 200.

151. *Polnoe sobranie sochinenii*, xiii. 138.

CONCLUSION
AN UNFINISHED REVOLUTION

What is the meaning of the Russian Revolution a hundred years on? Communist party rule is long gone and the Cold War a fading memory, so the old political pressures on how we judge that history have weakened. At the same time, the events and passions of a century ago seem no longer to inspire political imagination and action. The centenary of 1917—I am writing these words on its eve—may change this, perhaps momentarily, but more likely not. I sometimes wonder: who cares now about the Russian revolution? Perhaps this is one of the reasons I ask in this book the same question of the people who made and experienced that revolution: what did it mean to them?

As I suggested in the Introduction, and as readers can see, my approach to narrating and interpreting this history has been more about uncertain interpretations by those who lived the past than solid conclusions in hindsight. Of course, I do identify patterns and make generalizations, even about the march of time through events and turning points. But I lean, for this is where I believe deeper truths are to be found, toward evidence that reminds us of the variety, flux, and possibility of the past. Readers might wish for a more straightforward narrative, where all the pieces fit together according a clear historical logic and direction. It might seem that I am avoiding the responsibility of the historian to make strong arguments and offer final conclusions. But my approach is a different type of argument: about the variety and complexity of meanings in every historical situation, about the diversity and instabilities of human experience, about the dangers of simple patterns and final conclusions. Some readers may find this way of telling the past unsettling, which is partly the point, if what are unsettled are simplifications and assumptions in how we approach history, including our own.

This is not to say that I do not have a point of view, judgments, and sympathies that have influenced the story I tell. My search for experience—for the complex mixtures of ideas, emotions, values, and ideals that shaped how people inhabited and acted in the world—is itself a point of view and even a political stance. So is my tendency to see in these stories important questions about the human person, justice and injustice, violence, freedom, and the meanings of history. I try to keep overt political appeals out of my teaching and writing. But it is not hard to detect my leanings: my admiration for those who fought for something better in life for themselves and for others, especially for human dignity and rights, freedom, equality, and fairness, and who believed that these were not impossible goals. But I have also not hidden my recognition that history tends to bring disappointment, or worse. Daring "leaps into the open air of history" (Walter Benjamin's phrase that I have brought into this story more than once) have tended to end not in soft landings in the utopian "kingdom of freedom," but hard falls back into the "kingdom of necessity" (the leap that socialist revolution was supposed to make, we have seen, according to Marxism). I admit to finding this rather sad. Hence my admiration for those who try to leap anyway.

It is a reflection of these patterns of idealism and disappointment that the Russian revolution has been often judged "unfinished."[1] This is evident in the history that followed the stopping point of this book in 1921. Though many Communists criticized the New Economic Policy as a compromise and retreat, it was not as unrevolutionary as it might look. Because this new course reflected an awareness that the majority of the population was not ready for socialism, it came with a "cultural revolution," as Lenin called it, to transform how people lived and thought. From the point of view of the peasant majority, this cultural revolution felt like the town invading the village: assaulting religious practices and beliefs, using schools to inculcate new values in children, and trying to impose a radically "new everyday life" (*novyi byt*) in family relationships, sexual and gender norms, styles of work, drinking traditions, reading tastes, and more. The fact that these cultural campaigns altered very little in people's actual lives during the 1920s led a great many Communists to fear that that their goal of creating a modern socialist society was drowning in a vast and dark peasant ocean.

The situation among workers was not much better. Whether one looked at what workers preferred to read (mostly entertaining fiction), or how they organized their family life (such as men insisting that their wives had no place in public life), or the persistence of heavy drinking, the proletariat seemed to have wandered off the revolutionary path. In turn, workers joked that NEP stood for the "New Exploitation of the Proletariat." Though the working class was politically privileged—lionized as the "ruling class" and enjoying preferential treatment in access to education, positions of authority, and other paths of upward mobility—most workers endured low wages, high levels of unemployment, and working conditions that resembled those before the revolution. Outside of work, housing was cramped and urban crime was rampant. The unfinished nature of the social revolution was especially visible in the rise of the "new bourgeoisie" of so-called Nepmen (mostly small business owners and traders) enjoying the pleasures of an urban life adorned once again with exclusive restaurants, cafes, casinos, and nightclubs.

Stalin's "Great Turn" cut through the compromises and complexities of NEP to revive the militant spirit of class struggle, collective and individual heroism, and utopian enthusiasm. The First Five-Year Plan, launched in 1928, to create an entirely state-run collective economy, was less about "planning" than mobilizing the population for a radical economic leap into a new economy, society, and culture. This revolutionary spirit, which mixed utopianism and militarism, was expressed well by Stalin's chief economist, Stanislav Strumilin: "Our task is not to study economics but to change it. We are bound by no laws. There are no fortresses that Bolsheviks cannot storm." Stalin embraced this mentality as a slogan for his revival of revolution. Stalinism rejected the limits of what scientific economics considered possible, the limits of nature, even the limits of the human body. Plan targets were repeatedly raised; then, the whole Five-Year Plan was to be completed in four years; and, at every step, the "plan" was to be "over-fulfilled." Like War Communism, the "Great Turn" politicized economics—and politics meant revolutionary war: industry and agriculture were "fronts" with "campaigns" and "breakthroughs"; workers were "shock" workers; labor "battalions" were deployed to the "front lines" to "attack" areas of need; young people volunteered (and were encouraged to volunteer) to work on grandiose industrial projects or join the mass collectivization campaign, considering themselves heroic fighters; "class enemies" were battled and "liquidated"; and those who urged more rational policies (or who failed in their tasks) were treated as traitors in wartime. Everything was to be transformed in this new revived revolution: natural geographies remade, cultural authorities overthrown, and human beings "reforged."

This revolution, which brought much suffering and harm into people's lives, turned increasingly conservative in the 1930s: toward greater emphasis on political authority, order, and repression (briefly exploding in open terror against opponents in the late 1930s); uniformity and ideological orthodoxy in cultural and intellectual life; traditional values in social life (especially in the family, where divorce was made more difficult, homosexuality and abortion criminalized, and the role of women as mothers extolled); and rising income inequality and material privileges for loyal elites. During World War II, when the USSR's survival was threatened by Nazi invasion and occupation, ideology and policy shifted even more strongly toward nation, home, and family as the foundations of Soviet life. At the same time, people were told, and many surely felt, that life in the 1930s was the realization of at least some of the original revolutionary dream. "Life has become better, life has become more joyful, comrades," Stalin pronounced. The Soviet people were expected to express their happiness publicly and were regularly assured that they had good reasons to be happy, for they enjoyed (or so said the new 1936 constitution, for example) freedom of speech, press, assembly; social rights that included a guaranteed right to a job, leisure time, health protection, care in old age and sickness, housing, and education; and complete equality for women and non-Russians. It seemed, as propaganda insisted, that now everyone could "live like a human being."[2]

The decades after Stalin's death in 1953 were marked even more by conservative stability, punctuated by two brief and unsuccessful attempts to convince the party and the people that the revolution was not finished and to revive its spirit and goals. Nikita Khrushchev rejected Stalinist "tyranny," encouraged a revitalizing "thaw" in intellectual and cultural life, and launched vigorous economic campaigns to overcome inertia and bureaucracy. Believing (or claiming to believe) that these efforts would enable the Soviet Union to overcome persistent economic backwardness and leap from necessity into prosperity, in 1961 he declared that "the present generation of the Soviet people shall live under communism," under conditions of such abundance that social life could be run according to the communist principle "from each according to their abilities, to each according to their needs."

In 1985, at a time of even more entrenched conservatism, Mikhail Gorbachev launched another "revolution," calling on party members to join in his campaign of "reconstruction" (perestroika) in order to overcome "stagnation." Most people experienced the "era of stagnation" as not so terrible: Soviet society had become a welfare society that provided the majority of people tangible if modest benefits, including free medical care, guaranteed employment, a pension at retirement, low-cost housing, subsidized food, and consumer goods. Gorbachev disrupted this tolerated order with bold speeches ending the conspiracy of silence about serious problems in the socialist system: slowing rates of economic growth and an "erosion of ideological and moral values." Gorbachev and his allies railed against a public mood of cynicism and pessimism. The solution, he insisted, was a "revolution" in which people would achieve great things because they know they are masters of their fate building "a shining temple on a green hill." Gorbachev imagined, as Lenin had (whom he often quoted), unleashing "mass initiative" and enthusiasm in order to finally achieve the dream of a socialist society made by "the living creativity of the masses" for the good of the Soviet people and the whole world.[3] He insisted that the original socialist dream of a prosperous, democratic, and just society was still attainable. He believed that "the healthy forces of the people" were ready to come together under the party's leadership "to accomplish the historic task of renewing socialism."[4] But Gorbachev could not control the "creativity" he unleashed. With the small amount of new freedom allowed, the press and the streets became spaces for political activity such as Russia had not seen since the revolution itself. "Informal" democratic organizations emerged, street demonstrations broke out in Moscow and other cities, workers went on strike, nationalist movements revived among both non-Russians and Russians, and intellectuals, journalists, and writers published daring statements. Very few of these endorsed Gorbachev's vision of revitalized Leninism.

Communist party rule in Russia ended in a revolution fueled partly by what Gorbachev had hoped to heal: deep disenchantment with Soviet socialism. On coming to power in 1991, Boris Yeltsin, himself a disenchanted communist official, offered a condemning verdict on why Gorbachev failed: "He wanted to combine things that cannot be combined—to marry a hedgehog and a grass snake—communism and a market economy, public-property ownership and private-property ownership, the multiparty system and the Communist Party with its monopoly on power."[5] Gorbachev had insisted that he would not question Russia's "socialist choice" of 1917. The trouble was that the Soviet experience had left too few people inspired any longer by that choice, too few people who still believed that socialism would liberate the human spirit and enrich human life, who believed that what 1917 started should be finished.

Under Yeltsin, this political disenchantment with the promises of communism inspired yet another revolution—to dismantle the old regime, suddenly and swiftly. With the fervor of a convert, Yeltsin led the charge to tear down one-party rule and dismantle the state-controlled economy, most of it redistributed to individuals with connections and influence. That widespread corruption and chaos resulted was of less concern to him and his allies than that the old order was shattered. This was a destroying revolution, a counter-revolution. Its idealists believed this demolition would unleash new freedoms and energies to build a new society. Yeltsin's revolution had its enthusiasts and supporters (and a great deal of European and American support, unlike any previous Russian revolution), but it was experienced by most people as a catastrophe visited upon the population by leaders still experimenting ideologically with other people's lives. The 1990s brought freedom but also economic disorder, financial corruption, the collapse of healthcare and other social services, and widespread crime and violence. Many found these conditions frightening and unbearable. Others accepted all this as the necessary price for freedom. Some took advantage—to gain personally or to leave.

Vladimir Putin, Russia's dominant leader since the start of the new century, declared himself opposed to all revolutions. "Russia in the past century over-fulfilled its plan for revolutions," he declared in 2001. Looking over Russia's history of revolutions and counter-revolutions, reforms and counter-reforms, he proclaimed that "it is high time to say firmly that this cycle has ended. Enough is enough!"[6] Putin justified his drive for greater stability, order, tradition, and authority (authoritarianism, in the view of critics) by recalling the emotional and psychological strains of living in times of revolution. The radical dismantling of communism in the 1990s, which was meant to be a new leap into the kingdom of freedom but was experienced by most people as chaos and crisis, shaped Putin's anti-revolutionary stance and that of many of his contemporaries. They might have found the account of the experience of revolution written in 1918, quoted in Chapter 4, as describing their own state of mind: "Nerves are pulled tight. Thoughts coil into a tangle. No beginning, no end, no exit, no solution....Everyone wants to simply shout: 'Can't you finally just leave us alone. I don't want a thing—not peace, not war, not joy, not despair, not your damned politics!'"[7] Putin seems to have understood this mood, that people were tired of "leaps" into the unknown, even when they promised spectacular new happiness.

It is not the work of the historian to predict the future—the past's futures are hard enough to predict. Yet somehow in our times we see a remarkable number of people across the world, mostly young, acting as if they believe that one must venture beyond the limits of life as it is to create life as it ought to be—whether that "ought" comes from moral beliefs, religious convictions, political values, or some other impulse that says that the present is not enough and this is not the best we can be. These dreamers challenge all they judge to be negative in the world, occupy public squares with demands for local and global change, create alternative communities and practices, and, not least, resist what we tell them is impossible to achieve. In Russia, too, despite all the disappointments and failures of revolution, we see people who still believe, and even take to the streets to say, that the way things are fall short of the way things ought to be. Very few of these movements look back, as many once did, to the Russian revolution for inspiration. And yet, could we awaken from the dead the idealists of those days, they might recognize the spirit, values, and hopes animating protests around the world today. So, perhaps, the Russian revolution is still an open story and unfinished.

Notes

1. See Isaac Deutscher, *The Unfinished Revolution: Russia, 1917–1967* (New York, 1967), but also Michael McFaul, *Russia's Unfinished Revolution: Political Change from Gorbachev to Putin* (Ithaca, NY, 2001).
2. See e.g. the 1934 poster, "Every Collective Farm Peasant or Individual Farmer Now Has the Opportunity to Live Like a Human Being," in Victoria E. Bonnell, *Iconography of Power: Soviet Political Posters Under Lenin and Stalin* (Berkeley, CA, 1997), plate 4, discussed 118–20.
3. Mikhail Gorbachev, *Perestroika: New Thinking for our Country and the World* (New York, 1987), 29.
4. Quotations are from speeches made between 1987 and 1989 collected in various Russian editions of his writings and from his book in English, *Perestroika*.
5. M. Parker and F. Coleman. "'We are taking over'" (interview with Boris Yeltsin), *Newsweek*, 118/27 (30 December 1991), 21.
6. Richard Sakwa, *Putin: Russia's Choice*, 2nd edn (London, 2008), 47.
7. Isaiia Gromov, "Ostav'te nas v pokoe," *Gazeta dlia vsekh*, 8 February 1918, 1.

BIBLIOGRAPHY

SELECTED READINGS IN ENGLISH ON THE RUSSIAN REVOLUTION, 1905–1921

The historiography of the Russian Revolution is immense and rich in diverse (often conflicting) perspectives and interpretations, many of which have been considered along the way in this book. Scholars have explored the revolution's long-term and immediate causes; analyzed the ideologies that guided various political parties and leaders; described the role and goals of different social groups; turned away from the traditional focus on the capital cities and central provinces to explore more distant spaces of nation and empire; and sought deeper and more complex mentalities and attitudes beneath the surfaces of events, behaviors, and formal ideologies. The tendency over time, as in most other areas of historical writing, has been to move from the study of individuals to society, from events to experiences, from the center to the margins, from surfaces to depths—even when causes and outcomes have remained key questions. Of course, scholars continue to argue about approaches and interpretations (usually politely, but not always) and to research new sources. This bibliography, though limited to works in English, tries to reflect many of these directions and perspectives. Most of all, I hope readers might find paths to explore. I have not included every work cited in the notes, which can also be used to pursue further reading on particular questions.

WEBSITES

<http://web.mit.edu/russia1917/AboutProject.html> [accessed 26 August 2016]
Deepening of the Russian Revolution, 1917: a student project at MIT with many useful links.
<https://www.hathitrust.org> [accessed 13 August 2016] Digitized copies of a wide range of books (search e.g. "Russian Revolution").

BIBLIOGRAPHY

<https://www.marxists.org/history/ussr/events/revolution> [accessed 13 August 2016] Writings in translation by many Russian socialists and other documents.
<http://soviethistory.msu.edu/> [accessed 13 August 2016] Seventeen Moments in Soviet History: a valuable and carefully built site with documents, visual material, analysis, and more covering the years 1917–91.

DOCUMENTS IN TRANSLATION

Ascher, Abraham, ed. *The Mensheviks in the Russian Revolution.* Ithaca, NY, 1976.
Avrich, Paul, ed. *The Anarchists in the Russian Revolution.* Ithaca, NY, 1973.
Bing, Edward, ed. *The Secret Letters of the Last Tsar: Being the Confidential Correspondence between Nicholas II and his Mother, Dowager Empress Maria Fedorovna.* New York, 1938.
Bonnell, Victoria, ed. *The Russian Worker: Life and Labor under the Tsarist Regime.* Berkeley, CA, 1983.
Browder, Robert Paul, and Alexander F. Kerensky, eds. *The Russian Provisional Government, 1917: Documents.* 3 vols. Stanford, CA, 1961.
Bunyan, James, and H. H. Fisher, eds. *The Bolshevik Revolution, 1917–1918: Documents and Materials.* Stanford, CA, 1961 (1st edn 1934).
Clark, Katerina, and Evgeny Dobrenko. *Soviet Culture and Power: A History in Documents, 1917–1953.* New Haven, 2007.
Daly, Jonathan, and Leonid Trofimov, eds. *Russia in War and Revolution, 1914–1922: A Documentary History.* Indianapolis, 2009.
Freeze, Gregory. *From Supplication to Revolution: A Documentary Social History of Imperial Russia.* Oxford, 1988.
Gorky, Maxim. *Untimely Thoughts: Essays on Revolution, Culture, and the Bolsheviks, 1917–1918.* New Haven, 1995.
Harcave, Sidney. *First Blood: The Russian Revolution of 1905.* London, 1964.
Hickey, Michael C., ed. *Fighting Words: Competing Voices from the Russian Revolution.* Santa Barbara, CA, 2011.
Kowalski, Ronald. *The Russian Revolution, 1917–1921.* London, 1997.
Pipes, Richard, ed. *The Unknown Lenin: From the Secret Archive.* New Haven, 1996.
Rosenberg, William G., ed. *Bolshevik Visions: First Phase of the Cultural Revolution in Russia,* 2nd edn. Ann Arbor, 1990.
Steinberg, Mark D. *Voices of Revolution, 1917.* New Haven, 2001.
Steinberg, Mark D., and Vladimir M. Khrustalev. *The Fall of the Romanovs.* New Haven, 1995.
Tucker, Robert C., ed. *The Lenin Anthology.* New York, 1975.

Žižek, Slavoj, ed. *Revolution at the Gates: A Selection of Writings from February to October [by] V. I. Lenin.* London, 2002.

MEMOIRS AND ACCOUNTS BY PARTICIPANTS

Babel, Isaac. *1920 Diary.* New Haven, 1995.

Beatty, Bessie. *The Red Heart of Russia.* New York, 1918.

Botchkareva, Maria, as set down by Isaac Don Levine. *Yashka: My Life as a Peasant, Officer, and Exile.* New York, 1919.

Bunin, Ivan. *Cursed Days: Diary of a Revolution,* tr. and ed., Thomas Gaiton Marullo. Chicago, 1998.

Dune, Eduard M. *Notes of a Red Guard,* tr. and ed. Diane P. Koenker and S. A. Smith. Urbana, IL, 1993.

Lyandres, Semion. *The Fall of Tsarism: Untold Stories of the February 1917 Revolution.* Oxford, 2013.

Reed, John. *Ten Days that Shook the World.* Harmondsworth, 1977 (orig. publ. 1919).

Serge, Victor. *Memoirs of a Revolutionary, 1901–1941,* tr. Peter Sedgwick. Oxford, 1963.

Shklovsky, Victor. *A Sentimental Journey: Memoirs, 1917–1922,* tr. Richard Sheldon. Ithaca, NY, 1970 (orig. publ. 1922).

Steinberg, I. N. *In the Workshop of the Revolution.* New York, 1953.

Sukhanov, N. N. *The Russian Revolution: A Personal Record,* ed. and tr. Joel Carmichael. Oxford, 1955 (originally published in Russian in 1922).

Trotsky, Leon. *History of the Russian Revolution,* tr. Max Eastman. Chicago, IL, 2008 (orig. publ. 1932).

Zelnik, Reginald, ed. *A Radical Worker in Tsarist Russia: The Autobiography of Semen Ivanovich Kanatchikov.* Stanford, CA, 1986.

GENERAL SCHOLARLY HISTORIES

Acton, Edward, Vladimir Cherniaev, and William G. Rosenberg, eds. *A Critical Companion to the Russian Revolution, 1914–1921.* Bloomington, IN, 1997.

Ascher, Abraham. *The Revolution of 1905,* i. *Russia in Disarray;* ii. *Authority Restored.* Stanford, 1988, 1992.

Badcock, Sarah. *Politics and the People in Revolutionary Russia: A Provincial History.* Cambridge, 2007.

BIBLIOGRAPHY

Badcock, Sarah, Liudmila G. Novikova, and Aaron B. Retish, eds. *Russia's Home Front in War and Revolution, 1914–22*, vol. 1. *Russia's Revolution in Regional Perspective*. Bloomington, IN, 2015.

Burdzhalov, E. N. *Russia's Second Revolution: The February 1917 Uprising in Petrograd*, tr. and ed. Donald Raleigh. Bloomington, IN, 1987.

Chamberlain, W. H. *The Russian Revolution*, 2 vols. Princeton, 1987.

Ferro, Marc. *The Russian Revolution of February 1917*. Englewood Cliffs, NJ, 1972.

Ferro, Marc. *The Bolshevik Revolution: A Social History of the Russian Revolution*. London, 1980.

Figes, Orlando. *A People's Tragedy: The Russian Revolution, 1891–1924*. Harmondsworth, 1996.

Figes, Orlando, and Boris Kolonitskii. *Interpreting the Russian Revolution: The Language and Symbols of 1917*. New Haven and London, 1999.

Fitzpatrick, Sheila. *The Russian Revolution*, 3rd edn. Oxford, 2008.

Frankel, Edith Rogovin, Jonathan Frankel, and Baruch Knei-Paz, eds. *Revolution in Russia: Reassessments of 1917*. Cambridge, 1992.

Harcave, Sidney. *First Blood: The Russian Revolution of 1905*. London, 1964.

Hasegawa, Tsuyoshi. *The February Revolution: Petrograd, 1917*. Seattle, 1981.

Holquist, Peter. *Making War, Forging Revolution: Russia's Continuum of Crisis, 1914–1921*. Cambridge, MA, 2002.

Koenker, Diane P., William G. Rosenberg, and Ronald Grigor Suny, eds. *Party, State, and Society in the Russian Civil War: Explorations in Social History*. Bloomington, IN, 1989.

Lincoln, W. Bruce. *Passage through Armageddon: The Russians in War and Revolution, 1914–1918*. New York, 1986.

Lindenmeyr, Adele, Christopher Read, and Peter Waldron, eds. *Russia's Home Front in War and Revolution, 1914–22*, vol. 2. *The Experience of War and Revolution*. Bloomington, IN, 2016.

Pipes, Richard. *The Russian Revolution*. New York, 1990.

Raleigh, Donald J. *Revolution on the Volga: 1917 in Saratov*. Ithaca, NY, 1986.

Raleigh, Donald J. *Experiencing Russia's Civil War: Politics, Society, and Revolutionary Culture in Saratov, 1917–1922*. Princeton, 2002.

Read, Christopher. *From Tsar to Soviets: The Russian People and their Revolution, 1917–1921*. New York, 1996.

Schapiro, Leonard. *The Russian Revolutions of 1917: The Origins of Modern Communism*. New York, 1984.

Service, Robert, ed. *Society and Politics in the Russian Revolution*. New York, 1992.

Shukman, Harold, ed. *The Blackwell Encyclopedia of the Russian Revolution.* Oxford, 1994.

Siegelbaum, Lewis. *Soviet State and Society between Revolutions, 1918–1929.* Cambridge, 1992.

Smith, S. A. *The Russian Revolution: A Very Short Introduction.* Oxford, 2002.

Suny, Ronald Grigor. *The Baku Commune, 1917–1918: Class and Nationality in the Russian Revolution.* Princeton, 1972.

Suny, Ronald Grigor, and Arthur Adams, eds. *The Russian Revolution and Bolshevik Victory.* Lexington, MA, 1990.

Wade, Rex A. *The Russian Revolution, 1917.* Cambridge, 2000.

Wade, Rex A. *The Bolshevik Revolution and the Russian Civil War.* Westport, CT, 2001.

Weinberg, Robert. *The Revolution of 1905 in Odessa.* Bloomington, IN, 1993.

POLITICAL PARTIES, LEADERS, INSTITUTIONS, AND IDEOLOGIES

Abraham, Richard. *Alexander Kerensky: The First Love of the Revolution.* New York, 1987.

Ascher, Abraham. *Pavel Axelrod and the Development of Menshevism.* Cambridge, MA, 1972.

Ascher, Abraham. *P. A. Stolypin: The Search for Stability in Late Imperial Russia.* Stanford, CA, 2001.

Brovkin, Vladimir M. *The Mensheviks After October.* Ithaca, NY, 1987.

Brovkin, Vladimir M. *Behind the Front Lines of the Civil War: Political Parties and Social Movements in Russia, 1918–1922.* Princeton, 1994.

Clements, Barbara Evans. *Bolshevik Feminist: The Life of Aleksandra Kollontai.* Bloomington, IN, 1979.

Daniels, Robert V. *The Conscience of the Revolution: Communist Opposition in Soviet Russia.* New York, 1960.

Deutscher, Isaac. *The Prophet Armed: Trotsky, 1879–1921.* Oxford, 1954.

Farnsworth, Beatrice. *Aleksandra Kollontai: Socialism, Feminism, and the Bolshevik Revolution.* Stanford, CA, 1980.

Galili, Ziva. *The Menshevik Leaders in the Russian Revolution.* Princeton, 1989.

Haimson, Leopold H. *The Russian Marxists and the Origins of Bolshevism.* Cambridge, MA, 1955.

Hildermeier, Manfred. *The Russian Socialist Revolutionary Party Before the First World War.* New York, 2000.

Hoffmann, David. *Cultivating the Masses: Modern State Practices and Soviet Socialism, 1914–1939.* Ithaca, NY, 2011.
Knei-Paz, Baruch. *The Social and Political Thought of Leon Trotsky.* Oxford, 1978.
Pipes, Richard. *Struve*, i. *Liberal on the Left, 1870–1905*; ii. *Liberal on the Right, 1905–1944.* Cambridge, MA, 1970, 1980.
Rabinowitch, Alexander. *The Bolsheviks Come to Power.* New York, 1976.
Rabinowitch, Alexander. *Prelude to Revolution: The Petrograd Bolsheviks and the July 1917 Uprising.* Bloomington, IN, 1978.
Rabinowitch, Alexander. *The Bolsheviks in Power: The First Year of Soviet Rule in Petrograd.* Bloomington, IN, 2007.
Radkey, Oliver. *The Agrarian Foes of Bolshevism.* New York, 1958.
Rosenberg, William. *Liberals in the Russian Revolution: The Constitutional Democratic Party, 1917–1921.* Princeton, 1974.
Ryan, James. *Lenin's Terror: The Ideological Origins of Early Soviet State Terror.* London, 2012.
Sakwa, Richard. *Soviet Communists in Power: A Study of Moscow during the Civil War, 1918–21.* London, 1988.
Wortman, Richard. *Scenarios of Power: Myth and Ceremony in Russian Monarchy*, ii. *From Alexander II to the Abdication of Nicholas II.* Princeton, 2000.

ECONOMY, SOCIETY, AND CULTURE

General

Beer, Daniel. *Renovating Russia: The Human Sciences and the Fate of Liberal Modernity, 1880–1930.* Ithaca, NY, 2008.
Bonnell, Victoria E. *Iconography of Power: Soviet Political Posters under Lenin and Stalin.* Berkeley, CA, 1997.
Bradley, Joseph. *Muzhik and Muscovite: Urbanization in Late Imperial Russia.* Berkeley, CA, 1985.
Clowes, Edith, Samuel Kassow, and James West, eds. *Between Tsar and People: Educated Society and the Quest for Public Identity in Late Imperial Russia.* Princeton, 1991.
Corney, Frederick C. *Telling October: Memory and the Making of the Bolshevik Revolution.* Ithaca, NY, 2004.
Engelstein, Laura. *Keys to Happiness: Sex and the Search for Modernity in Fin-de-Siècle Russia.* Ithaca, NY, 1992.

Frame, Murray, Boris Kolonitskii, Steven G. Marks, and Melissa K. Stockdale, eds. *Russian Culture in War and Revolution, 1914–1922*. 2 vols. Bloomington, IN, 2014.

Gatrell, Peter. *Russia's First World War: A Social and Economic History*. Harlow, 2005.

Gleason, Abbott, Peter Kenez, and Richard Stites, eds. *Bolshevik Culture: Experiment and Order in the Russian Revolution*. Bloomington, IN, 1985.

Gurianova, Nina. *The Aesthetics of Anarchy: Art and Ideology in the Early Russian Avant-Garde*. Berkeley, CA, 2012.

Healey, Dan. *Homosexual Desire in Revolutionary Russia: The Regulation of Sexual and Gender Dissent*. Chicago, 2001.

Hessler, Julie. *A Social History of Soviet Trade: Trade Policy, Retail Practices, and Consumption, 1917–1953*. Princeton, 2004.

Kelly, Catriona, and David Shepherd, eds. *Constructing Culture in the Age of Revolution, 1881–1940*. Oxford, 1998.

Lih, Lars. *Bread and Authority in Russia, 1914–1921*. Berkeley, CA, 1990.

McAuley, Mary. *Bread and Justice: State and Society in Petrograd*. Oxford, 1991.

McReynolds, Louise. *Russia at Play: Leisure Activities at the End of the Tsarist Era*. Ithaca, NY, 2002.

McReynolds, Louise. *Murder Most Russian: True Crime and Punishment in Late Imperial Russia*. Ithaca, NY, 2013.

Malle, Silvana. *The Economic Organization of War Communism, 1918–1921*. Cambridge, 1985.

Mally, Lynn. *Culture of the Future: The Proletkult Movement in Russia*. Berkeley, CA, 1990.

Mironov, Boris, with Ben Eklof. *The Social History of Imperial Russia, 1700–1917*. Boulder, CO, 2000.

Neuberger, Joan. *Hooliganism: Crime, Culture, and Power in St. Petersburg, 1900–1914*. Berkeley, CA, 1993.

Steinberg, Mark D. *Proletarian Imagination: Self, Modernity, and the Sacred in Russia, 1910–1925*. Ithaca, NY, 2002.

Steinberg, Mark D. *Petersburg Fin de Siècle*. New Haven, 2011.

Stites, Richard. *Revolutionary Dreams: Utopian Vision and Revolutionary Life in the Russian Revolution*. Oxford, 1989.

Stites, Richard. *Russian Popular Culture*. Cambridge, 1992.

Sylvester, Roshanna. *Tales of Old Odessa: Crime and Civility in a City of Thieves*. DeKalb, IL, 2005.

Von Geldern, James. *Bolshevik Festivals, 1917–1920*. Berkeley, CA, 1993.

BIBLIOGRAPHY

Workers

Aves, Jonathan. *Workers Against Lenin: Labour Protest and the Bolshevik Dictatorship*. London, 1996.

Bonnell, Victoria. *Roots of Rebellion: Workers' Politics and Organizations in St. Petersburg and Moscow, 1900–1914*. Berkeley, CA, 1983.

Chase, William J. *Workers, Society, and the Soviet State: Labor and Life in Moscow, 1918–1929*. Urbana, IL, 1987.

Engelstein, Laura. *Moscow, 1905: Working-Class Organization and Political Conflict*. Stanford, CA, 1982.

Kaiser, Donald H., ed. *The Workers' Revolution in Russia, 1917*. Cambridge, 1987.

Koenker, Diane P. *Moscow Workers and the 1917 Revolution*. Princeton, 1981.

Koenker, Diane P. *Republic of Labor: Russian Printers and Soviet Socialism, 1918–1930*. Ithaca, NY, 2005.

Koenker, Diane P., and William G. Rosenberg. *Strikes and Revolution in Russia, 1917*. Princeton, 1989.

Mandel, David. *The Petrograd Workers and the Fall of the Old Regime*. London, 1983.

Mandel, David. *The Petrograd Workers and the Soviet Seizure of Power*. London, 1984.

McDaniel, Tim. *Autocracy, Capitalism, and Revolution in Russia*. Berkeley, CA, 1988.

Murphy, Kevin. *Revolution and Counterrevolution: Class Struggle in a Moscow Metal Factory*. Chicago, 2007.

Smith, S. A. *Red Petrograd: Revolution in the Factories, 1917–1918*. Cambridge, 1983.

Surh, Gerald D. *1905 in St. Petersburg: Labor, Society, and Revolution*. Stanford, CA, 1989.

Wynn, Charters. *Workers, Strikes and Pogroms: The Donbas-Dnepr Bend in Late Imperial Russia, 1870–1905*. Princeton, 1992.

Peasants

Burbank, Jane. *Russian Peasants Go to Court: Legal Culture in the Countryside, 1905–1917*. Bloomington, IN, 2004.

Burds, Jeffrey. *Peasant Dreams and Market Politics: Labor Migration and the Russian Village, 1861–1905*. Pittsburgh, PA, 1998.

Eklof, Ben. *Russian Peasant Schools: Officialdom, Village Culture, and Popular Pedagogy, 1861–1914*. Berkeley, CA, 1986.

Figes, Orlando. *Peasant Russia, Civil War: The Volga Countryside in Revolution.* Oxford, 1989.

Frank, Stephen. *Crime, Cultural Conflict, and Justice in Rural Russia, 1856–1914.* Berkeley, CA, 1999.

Gill, Graham. *Peasants and Government in the Russian Revolution.* London, 1979.

Retish, Aaron B. *Russia's Peasants in Revolution and Civil War: Citizenship, Identity, and the Creation of the Soviet State, 1914–1922.* Cambridge, 2008.

Worobec, Christine. *Peasant Russia: Family and Community in the Post-Emancipation Period.* Princeton, 1991.

Young, Glennys. *Power and the Sacred in Revolutionary Russia: Religious Activists in the Village.* University Park, PA, 1997.

Soldiers and Sailors

Mawdsley, Evan. *The Russian Revolution and the Baltic Fleet.* New York, 1978.

Sanborn, Joshua A. *Drafting the Russian Nation: Military Conscription, Total War, and Mass Politics, 1905–1925.* DeKalb, IL, 2003.

Saul, Norman. *Sailors in Revolt: The Russian Baltic Fleet in 1917.* Lawrence, KS, 1978.

Wade, Rex. *Red Guards and Workers' Militias in the Russian Revolution.* Stanford, CA, 1984.

Wildman, Allan. *The End of the Russian Imperial Army,* i. *The Old Army and the Soldiers' Revolt (March–April 1917)*; ii. *The Road to Soviet Power and Peace.* Princeton, 1980, 1987.

Women

Bernstein, Laurie. *Sonia's Daughters: Prostitutes and Their Regulation in Imperial Russia.* Berkeley, CA, 1995.

Chatterjee, Choi. *Celebrating Women: Gender, Festival, and Bolshevik Ideology, 1910–1939.* Pittsburgh, PA, 2002.

Clements, Barbara, Barbara Engel, and Christine Worobec, eds. *Russian Women: Accommodation, Resistance, Transformation.* Berkeley, CA, 1991.

Engel, Barbara Alpern. *Between Fields and the City: Women, Work, and Family in Russia, 1861–1914.* Cambridge, 1995.

Glickman, Rose. *Russian Factory Women: Workplace and Society.* Berkeley, CA, 1984.

Ruthchild, Rochelle Goldberg. *Equality and Revolution: Women's Rights in the Russian Empire, 1905–1917.* Pittsburgh, PA, 2010.

Stites, Richard. *The Women's Liberation Movement in Russia: Feminism, Nihilism, and Bolshevism, 1860–1920*. Princeton, 1978.

Wood, Elizabeth A. *The Baba and the Comrade: Gender and Politics in Revolutionary Russia*. Bloomington, IN, 1997.

Empire

Avrutin, Eugene M. *Jews and the Imperial State: Identification Politics in Tsarist Russia*. Ithaca, NY, 2010.

Brower, Daniel R., and Edward J. Lazzerini, eds. *Russia's Orient: Imperial Borderlands and Peoples, 1700–1917*. Bloomington, IN, 1997.

Burbank, Jane, and David Ransel. *Imperial Russia: New Histories for the Empire*. Bloomington, IN, 1998.

Campbell, Elena. *The Muslim Question and Russian Imperial Governance*. Bloomington, IN, 2015.

Geraci, Robert P. *Window on the East: National and Imperial Identities in Late Tsarist Russia*. Ithaca, NY, 2001.

Gerasimov, Ilya, Jan Kusber, and Alexander Semyonov, eds. *Empire Speaks Out: Languages of Rationalization and Self-Description in the Russian Empire*. Leiden, 2009.

Hirsch, Francine. *Empire of Nations: Ethnographic Knowledge and the Making of the Soviet Union*. Ithaca, NY, 2005.

Kamp, Marianne. *The New Woman in Uzbekistan: Islam, Modernity, and Unveiling under Communism*. Seattle, 2006.

Kappeler, Andreas. *The Russian Empire: A Multiethnic History*, tr. Alfred Clayton. Harlow, 2001.

Keller, Shoshana. *To Moscow, Not Mecca: The Soviet Campaign Against Islam in Central Asia, 1917–1941*. Westport, CT, 2001.

Khalid, Adeeb. *The Politics of Muslim Cultural Reform: Jadidism in Central Asia*. Berkeley, CA, 1998.

Khalid, Adeeb. *Making Uzbekistan: Nation, Empire, and Revolution in the Early USSR*. Ithaca, NY, 2015.

Lohr, Eric, Vera Tolz, Alexander Semyonov, and Mark von Hagen, eds. *The Empire and Nationalism at War*. Bloomington, IN., 2014.

Martin, Terry. *The Affirmative Action Empire: Nations and Nationalism in the Soviet Union, 1923–1939*. Ithaca, NY, 2001.

Meier, Natan N. *Kiev, Jewish Metropolis: A History, 1859–1914*. Bloomington, IN, 2010.

Nathans, Benjamin. *Beyond the Pale: The Jewish Encounter with Late Imperial Russia*. Berkeley, CA, 2002.

Norris, Stephen M., and Willard Sunderland, eds. *Russia's People of Empire: Life Stories from Eurasia, 1500 to the Present*. Bloomington, IN, 2012.

Plokhy, Serhii. *Unmaking Imperial Russia: Mykhailo Hrushevsky and the Writing of Ukrainian History*. Toronto, 2005.

Sahadeo, Jeff. *Russian Colonial Society in Tashkent, 1865–1923*. Bloomington, IN, 2007.

Slezkine, Yuri. *Arctic Mirrors: Russia and the Small Peoples of the North*. Ithaca, NY, 1994.

Stanislawski, Michael. *Zionism and the Fin de Siècle: Cosmopolitanism and Nationalism from Nordau to Jabotinsky*. Berkeley, CA, 2001.

Stein, Sarah Abrevaya. *Making Jews Modern: The Yiddish and Ladino Press in the Russian and Ottoman Empires*. Bloomington, IN, 2004.

Suny, Ronald Grigor, and Terry Martin, eds. *A State of Nations: Empire and Nation-Making in the Age of Lenin and Stalin*. Oxford, 2001.

Tuna, Mustafa. *Imperial Russia's Muslims: Islam, Empire, and European Modernity, 1878–1914*. Cambridge, 2015.

Veidlinger, Jeffrey. *Jewish Public Culture in the Late Russian Empire*. Bloomington, IN, 2009.

INDEX